Matanzas

UNIVERSITY PRESS OF FLORIDA
Florida A&M University, Tallahassee
Florida Atlantic University, Boca Raton
Florida Gulf Coast University, Ft. Myers
Florida International University, Miami
Florida State University, Tallahassee
New College of Florida, Sarasota
University of Central Florida, Orlando
University of Florida, Gainesville
University of North Florida, Jacksonville
University of South Florida, Tampa
University of West Florida, Pensacola

MATANZAS

The Cuba Nobody Knows   MIGUEL A. BRETOS

UNIVERSITY PRESS OF FLORIDA   *Gainesville · Tallahassee · Tampa*
Boca Raton · Pensacola · Orlando · Miami · Jacksonville · Ft. Myers · Sarasota

Copyright 2010 by Miguel A. Bretos
Printed in the United States of America. This book is printed on
Glatfelter Natures Book, a paper certified under the standards of the
Forestry Stewardship Council (FSC). It is a recycled stock that con-
tains 30 percent post-consumer waste and is acid-free.

15   14   13   12   11   10   6   5   4   3   2   1

Library of Congress Cataloging-in-Publication Data
Bretos, Miguel A.
Matanzas: the Cuba nobody knows/Miguel A. Bretos.
p. cm.
Includes bibliographical references and index.
ISBN 978-0-8130-3432-4 (alk. paper)
1. Matanzas (Cuba)—History. 2. Matanzas (Cuba)—Description
and travel. 3. Matanzas (Cuba)—Social life and customs.
4. Matanzas (Cuba)—Biography. I. Title.
F1819.M4B74 2010
972.91'39-dc22   2009034633

Frontispiece: Matanzas sugar mill owner Laurentino García Alonso
and daughters Consuelo and Amalia María in Seville, 1909. (Photo by
Gómez Studio, Seville)

The University Press of Florida is the scholarly publishing agency
for the State University System of Florida, comprising Florida
A&M University, Florida Atlantic University, Florida Gulf Coast
University, Florida International University, Florida State University,
New College of Florida, University of Central Florida, University of
Florida, University of North Florida, University of South Florida,
and University of West Florida.

University Press of Florida
15 Northwest 15th Street
Gainesville, FL 32611-2079
http://www.upf.com

Para mis nietos y todos sus primos nacidos y por nacer,
y para todos los matanceros habidos y por haber.

Buscando el puerto en noche procelosa
puedo morir en la difícil vía,
mas siempre voy contigo, o Cuba hermosa,
y aferrado al timón espero el día.

Searching for haven in the stormy night,
I may well perish as I make my way;
But always to you, Fair Cuba, holding tight,
Fast by the rudder, I await the day.

—José Jacinto Milanés (Matanzas, 1814–1863)

Contents

Illustrations

Preface

OVER THE YEARS, the allure of the Cuban capital has seduced all comers to the point of nearly subsuming the nation's identity, as if Cuba were the hinterland of Havana instead of Havana the capital of Cuba. Cuban cigars are called *habanos*, the national dance is the *habanera*, and the only native dog breed the Havanese. When the Countess of Merlin wrote her influential book (published 1844), she called it simply *La Havane*. Andy García produced a movie about Castro's takeover (script by the late Guillermo Cabrera Infante) unselfconsciously titled *The Lost City*.

Equating Havana with Cuba is a habit. The resulting distortion is not unlike that brilliantly captured on the classic *New Yorker* magazine cover (March 29, 1976): the Upper West Side appears in vivid detail in the foreground. The Jersey shore is a nondescript band across the river. Chicago, Utah, Nebraska, and California are dots strewn about a vague landscape. Russia, China, and Japan appear on the far horizon across a Pacific Ocean about as wide as the Hudson.

This book is about my hometown of Matanzas, one such dot in Cuba's interior. Known as "the Athens of Cuba," Matanzas is a maritime, culturally significant provincial capital one hundred kilometers east of Havana. The city's name means "slaughters" or "killings." How that peculiar place-name came to be is discussed in chapter 2.

Congressman Tip O'Neill's aphorism that "all politics is local" is profoundly insightful. With caveats, locality can help us understand not only politics but history as well. For example, one cannot understand Fidel Castro's mindset and worldview and, consequently, the history that he made, without taking into account the unique context of Oriente province, where he was born and grew up. His father, Ángel Castro, was a Spanish veteran who had fought the Yankees in the War for Independence (1895–1900), made a fortune in sugar,

Fig. 2. Cuba on a 1930s Baquedano brand coffee label.

and begat two broods, one within and one outside of wedlock. Fidel belonged to the latter. Northern Oriente in the 1920s had just undergone the ecological and social tidal wave that Big Sugar brought in its wake. Social inequities were brutal and raw. Just as important, the American presence was overwhelmingly palpable and far from benign. Guantánamo was nearby. The United Fruit Company's Preston and Boston sugar mills were a few kilometers away from Castro's home at Birán, their tall smokestacks visible for kilometers around. It was the perfect incubator for the visceral anti-Yankee animus that energizes him. One wonders if history might have turned out differently had Castro been the product of a gentler, more sedate place such as Matanzas.

Just as the preeminence of Havana distorts our perspective of Cuba across the map, the preeminence of the Cuban Revolution distorts our understanding of Cuba across the calendar. If Havana reduces the rest of Cuba to a backyard, the revolution reduces all pre-1959 Cuban history to a preface. That is patently absurd.

This book begins with the first of many historical tidal waves that have washed over Cuba: the European invasion that began in 1492. It ends, as 1958 did, with Batista's plane idling on the tarmac and another big wave about to break into a tsunami. Ending my book where I do is no crude attempt to redress the balance but a recognition that my knowledge of postrevolutionary Matanzas is slender and my firsthand experience limited. "Revolutionary Matanzas" is in any case an oxymoron.

Not having experienced Matanzas in that era is no excuse for not writing about it, of course. If firsthand experience were a prerequisite for historians to function, the scope of history would be limited indeed. No one has firsthand experience of the reign of Shi Huangdi, the Empire of Oyo, or the Franco-Prussian War. Drawing the line where I do is a positive statement of my conviction that there are people far better equipped than I to do justice to the theme. Taking stock of Cuba's experience under Castro will be a priority for Cuban historians—indeed, an urgent national priority—as soon as it is possible for them to do so without fear.

Historians "do it with footnotes," but in my case you will find the darned little things at the end of the book. As a scholar I have read as much as possible about the part of Cuba I most relate to, but not everything I know about my hometown has come from conventional sources. In hindsight, the most fundamental things I know about Matanzas I learned from my father, my two grandmothers, and a darling grandaunt who was blind like Homer and, like the Greek bard, a great spinner of yarns.

Her name was Antonia Batista Díaz. We called her Tía Ñiquita. She died in Miami in 1968 at a remarkably lucid one hundred years of age after a short and pointless exile. She was reliable, a woman of her word. In the 1930s doctors told her she would never walk again, but she made a deal with St. Francis of Assisi. St. Francis delivered—she got back the use of her legs—and she did as promised. She dressed only in brown until the Miami morning when someone brought her lunch and found her dead. She had become a bride three times and a widow just as many but she had no children. Her fair skin clung to her bones as if flesh were superfluous. She was proud of her hair, which many a younger woman would have envied. She wore it in a bun but would let it loose every now and then, in a white cascade to her waist, and sensuously comb it.

Tía Ñiquita was renowned for her quilts, which she bravely kept on making although she could barely see. The stitches my aunt applied with eyes dimmed by age and fingers lit by memory had a sinuous, organic beauty. As a child I would sit next to her on her old-fashioned iron bed outfitted for mosquito netting—a necessity in Cuba—and cut little squares of cloth. "I need a green one," she would ask. "Now a yellow one. See that they go well together." Meanwhile, she told one story of old Matanzas after another. She had prodigious recall. I only wish that my own storytelling—history is, at least partially, telling stories—were half as good as hers.

This book is in a limited sense also a memory. The opening chapter seeks to recapture the last impressions of Matanzas that a young man, then eighteen years old, carried with him into exile one rainy August day in 1961. The last explores the city and setting to which he returned forty-two years later.

That young man is alive today. He grew up to become me. We share a heart, a mind, and—much to his pointless regret—an aging body. I am an American citizen and have lived all over the world, from Nebraska to Australia, and from Colombia to Québec. But he is still resolutely Cuban and obstinately *matancero*.

Personal considerations aside, Matanzas is a very worthwhile subject. A century and a half ago, Samuel Hazard, author of a classic travel account, noted ruefully that Matanzas received much less attention than it deserved. This is still the case today. Sandwiched between Havana and Varadero, it is easy to find. Ironically, it is just as easy to miss.

Much of importance has happened in the city and environs. Matanceros have played a key role in the development of Cuba's music (there is a whole chapter on that). The place is important architecturally, monumentally, and as urban enterprise. It is a preeminent seat of Afro-Cuban culture. It has produced a rich literature and has been called—among many other things—"the City of Poets." Modern Cuban art and Cuban baseball began there.

Matanzas is Cuba in microcosm. Many of the forces that have made the country what it is, from colonial contraband to sugar monoculture to modern Santería, are found there in sharp relief and, I may add, in living color. This book seeks to be not so much the history of a Cuban locality as an approach to Cuban history from a local perspective.

Except where otherwise indicated, all translations are mine. This includes both prose and poetry. Readers will find numerous poems cited at some length. They are part of Matanzas' literary canon, more often than not the things people memorize. Most can be readily accessed in <www.Cubaliteraria .com>. Also, except where otherwise indicated by a credit line, all illustrations are from my personal collection.

It is customary for authors to acknowledge their debt to their benefactors, and I can do no less. Several people encouraged me to write this book. Jere and Katharina Bruner of Oberlin, Ohio; Norman and Carolyn Carr of Washington, D.C.; and Fabiola Santiago of the *Miami Herald* must be mentioned. Amy Gorelick of the University Press of Florida had a contract ready for my signature within hours of my initial proposal. I am grateful to her for sticking it out with a project that took longer than anticipated. I could not have asked for better author support than that provided by the University Press of Florida. Kirsteen E. Anderson, my copy editor, did much for the manuscript, making the crooked straight and the rough places plain.

Many people facilitated my research. Working at the Archivo General de Indias in Seville, where most of my research on early colonial Matanzas was carried out years ago, was an experience to be treasured. The same is true for the Library of Congress' Hispanic, Prints and Photographs, and Maps and Geography Divisions. I am especially grateful to John R. Hébert, head of the latter. The Cuban Heritage Center at the University of Miami is indispensable to anyone interested in Cuba. My thanks to Esperanza de Varona and her staff.

I am grateful to my son Fernando for his fruitful suggestion that I look into ocean thermal energy conversion (OTEC) and its remarkable link to Matanzas, and to Vanessa Vallejo for her photographic talent. Manuel Barcia's and Dick Cluster's readings of the manuscript led to numerous and ever-welcome improvements. The latter, in particular, was generous in sharing, guiding, and suggesting. Stephen Stumpfle of Indiana University, Carlos Giménez, and Jorge Musa Lambert offered immensely useful suggestions on matters musical. I am grateful to J. León Helguera for his interest and comments; to Julia Prieto Gómez for valuable input about Governor Severino de Manzaneda; to Dayton Hedges for his information about his family's businesses in Matanzas; to Antonio Bechily; to Juan de Zárraga, the current Marquis of Jústiz de Santa Ana; to Lorne Bedard of B. L. Graphics; to Ramón Cernuda; to Emilio Cueto, the breadth of whose collection is only surpassed by the depth of his learning; to my good friend Alberto Sánchez de Bustamante for his unwavering encouragement; to the late Raúl Ruiz, Matanzas' distinguished city historian, who honored me with his correspondence and both delighted and enlightened me with his works; to Dan Whittle of the Environmental Defense Fund; to Julio Díaz Díaz of the University of Matanzas; and especially to my cousin once removed, Carmen García Blanco de Galindo, of Matanzas. It was in Carmucha's living room, within sight of Matanzas Bay, surrounded by the warmth of family long unseen or newly met, that I believe I made the decision to write the book you now hold. It begins as my sister, Raquel, and I left Matanzas for exile in 1961 and is therefore her story as well as mine.

My benefactors range from titled nobility to former professors of Marxism. They are innocent of my opinions and in no way responsible for my errors.

Finally but endlessly, I owe thanks to my wife, Raquel Vallejo, who has shared me with this book and Dr. Parkinson's damned disease for the past several years. The former she has done with exemplary patience, the latter with love abounding.

1 One Last *Vuelta*

MY SISTER RAQUEL AND I left Matanzas for exile in the United States one rainy August Tuesday in 1961. We were booked on an afternoon flight to Miami, but we had to report to the immigration desk at Havana's airport at eight in the morning. It took one and a half hours to travel from our home to the airport by the brand-new expressway and the Havana Harbor Tunnel but, just in case, we left at five.

It was dark when we got into the car. Antonia, our nanny, had prepared *café con leche* with buttered toast. Antonia was proud of her Canary Islander ancestry but a bit uneasy when told that she was "the last of the Taínos" because of her native-like features. She handed us the poor excuse for a breakfast with which Cubans energize their mornings in a Thermos bottle and a paper bag. Her eyes were full of tears. "You will see them soon again," said my father, half-jokingly. "I don't think so," answered Antonia, wiping away her tears. "I will never see them again." She must have known something my folks did not.

Mother, ever impractical, asked that we go for a *vuelta*—a spin around the town. "It may be our last for a very long time," she argued. Father protested—it was raining hard and time was pressing—but at last he gave in. At five in the morning, in darkness and rain, we began our last spin around the town.

The vuelta was a cherished tradition. There were established circuits in Matanzas' own version of this universal social ritual. Families with cars would range from one end of town to the other. Others would walk the neighborhood. Where sidewalks were wide enough, people did not think twice about bringing out their caned Cuban rocking chairs and settling down outside—the city as living room. The ultimate Matanzas vuelta, of course, was *la vuelta al parque*, a promenade around the town's central square, the Parque de la Libertad (Liberty Square). Once upon a time, women and couples would walk clockwise, men counterclockwise, exchanging glances and pleasantries. This custom was but a quaint memory when I had my turn at the park. Generations come and go but the park remains; people die, the city goes on.

Our own version of the motorized vuelta was predictable enough. Up Contreras Street one went, all the way to Machado Park. From there one could see the entire town lying below. (One still can, of course; exiles just have this habit of speaking in the preterit.) Contreras was officially Bonifacio Byrne Street, honoring the Matanzas-born "Poet of the Flag," but the name of colonial-era vintage lived on. Machado Park was—is—a gem. Designed by Jean Claude Nicolas Forestier, it was his most important Cuban commission outside of Havana.[1] The park is laid out on several levels carefully defined by monumental stairways. It was a balcony open to the city below. At the park we would get out of the car, walk about the belvederes, and enjoy the view before heading down Milanés Street, the city's main thoroughfare. Formerly Gelabert Street, it was renamed after another Matanzas poet, José Jacinto Milanés. Being a poet in Matanzas is serious business. The city, after all, is known as "the Athens of Cuba" (la Atenas de Cuba). Local wits suggest "the Antenna of Cuba" would be more apropos because Matanzas' Athenian days are long past but the radio signal from Miami comes in strong. Matanzas, after all, is the Cuban provincial capital nearest the United States. The legendary ninety-mile width of the Florida Straits is measured from Key West to a point on the Matanzas shore.

One could see the entire blue expanse of Matanzas Bay from the park. It was there that the Dutch admiral Piet Heyn captured the entire Spanish transatlantic fleet one bright September day in 1628, dealing Spain a disastrous defeat. Sometimes we would take the road to La Cumbre, literally "The Summit," past the palatial villas built by Matanzas sugar barons during the nineteenth-century sugar boom, or go to the hermitage dedicated by the town's Catalonian community to house their black Madonna, the Virgin of Montserrat, in 1875. The view from there is breathtaking, the harbor and the city sprawling to one side and the Yumurí River valley to the other.

The city was deserted as we headed down Milanés Street that rainy morning long ago, past the Central Presbyterian Church at Milanés and Dos de Mayo on our way to Liberty Square. José Martí's fine bronze statue (one of the first to

Fig. 3. José Jacinto Milanés *(left)* and Bonifacio Byrne on Cuban postage stamps. To be a poet in "the City of Poets" is serious business.

be erected anywhere in Cuba) has kept watch over the square since 1908 from the same spot where King Ferdinand VII's marble one by Peschieri used to be. Ferdinand now resides at the provincial museum—unfairly perhaps, because he would probably understand the way Cuba is run these days better than Martí would.

Every Friday night, the band from the local garrison offered a *retreta* at the square, a mélange of popular airs that ended with the national anthem. Splice the theme of a Mozart aria to ferocious Spartan lyrics calling for struggle unto death for the Fatherland and you get the idea. When it was played, everyone doing the vuelta at the square abruptly stood at attention, only resuming motion when the last martial notes died down, like a carousel to which power was temporarily cut off. The cars that happened to be driving around stopped also. The anthem is short, a virtue in the genre.[2]

We drove around rain-drenched Liberty Square, past the Triolet French Apothecary, and the adjoining Louvre Hotel and restaurant. The Louvre was famous for its sweets, especially the *capuchinos*, the outrageously sweet Cuban cupcakes, baked in little paper cones and thoroughly drenched in syrup. Triolet, a working pharmacy then, is now Cuba's Pharmaceutical Museum. The predominance of French names is not accidental. Matanzas received major French influences over time, especially during the first quarter of the nineteenth century, when numerous exiles from Louisiana and the slave rebellion in French Saint-Domingue made Matanzas their home and introduced coffee culture there.

Government House rose on one side of the square, the Artistic and Literary Lyceum and the Spanish Casino (the town's *criollo* and Spanish clubs, respec-

Fig. 4. Generations come and go but the vuelta stays. *Left:* The vuelta in a *volanta* (ca. 1898). *Right:* Matanzas' first Model T (1912). (Left photo courtesy of Prints and Photographs Division, Library of Congress)

tively) on the other. On the corner of Contreras and Santa Teresa streets stood the Ramón Guiteras Public Library, a gift to Matanzas by the descendants of an illustrious expatriate. The former Spanish Casino is now the home of Matanzas' Biblioteca Gener y del Monte. Named after two Matanzas patrician literati from the city's golden age, it houses one of the island's best research collections. It is fitting that two important libraries face the city's main plaza, for matanceros have always been devoted to books. The colonial Matanzas elite was famously bibliophile. Matanzas had Cuba's first public library.

Milanés Street took us down to Vigía (Watchtower) Square, where the city was settled one October day of 1693. The memorial to Independence War hero Pedro Betancourt stood in the middle of the square, topped by a Cuban insurgent soldier from 1895 holding a billowing flag frozen in marble. Crossing the iron bridge spanning the San Juan River—one of the city's two substantial waterways—we drove the length of Pueblo Nuevo to the main railroad depot at the end of Tirry Boulevard. The depot is an English folly with an impressive cast iron sculpture of Britannia in the front garden. Pueblo Nuevo, one of the city's three classic neighborhoods, was a product of the nineteenth-century sugar boom and the resulting expansion of railroads.

An obligatory stop on the traditional vuelta was the Chinese gelateria next to the Grand Hotel París, which made what were reputed to be the best fruit sherbets in Cuba. The Chinese were conspicuous in Matanzas. The region, in fact, had been a major destination for the tens of thousands of Chinese brought to Cuba during the nineteenth century as indentured laborers to work the cane fields. Between 1847 and 1873, more than 120,000 Chinese were imported into Cuba, a significant portion of whom ended up in Matanzas city and province.[3]

The cultural importance of the Chinese to Matanzas can be demonstrated in many ways, but this is definitive: Matanzas was the only Cuban city to have its own *charada*, a numerological key to dreams and enigmas introduced in Cuba by the Chinese in the 1870s. Also known as Chiffá, it consists of thirty-six numbers to each of which a meaning is attached. The Cuban charada extended the numbers to one hundred; the Matanzas one to sixty. Its main practical application was in gambling, an evergreen Cuban concern. (Not surprisingly, a Cuban American legislator from Miami was one of the cosponsors of the Florida Lottery Bill and introduced it in the state legislature.)[4]

On our way back we followed Esteban Boulevard to the Palmar de Junco, where a baseball game was first recorded in Cuba in 1874—another legacy of the city's connections with the United States. The record shows that the strictly amateur Matanzas club was slaughtered by the visiting Havana team, which showed up with the great Esteban Bellán, the first Cuban to play in the Big Leagues, and another early Cuban baseball luminary, Emilio Sabourin. You should never trust those Havana slickers.

It was drizzling when we crossed Concordia Bridge over the Yumurí River and entered the suburb incongruously named Versalles, another important milestone in the city's urban history. The bridge was inaugurated in 1878 and named to honor the armistice that ended the Cuban insurgency known as the Ten Years' War (1868–1878). Its deliciously eclectic columns by Matanzas architect Pedro Celestino del Pandal have become a logo for the city. The bridge marked the edge of the Barrio de la Marina, an important site of Matanzas' vibrant Afro-Cuban culture, one of the city's glories.

Several blocks into Versalles was the Goicuría Barracks, the headquarters of the military garrison since colonial days, when it was known as Cuartel de

Fig. 5. Celebrated on a 1957 postage stamp, Concordia Bridge over the Yumurí (1878) has become the city's emblem. The stonework was designed and made in Matanzas but the prefab metal spans were cast overseas. Matanzas is known as "the City of Bridges."

Cristina. The barracks complex was attacked by a revolutionary group quite unrelated to Fidel Castro in 1956. It was a spectacular milestone of the struggle against the dictatorship of Fulgencio Batista. Not far beyond the barracks was the Hershey Railroad Station, built by the American chocolate magnate Milton Hershey to connect Havana to Matanzas via his vast sugar mill in Havana province.

Fig. 6. Goicuría attack commemorative stamp.

Gabriel de la Concepción Valdés, known as "Plácido," Matanzas' tragic mulatto poet, was executed in front of the barracks during the reign of terror launched by the colonial government in 1844. It was a preemptive measure against a vast slave conspiracy, the existence of which was long in doubt but which scholars increasingly accept as fact. The plot, known as La Escalera (The Ladder) because of the method used by the authorities to extract confessions, was a bloody chapter in the sordid annals of slavery. The victims would be mercilessly flogged while tied down to a ladder. The year 1844 went down in history as *el año del cuero* (the Year of the Lash).

As our car climbed the hills beyond Versalles, I made out the ramparts of San Severino Castle below, a hulking silhouette in the semidarkness. As I looked back to catch one last glimpse of my hometown, tears and the drizzle blurred the view. Far in the distance, across the wide bay, the Maya Point lighthouse winked its electric eye.

We reached the expressway with the first light of morning. The rain had eased. A truck full of Castro militiamen in their blue and olive green uniforms was coming towards us in the opposite lane. They were waving their arms and banging on the sides of the flatbed. Our car windows were open when we passed the truck, so we could hear the militiamen shouting slogans as they swooshed by, the syllables trailing off in a rush of moisture-laden wind: "Fidel, seguro, a los yanquis dale duro." ("Fidel, for sure, hit the Yankees hard.")

Exile breeds nostalgia, a longing for that which is left behind beyond recovery, and nostalgia can be painful. No wonder the ancient Greeks were said to prefer death to ostracism. For years after leaving Cuba, I grieved the loss of my homeland, my hometown, my family's heritage of hundreds of years in the country, my friends, in short, my Fatherland. Matanzas, the *patria chica,* the "small fatherland," being closer, hurt the most.

I haven't changed my fundamental view that Cuba would have been much better off without the turmoil and needless destruction inflicted in the name of the revolution. But I decided to see the results for myself in 2003, and returned to Cuba with another Raquel, my wife, Raquel Vallejo. The Vallejos are from Matanzas, but the family moved to Havana in the 1930s in search of better business opportunities. The times were not good for the erstwhile Athens.

The Castro brothers were still there when I returned, of course. Raúl is now president—proof that the revolution has a strong commitment to Fraternity, although Liberty and Equality are problematic. Fidel hangs on, however, and sometimes it seems as if he might never go away. He never will in the sense that he will haunt Cuban life for generations to come. Crossing Concordia Bridge over the Yumurí on a glorious, sunny morning made it seem as if he did not matter at all; as if his revolution did not matter at all; as if nothing mattered but the sky, the sunshine, and the gentle Cuban breeze ruffling the royal palms.

The reality of actually returning home was an intense emotional experience at once depressing and uplifting. Everything seemed so shabby and worn out relative to the Cuba I once knew, but Cuba's beauty and the human quality of the Cuban people more than compensated. Cuba has changed a lot, in a few cases for the better, in others for the worse. The social, political, and economic costs of almost five decades of what is officially called "socialism" are enormous, but some progress has been made. As usual, one must search for understanding in the shades of gray.

One must applaud Cuba's commitment to universal health care and universal education but be aware that both are used ruthlessly as mechanisms of social control. The Committees for the Defense of the Revolution do a lot of useful community work, but their primary task is to snitch on the citizenry. One can rejoice that the regime now allows the celebration of Christmas, but why was it ever forbidden? Or applaud City Historian Eusebio Leal's effort to restore Old Havana, but why was its ruination ever allowed and even encouraged? Severing Cuba's links to its meddling neighbor and occasionally obtuse rich uncle, the United States of America, was undoubtedly heroic, but one wonders whether it was not in equal measure stupid.

The Casa Cabañas, the big house in downtown Matanzas where I spent my childhood, was one block from Vigía Square, the town's former *plaza de armas*, on Milanés Street. It was designed to house a store and commercial offices at street level and two large luxury residential apartments on the top floor. The Beaux Arts faux-palatial façades are full of garlands, urns, and whatnot. It was built by my mother's father, Tomás Cabañas Vallín, and his brother, José, in 1917.

My grandmother Lola—her name was Dolores Batista, no relation to Fulgencio—and her sister-in-law, Florita, both recently widowed and struggling to stay afloat, had sold the building during the Depression, but we leased the living quarters back during the 1950s. In those days the street floor housed the offices of *El Republicano*, one of Matanzas' three dailies. Like so many Cuban families, the Cabañas were divided by the revolution. Tomás' descendants went to Miami; José's remained in Cuba. One of the Cuban Cabañas is a top diplomat who for a while ran the Cuban government's office dealing with exile affairs.

My sister and I were forbidden from standing on the Casa Cabañas' seemingly endless rows of balconies because—so they said—they had been pronounced unsafe by some engineer. The balcony doors were all padlocked; one could open only the louvered panels. Fifty years later the balconies are still there, perfectly solid and safe, weighing down on their presumptuous brackets. They will be there in another five hundred, when my memories and those of the house's current occupants will be long vanished.

Back in the 1950s, the sacred image of the Virgin of Charity of El Cobre, the patroness of Cuba, toured the island. "Cachita," as the Virgin is known familiarly by her devotees, was scheduled to go by in solemn procession under our balconies, followed by the bishop, his clergy, and thousands of the faithful. It was billed as a once-in-a-lifetime event. The Casa Cabañas was then the only two-story building along a key stretch of Milanés Street and had a privileged view. My mother threw caution to the winds and opened the balconies to our family, friends, and neighbors. Faith supplied what engineering would not guarantee. The same old Cuban flag that had greeted holidays at home since 1902 hung from the corner balcony and fluttered gently in the evening breeze. In the following days, nobody can remember exactly when, Mother removed the padlocks from the louvered doors.

"La Casa CABAÑAS"

— CALZADO COSIDO PARA CABALLEROS —

CALIDAD - - BUEN GUSTO - - ECONOMIA

FABRICACION NACIONAL
ESPECIAL DE ESTA CASA

Este Calzado es hecho en nuestra Fábrica de Matanzas.

PROTEJA LA INDUSTRIA LOCAL

Fig. 7. The Casa Cabañas, ca. 1925.

Another Cuban flag, big and subdued by the rain, hung from the flagpole at the Rancho Boyeros Airport when we arrived. Kids and their families were alighting from cars. We immediately knew they were our fellow passengers because for every kid there was a duffel bag just like ours. Called chorizos, or "sausages," they had been created by some enterprising luggage maker to contain the eighty pounds of luggage permitted per Miami passenger—not an ounce more.

Everybody called the Miami departure gate *la pecera* (the fishbowl), and now we could see why. Passengers were sequestered behind a glass wall. It was hot and muggy for us fishes. Little kids traveling alone—there were many—screamed for their parents visible on the other side of the glass partition. Raquel and I were on our own, too. Although we were not aware of it then, we were part of one of the most remarkable episodes in U.S. immigration history, Operation Pedro Pan. The brainchild of Monsignor Brian Walsh, a genial Irish priest based in Miami, Pedro Pan spirited out of Cuba some eighteen thousand children snatched, as it were, from the maw of godless, brainwashing, snitch-on-your-parents Communism.

A gruff official asked if I had any jewelry. I produced a little birthstone ring, a gift from my grandmother, which was promptly confiscated. Nearby, a fat woman in her fifties was in tears. She could not remove her wedding band, embedded in her finger. The officials offered her a mushy bar of soap. "If that does not work, we will have to clip your ring off, or you can stay," said a militia-woman with a half-smile on her face. After much soapy effort, and doubtless some pain, finger and ring were absolutely divorced. She turned towards her husband, her eyes full of tears, and showed him her chubby finger, now naked and inflamed. He shook his head. The fat woman and her man boarded immediately before us. "Hijos de puta" she was muttering. Sons of whores.

At long last the Pan Am Miami flight was cleared and began taxiing for takeoff.[5] When the landing gear retracted with a metallic thump and we were safely airborne, everyone began singing the Cuban national anthem as if on cue. Carried by voices choked with emotion, out of tune, and muted by the drone of the engines, the irony of our rousing ourselves to combat as we fled was lost on everybody.

As the DC6 climbed through the gray clouds, the skies turned suddenly deep blue and bright sunshine gilded the aircraft's wings. Soon enough, the plane began its descent and we were reimmersed in the wet darkness from which we had been temporarily delivered. As we broke through the low clouds, we could see Miami sprawl below, flat and unimpressive. Like Matanzas, Miami was drenched that August afternoon. The same storms dump rain in both places.

2 The Bay of Slaughters

BEFORE IT WAS A SPANISH colonial settlement, Matanzas was a bay with a sinister name, and before that it was Guánima. That is what the aboriginal Taínos called it. *Gua-* is a tenacious Taíno prefix that lives on in place-names and everyday speech throughout the Caribbean. As to the *nima* in *Guánima,* it could mean "heights." At any rate, the euphonious Guánima became the menacing Bahía de Matanzas (Bay of Slaughters) in the early sixteenth century. It is a pity that, unlike at Abana (Hispanicized as La Habana), the lovely native place-name did not prevail. It would have been fun to be a *guanimero* instead of a matancero. It sounds deliciously Taíno, and there would have been no need to explain the slaughters away.

The unusual colonial name, which I will discuss in some detail later on, resulted from an equally unusual event—whether heroic or tragic depends on your point of view—that took place in the bay's environs around 1510. Matanzas had another fifteen minutes of fame on September 9, 1628, when a Dutch West India Company fleet under Pieter Pieterszon Heyn—"Piet Heyn" for short—bottled up the Spanish *flota* at the harbor and captured the vast wealth it was carrying. The spectacle, no doubt frightening to the people living in the scattered hamlets around the big bay, must have lived on in long-recounted tales.

That was a long time ago. Before the Dutch presented to the city a superb bronze statue of their hero, most contemporary matanceros were blissfully unaware of that event and its vast ramifications. Heyn now stands next to the seawall, his bronze eyes gazing into the blue yonder. There is no plinth supporting the statue; he shares the sidewalk with passersby. The sculptor imagined the victorious admiral facing the wind of some remote horizon, his ruffles agitated by a wind long becalmed.

By the time the Dutch left Matanzas Bay, their ships heavy with Spanish booty, the native way of life that had unfolded there for ages was all but gone.[1] A century after the Spanish invasion, the Cuban aboriginals had been nearly wiped out in one of history's worst demographic tragedies. Nearly but not quite. The demise of the Taínos is a myth which, like all myths, contains a great deal of untruth. Native communities survive to this day, especially in the eastern part of the island.

There had been several waves of migration into Cuba before the Spanish showed up. Native settlers island-hopped by canoe all the way from South America as far north as the Bahamas. The Taínos were latecomers who imposed their hegemony and superior technology on earlier inhabitants. Eventually, they might have made it north to the homeland of the fierce Calusas of South Florida, but the Calusas beat them to the punch, raiding Cuban Taíno villages in their seafaring dugouts. The Postclassic Mayas, another great canoeing civilization, might in time have colonized Cuba, with incalculable consequences. The arrival of the Spanish foreclosed any such possibilities. Cuba's destiny as the "Key to the Gulf" would be fulfilled in the age of galleons, not the age of canoes.

Guánima was surrounded by tall primary rain forest. The trees grew all the way to the shoreline, there to meet with the pristine ocean. Three large rivers, the Guainey, Babonao, and Jibacabuya—otherwise the San Juan, Yumurí, and Canímar—and another tiny one, the Guaybaque, guaranteed an abundant supply of water. Yet another river, the Sabicú, now subsumed by the city itself, existed at contact.[2] The original Matanzans lived in several settlements around the bay. The rivers connected coastal dwellers with other groups living in the fertile adjacent valleys.

Clever agriculturists, the first Matanzans had mastered at contact the technique of the *conuco*, building the marvelously productive mounds where the ancient circum-Caribbean people grew their food with remarkable efficacy and economy of means. They were legendary fishermen who mined the protein wealth of their fluvial and maritime environment with consummate skill.

From time to time a hurricane would roar by, disrupting the lives of the people and reminding them of the power of that capricious deity Juracán, whence

Fig. 8. Cast in bronze, Piet Heyn surveys the Bay of Slaughters.

the modern name for these tempests derives. With remarkable insight, they expressed Juracán as a vortex. Any modern meteorologist would recognize his glyph as a brilliant logo. Juracán's visitations wrought much havoc but could not destroy the usual rhythms of wet and dry seasons, planting and harvesting, work, worship, rest, and the things people do whether they dress in guayaberas or loincloths.

One day another hurricane of sorts made landfall not far from Guánima, at a place known as Abana, towards the setting sun. Like the high waters of Juracán, this whirlwind also came from the sea. It came in strange canoes. The people must have been quite amazed, for they had never seen the likes of those before. They had no idea that they were living in something called the year of our Lord 1508, which was just too bad. Much pain and suffering would be inflicted on them to remedy that deficiency.

The leader of the pale folks aboard the weird canoes was a native of Noia, a small seafaring town of Galicia, in the kingdom of Castile and Leon. His name was Sebastián de Ocampo.[3] He had orders from Nicolás de Ovando, the governor of Hispaniola, to circumnavigate the land Columbus had earlier called "Juana" after the crazy princess of Castile. It is certain that he put in at Havana, where he careened his flotilla, less certain that he actually made it to Matanzas. The news of the strangers' arrival, however, must have traveled swiftly on foot among the interconnected native villages.

Ovando wanted a key question settled: was Cuba, in fact, an island or a peninsula? He needed better intelligence as to its resources. The governor's instructions came directly from King Ferdinand of Aragon himself, who was keenly interested in the economic potential of the land. Ocampo established Cuba's insularity for the record and became the first *gallego* to play a role in Cuba's history. He would not be the last, of course.

The land now known for sure to be an island attracted other Spanish visitors in the following years. Between 1511 and 1513, Diego Velázquez de Cuéllar, *adelantado* of Cuba, settled the first cities. In 1513, his lieutenant, Pánfilo de Narváez, visited Guánima, which soon acquired a reputation among the Castilians for the fertility of its soils and abundance of its agricultural produce. Velázquez himself went there in 1519.[4]

The year before Velazquez' visit, four vessels had put into the bay to collect supplies for Juan de Grijalva's planned expedition to the Yucatan. Guánima was already being referred to as "Puerto de Matanzas" among the Spanish. Much ink has been shed regarding the origin of the sinister name. Bernal Díaz del Castillo was aboard one of the vessels. He recorded the tragic story behind the name's origins in his *Verdadera historia de la conquista de la Nueva España* "although," he dutifully protested, "it is beyond my subject matter." This is what Bernal had to say:

> Before this island was conquered, a ship was wrecked upon this shore, near the river and harbor, and it happened that some thirty Spanish individuals were aboard, including two women. So, in order to get them across the river [that is, the bay], which in this place carries a lot of water, many natives came over from Havana and other towns. They had the secret design of killing the Spaniards but fearing to attack them on land, they lured them into their canoes. And then, when they were in mid-stream, the Indians overturned the canoes and killed all the Spaniards save three men and a woman, who was very beautiful. One of the treacherous chiefs took her, and they allocated the three Spaniards among the others. . . . I

knew the woman. After the island was won over, she was taken back from her captor, and I saw her married to a Pedro Sánchez Farfán in the town of Trinidad. And I also met the three Spaniards, one so-called Gonzalo Mejía, an elderly native of Jerez and a Joan de Madrigal, single, and another fellow by the name of Cascorro, a sailor born in Moguer.[5]

Fray Bartolomé de las Casas in his famous *Historia de las Indias* offers a variant of this narrative. According to Las Casas, two Spanish women were rescued by the Spanish, one of them around forty, the other around eighteen years old. Las Casas describes in considerable detail the fact that they were stark naked "liked their mothers brought them to the world." This is their story, as told by the great padre:

> The Indians had killed certain Spaniards with whom they had come to that harbor, which was therefore named, or so I believe, of the Slaughters, which is an arm of the sea. The Spaniards wanted to go somewhere else, so they got with the Indians in canoes, and once they were in the middle of the lake [that is, the bay], the Indians flooded [the canoes], and since so few of them knew how to swim, they drowned, and [the Indians] with their oars helped them exit this life. Only the two women, being women, were allowed to live. Seven Spaniards who could swim swam to land with their swords, which they never left behind, and once they were safely on land, they went to a village. The cacique or chief asked them to drop their swords, and once they had done that, the chief hung them from a great tree called a ceiba.[6]

Like Bernal, Las Casas also reports that both women were happily married after their rescue, in spite of their harrowing experience.

That is all. Both Bernal and Las Casas agree on the fundamentals: a substantial number of Spaniards were dispatched by drowning when the canoes in which they were traveling were overturned in mid-harbor. The women—whether one or two is an open question—were retained for sexual services by the natives. The male survivors—three or seven—were either enslaved or hung from a ceiba (*Ceiba pentranda,* or kapok). When one considers what the thorny trunk of a ceiba can do to human flesh, that would not have been a pretty sight.[7] In spite of their discrepancies, Las Casas' titillating tale and Bernal's reluctant account give us enough clues to fix with some accuracy the date of the arrival of this mysterious and ill-fated vessel.

That it was not part of the Ocampo expedition is certain. Ocampo sailed on two vessels, both accounted for. Could the ship have been part of the Vicente Yáñez Pinzón expedition which, according to Peter Martyr, circumnavigated Cuba even before Ocampo did so?[8] By the time Velázquez and his redoubtable lieutenant, Narváez, embarked on the exploration and settlement of Cuba, the story of the shipwrecked Spaniards was already known. In fact, Narváez was on the lookout for survivors. What the mystery ship was, who had sent it, and where it was going are tantalizing questions for which no one has provided answers.

The massacre, however, was a certain and dreadful event. It reveals that the original guanimeros were tough people not to be trifled with. Throughout the tragic conquest of the Caribbean, native people were normally on the receiving end of atrocities. We need look no further than Narváez' bloody march across Cuba. He outdid himself at a place called Caonao, where, according to Las Casas' estimate, some two thousand natives were wasted. (Velázquez gives the much more modest and likely more accurate figure of 168, still quite a performance.)[9]

The lost ship's impact on the Spaniards' imagination was great and fixed the awful name "Bay of Slaughters" upon that arm of the sea. In time, the name would encompass the city and province as well. Guillermo Cabrera Infante once asked himself whether there was another country in the world with a place named "Slaughters."[10] The answer is yes: there is La Matanza near Buenos Aires and Fort Matanzas on Matanzas Inlet near St. Augustine, Florida. Though clearly not unique, the name is certainly unnerving. Maybe matanceros are secretly haunted by its sinister implications and, like children with odd names, have always been on the lookout for a neat alias. It is not coincidental that Matanzas is renowned as "the Cuban city of nicknames."

The name appears on maps from a very early date. This was not a recognition of the place's notoriety but an acknowledgment of the fact—important to mariners—that the only reference point on Cuba's northern coast is the nearby hill Pan de Matanzas. According to Trelles, Matanzas' cartographic debut was in Girolamo Benzoni's *Historia del Nuovo Mondo* (Venice, 1565).[11] It also appears in the work of Benzoni's contemporary and fellow Venetian Giacomo Gastaldi (ca. 1500–ca. 1565). A Gastaldi map, otherwise clueless as to the island's true aspect—his Cuba looks a bit like an overcooked sausage—shows Matanzas in its correct location. Havana ("San Cristóbal") still appears in its

Fig. 9. *Isola di Cuba* by Giacomo Gastaldi (Venice, 1565). Cuba looks like an overcooked sausage but Matanzas is correctly located. (Courtesy of Geography and Maps Division, Library of Congress)

original location on the southern shore of the island, whence it was moved after a few years.[12]

Although obviously unknown to Trelles (and Gastaldi, for that matter), the commendably accurate map of Cuba offered by Alonso de Santa Cruz in his famed *Islario general de todas las islas* of 1539–1565 shows Matanzas correctly located and richly detailed. The harbor and the San Juan and Yumurí rivers are clearly rendered, the "Ycacos" peninsula is identified and, what is more remarkable, Matanzas is indicated as a settled town with its castle and moat. Not yet, don Alonso. The building of the castle was still almost a century and a half into the future but the acknowledgment that a community, although not a formal city, existed there is important.[13]

Matanzas Bay—or if you prefer, Guánima—is wide open and inviting, like a friend's embrace. Punta Gorda marks its western tip and Punta de Maya its eastern one. Punta Gorda is a rugged headland. Punta de Maya is the flat top of an emerging marine terrace barely rising above the sea level. The two are separated by a distance of six kilometers. An elegant little lighthouse at Punta de Maya locates the entrance to the harbor and warns mariners of the reefs lying offshore.

The southern shore is flat. The immediate hinterland is a typical Karst formation. This accounts for the many caves in the city's environs, including the famous Bellamar Caverns, a great tourist attraction of times gone by. A spelunker's paradise since native days, Matanzas' caverns have yielded much information about aboriginal Cubans. Local folk love their caves. Dr. Ercilio

Vento Canosa, the city's Renaissance man in residence, also presides over the Cuban Speleological Society.

The northern shore of the bay is hilly, rising up to the gentle heights of the Havana-Matanzas range at La Cumbre. The hills form a huge amphitheater around the adjacent Yumurí Valley with its meandering river. From the summit (which is what *la cumbre* means), a spectacular view of the harbor may be had and, if you turn around, one of the valley that is just as breathtaking. Grand Duke Alexis Alexandrovich of Russia, who visited Matanzas in the 1870s famously remarked that the valley, Matanzas' Eden, "only lacked Adam and Eve."[14] Fortunately, it also lacks malignant serpents. A blessing of the Cuban countryside is that, with the exception of one species of spider, poisonous animals do not exist.

The Yumurí River empties into the bay through a lovely gorge called El Abra, a local landmark. The lush, green expanse of the valley is dominated by the impressive Pan de Matanzas, visible in the far distance with its profile reminiscent of a sleeping woman. For almost five hundred years, ships have been guided by the Pan into Matanzas Bay; you can see it for miles offshore. Playing Popocatépetl to this Ixtlacíhuatl is the rugged Palenque. As its name indicates, the Palenque was a refuge of runaway slaves during the colonial period.

Matanceros have a close relationship to their little corner of the vast ocean. Couples court on the *malecón* (seawall), modeled after Havana's but in a minor key. In Cuba, malecones seem to have a distinctly romantic aura. Generations of local kids have cast their lines into the harbor seeking yellowtails, snappers, and groupers, or have gone swimming in the charming, tiny horseshoe beach at Bueyvaquita or skin-dived at the Laja, a shallow reef-like formation in the middle of a bay otherwise known for its remarkable depths—more than eight hundred meters off Rubalcava Point at the entrance.[15]

Local devotees of Olokún and Yemayá, the marine deities of the Yoruba, have entrusted their offerings to the harbor for generations, hoping to please the holy orishas. Matanzas Bay is especially favored by Olokún devotees. Olokún, one of Yemayá's *caminos,* or manifestations, presides over the abyssal oceans. Matanzas Bay is a fitting abode, given the harbor's enormous marine depths. It is not unusual to run into flotsam that clearly came from such offerings. People who are not Santería devotees stay respectfully clear of it. No one wants to offend the lovely but capricious Yemayá, let alone Olokún, the irascible deity of the blue.

People of all ages have sat on the malecón in the still of night when, if you paid attention, you could hear conversations carried on the water from far away. At eleven o'clock taps was played at the military garrison in the Versalles sector of town. The night air would carry the brassy, melancholy notes across the water, and everybody would look at their watches.

Many a *balsero* (freedom rafter) has seen the city's lights disappear over the horizon. Matanzas Bay has been a favored point of departure because of the relatively short distance to the United States. La Boca de Camarioca—the town of Camarioca proper is a few kilometers inland—lies not far from Maya Point, on the southeastern edge of the bay but technically outside of it, some twenty kilometers from Matanzas city. The first organized boat exodus from Cuba was the Camarioca event of 1966, a predecessor and dress rehearsal for the much larger Mariel episode of 1980, when 125,000 Cubans were picked up by relatives from the United States. In the summer of 1994 thousands more left on literally anything that would float.

Watching the movement of ships at the port has always been great free entertainment and the melancholy wail of foghorns very much a part of the city's soundtrack. When I was a kid, large ocean liners would routinely put in at Matanzas Bay because Havana was too tight for them. I vividly remember the *Ile de France* riding at anchor in the harbor, all lit up like a Christmas tree. A 1936 stamp issue shows the gigantic *Rex* at anchor in the deep bay. The bay's depth and draught, strategic location within the Havana-Varadero corridor, and latent tourist appeal suggest Matanzas' potential as an ideal cruise port in an as-yet unlikely but imaginable future. The sea was in the beginning, is now, and ever shall be the main protagonist of the Matanzas story.

Creating a system of transatlantic convoys was possibly the single most important policy decision affecting Cuba made by Spanish authorities in the entire colonial period. In 1543, the king decreed that all navigation between Spain and the Indies should be in convoys. Four years later, an armed naval escort was mandated for all crossings.

Rather than sailing alone or in small groups across the Atlantic, Spanish ships were to sail in a large company. The reason is all too clear: it was an attempt to foil the designs of Spain's enemies in the New World and to frustrate the pirates and privateers of the Caribbean. Seek safety in numbers. The doctrine was that simple, and that effective.

There was a downside to this practice. Putting all your ships in one fleet is the equivalent of putting all your eggs in one basket. It raised the ominous possibility of losing the entire fleet at one go. It happened once, and it happened in Matanzas Bay. That fateful day was September 9, 1628. The catastrophe made Matanzas a household word in the Netherlands and Piet Heyn a Dutch hero for the ages.

What was especially noteworthy about the Matanzas debacle was not only its scope—which was enormous—but, in hindsight, its exceptionality. On the whole, the system of the flotas worked. Any doubter should consult that work of titanic scholarship by the French historians Pierre and Hughette Chaunu: *Seville et l'Atlantique*. The Chaunus, a husband-and-wife team, meticulously and with infinite patience and skill traced the patterns of Spain's transatlantic trade for the entire Spanish colonial period, revealing its complexity and remarkable scope.

This is how it functioned: a convoy carrying the products of Mexico and the Orient (sent to Mexico via Acapulco on the transpacific Manila galleon) was to sail from Veracruz to Havana every year. It was joined there by another fleet sailing from Cartagena de Indias, carrying the precious metals and merchandises of South America. The first of these formations was the flota par excellence—la Flota de la Nueva España. The second was referred to as the Galeones de Tierra Firme (or simply, "the Galleons"). There were some subsidiary formations, for example, a small flotilla sailed from Honduras to Havana carrying the produce of that portion of the empire, there to join the others.

Once assembled at Havana, the transatlantic convoy would depart, sail the New Bahama Channel and head for the ocean blue. It was sped along by the Gulf Stream and prevailing winds, not to mention the intercession of Our Lady of Fair Winds (Nuestra Señora del Buen Aire), the patroness of mariners. After weeks at sea, the lumbering ships would sight the shores of Spain.

The wait in Havana could extend for weeks or months, to the delight of local merchants and all and sundry residents. No need to wonder why Havana's whores have always been renowned. They have had abundant custom from the earliest of colonial times. The massive fleet would cross the great water and enter the mouth of the Guadalquivir in sight of Palos de la Frontera. A little longer and the Giralda and Seville's Torre del Oro came into view. Seville was the Spanish terminus of the route and was the only port in Spain authorized to trade with the New World. It was the emporium of the Indies.

The outbound leg followed essentially the same itinerary in reverse, except that the ships sailed down to the Canaries before heading west, in order to take advantage of winds and currents. That, in a nutshell, was *la carrera de las Indias*. Matanzas had a cut in the action, of course. The little settlement by the broad harbor was one of the Cuban localities that grew the foodstuffs and salted the bacon that ended up in the holds of the big galleons. (Meanwhile, it carried on brisk side trades with whoever else entered the harbor—but hush-hush, of course. This was the infamous *comercio de rescate* in Spanish colonial terminology, otherwise contraband.)

In 1621, events took place in Europe that would directly impact the history of the New World. At the end of their truce with Spain, the Dutch formed the West India Company, modeled after their very successful East India counterpart, whose activities had secured a Southeast Asian empire for the Hollanders. A main objective of the West India Company was to capture one of Spain's transatlantic fleets. An attempt in 1626 proved unsuccessful when the Spanish vessels cleverly eluded the Dutch in the Old Bahama Channel. The Dutch commander was Rotterdam's Pieter Pieterszon Heyn, an East India veteran. He would be back.[16]

In 1628, the fleet from New Spain gathered at Veracruz under the protection of San Juan de Ulúa's bastions, ready to begin its crossing of the Atlantic. The ungainly galleons rode low on the water. They were loaded with precious metals: two years' worth of treasure from the Orient, Mexico, and Guatemala. The Spanish admiral, Juan de Benavides y Bazán, was a veteran of the carrera de las Indias and a scion of one of Spain's great seafaring families. On July 21, 1628, Benavides gave orders to weigh anchor at Veracruz but ran into a gale that sent the *capitana* to the bottom and damaged several other vessels, delaying the fleet's departure for weeks while repairs were undertaken. (In Spanish naval protocol, the *almiranta* is the admiral's flagship, the capitana that of his second in command.)

Unbeknownst to Benavides when his ships finally left, a trap had been set for him in Cuban waters by the West India Company fleet, again under Heyn's command. The governor of Cuba, Lorenzo de Cabrera, was aware that two Dutch fleets operated in the waters to the north of the island, one consisting of nine sails and the other of twenty-nine. It was a fearsome situation. Cabrera, ever diligent, dispatched couriers to Veracruz and Cartagena with a warning. A courier made it to Cartagena, but none came to Veracruz.

Heyn knew what he was doing. He knew Havana well. He had spent two years as a prisoner in Morro Castle, learned Spanish, understood the Spanish psychology, and had committed to memory as much as he could learn about the fleet's routine. Acting on his remarkable local knowledge and peerless seamanship, the Dutch commander ordered the smaller of his two fleets to patrol the northern coast of present-day Pinar del Río while he waited out at sea northeast of Havana.

On August 1, the commander of the smaller fleet, Pieter Andrianszon Ita, sighted the Spanish galleons from Honduras and closed in on them. The Spanish commander, Álvaro de la Cerda, cleverly assessing that the large Dutch battleships could not operate close to shore, ordered his smaller vessels to hug the coast. They almost made it to haven while fiercely exchanging gunfire with the enemy. The Spanish flagship caught fire and sank in full view of the horrified Havana citizenry. The encounter was commemorated in an anonymous print commissioned, no doubt, on Ita's behalf.[17]

Meanwhile, the New Spain fleet was sailing into Heyn's trap. At dawn on September 9, Benavides sighted the Pan de Matanzas to starboard and knew immediately he was off-target—he was too far east. As it turned out, the Spanish had mistaken the lights of the Dutch fleet for those of Havana and overshot their mark. The Spanish fleet would have to turn around now in order to make Havana's harbor. The cumbersome maneuver was underway when, toward ten o'clock in the morning, Dutch sails appeared on the horizon. It was an awe-inspiring sight.

Heyn had maneuvered his ships masterfully. To the east, a Dutch formation prevented the Spanish fleet from escaping toward the Old Bahama Channel. To the west, another had taken position between the Spanish vessels and the safety of Havana. A few of the Spanish merchantmen managed to sneak through in the knick of time, but the bulk of the Spanish fleet remained behind, quite well and truly surrounded.

Benavides had no time to call a formal war council. There were two judges from the Audiencia of Mexico aboard his flagship, so a hasty meeting was convened. Three options emerged. The first was to break through towards Havana, hoping to make it to the Cuban capital, guns blazing. The second was to sail onward towards the Atlantic and run the gauntlet of the Dutch fleet. Losing some, maybe most, of the Spanish ships was a virtual certainty in the first scenario. To cross the Atlantic with the agile Dutch fleet in hot pursuit was obviously foolhardy, and that option was promptly discarded.

The third option was to sail south towards Matanzas, make the harbor, hold the Dutch ships at bay, unload the treasure, and seek military support from Havana. The problem with this plan was that no one aboard the Spanish fleet knew Matanzas harbor with one exception: a certain Andrés de Agujetas, who was being transported to Spain as a prisoner for insubordination. Agujetas participated in the deliberations from his cage.

This shady character promised to lead the ships to a place where they could unload while the battleships trained their artillery on the Dutch. The Spanish would sail into the harbor with the breeze, but the Dutch would find it impossible to enter the harbor immediately because of the nightly *virazón*, when the prevailing *terral* winds would blow off the land. This, argued Agujetas, would give the Spanish enough time to save the cargo, position the warships, and meet the Dutch with a wall of fire.

With time ticking away and the Dutch pressing down on him, Benavides issued the order to sail into Matanzas Bay. As it turned out, Agujetas' knowledge of the bay was considerably less than precise. Unlike my friends and me, he had not gone fishing near the Laja, the shallows in the middle of the bay. And that's exactly where he led the Spanish men-of-war. One after another, they were caught between the shallows and the shore with their fore castles pointing toward land and the rear castles towards the sea. Unable to deliver a broadside except into each other, they became sitting ducks for Piet Heyn's ships. That night, a bright full moon lit the immobile Spanish fleet. The Dutch spent the night lodging sporadic, unnerving volleys into the helpless Spanish vessels.

With his men-of-war paralyzed and his merchantmen in disarray, Benavides was lost, and he knew it. All through the moonlit night and well into the morning, something completely unprecedented in Spain's naval annals happened: a thorough panic aboard. As the Dutch cannon boomed, sailors, bigwigs, and even the admiral himself clambered overboard into boats and anything that would float. The Dutch boarded nearly empty vessels. They had all the time in the world to board the Spanish bottoms, ransack the ships, take as many prizes as they could possibly sail, sink the rest, and depart leisurely back home. Their already sizable fleet was augmented by four captured men-of-war and four large merchantmen fully loaded with bullion and precious merchandise. The contents of each captured ship were proudly and meticulously noted in some of the broadsides circulated at the time: this one loaded with bullion, that one with indigo, the other with cacao—a king's ransom.[18]

Piet Heyn's return to Holland in triumph was the West India Company's finest hour. The sale of the booty produced fifteen million florins and meant that the West India Company could pay its stockholders an unprecedented div-

Fig. 10. Dutch capture of the *"Zilvervloot"* (Silver Fleet), in Matanzas harbor, September 1628 (detail). (Engraving by Claes Visscher, courtesy of Geography and Maps Division, Library of Congress)

idend. Medals were struck in Heyn's honor. Engravings showed the Matanzas harbor, Heyn's portrait, and the great Dutch victory. The mountains are much too tall in these artistic renderings perhaps, but some leeway must be allowed for patriotic enthusiasm and the aesthetics of propaganda. In one particularly lovely engraving, Benavides and his men are shown running away on a distant beach, like tiny little ants.[19]

Heyn's apotheosis was matched by Benavides' dishonor. He had to answer to his sovereign, who was determined to have his head. "I do not even remember how much treasure was lost, for that is of minor consequence," remarked Philip IV, no doubt disingenuously, "but for the loss of our honor . . . for that he must pay."[20] And pay he did. The king understood the values of his age very well, and knew what the real issues were.

So indeed did the great Spanish jurist Juan de Solórzano Pereira, who was in Havana when Benavides showed up after his spineless performance. Benavides was sent to Spain in chains and Solórzano led the prosecution. This is the late Manuel Moreno Fraginals' take on his efforts:

> Solórzano Pereira's legal brief might well be considered one of the age's greatest legal monuments, one in which the norms dictated by honor, reputation, noblesse, family tradition, courage, manhood, moral authority before subordinates, the power of example, willingness to defend one's reputation and that of those under one's authority, and the refusal to endure humiliation constitute an inviolable supra-legal code. Although true to the procedural norms of the age, the brief against Benavides y Bazán was in a way a moral judgment, where traditional knightly values supplanted the penal code. We are therefore in the presence of a masterpiece of baroque art which no literary critic has ever cited.[21]

The hapless admiral was executed with imposing solemnity at Seville's San Fernando Square on May 18, 1634. If Philip had had his way, Benavides' head would have been displayed in Matanzas in perpetuity. Fortunately, that did not happen; it would have been terrible for a place with such a name.[22]

Heyn did not live long to enjoy his well-deserved fame. He died in 1629. His glory will live for as long as soccer is played and beer drunk—which is to say forever—in "De Zilvervloot," a Dutch evergreen and a perennial favorite of cheering fans:

> Piet Heyn, Piet Heyn,
> Piet Heyn, so short his name
> So truly great his deed,
> 'Twas he who captured the silver fleet.[23]

3   Governor Manzaneda's Castle

Founding a city in the Indies was a solemn event. Matanzas had existed as a populated place since early colonial days but was not formally settled until 1693, a belated response to the lessons of 1628. The city of the two rivers belongs to a second wave of Cuban urban foundations that included also Santa Clara (1689) carried out by a remarkable colonial governor, Severino de Manzaneda, towards the end of the Hapsburg era.[1]

Havana was essentially a fortified supply depot, and Matanzas part of its productive backyard. The fleets' demand for foodstuffs, hides, and tallow—the last essential for making candles—far exceeded the productive capacity of the modest Havana population. Raising cattle and swine for the fleets consequently became the matanceros' livelihood since early on. The preservation of meat required salt, and the exploitation of salt pans engaged local energies since at least 1587, when a Luis Herrera was authorized to extract salt from Punta de Hicacos.[2] The salt pans near modern-day Varadero functioned until the early 1960s.

Before too long, Matanzas' produce, deep harbor, and abundance of fresh water caught the eye of buccaneers and filibusters. Dutch, French, and English ships called to replenish their water supplies and trade with the locals, the latter ever willing to operate on the margins of the law to obtain much-needed supplies, including an occasional slave. Matanzas consumers and their smuggling partners had it all figured out, as the royal officials in Havana reported to the crown in 1679:

Ships of the Dutch and other nations enter the harbor with the pretext of loading water and wood before venturing into the Bahama Channel and, while there, trade with the local folks, who take advantage of the prices of cloth and merchandise. Even though the owner of a neighboring estate invariably sends word of the goings-on to the governor and Captain-General, the smugglers have plenty of time to unload their wares in places where they cannot be caught, availing themselves of the many coves and hideaways along the vast shoreline with the full connivance of the local people, which makes law enforcement impossible no matter how hard we try.[3]

In August of 1678, two French pirate vessels, frustrated by their inability to attack Havana, fell upon three Dutch ships carrying on illicit trade at Matanzas, boarded them, and sailed away with their cargo. That a Dutch merchant flotilla could sail into the harbor and set up shop with such brazen impunity gives a measure of the free-for-all that Matanzas' harbor was in those days.

It was not the Dutchmen's lucky day. The pirates put fifty Dutch sailors ashore, there to await their fate. Unwilling to put them to work on the Havana walls for security reasons, the governor allowed the stranded mariners to be rescued by another Dutch ship shortly thereafter, and good riddance. He must have been thoroughly delighted at the discomfiture inflicted on the despised Dutch at Matanzas Bay precisely fifty years after the disaster of 1628.[4]

The Cuban landscape was very different then from what we see today. The open fields, palm groves, and savanna-like environment of western Cuba are the successors of lush tropical rain forest. Cuba then was blanketed by first-growth forest, undisturbed by human activity for eons of time save for the few clearings where the native folks would settle their villages. Matanzas was the green heart of the great forest, her binding red soil nurturing the giants that shot ever upwards in search of light in the upper canopy. It looked not unlike those paintings by Tomás Sánchez that so powerfully evoke a wild, primeval Cuba.

The quality of Cuban timber became legendary. Philip II insisted on Cuban precious woods for the joinery of El Escorial and took a personal interest in the matter. His royal hand often appeared on the pages of Escorial accounts insisting on Cuban timber or demanding that "without discussion or difficulty of any kind," skippers load the materials His Majesty required.[5] Timber was a strategic material—it went into ships and became the basis of the advanced shipbuilding industry that flourished in Cuba during the colonial period.[6] Eighteenth-century maps show virtually the entire region as "los cortes de madera del Rey" (the king's timber reserves) until the eve of the nineteenth-century sugar boom.

Encomiendas, the thinly disguised form of slavery under which the natives rendered tribute to Spanish landowners—supposedly in exchange for religious instruction—were granted to early settlers, but the rapid decline of the native population made them worthless.[7] No Indians, no tribute: Cuba was not to be encomienda country. Acreage was another story. Land was essential to cattle raising and agriculture, and it was allocated in usufruct by local authorities in the monarch's name.[8] The key to obtaining grants, or *mercedes,* was access to the government in Havana.

The first merced in Matanzas, awarded in March 1558, went to Inés de Gamboa, the widow of Pedro Velázquez. It included the site of Canímar and the savanna of Macuriges. Thinly populated Matanzas became a milch cow for Havana interests with access to official largesse and capable of persuading, extorting, or bribing their way into the land-grant sweepstakes. The small oligarchy that ran the Havana city council was in a privileged position to play the game. So was the church, which claimed a slice. Major mercedes of land in the Matanzas region were made to the powerful convent of Santa Clara de Asís in Havana.[9]

Grants came in two kinds: *hatos* if meant for the raising of range cattle; and *corrales,* essentially for pigs. In either case, grants were carved out in circles generated from a central point marked by a *bramador,* or marker. This typically Cuban system left a lasting trace on the landscape. Well into the twentieth century, it was not uncommon for rural properties to have boundaries in the shape of an arc of a circle. Where two such circumferences intersected, a *realengo* was created—the source of much litigation.

Sugarcane arrived early, if on a modest scale. By 1598, Governor Juan de Maldonado Barnuevo reported to the crown that cane fields had existed in Matanzas for more than forty years.[10] Around 1620, Francisco Díaz Pimienta, a colorful Cuban-born navigator, soldier, smuggler, and pioneering writer, built a *trapiche,* or sugar mill, operated by water from the Cañas River, a tributary of the San Juan.

Benavides stopped at the Díaz Pimienta mill in his hasty flight from the Dutch in 1628. He is said to have buried some treasure nearby. One wonders how he could have done so without anyone noticing and in the short time he had. Yet tales of buried treasure live on, however improbable their script. Rumors of *entierros* were still part of the region's folklore at least well into the 1950s, when I went camping there with my friends.

Matanzas' vulnerability was simultaneously a fiscal headache and a security concern. The local population was dispersed and difficult to control. Vigías had been located in the region since at least the 1570s, but the lookouts were difficult to supply and manage. One was located at the tiny sugar mill of Juan Pérez Borroto, who tried his best to keep the government in Havana more or less informed of the local scene.[11]

Colonial authorities could tolerate fiscal evasion in a backwater, but what if an organized force used Matanzas as a base to threaten Havana itself? Thomas Gage, the renegade friar and English spy, discussed such an eventuality in some detail. For the Spanish, it was a nightmarish scenario.[12]

The debacle of 1628 had demonstrated the potential vulnerability of Havana from its unfortified land side. No matter how fierce and forbidding the bastions protecting the shoreline, taking the city would be a cakewalk for a determined and large enough force coming in from the south, the "soft underbelly" of Havana, to use Churchill's terminology. Cromwell's occupation of Jamaica in 1655 served as a reminder that there was no dearth of enemies angling for control of such a critical parcel of the Spanish Empire. Whoever controlled Havana controlled access to the Caribbean, and whoever did that had a stranglehold on the Spanish New World empire.

As early as 1653, Governor Francisco Xelder had recommended the fortification of Matanzas to no avail. In October 1680 Governor Joseph de Córdoba Ponce de León urged the fortification and settlement of the Matanzas harbor as part of a comprehensive plan to defend Havana itself.[13] He discussed in greater detail than anyone before him the project's topographic, strategic, and financial aspects. For good measure, he attached to his proposal a map of the harbor with precise suggestions for the location of a fort at Punta Gorda.

The urgency of the matter was underlined the following year when a French privateer visited the harbor and laid the Pérez Borroto mill waste. This left the region with no surveillance whatsoever. Local smugglers must have been secretly delighted: the snitch was gone. Pérez Borroto was understandably chastised. He steadfastly refused to go back unless security was provided.[14]

Córdoba's plan landed on the desk of Joseph de Veytia Linage, Spain's foremost expert on colonial trade and defense. Veytia immediately commissioned two studies of the proposal. The studies concurred that the fortification and settlement of Matanzas could not be postponed and that it must be carried on swiftly "to prevent any enemy from damaging the works while [they are] still vulnerable." Veytia's resolute endorsement cut through the red tape. On April 14, 1682, a royal order commanded the governor in Havana to build a stone fort in Matanzas and appropriated thirty thousand pesos for that purpose. And, the royal order went on:

> under the protection of said castle you should plant a settlement on the site indicated in [Córdoba's] map, a fertile and pleasant location adjacent to the river of Matanzas, easy to defend and healthy, with clean air and good aspect. And you should settle the place with 30 families that are to go there from the Canaries, joining to them the dispersed population of said region to which others will no doubt join, seeing that the land is secured.[15]

The order left no doubt as to the location of the fort: it had to be where indicated on the 1680 map. The government obviously wanted no deviations that might delay the works. Almost one year later, the governor informed the crown that a ship had arrived from Mexico with the stocks, gunpowder, and ordnance to supply the proposed Matanzas fort, and asked for one hundred slaves to complete the Havana walls and begin the Matanzas project.

Not much happened over the next few years. Córdoba left office in 1685 and his successors, Manuel de Murguía y Mesa (1685–87) and Diego Antonio de Viana e Hinojosa (1687–89), proved either unwilling or unequal to the task. It would take a new governor, Severino García de Manzaneda Salazar Salinas de Zumalabe y Rozas, Knight of Santiago, Field Master of Spanish Infantry, to re-energize the project.[16]

Don Severino was born in Balmaseda, in the ancient señorío of Biscay, in 1644. Balmaseda is famed throughout Spain for its passion play. He was christened in the imposing local parish church and was given the name of the town's patron, Saint Severinus, which he would later on transmit to Matanzas. Manzaneda was the patron of the *anteiglesia* of nearby Galdácano. The church for which don Severino was responsible was Andra Mari de Elejalde, one of Biscay's Romanesque jewels. Patronage of the church in Spain was a realengo, that is, a royal prerogative. His patronage of a modest but old and encrusted church suggests that Manzaneda belonged to an ancient and distinguished if not necessarily affluent lineage.

A veteran of many battles in Flanders, Sicily, and the Roussillon, Manzaneda took office in Havana in 1689 and held it until 1697. The late Leví Marrero, one of the smartest and most constructive scholars Cuba ever produced, hails him as "one of the smartest and most constructive governors of the Cuban colonial period."[17]

Energetic and efficient, Manzaneda took nothing for granted, beginning with the suitability of the proposed location for the Matanzas fort. In a lengthy and tightly reasoned letter written on August 11, 1691, he ventured a cogent criticism of the existing proposal. The 1680 map was wrong. There were shallows in the harbor but not where Córdoba had indicated. They defined two channels, one to the north and another to the south, permitting ships of reasonable draft to enter deep into the bay. Isolated Punta Gorda therefore made no sense as the location for the castle. A location closer to the bottom of the harbor and, consequently, to the Yumurí and San Juan rivers, certainly did.[18]

The governor proceeded to Matanzas in January of 1693 with an entourage that included don Juan de Herrera Sotomayor, a military engineer responsible for the technical aspects of the project; don Bartolomé de Arriola, accountant; and don Diego de Peñalver Angulo, controller of the royal exchequer. On launches commandeered from one of the fishing villages along the shores, Manzaneda and his companions rowed out to the middle of the harbor, where they took sounds. At the proposed site for the castle they found a thatched hut belonging to a Juan de Mirabal. The poor fellow was immediately ordered to clear the site.[19]

The preliminary decision making extended for several weeks in October and November 1693. The governor, Bishop Fray Diego Evelino de Compostela, and their entourages lodged in a campsite next to the San Juan River. The feast of St. Charles Borromeus fell on November 4, and the saintly archbishop of Milan, one of the heroes of the Counter-Reformation, was invoked as the new city's patron and co-namesake (with Saint Severinus, after the governor's patron saint).

The first book of baptisms of the new parish records that, on October 14, Fray Diego Evelino baptized a black, native of the Congo, slave of don Santiago de Arrate, who was named Joseph. A few days later, the prelate joined

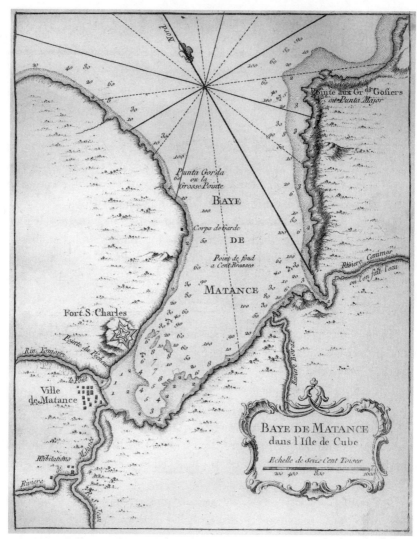

Fig. 11. Map of Matanzas Bay from Jacques Nicholas Bellin's atlas, Paris, 1764.

in matrimony Domingo Rodríguez, a widower from Tenerife, and Josefa Rodríguez, legitimate daughter of Domingo Alfonso and Catalina Rodríguez, both natives of San Francisco de la Rambla, on the island of Tenerife. One of the witnesses was Captain Diego Méndez de León Illada, of whom we shall hear more later.[20] The original parish church, a poor hut made of wattle-and-daub walls and a thatched roof, was ready for services on September 8, 1695, when the first parish priest, Br. Sebastián Ruiz Benítez, installed the Blessed Sacrament in the presence of the *cabildo* (council) and authorities.

No effete cavalier with a plumed hat, Governor Manzaneda was a classic type A personality who often came close to impertinence. His correspondence with Madrid reveals the "thinking outside the box" that is the mark of every successful executive, but he could get carried away. After the conclusion of the foundational formalities, he virtually granted a coat of arms to the new city. "Me pareció darle por armas," he wrote:

> I saw fit to grant [the new city] for arms two gates instead of the two keys that this city [of Havana] bears, and which symbolize the two kingdoms [of Spain and the Indies] and, since Matanzas and its castle are located in the port that controls both the Old and the Bahama Channels, which is the way through which fleets, treasure, and trade travel to those kingdoms [of Spain], the new city, it being Your Majesty's pleasure, could be so honored.[21]

Bravo, don Severino! Good try but bad form. Granting honors and privileges of arms is a prerogative of the monarch that cannot be usurped or preempted. *Me pareció darle por armas* is too presumptuous an expression for a governor, and dabbling in heraldry is not part of a governor's job description. No wonder that arms were not granted. Matanzas would have to wait more than a century for that recognition of honorable urban existence.

It is a commonplace of Matanzas history that the city was settled with thirty families from the Canaries recruited for that very purpose, as authorized by the royal order of 1682. The settlement of the proposed city was an assisted, government-subsidized migration scheme, part of a larger plan to stimulate Canary Islander migration to the Caribbean island. The program lasted several years and, as a result, a great many more people than had been intended crossed over to Cuba at government expense. Somebody in the Canaries was doubtlessly doing well loading would-be settlers bound for the Bay of Slaughters.

The first ship bringing Canary settlers specifically for the Matanzas project was the *Nuestra Señora del Rosario, San Diego y San José*. She sailed from Tenerife under skipper Pascual Ferreira on July 15, 1684, and landed in Havana with four families—thirty-six persons—bound for Matanzas.[22] In the course of a little less than a decade, between 1684 and 1693, a total of 470 would-be settlers—seventy-three families in total—made the crossing to Havana, there to await settlement, surviving as best they could until that time.

Because of the crown's interest in keeping track of the potential colonists—they would be needed eventually—each was painstakingly described. There were no passport photos then. Thus, the *Nuestra Señora del Rosario y San Francisco Xavier,* sailing from Tenerife on September 24, 1689, under skipper Luis Cordero brought nine families and fifty-six individuals aboard, including

> Domingo Rodríguez, crooked, stooped shoulders, wavy brown hair, white face, brown eyes, thirty years old. Francisca Hernández Felipe, his wife, dark complexion, short stature, stooped, black-haired, black eyes, twenty-one years old and a native of the city of La Laguna on the island of Tenerife. Ursula Felipe de Llarena, thin body, medium height, white skin, small black eyes, black-haired, and fifteen years old [and] Diego Felipe, twelve years old, dark complexion, brown wavy hair, brown eyes, her children. María Felipe, her mother-in-law, tall, white, bearing a few smallpox pockmarks, black-haired, big black eyes, and forty-five years old.[23]

Sharing the discomfort of the crossing was the Núñez de Villavicencio family: Gonzalo, the father,

> tall, dark, black-haired, brown eyes, forty-eight years old [and] his wife, Catharina García, shortsighted, white, scarred by the pox, of medium height and forty years old, both of La Laguna [and] Pedro Núñez, dark complexion, brown eyes, black wavy hair and fourteen years old, Inéz Núñez, eleven years old and Gerónimo Núñez, six years old, their children.

The dry records tell us much about how the passengers looked but are silent about how they felt. What their emotions were as the ship weighed anchor and they caught their last glimpse of their home we will never know. The fright of the first night on the high seas, or the joy and relief of arrival, is beyond the power of documents to convey but not beyond our ability to imagine. After their long crossing, Havana must have seemed like paradise.

When the time came to physically move the families to their new home, identifying them proved to be something of a challenge to the colonial authorities. By a decree of May 15, 1693, the governor ordered thirty named families culled from the larger group to proceed forthwith to Matanzas. Of the thirty, fourteen came up with all manner of excuses not to go to Matanzas at all. Fortunately, enough families from the large reservoir available were found to make up the mandated number. Their inducement was the subsidy promised by the crown to settlers: a building lot in the city itself and a *caballería* (33 acres, or 7.8 hectares) of good agricultural land nearby.

The management of the Canary Islanders became the responsibility of a remarkable character, Captain Diego Méndez de León Illada, a veteran with seventeen years' military experience in Havana, fifteen as a cavalryman and two as *alférez* (standard-bearer) of the city's garrison. On June 21, 1693, he was appointed "captain of the thirty families . . . in which employment he served for the nine following years with singular success and approval from his superiors."

The military implications of his appointment as "captain" of the settler cohort are evident. The settlement was a semi-militarized operation, and the government wanted tight control. His appointment cost him dearly, for he was forced at one point to sell his assets and those of his wife and children "to keep the said families fed and dressed because, even though each family was promised fifty pesos, this was not implemented for more than two years."[24] The colonial government, ever quick to demand, was slow to deliver. The good captain was elected *alcalde de primer voto* in Matanzas' first city council meeting, so he is the first of Matanzas' mayors.

When completed, the castle, or *alcázar,* of San Severino was the easternmost of Havana's defenses, marking the capital city's outer defensive perimeter in that direction. As such it bears comparison with its almost twin, the somewhat earlier Castillo de San Marcos at San Agustín de la Florida (built 1672–1695). San Severino's immediate mission was to keep watch over Matanzas harbor, prevent alien activities there, and put a stop to contraband. But it did so much more than that. It would be difficult to exaggerate the large stone castle's importance to the fledgling village. For the first time in its short history, a major social investment was being made in the settlement. The fort's presence was reassuring, not to mention the obvious fact of its political and economic significance. Matanzas was no longer a precarious frontier settlement and a nest of fiscal malefactors but a young and dynamic new city, castle and all. Down the centuries the fortress has retained its hold on the town's imagination as one of Matanzas' truly iconic corners. The castle has been designated as a stop on UNESCO's "Slavery's Route" program.

Just as Matanzas filled a niche in the larger scheme of Havana's defenses, a defensive network grew up around Matanzas itself. It included the tower and battery of San José de la Vigía, which stood essentially where the fire station stands today on Vigía Square. Fréderic Mialhe depicted it in the 1840s as a horseshoe-shaped platform with a parapet. The other components were the battery of Peñas Altas and, finally, the gracious little fort of San Felipe del Morrillo, built where the Canímar meets the harbor.

The settlement greeted the new century on a new footing. It had a cabildo (town council), a mayor, a parish priest, a castle, a garrison, a *traza* (town layout), birth papers properly recorded by notaries, and saintly advocates in heaven. The cluster of huts around a miserable church was now a city. Her district extended for six leagues in the round measured from the church door. Like Seville, Toledo, or even Rome itself, San Carlos y San Severino de Matanzas was now *urbe condita*, the starting point of serious history.

4   Green Tobacco and a Clever Marquis

IN 1700 THE FRAIL MONARCH IN WHOSE NAME the city was founded died without an heir. On his deathbed, Charles II named his French Bourbon grandnephew, Philippe, Duke of Anjou, as his heir and successor. This delighted the French, disappointed the Austrians, and alarmed the English with the prospect of a supermonarchy. A decision made by a feeble-minded king on his deathbed was not enough to keep the peace, so off to war the great powers marched, dragging many a smaller one into the mess. The lengthy conflict lives on in the French children's song "Malbrough s'en vat-en-guerre," originally a mockery of the "hero of Blenheim" (1704), Britain's "First Churchill," John, Duke of Marlborough.

The 1713 Peace of Utrecht that brought the War of the Spanish Succession to a conclusion was consequential indeed, a crossroads of European and colonial history. Anjou became Philip V of Spain after all and, in recognition of French support, he ceded to France the western third of Hispaniola. This act would have major consequences for Matanzas far into the future.

At the newly minted city, the first quarter of the century went by like the Yumurí's lazy flow. Then, on October 19, 1730, the colonial routine was shaken by a visitation from the old Taíno deity Juracán. Folks watched in anguish as the winds rose and huge waves roared through the town, a village of crudely built, mostly thatched structures. The precarious bridge that had spanned the Yumurí since 1722, connecting the castle to the village, was swept away. Only one building stood up to the hurricane: the stone dwelling of Diego García de Amoedo on the corner of modern Medio and Matanzas streets, one block away from the future site of the Casa Cabañas.

The Blessed Sacrament was installed at the García de Amoedo manse with as much dignity as the surrounding devastation allowed. For their home to become a makeshift tabernacle became a source of great pride and honor to the family. A plaque was eventually installed on the wall bearing the image of a chalice and the legend "On October 19 God honored this house. Year 1730."[1] Six years after the storm, the house was granted the *privilegio de cadenas*, that is, it became a sanctuary for fugitives from justice provided they could touch the chain hanging on the portico. A faint reminder of the old chain was La Cadena, the big grocery store located one block away on the corner of Milanés and Matanzas. In 1957 it was thoroughly remodeled to become Cuba's first supermarket outside of Havana.

Under the new dynasty, as under the old, matanceros continued to practice their time-honored calling as smugglers, though more discreetly now on account of the castle and garrison. Salt continued to be mined, meat salted, and hides scraped and hung to tan under the sun. Modest sugar mills sprouted here and there. Change was coming, however. In the closing years of the seventeenth century, the region's original cattle-based economy was transformed by a surge in the production of tobacco. In 1699, Juan González, the alférez of Matanzas, sold to the Royal Exchequer thirteen *arrobas* of tobacco for 164 *reales* (an arroba equals 25 pounds).[2] Tobacco was grown on small family farms (*vegas*). In a short time, and for the rest of the 1700s, it became the mainstay of the local economy.

Tobacco was big in the Canaries, and the Canary settlers had brought with them knowledge of its cultivation and processing. Matanzas' tobacco, known as *verdín* because of the light green coloring of the leaf, was perfect for snuff but required a delicate processing. Only Güines in the Havana district rivaled Matanzas in its production.[3] As long as consumers enjoyed snorting the green powder and soiling their handkerchiefs and sleeves with nicotine-enriched mucus, demand and prices remained high.

Producing snuff required milling, and milling required efficient, reliable power. In the early days of tobacco, some thirty mills were established along the banks of the Almendares River near Havana to take advantage of the stream's hydraulic potential. As Havana became saturated, enterprising eyes looked east. In February of 1715, Juan José de Jústiz y Umpiérrez, Havana's *sargento mayor*, applied to the Matanzas council for a grant of the flow of the

San Juan River in the environs of some land he owned, in order to operate a tobacco mill. The land was the old Díaz Pimienta sugar estate. The council granted Jústiz the required permission but prudently restricted riparian rights to only the part of the river that flowed over his property. There was one condition: Jústiz had to build the mill within two years. He did; he actually built two for good measure and sold the second to a fellow habanero and kinsman, Jerónimo Espinosa de Contreras y Jústiz. Since ownership of land was the key to prosperity, Jústiz and Espinosa simply set out to buy as much of it as possible. Before long they owned most of the land granted to the original settlers.[4]

Tobacco initially promised a new era of prosperity and development until an added factor entered the equation. In 1717, a royal decree created the Estanco, or royal tobacco monopoly. The Estanco was to be the only buyer at prices artificially fixed, and the only authorized seller of the product. This monopoly was so unpopular that it led to the first Cuban revolt when enraged tobacco farmers forced the resignation of Governor Vicente Raja, who was unceremoniously shipped to Spain. The last of several riots ended in an armed confrontation and the hanging of ten *vegueros* (tobacco farmers) at Jesús del Monte in 1723. Four years later, the state ratcheted up its monopolistic aims: the Estanco would no longer buy processed snuff, but only whole leaf. In one fell swoop Cuban tobacco millers would be out of business.

Jústiz came up with a daring idea. He offered to send the king a sample of his mill's product. If the king did not like it, he could burn it. But if he did, the crown could buy his snuff at a fair price to be set by the authorities. The king must have liked it, for the Estanco agreed to make an exception and buy Jústiz' product for six pesos per arroba.[5]

Local tobacco, although not of global importance, could certainly make two already rich families richer, especially if they owned the only two mills around. To maintain this modus vivendi, a cozy relationship with the authorities was essential. A little gift here, a little something there, a good word by an influential friend could do wonders. Public relations mattered, and it was in that spirit, no doubt, that don Juan José de Jústiz underwrote the construction of Matanzas' parochial church, now the Cathedral Church of San Carlos. It was finished in the 1750s. This philanthropy was the rationale for the award of the title Marquis of Jústiz de Santa Ana, which he received one year before his death in 1759. He was succeeded by his nephew, Manuel José Aparicio del Manzano y Jústiz, the second marquis. His kinsman and partner, don Jerónimo, was also a generous donor to visible public initiatives, and went on to become the Count of Gibacoa (also spelled Jibacoa) in 1764. He died in 1787.

As to the growers, while selling contraband tobacco leaf to the English or the Dutch may have been exciting and financially rewarding, selling it to the Jústiz-Gibacoa group for milling was far more secure and reliable. Every party to the scheme had a sniff, and it worked. Matanzas' tobacco economy flourished in consequence. Bishop Pedro Agustín Morell de Santa Cruz's 1755 inspection of the diocese reported some 207 estancias where tobacco was grown. By 1771, the last generation before the great sugar boom, the *tazmía,* or estimate of the annual tobacco crop, in the locality of Naranjal alone rose to a bit less than 60,000 *cujes* of tobacco (a cuje was a stick with no more than 150 leaves). Many free blacks and mulattoes were involved in tobacco culture. In 1774, the Jústiz-Gibacoa mills were worth a whopping 200,000 pesos.

In August 1762, the eventuality that had motivated Matanzas' foundation in the first place actually materialized. A large British amphibious force under the command of George Keppel, third Earl of Albermarle, showed up before Havana. Their mission: to take the Cuban capital. Matanzas' castles, while perhaps effective in the naval scenarios of the seventeenth century, proved irrelevant when the clock struck what Cuban lore knows as "the hour of the mameyes."[6]

When His Britannic Majesty's ships came calling with overwhelming force, the redcoats did not so much as bother with Matanzas. They landed at exurban Cojímar and Bacuranao and blockaded Havana. *Check.* British sappers then spectacularly breached the Morro's walls. *Check.* With the Union Jack flying over Morro, Albermarle threatened to bomb Havana at will from the heights of La Cabaña. *Checkmate.* The city was lost and Governor Juan del Prado Portocarrero surrendered. Sure, he could have fought to the death at the cost of enormous damage and loss of life, but that was not the spirit of eighteenth-century warfare. The horrors of the twentieth century were mercifully as yet unimaginable.

The fall of Havana could not but impact the Matanzas region, even though the settlement itself was only perfunctorily occupied. On September 28, a British force under the command of Major Alexander Monypenny of the 22nd Regiment, Royal Marines, accepted Matanzas' surrender and removed its ordnance to Havana. Perhaps anticipating a full-fledged occupation that never came, local military authorities disabled San Severino Castle and retreated to the Morrillo on the eastern side of the bay, where they were by all accounts unmolested. Indeed, as far as the British were concerned, Matanzas was outside their jurisdiction.[7]

A fascinating testimony of the British presence in the environs of the Bay of Slaughters is a beautifully carved powder horn with a view of "Matansia" currently among the treasures of the noted collector and scholar Emilio Cueto of Washington, D.C. (A similar horn with a carved plan of Havana is at the Library of Congress.) The Cueto powder horn belonged to a William Waite, probably a British officer, and was carved by a member of the 1762 invading force, possibly one of Major Monypenny's men.[8]

The city's somewhat less than epic defense generated two extraordinary documents, both written from a feminine criolla perspective and addressed to King Charles III. The first, called "Memorial dirigido a Carlos III por las señoras de La Habana," was in all probability written by a criollo cabal that may have included historian José Martín Félix de Arrate. Feminine authorship was a canard. The second, "Dolorosa métrica expresión del sitio y entrega de La Habana," presents a scathing criticism of the colonial government's performance contained in twenty-four *décima* stanzas. (A discussion of the décima appears near the beginning of chapter 11.) It circulated anonymously but there is little doubt that it was indeed written by a woman, Beatriz de Jústiz Zayas Bazán, the Marchioness of Jústiz de Santa Ana, wife of the second marquis. Life is about more than making money and milling snuff.

The 1763 Treaty of Paris that ended the war brought a significant boost to the Matanzas population from an unexpected source. The treaty stipulated that the British return Havana to Spain in exchange for Spanish Florida. Virtually the entire Spanish population of La Florida was consequently evacuated. By late 1764, some 3,104 persons had been ferried to Cuba or elsewhere in the empire. Eighty-four Spanish Florida families (almost four hundred warm bodies) settled near Matanzas on land donated by Jerónimo Espinosa de Contreras, whose resources also financed the postwar repairs to San Severino Castle. Don Jerónimo had a very significant stake in the Matanzas economy and, like many fellow Havana aristocrats, was eager to court favor with Madrid after collaborating more or less openly with the British occupation.[9] As a tangible reward he got his coveted title: Count of Gibacoa. Contreras, one of Matanzas' main streets, bears his family name.

The Florida settlers were a diverse group that included peninsular Spaniards, Canary Islanders, and Afro-Floridians. Among the settlers was a Francisco Menéndez, a free African settler of Fort Mose, the remarkable freedmen's community north of St. Augustine.[10] Each family received a lot of one caballería of virgin farmland, sixty-six pesos in cash, and the means to buy a slave and farming tools. The new settlement, now known by the pedestrian name of Ceiba Mocha, was elegantly named San Agustín de la Nueva Florida.

The parish church celebrates the town's origins. A much-venerated image of St. Augustine still presides over the main altar. In time, however, the saintly Bishop of Hippo was challenged for first place in the people's devotion by Our Lady of Candlemas (La Candelaria). In the old days thousands of people would make the pilgrimage to la Fiesta de la Mocha every Candlemas (February 2). At dusk, following a mass, the holy images of La Candelaria and St. Augustine (who always had precedence) would be borne in procession. Set on palanquins, the images jerked along amidst a sea of lit candles, clouds of incense, the drone of Hail Marys, and heavy-handed renditions of hymns accompanied by a trumpet, a tuba, cymbals, and a couple of drums.

The feast's secular culmination was a famed *tómbola,* or flea market, where delicacies and preserves made by Catholic ladies of the city would be sold to benefit the parish. The last couple of weeks in January were a busy time in my grandmother Consuelo's kitchen, where literally hundreds of jars of mango, orange, papaya, grapefruit, and guava preserves would be labeled. Containers were saved throughout the year for my grandmother's justly famed preserves. As each fruit came into season, the house would become a little factory with jars and bottles of all sizes taking up every available surface. A heavy, sweet, delicious smell permeated every corner and would linger for days on end.

In the years that followed the British occupation, Matanzas city life picked up and local infrastructure was improved. A bridge across the San Juan was built under Captain-General Felipe de Fondesviela, Marquis de la Torre. It was finished by the time the marquis left office in 1777. Made of local hardwood, it measured 1,300 feet in length by 24 in width and cost 7,500 gold pesos. Matanzas was home to 3,249 souls then.

In those days the formal traza, or city grid, was limited to the land between the San Juan and Yumurí rivers. The marshy Yumurí shore was a *ciénaga* (swamp); south of the San Juan it was *monte* (forest). The traza began at the shore in the point of a triangle that gradually extended into the surrounding hills. The San Juan River formed one side and the Yumurí the hypotenuse. At the vertex was the Plaza de la Vigía, the spot where Manzaneda had settled the city in 1693. Although irregular, the dusty space served as the plaza de armas and civic center. The completion of the fortress of San José de la Vigía in 1748 gave it a much-needed focal point.

The fortress of San José de la Vigía was nowhere near San Severino in quality and sophistication.[11] It was essentially a battery deployed on top of a horseshoe-shaped platform. It had two moats, a drawbridge with a gate, and an *aljibe,* or water reservoir. The actual building was the work of don Felipe del Castillo, *capitán de milicias,* who was commemorated on a plaque at the entrance. The fort building was afflicted with all kinds of problems throughout the century of its life. In 1805 the inner door collapsed. Most of the timbers were by then thoroughly infested with termites. Major repairs were urgently requested in 1831. The fort was eventually demolished between 1854 and 1858.

For all its defects, however, the fort was an important addition to city life. One of its functions was to mark the time for the city's inhabitants. Back in those days people depended on public clocks and the pealing of bells. The fortress had a bell for that purpose. Time was kept by a mechanical clock inside. At the right moment, somebody would go to the bell and ring in the hour.

The years that followed Spain's recovery of Havana witnessed a thorough reorganization of Cuba's military establishment. Chastised by the humiliation of 1762, Charles III of Spain was determined not to let it happen again. Defense therefore became a top government priority. Matanzas' newly gained significance was reflected in the creation of the Matanzas dragoon regiment in the 1770s. The outfit was assigned a white uniform with blue collar and lapels and golden buttons. A colonel's flag with the cross saltire of Burgundy, the royal arms, and the motto "I profess valor and fidelity" became the regimental colors.[12]

The church had also made significant progress by the second half of the eighteenth century. Unlike the original building, the new church could stand up to any hurricane, as indeed it has, including the catastrophic ones of 1846, 1870, and 1926—but it has proved no match for neglect. The church's vaults partially collapsed in the 1970s, the consequence of water filtering through the outer tile roof.

When finished, the church was a noble edifice with a cruciform plan and a grand dome. It was begun in 1730 and the vaults closed by 1750, a remarkable building effort for so small a settlement. The towers, portico, clock, and Carrara marble floors date to the middle of the nineteenth century and were built by the dynamic parish priest Manuel Francisco García.[13] The remarkable murals, now severely damaged by moisture and mildew as a result of the roof's

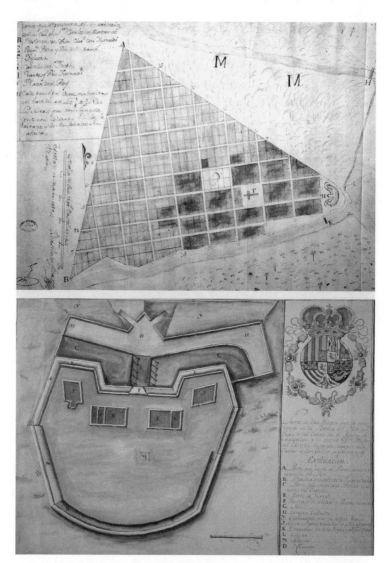

Fig. 12. *Above:* traza, or city layout, of Matanzas in the mid-eighteenth century. *Below:* plan of the fortress of San José de la Vigía, 1748. Note the fort's location at "NG" on the city layout. (Courtesy of Spanish Government, Ministry of Culture, Archivo General de Indias, MP–Santo Domingo, 268 and 227)

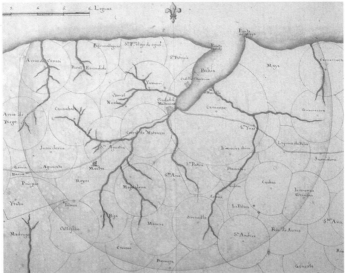

Fig. 13. *Above:* The parish church, later the cathedral, of Saint Charles Borromeus is shown in a 1905 photograph. *Below:* Matanzas' original district encompassed the area of a circle with a six-league radius centered at the parish church's main door. Note the circular land grants dating to the sixteenth century. (Upper photo courtesy of Prints and Photographs Division, Library of Congress; lower photo courtesy of Spanish Government, Ministry of Culture, Archivo General de Indias, MP–Santo Domingo, 323)

failure and the partial collapse of the vaulting, date to the twentieth. The parish church contains a shrine to the venerated Cristo de la Misericordia, a brooding image of the Crucified Christ that is said to have been carved miraculously in the 1730s (which was probably the only way the church could have obtained it in those struggling days).

Numerous and fruitless attempts were made to settle Franciscan and Dominican convents in colonial Matanzas. Only the friars of St. John of God took the bait and built a hospital in the town in 1749. Before their arrival, health care was the responsibility of a lone physician, a Juan García, who is recorded there in 1740. The friars' hospital was not much to write home about. Bishop Morell de Santa Cruz visited the facility and reported that the hospital was "thatched with straw . . . with one foyer and three rooms, all very narrow: six beds, five bed sheets, four pillows, and no patients."[14] The lack of patients at the miserable house for the sick could mean that the people of Matanzas were very healthy, but more likely that they were unwilling to risk their lives in such a place.

In 1747 Matanzas worthily celebrated the accession of King Ferdinand VI. The bill was footed by Captain del Castillo, the benefactor of Vigía fort. The program included fireworks, a pageant with knights on horseback, and the first dramatic performance in Matanzas' history. The play staged was a court comedy with a mythological theme, *Hado y divisa de Leonido y de Marfisa*, by Pedro Calderón de la Barca. The piece in question, with a complex plot and a large cast, debuted at the Palacio del Buen Retiro in Madrid in the presence of King Charles II on March 3, 1680. Why it became Matanzas' initiation into theater is a mystery. Did the players come from Havana? Was it locally produced? It would be fascinating to have answers.

Matanceros observed with as much pomp and circumstance as local conditions allowed the feast of Corpus Christi. By 1751 they had an appropriate setting for the great civico-religious display in the newly finished parochial church. The procession featured a *tarasca*, a winged monster or dragon reminding those present of the Evil One defeated by Christ's resurrection.[15] Black folks dressed up as *diablitos* (little devils) took part in the pageant, an indication that something close to African *cabildos de nación* (African ethnic mutual-aid societies) were already functioning.

In 1778, Matanzas experienced its first recorded homicide: a crime of passion with aggravating circumstances. The principals were José de Quintana; his much younger wife, Antonia María Unsiga Gálvez; and José Giménez, a native of Trinidad, known as "El Tierradentro."[16] Giménez and María Antonia were lovers. They decided to get rid of the old man, so Giménez knifed and castrated Quintana, bundled up the remains weighted with stones, and threw them into the Cañas River. He either did not go out far enough or did not put enough stones in the bundle, for a passerby found the corpse nibbled on by fishes. Discovered, the murderer was sentenced to death by hanging and executed at Vigía Square. "La Unsiga" was sent in chains to Havana to meet her fate. Whatever happened to her must have been considered as of lesser consequence, for the remarkable source that recorded the events is silent about that.

Notable for its unique place in Matanzas' forensic history, this Macbeth at the Bay of Slaughters also inspired décimas. Not surprisingly, they were encrusted with the deepest prejudices of a patriarchal society. Giménez may have wielded the knife but it was María Antonia, the evil woman, who bears the heaviest burden of responsibility. The moral of the story:

> Let God take unto his bosom
> Giménez the swiftly passing;
> And the living learn their lesson,
> In women there is no trusting.[17]

Published in 1854 by pioneer Matanzas historian Pedro Antonio Alfonso, this is among the earliest known exemplars of Cuba's most characteristic genre.[18] Not quite the earliest, though. The Marchioness of Jústiz de Santa Ana wrote one first.

Matanzas rightly claims to be the birthplace of Cuba's first historian, first grammarian, and first author of a mathematics treatise. All three distinctions converge on a single remarkable individual, Antonio José Valdés. Born in Matanzas in 1780, he was entrusted as a babe to the Havana Foundlings' Asylum, hence the Valdés surname. (Valdés has been the name given to foundlings in Cuba since the foundation of the House of Maternity and Beneficence in Havana in the late eighteenth century.) Elite women sponsored foundlings as a charity. His godmother was Antonia María Junco y Morejón, a member of the emerging Matanzas patriciate and an enduring link to the Matanzas community. Valdés led a remarkable career as a teacher, writer, printer, and revolutionary. He traveled far and wide, entering the service of the patriot junta of Buenos Aires and later on that of the Mexican empire of Agustín de Iturbide. His *Historia de la isla de Cuba y en especial de La Habana* was published in

Havana in 1813 before he began his Latin American adventures. It is a substantive work, unusual in that it was the first such book not written from the perspective of the criollo aristocracy.[19]

My paternal lineage arrived in Cuba at this stage of the island's history. Ramón Bretós y Marsal traveled to the island colony as a servant of don Juan Ignacio de Urriza, naval *comisario* for Cuba, sometime in late 1773.[20] He was born in Tavares, near Huesca, in the kingdom of Aragón. In Cuba he married Bárbara Almirante Fernández del Campo, whose family had come from Caracas in the seventeenth century.[21]

Ramón Bretós did well, considering his modest beginnings. As his career demonstrates, the dynamic Cuban society of the late eighteenth century offered numerous opportunities to those capable of taking advantage of them. From household servant he rose to *teniente guarda mayor de la Real Hacienda* (chief constable of the Royal Exchequer) with ten corporals, thirty-two guards (five mounted), and six supernumeraries under his command.[22] On January 25, 1790, he was personally in charge of a pack of seven mules carrying a substantial amount of cash from the *situado*, a subsidy sent from Mexico to Cuba every year.[23] The detail included two muleteers, one corporal, and two dragoons.

Near Sabanilla in the Matanzas district, two of the animals apparently lost their footing and ended up at the bottom of a ravine. One vanished; the other was found, dead from a machete blow. Some of the money was never recovered. An investigation followed and a hearing held in 1792, at which don Ramón was cleared of malfeasance. Then, two years later, the *fiscalía* (prosecutor's office) reopened the case and demanded a bond. The copious dossier, documenting all but the outcome of the proceedings, ended up in Seville at the Archivo General de Indias.[24] Was Bretós a fool who lost the mules or a crook who stole the money?

In June 1794 he offered for sale two clavichords, a book cabinet, and a *negra* (female slave) in Havana's *Papel Periódico*. Be that as it may, it is good to learn that his family had a taste for music and books, however distasteful their complicity in the crime of slavery. Books, music, and sadly slavery would be very much a part of the Matanzas story during the century about to begin. His career does not seem to have been affected. In the Cuba of his day that was a good sign either way.

5 Coffee Cup and Sugar Bowl

FOR MOST OF THE 1700s, growing verdín and milling snuff had sustained the local economy but, like powdered wigs and lace ruffles, snuff was destined to go out of style. The changes in taste brought about by the French Revolution drove the habit of snorting powdered nicotine out of fashion. Demand for verdín died out, but the same forces that doomed it opened the way for coffee and sugar. Between the two they would transform the city and its hinterland in the course of a generation. When Matanzas received a grant of arms in 1828, the field showed a schematic representation of the city in its topographic setting. A castle flanked by two rivers and two bridges occupied the foreground with the Pan, the local version of a mountain, in the background. Cane stalks and coffee branches supported the shield. It was heraldry's tribute to economic history.

Cane had been grown and sugar made locally for generations. Primitive sugar mills had existed in the region since early times, but production had never been of any consequence. Coffee, by contrast, was a newcomer. Despite its global history, it was unheard of commercially in Cuba until the second half of the eighteenth century. *Caffea arabica* is a native of the Horn of Africa. The brewing of roasted and ground coffee berries into a stimulating infusion developed in the Middle East and reached northern Europe by the 1600s. By the following century it was the rage throughout the Continent. The French introduced coffee in the Caribbean by the early 1700s. As demand grew, their island colony of Saint-Domingue became the world's number-one supplier of

Fig. 14. Granted in 1828, Matanzas' arms featured local topographic landmarks. The supports of coffee branches and sugarcane stalks celebrated the region's agricultural prowess. (Courtesy of Spanish Government, Ministry of Culture, Archivo General de Indias, MP-Escudos, 165)

the mighty berries. Saint-Domingue was also the world's prime producer of sugar, but its days of fabulous prosperity were numbered. When the French revolutionary ideals of Liberty, Equality, and Fraternity penetrated a colony where slavery, inequality, and exploitation were the norm, the result was the New World's second successful revolution. The lucrative dual plantation system was collateral damage; it was ruined beyond recovery.

The events in Saint-Domingue were greeted in Cuba with a mixture of apprehension and Schadenfreude. Slave revolts were always frightening but this one was perversely opportune. When the bloody dust settled, many Saint-Domingue planters found themselves in Cuba as refugees. They carried coffee know-how to places like Santiago, Pinar del Río, and Matanzas, where exile colonies emerged. With expertise available and competition from Saint-Domingue coffee and sugar out of the game, Cuba was poised to move into the vacuum.

Let us pause briefly and consider the geography of Cuba circa 1790, just before Haitian independence altered the course of history. We do not need a map, really. The same cartographic imagination that has turned the Netherlands into a lion, Italy into a boot, and China into a dragon has turned Cuba into a crocodile, head to the east, tail to the west. The croc's tail, known then as Nueva Filipina and today as Pinar del Río, was a near-vacant wilderness covered with pine forests. Immediately to the east, where the island begins to widen, lies the Llanura Roja de La Habana–Matanzas. These "Red Plains" are a vast expanse of rich lateritic soil wedged between Pinar del Río's Sierra del Rosario to the west, the Escambray range to the east, the island's coastal swamps to the south, and a complex littoral to the north. The iron-rich soil is the color of red oxide. Its high clay content makes it stick to everything.

In croc cartography this is essentially the ancient reptile's belly and rump. The flat landscape is broken by the Bejucal-Madruga-Limonar and Habana-Matanzas heights, the latter a gentle range of hills and intermountain valleys running from the eastern shore of Havana harbor to the spectacularly beautiful Yumurí Valley abutting Matanzas, in the 1700s still a sparsely populated town. Adjacent to Matanzas on the south and east is the Valle de la Magdalena, a stretch of gently rolling country all but made to order for cane fields. The rocky coastline is broken by occasional gorges, or *abras,* such as the ones at Santa Cruz del Norte, Jaruco, Jibacoa, and Puerto Escondido. Rivers of great beauty but little consequence flow through them as colonial contraband once did. The abra of the Yumurí at Matanzas forms a dramatic backdrop to the city itself. Today, the stretch of coast between Havana and Matanzas is full of oil pumps. Offshore, vast reserves of black gold are said to exist, waiting to become gasoline and greenhouse gases and, Cubans hope, re-energize a chronically anemic economy.

In 1790 Havana was the only city of any consequence in the region. The capital's hinterland was the western tip of the Llanura Roja, the point where the crocodile's tail joins the abdomen. Havana is near where the island is at its narrowest, a mere thirty-five kilometers across. The British occupation of 1762–63 did not extend beyond this immediate region. Mariel to the west and Matanzas to the east were the "boundaries" of British-occupied Havana. With minor adjustments this approximates the modern province of that name.

A result of the British presence was the dramatic and swift development of this lush but tiny region. Even before the collapse of Saint-Domingue catapulted Cuba to global sugar prominence, a significant plantation economy had developed in Havana's backyard. Settled towns such as San Antonio de los Baños, Santiago de las Vegas, Santa María del Rosario, San Felipe y Santiago de Bejucal, and San Julián de Güines dotted the region and served the needs of a growing rural economy. By 1790, Havana's original forest cover was gone, eaten up by an expanding agricultural frontier.[1]

The Matanzas region offered a sharp contrast. Although topographically and morphologically all but identical to Havana, what is now Matanzas province was then a green wilderness. The tall forests that provided Philip II's Escorial with timber were still standing, for tobacco had barely made a dent on the magnificently primeval landscape. The forest was under direct crown protection as the source of strategic naval stores. Matanzas was undeveloped for a very good reason: nothing else that was in demand could be produced there.

That would radically change. Coffee's debut and sugar's initial forward push hit Matanzas almost simultaneously around 1800. The Yumurí Valley had ideal conditions for growing both coffee bushes and sugarcane. Its proximity to Matanzas' port, opened to peninsular trade in 1794 and to global operations in the early 1800s, facilitated agricultural development. The Bilbao-born Matanzas merchant José Matías de Ximeno y Uzaola,[2] a key proponent of the port's opening, went on to amass one of the town's great fortunes.

The importance of coffee to the island's economy grew dramatically between 1800 and the mid-1840s. In 1790 Cuba's coffee exports were a mere 80 tons. By 1815 the figure was 15,000 tons, and by 1827 more than 20,000 tons.

Meanwhile, internal demand grew apace. It is around this time that Cubans became prodigious gulpers of caffeine.

Unlike the production of sugar, which required a massive investment in machinery, land, and slaves, coffee's demands were modest. A lucrative *cafetal,* or coffee plantation, could be established on a relatively small area of farmland. It is less wasteful of energy and requires less forest clearing than cane fields. Coffee bushes love shade.

The labor requirements of coffee, like those of sugar, were met by Africans in bondage. The demands of the cafetal on its slave crew, however, were nowhere near the crushing burdens of the cane field and the increasingly mechanized sugar mill.[3] Offering a relaxed lifestyle by comparison, the coffee plantation encouraged gracious country living. Numerous travel accounts capture the cafetal's sybaritic ways and elegant settings: the rows of palm trees that graced the approaches, the gated entrances, and the commodious *vivienda* (main house, but by no means mansion). Guests would be entertained and lodged amidst fronds and cool porches in a garden-like environment that softened the harsh edges of a working plantation's routines. Coffee, like sugar later on, attracted considerable foreign participation, especially from North Americans.[4]

Until about the middle of the nineteenth century, sugar and coffee shared top billing in Cuba's and Matanzas' agriculture, but coffee would not endure. Had coffee maintained its position as the island's key export, Cuba's future would have been vastly different. It was not to be: the emergence of more efficient competitors such as Brazil, the imposition of punishing tariffs by the United States in the 1830s, and the extraordinarily active hurricane seasons of the 1840s doomed Cuban coffee agriculture. In addition, the considerably higher profitability of sugar as railroads cheapened carriage of heavy sugar boxes from mill to dockside crowded coffee out of the race for best return on investment. By mid-century coffee had declined drastically relative to sugar and had lost its position as a key export.

Sugar originated in the ancient Indus Valley, where the locals came up with a clever invention to extract juice from the stalks of giant grasses: two rollers grinding against each other under human or animal traction. The medieval Arabs added a third roller. This dramatically increased the stability of the grinding mechanism and the efficiency of the operation. Modern grinding mills operate on that principle. In old-fashioned trapiches, the raw juice, or *guarapo,* flowed to a cauldron where it would be boiled. The fiber (*bagazo*/bagasse) would be used for fuel.

Making sugar the traditional way demanded extracting the impurities, or *cachaza,* from the boiling guarapo and reducing the latter to the point where sugar crystals formed. The resulting sticky goo would be put into funnel-like cone molds (*hormas*). The contents of the molds drained into a trough. The liquid molasses would flow there, leaving the solids inside the cone. When dried, the mold would be emptied, and the sugar sorted according to its quality, whiteness, and consistency. Sugar would then be packed in heavy *cajas,* or boxes, weighing from 440 to 550 pounds. The sheer weight of the exportable unit required proximity to a port until railways made inland production profitable.

In 1760 Cuba produced 4,964 tons of sugar. Almost one hundred years later, in 1856, the output was 359,397 tons, fully 25 percent of the world's production and almost as much as the combined output of the British West Indies, Brazil, and Louisiana.[5] The history of Cuban sugar in the nineteenth century is essentially the history of the opening of the Matanzas and western Las Villas agricultural frontiers. Sugar (and, for a while, coffee as well) provided the energy for the amazing nineteenth-century growth of cities such as Matanzas, Cárdenas, and Cienfuegos. By mid-century, Cárdenas rivaled Matanzas as a sugar-exporting port. Like Matanzas, Cienfuegos became a handsome town of broad boulevards, splendid mansions, and rich urban amenities. The city's Terry Theater was one of the best in Cuba.

The coming of Big Sugar represented a break with the past in substance and scope. Sugar catapulted Matanzas from an obscure coastal settlement to Cuba's third largest city in population and, arguably, second in importance by 1850. Nearness to Havana created unique challenges and opportunities. Sugar export patterns linked the city to American ports with important consequences. From a small subsidiary farming economy, Matanzas entered the global realm where sugar was king, and she did it in grand style.

This growth would not have happened at quite the scale that it did but for the presence of an articulate criollo lobby that led the way: figures such as the Havana economist Francisco de Arango y Parreño (later ennobled as a marquis) and institutions such as the Royal Economic Society of Friends of the Country. Matanzas had its own affiliate of the Economic Society, the Sociedad Patriótica. They secured concessions and support, and succeeded in dismantling Spanish policies that impeded progress as they understood it. To them, the country's interest and those of the sugar plantation on which they had placed their bets for developing the economy and becoming rich were one and the same.

A major barrier that fell by the wayside before their onslaught was the traditional protection of the forest under Spanish law. A royal order of August 30, 1815, the Real Cédula de Montes y Plantíos,[6] opened to exploitation all the forests under the jurisdiction of the navy. For the forest this was tantamount to a death sentence. Towards the close of the eighteenth century, approximately five hundred caballerías of forest were felled and burned in Cuba each year. In 1840, the area of forest going up in smoke had risen to four thousand caballerías yearly. By then those caballerías were predominantly around Matanzas.[7]

Thoughtful Cubans such as José Antonio Saco, writing in the 1820s, and the Countess of Merlin a decade later deplored the massive deforestation and sounded a cry of alarm that, however, did not stand a chance against the power of sugar.[8] What to Phillip II had been a precious material worthy of a royal altarpiece was now mere firewood for a boiler or sleepers for a railway. Felling of the forests, moreover, created a vicious cycle. The yield of the first few years' crops planted in the rich *tierra colorada* of the great red plain was stunning, but it declined notably thereafter. This pushed the frontier outwards in search of the windfall accruing to those lucky enough to deflower virgin forest.

They had no idea—nor did they for the most part care—about the long-term ecological damage they were causing.[9] The central-south region of the province is a bowl, and it rains a lot in Cuba in the wet. While the forest stood, it absorbed vast amounts of moisture or released it into the atmosphere as vapor. With the forest gone, moisture accumulated at the bottom of the bowl—essentially the modern municipality of Perico and adjoining areas—producing catastrophic floods. The center of the province, in fact, became a lake when the rains were heavy until the Roque Canal was built in the early twentieth century. The "canal" is essentially an artificial riverbed to drain the excess water to the ocean.

Another concern of the tireless criollo economic intelligentsia was the procurement of labor, a polite way of saying expanding slavery to meet demand. Labor scarcity had always been an issue in colonial Cuba until the British occupation of Havana opened the floodgates to African slavery on a grand scale. In 1789, thanks in no small measure to criollo advocacy, free trade in slaves was authorized by the Spanish crown. It would eventually be extended until 1820, at which time it was supposed to end according to the terms of a solemn treaty with Great Britain. Illegal trade, however, continued to flourish for many years thereafter—in fact, for most of the nineteenth century.[10] Under criollo elite pressure, the laws regarding property and land were reformed to show clear and full title, not merely usufruct. Cuban ports were opened to world trade.

Very little of this affected the island's eastern districts, that is to say, the crocodile's back, head, and shoulders. The sugar history of eastern Cuba would be written with bold strokes, but not until almost a century later. With western Cuba's productive capacity laid low by the 1895–1898 independence war, a new chapter in the story of Cuban sugar opened in the east. As had happened before in the west, mighty forests were felled to clear the way for the mammoth sugar mills of Oriente and Camagüey, only this time around, the deforestation was done more quickly and efficiently with chains and bulldozers. Whereas the demand for labor had been met before by means of slavery and indentured Chinese labor, the twentieth-century sugar complex opted for Antillean immigration. Hundreds of thousands of laborers entered eastern Cuba from places like Haiti and Jamaica. That, however, is another story. We need to get back to nineteenth-century Matanzas.

As with coffee, the development of large-scale cane sugar cultivation in Matanzas began in the 1790s in areas adjacent to the city such as the Yumurí Valley, Corral Nuevo, and Ceiba Mocha. With the Havana hinterland just about colonized by sugar plantations, the eyes of investors began to look eastward to Matanzas.[11] The topography was favorable there, land abounded, and distances to port were manageable. By 1796, eighteen *ingenios* were operating in the Matanzas district. They belonged in some cases to patrician Havanans, such as the marchioness of Jústiz de Santa Ana, grand niece of the pioneer entrepreneur, the first marquis. In other cases, families that would become prominent in Matanzas society were among the mill owners, such as the Lamars, del Portillos, Ximenos, Alfonsos, and Juncos, the last a lineage that had first settled at San Agustín de la Florida, moved to Cuba in the 1600s, and settled in Matanzas at the close of the 1700s. Bernardo Junco, the paterfamilias, became Matanzas' *alcalde ordinario* and built the Junco Palace on Vigía Square. By 1827, the number of mills in the Matanzas district had jumped to 111.

It has been convincingly argued that the Matanzas sugar industry was substantially controlled by Havana interests.[12] It is equally true, however, that many of the individuals involved became thoroughly invested in the life of Matanzas, kept homes there, and came to consider themselves at least part-time matanceros. Such was the case of Domingo del Monte, an in-law of the powerful Havana Aldama family and a resolute Matanzas promoter. Prominent among them also was an Irish immigrant, Joaquín Mádan, who ran a lucrative business on the sidelines as a *negrero,* or slave trader. Also involved as investors or financiers were the firms of Fesser Hermanos and Santiago Drake y del Castillo, the latter in association with Henry Coit of New York, and the de la Torriente family, who eventually moved their operation to Matanzas and built the massive San Juan River sugar warehouses, Matanzas' largest structure under a single roof.

Like coffee before it, the sugar boom attracted a fair share of foreign investors, mostly American. Laird Bergad has identified a number of them. William Schweyer and Joseph Day of Portland, Maine, for example, supplied Maine lumber for sugar boxes and hogsheads. James and John Bailey operated an import-export firm, as did Charles Parkinson, who became a Bailey partner in 1855. James Burnham opened a local branch of his trading firm in 1849.[13] Latting and Glen, Matanzas' pioneering American trading firm, submitted a proposal to construct port facilities when Matanzas was opened to international trade in 1808.

Many of the Americans assimilated. William Schweyer's descendants married into Matanzas elite families and became well established in Matanzas society. Traces of the American presence live on in city place-names such as the Alturas de Simpson (Simpson Heights), a classic Matanzas barrio propelled to celebrity as the title of the first *danzón.*

The impact of economic development on the city's growth was dramatic. Between 1817 and the 1860s, the urban population exploded. In 1817 it was 4,446. Thirty years later, in 1846, it had quadrupled to 17,600, then it nearly doubled again to 30,390 in 1862–63. By then the entire province had been planted with cane as the railroad pushed the sugar frontier farther south and east. Equally dramatic was the growth of the port. It became the point of export for a growing sugar hinterland relentlessly expanding to Camarioca, the nearby Magdalena Valley, and elsewhere. The production of sugar in turn generated several important spin-offs, including refining, distilling alcohol, and producing the mechanical and metallurgical resources the maintenance of the industrial plant required, from trapiches to locomotives.

All this required a vast slave labor force. Between 1817 and 1827, the slave population of Matanzas province[14] grew at three times the rate of the rest of Cuba, and it doubled between 1827 and 1841 (from 26,552 to 53,331). These numbers could not but impact population ratios: black to white, and slave to free. In 1817, slaves were approximately 50 percent of the Matanzas population; by 1841 almost 63 percent. In some outlying districts the proportion was grossly lopsided. Guamacaro had a proportion of 90 percent of its population in bondage.[15]

The labor demands of this vast agricultural and factory complex were met in several ways. As the Matanzas sugar frontier opened up, networks of Havana-based but Matanzas-invested sugar mill and commercial interests continued to participate in the same mechanisms that kept Havana reliably supplied with Africans. Slaves would be purchased at the Havana slave market and transported to Matanzas, often with financing from merchants based in the capital city. In time, however, Matanzas developed its own network with the participation of Joaquín Mádan and the American traders Zacarías Atkins and George Latting. This enterprising trio acquired their human merchandise from vessels calling at the port or at clandestine drop-off and pick-up sites along the coast, much in the old tradition of colonial contraband. They were top feeders as well, operating their own slave ships. Mádan's *San Joaquín* and Atkins' *Serenade* could be counted on for a reliable supply of slaves fresh from Africa. Theirs was in no sense a marginal operation. In terms of volume it was comparable to the large slave-trading syndicates in Havana.

Matanzas slaves came from all over Africa. Many subgroups of the Yoruba from Nigeria and Benin (known generically as Lucumí in Cuba) came in great numbers. Congos, Carabalíes, Minas, Gangás, Mandingas, Fulas, and many others were also heavily represented in the Matanzas slave population. This is evident from the remarkable diversity of cabildos de nación reported by Israel Moliner Castañeda to be operating in the mid- to late nineteenth century.[16]

Most slaves were deployed in the countryside at ingenios or cafetales. Matanzas city in its heyday, however, had a very large domestic slave population as well. Although the demands of an extended patriarchal family were numerous and varied, most of the domestic slave cohort was at the service of status, not need. Impressive in their numbers and dressed in what even sympathetic observers like the Countess of Merlin described as rather outlandish livery, the large domestic servile staffs proclaimed by their very presence their owners' social prominence. For all the miseries of their existence, however, domestic slaves were better off than their rural brothers and sisters. More modest families might manage a slave or two to cook, wash, and keep house. Colored freedmen artisans might likewise own a handful of slaves to help at the shop.

Before the 1840s, slaves were deployed in relatively small units of production. After 1850, most slaves worked on large-scale mechanized plantations with crews often in excess of two hundred. By then all slave crews were housed in high-security *barracones*. The Cuban catalogue of this sinister building type, a jail in all but name, dates back to the first quarter of the nineteenth century. In 1825 Matanzas Governor Cecilio Ayllón's slave ordinance made them mandatory. Consequently, the modern Cuban barracón was perfected, if not altogether invented, in Matanzas. A remarkable barracón survived intact at Central Progreso well into the twentieth century. It provided for secure, sexually segregated dormitory space; a courtyard; and a tower that doubled as belfry. One entered through a massive archway. Eight elegant urns around the tower parapet softened somewhat the building's severity. Some said that the archway and windows in front resembled a skull (see fig. 18, bottom, in chapter 6). Spectacular barracones featuring multistoried towers existed at the San Martín and Alava sugar mills, among others.[17]

When the clandestine slave trade finally began to decline in the 1840s, the labor demands of Cuba's sugar Moloch found an alternative source of supply. In 1847 the first shipload of Chinese coolies arrived in Cuba. Devastated by a horrendous initial mortality rate, the experiment seemed as if it might not work. By 1853, however, the importation of virtually enslaved Asian labor was a going concern that in the course of the next twenty years would inject more than 100,000 Chinese laborers into Cuba.[18]

Coolie labor would be recruited in such places as Canton and Portuguese Macao and transported to Cuba, where laborers would be hired on contract by Cuban employers. The contracts were harsh. Laborers engaged their work for terms typically of a year. They had to be available to their employers around the clock for misery wages rarely exceeding ten pesos for the term of the contract, two changes of clothing, and a blanket. Thousands of conscripted laborers were brought over from the Yucatan Peninsula also, where the native rebellion known as the Caste War produced a harvest of exportable native Maya prisoners. Both groups were heavily, though not exclusively, represented in Matanzas.

The *zafra,* or harvest time, in nineteenth-century sugar mills was a fearsome time of hard toil and little sleep. Cutting down the cane and stowing it for transportation to the mill demanded all available hands, women and children not excepted.[19] The ungodly exertion was compounded by Cuba's relentless

Fig. 15. Chinese coolies in the cane fields, 1875.

sunshine and suffocating heat. No one who has never been inside a cane field as the morning advances and the temperature rises can quite appreciate just what a killer fieldwork can be.

For three summers in the early 1960s, when I was a young and penniless exile, I worked as a field hand at the Talisman sugar mill near Belle Glade, Florida. My job was to weed the furrows inside the cane field. We got started at five or six in the morning because by ten o'clock the field felt like an oven. The dry leaves of the cane stalks cut like blades, and dehydration was par for the course. I was in excellent physical trim then, but a workday would still flatten me. How anybody could survive in a cane field poorly nourished; barefooted; dressed only in a loincloth, shirt, and perhaps a hat; without gloves and a canteen of fresh water is beyond me, but that is how the slaves worked. As bad as my labor was, I was earning money for college, and I knew it would end. They had no hope.

The field was harsh but conditions were worse inside the plant. In steampowered mills the relentless rhythm of the machine took over. The noise level was high twenty-four hours a day. Fatigue was chronic among the slaves, and sleep deprivation often the source of nasty accidents where a hand or an arm would be caught in the jaws of a trapiche. Once the boilers were turned on at the beginning of the zafra, they had to be kept at a constant temperature. Without modern thermostats or accurate gauges, this was a critical task requiring brawn and concentration, not to mention enormous amounts of fuel: timber from the fallen forests in the early years, coal from the United States and local bagasse later on. From time to time, the most dreaded sugar mill industrial accident would happen when one of the boiling vats, or *tachos,* would break up or explode, causing havoc and casualties. One such accident killed my great-great-grandfather, Miguel Bretos Núñez de Villavicencio at the San Juan Bautista sugar mill near Limonar in 1875.

It was Juan Francisco Manzano, the remarkable slave-poet, who probably best caught something of a working mill's infernal bedlam in his poem "El ingenio." One can almost hear the noise that made it seem "as if hell had enlarged her bounds." The poem evokes "the frightful bell,"

> The dismal conch's loud blast at change of spell,
> The crack of whips, the hurried tramp of men
> The creaking mill, the driver' threats, and then,
> The sudden scream, the savage bloodhounds' growl.[20]

Steam had been tried out at Cuban mills as early as 1817. Its first successful application took place that year at Acana mill near Sabanilla del Encomendador.[21] The introduction of steam power to the mills was a transformational innovation. In 1825, only 2.5 percent of existing mills utilized steam. By 1861, 70 percent did. Eager to increase profitability, planters were very much up-to-date on the latest innovations. An attempt to introduce power plows was made in 1863, and a demonstration conducted at La Concepción, an Aldama family mill at Sabanilla. Mechanized plows would have been eminently suitable for the pancake-flat fields of western Cuba; however, the high cost of the machines coupled with the need to import costly specialized operators dampened enthusiasm for the equipment.[22] The innovative spirit of the Havana-Matanzas elite sugar planters was further demonstrated by planter Patricio de la Guardia's plan to use camels in the transportation of harvested cane at San Ignacio, his Yumurí Valley sugar mill. Thirty of the beasts actually arrived in Matanzas.[23]

A major technical breakthrough was the introduction of the Derosne tandem (*tren Derosne*) in the 1840s. Based on the development of the vacuum pan in Great Britain a few years earlier, Charles Derosne (1780–1846) integrated the grinding of the cane and boiling of the juice into a single system operated by the same steam power plant. His revolutionary system had benefited from ideas developed by a Louisiana quadroon, Norbert Rillieux, whose own system competed with Derosne's.

The first Derosne tandem in Cuba was installed at La Mella mill near Limonar in 1841 and tried out the following year. Derosne himself was on hand to assemble the complicated machinery. It was a resounding success because, in addition to significant savings of fuel, the machinery offered the option of being operated by a single person and produced a superior, whiter quality of sugar.

The owner of the mill was Wenceslao de Villa-Urrutia y de la Puente (1788–1852), a resolute advocate of technological innovation. Born in Spain, he arrived in Cuba at the turn of the eighteenth century and led a remarkable career as secretary of Cuba's Junta de Fomento (Development Board) and project manager for the Havana-Güines Railway. Under Villa-Urrutia's leadership, La Mella became a veritable experimental laboratory. The system of two synchronous horizontal mills in tandem was developed there, a significant Cuban contribution to sugar technology.[24]

A further important addition to the manufacturing process was the invention of the *centrífuga*. This was in essence a drum connected to a steam engine that could turn at 2,000 rpm, doing rapidly and efficiently the job that the old hormas had done with the help of time and gravity. The first centrífuga in Cuba spun at Amistad sugar mill near Güines in 1849. Matanzas mills followed suit. By 1857, French-made centrífugas operated at Agüica, Alava, Armonía, Flor de Cuba, Ponina, San Martín, and Unión.[25]

Advanced manufacturing technology required expert handling and sophisticated maintenance. The need for the former was met essentially by foreign operators. In time, Americans came to dominate the sector. Mechanics, locomotive engineers, and other skilled personnel would head to Cuba during the harvest, work hard, and return home with a nice bundle. The complicated machinery, however, required capital maintenance and repairs on a predictable schedule. Gears had to be rectified, axles machined, and new parts cast. This was the origin of the Cuban-based repair shop, or *fundición*. Cuban fundiciones developed a remarkable technical capacity and played a significant and innovative role in mill mechanization. In the 1950s, Cuban-made parts were exported to mills in Latin America and the United States.

Some of the best fundiciones in all of Cuba were located in what became Matanzas province. The first such operation in the city itself was the Felipe Vallée shop at Tirry Boulevard in Pueblo Nuevo. It was also the first in the province and was in business by 1830. The Ojo de Agua and Zuaznábar, Labayén & Co. shops followed in the 1840s. The best fundición in the province, however, was the legendary Perret shop in Unión de Reyes. Founded in 1869, it remained a family business until the revolution and, in a manner of speaking, since. Although the business was nationalized by the revolutionary government—the name was changed to Primero de Mayo—members of the Perret family continued to manage it until a few years ago.[26] The fundición was a matrix of Cuba's renowned mechanical excellence. Master mechanics were trained—literally in the nuts and bolts of their trade—precisely at such places. Anyone who marvels at the ingenuity with which Cuban mechanics have managed to keep American cars of the 1950s running for half a century needs look no further for the historical root of their skills.

The mechanical revolution was mirrored by a revolution in transport and communications. The telegraph made virtually instantaneous communications possible. Many mills acquired telegraph stations. Besides the convenience, it was a safety measure. Surreptitious communications among slave crews by means of drums had been revealed in 1843 and, although drumming in the mills was forbidden in consequence, the Morse code might be handy in case the army was needed to quell a rebellion.

Railroads, introduced in Cuba very early, turned the world of sugar upside down. The first train in the world ran between Manchester and Liverpool in 1830. The same year the Junta de Fomento began considering the railroad's introduction to the island. The first railroad in the colony ran between Havana and Bejucal in 1837, was later extended to Güines, and finally came to Matanzas in 1862. Railroads grew swiftly. By 1860 there existed 1,281 kilometers of railways in service, 497 kilometers under construction, and 468 under study.[27]

The first railroad in Matanzas province was the Cárdenas-Bemba (later Jovellanos) line, developed by a consortium of powerful Havana criollo investors then developing mills in central Matanzas. The Empresa del Ferrocarril de Cárdenas had completed eighty-three kilometers of line to Bemba when a further concession to extend the line to Macagua was negotiated. The Ferrocarril de Júcaro ran from Júcaro, near Cárdenas, to Altamisal, Banagüises, and San José de los Ramos. The first line in Matanzas itself, the Ferrocarril de Matanzas, connected the city to Guanábana (1840), later on to Sabanilla del Encomendador (1843), and eventually to Unión de Reyes and Coliseo (1848), traversing the Magdalena Valley sugar-growing district. Matanzas and Cárdenas were not connected until 1858, and then by roundabout: Cárdenas-Bemba-Coliseo-Guanábana-Matanzas.[28]

The "Sabanilla line" illustrates the links between sugar and Cuba's railway history. In 1839, a concession was granted to Gonzalo Alfonso Soler to build a railway from Matanzas city to Las Piedras plantation in the *partido* of Sabanilla del Encomendador. Alfonso owned two sugar mills near Sabanilla: San Gonzalo and Majagua. His sister, Rosa María, was married to Domingo Aldama, the head of a powerful Havana family that owned the Santa Rosa, Santo Domingo, and San José mills, also in Sabanilla. Other members of the Alfonso clan owned Triumvirato, Acana, and Concepción in neighboring Guanábana. The proposed Compañía del Ferrocarril de Matanzas was so tightly bound to narrow family interests that the government made it a condition for approval that local mill owners unrelated to the Alfonso-Aldama circle be allowed to participate as stockholders.[29]

Matanzas city's first railroad is linked to one of the most venerable railway relics in the world, La Junta de Fomento, Cuba's ultimate locomotive, officially a national monument. La Junta was made by the Rogers Locomotive Works of Paterson, N.J., expressly for the Ferrocarril de Matanzas and arrived home in 1843. She began service on November 1 and remained in Matanzas for her entire working career. Kept at the Sabanilla Station until 1912, she was exhibited at Havana's main rail station for many years and is now the star exhibit at Cuba's Railways Museum.

It would be hard to overemphasize the importance of family links in the world of the sugar plantation. Even a cursory view of the genealogies of a handful of families at the core of the Havana-Matanzas sugar oligarchy reveals the close-knit family circles, the marriages among first cousins, and the business linkages that kept the group cohesive—perhaps much too cohesive for its own good. Their accumulation of power and wealth was enormous.[30]

Marriage offered an opportunity for entrepreneurial others to enter the inner circle. Women of the princely Ximeno family, for example, married the likes of

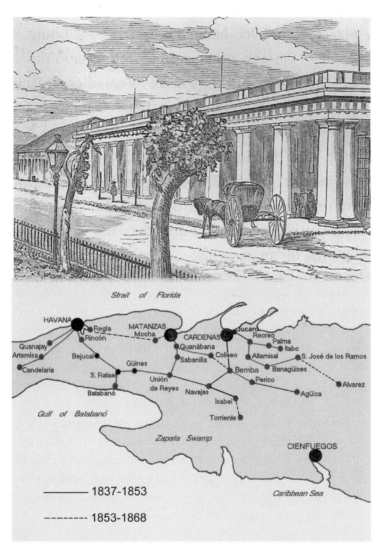

Fig. 16. *Above:* Sabanilla Station ca. 1870. *Below:* map of railways in the Havana-Matanzas region, 1837–1868.

William Updike Jencks and Nicolás Mahy y León—the former American, the latter Spanish—both dynamic businessmen. Rosa Aldama y Alfonso married the less affluent but very smart Domingo del Monte. Lola Cruz—a great deal more about her later—a member of the lesser sugar elite married a Ximeno at the very top of the food chain and became Matanzas' all-time hostess with the mostest. The connubial approach led a parvenu Dominican physician, Just Germán Cantero, to prominence as mill owner and gifted promoter.

The champion marriage entrepreneur in the tight little world of the Havana-Matanzas sugar plantocracy was a matancera, Elena Celestina Martín de Medina y Molina. Born in Ceiba Mocha in fairly modest circumstances in 1820, she married a city councilman, Juan de la Cruz van der Putter, who died leaving her childless and the mistress of two mills, Macutivo and Santa Elena. Beautiful, smart, and now well-heeled, Elena married José María Martínez de Campos y de la Vega, second Count of Santovenia, in 1854. On becoming the dowager countess in 1865—too bad for the count—she inherited a vast estate, including a palace in Havana and the Monserrate sugar mill in Matanzas. Her lock on the estate was absolute. Her son succeeded to the title, and she was his guardian during his minority. Her third marriage was viceregal: no less than the captain-general himself, Domingo Dulce y Garay, Marquis of Castell-Florit.

Back to the track. Cuban railways were not conceived as trunk lines joining population centers, like the British system, or as the complement of grand strategic designs and commercial schemes. Cuban lines served the ends of oligopolies. Their purpose was not so much to move people and merchandise as to move sugar to port and machinery to the mills. It was far more important to get a box of sugar from Banagüises to the docks at Cárdenas than to get a passenger from Matanzas to Cárdenas. Of course, the movement of passengers came as part of the package, with obvious social impact.

Railways dramatically expanded the sugar frontier, making it possible to bring into production remote areas hitherto uneconomical to exploit. They also had a major impact upon both the harvest of the cane and the industrial operation itself. Narrow-gauge trains would go into the fields to transport cane to the factory, while auxiliary locomotives in the environs of a mill were deployed to different ends. In the 1870s, portable rail systems developed principally by Henri Decauville in France were introduced at some mills. The Decauville system proved its mettle throughout the world, from the henequen haciendas of Yucatan to the Maginot line but failed to gain a foothold in

Cuba.[31] Outreach and greater efficiency meant larger mills and would account for the emergence of the *central* in the late nineteenth century.

The physical layout of the sugar ingenios, features of which would carry over to the massive centrales that began to appear in the 1870s, became standardized. A mill's "campus," or *batey,* would include the factory itself (*casa de calderas*), where the trapiches functioned and the industrial operations were carried out. A vivienda offered commodious lodging for the mill's administrator, or *mayoral.* Warehouses, a field office, a mechanical shop, and stables were part of the ensemble. Before the telegraph became available, many mills had colonies of homing pigeons.

Slaves were not so lucky. Originally housed in thatched huts, since the 1820s, and especially after 1844, slaves were increasingly housed in high-security barracks, where they could be locked up for the night, males on one side, females on the other. The urban equivalent of the barracón was the *entrepiso,* a high-security space inserted between the street floor and the upstairs apartments of palatial homes such the Junco mansion on Vigía Square.

The sheer scope of Matanzas' nineteenth-century sugar boom—its massive impact on everything from the economy to the landscape—can perhaps best be understood in numbers. On the eve of the Castro revolution, some 24 centrales operated in the province of Matanzas (out of 161 in all of Cuba). The largest ones, such as Tinguaro, Cuba, and España, were substantial by Cuban standards though nowhere near such titans as Camagüey's Jaronú in size or capacity. The two smallest, Elena and Puerto, both in the Yumurí Valley environs, were *cachimbos* (Cuban pejorative for small centrales).

There is no doubt that nineteenth-century mills were small by comparison, but what they lacked in size they more than made up for in smoke. Alberto Perret Moliner has determined the certain location of 618 mills in Matanzas province, with 73 others known from documentary references but as yet not located. That is almost 700 mills! A balloon ride over the flat Matanzas countryside at the height of the zafra of, say, 1857 would have revealed a manmade landscape where the ancient forest had once stood. Its most prominent feature would have been the countless plumes of smoke marking the spots where cane collected from an immense cane field was being ground into an endless stream of sweet crystals.

The classic Cuban ingenio can be compared to that other great Latin American agrarian complex: the mature hacienda. Like the hacienda, it depended on large landholdings and a captive labor force. Indeed, in Cuban usage a mill owner was a *hacendado* but one cannot extend the comparison much beyond that. Unlike the hacienda, the ingenio had no manorial pretensions nor did it serve as a source of honor. Status, yes, honor, no: the Cuban ingenio was essentially, if not exclusively, a commercial venture.[32] An intermediate type would be the classic Yucatan henequen hacienda which, like the Cuban ingenio, required mechanization, although the extraction of henequen fiber (*sosquil*) was nowhere nearly as complex as sugar making.

There is nothing in Cuban sugar mills to even suggest the lordly grandeur of Mexican—or, for that matter, Yucatecan—haciendas. One would also search in vain for that key component of the Latin American hacienda compound, the chapel. The Cuban ingenios and the slave population that made them work were essentially unchurched. Richard Madden, the British abolitionist, reported that to his knowledge in only two estates were slaves permitted to go to Sunday mass, and only one had a resident chaplain.[33] In 1839, Eulalia Bretton des Chappeles, a visitor to an ingenio on the San Juan River, formerly the property of an illustrious aristocratic family, was dumbfounded to find the chapel, "said to be one of the oldest on the island," in complete ruins.[34] Matanzas planter Pedro Hernández Morejón found it nearly impossible to locate priests in sufficient numbers and with the requisite qualities to be of any use.

White matanceros were not a particularly pious lot. Writing as early as 1828, the Rev. Abiel Abbot, a visiting Massachusetts minister, offered insightful and, given his Calvinist worldview and clerical status, remarkably objective observations about local religious practice. "Whatever benefit is to be derived from visiting the church," he concluded, "is shared by a very small portion of the people."[35] Matanzas in 1846 had the largest number of inhabitants per priest of any ecclesiastical jurisdiction in Cuba, (5,154 persons per priest, compared to 818 for the city of Havana and 1,760 for Santiago de Cuba).[36] This was in part a reflection of the profound secularization of Cuban society during the nineteenth century, a complex multi-causal phenomenon that needs thorough investigation. It could not but have facilitated the preservation of African culture.

Matanzas' centrality to the Cuban sugar empire is made manifest on the pages and plates of a luxurious volume published in 1857 and widely hailed as Cuba's most ambitious colonial publishing venture. *Los ingenios: colección de vistas de los principales ingenios de azúcar de la isla de Cuba*, sponsored by mill owner Justo Germán Cantero, offers exhaustive technical information about

Fig. 17. Ingenio La Santísima Trinidad ca. 1857. The tall tree and fallen trunk are remnants of the ancient forest. As old-growth forest disappeared, royal palms took over the landscape. Lithograph by Eduardo Laplante, ca. 1857. (Courtesy of Rare Books Division, Library of Congress)

Cuba's most advanced sugar mills. The printing by the Havana press of Luis Marquier was of an exceptionally high standard, and the stunning lithographs by Eduardo Laplante have become iconic. Matanzas province is represented in nineteen out of twenty-eight entries.

Sugar provided the energy that made Matanzas and attracted a population. International connections and prosperity propelled Matanzas into renown— as the "Athens of Cuba," no less. Profits built the palatial homes of the local elite, a.k.a. the "Señorío." It was a golden age for those in a position and with enough ethical anesthesia to enjoy it. But sugar was based on slavery and, on that account, there was the devil to pay.

6 The Year of the Lash

ASK ANYONE FAMILIAR WITH Cuban lore to freely associate, say "forty-four," and back comes the answer without missing a beat: "el año del cuero." The Year of the Lash is what 44 stands for in the charada, the Chinese divination scheme with which Cubans have made sense of dreams and omens for generations. It is a strange but compelling memorial to the horrible events of 1844.[1]

Seeking to defuse what was assumed to be a well-organized conspiracy and prevent an apocalyptic slave uprising, the colony's government launched an all-out wave of repression that claimed thousands of victims. According to the historian Vidal Morales y Morales, about four thousand people were arrested in the first few weeks of 1844 in Matanzas alone, including two thousand freedmen and seventy-five whites. By the end of the year—again, in Matanzas alone, which was said to be the epicenter of the conspiracy—seventy-eight victims had been formally executed, both slaves and free people of color, men and women. It did not stop there: 1,292 were sentenced to prison terms ranging from six months to ten years, and 435 banished. Floggings ran into the thousands, and hundreds of victims—mostly slaves—just disappeared, their deaths attributed to diarrhea. The victims would be whipped while tied down to a ladder (*escalera*), hence the name of this shameful episode: *la conspiración de la escalera*.[2]

As a young man I loved to cycle what was then known as the Old Guanábana Road across the former domain of the Aldamas and the Alfonsos, where the

Matanzas sugar plantation complex reached a climax.[3] A sense of the past hung about the place. Ceibas and algarrobos lined the road, lonely survivors of the ancient forest spared for their shade. The ride was a time warp meandering through the nineteenth century. The vintage macadamized road surface was pockmarked by one hundred years of potholes. Where scavengers had yet to remove rails and sleepers, fragments of old railway track survived alongside.

Along the road lay the ruins of Triumvirato, an old mill with an antique name founded in the early nineteenth century by Julián Luis Alfonso Soler, the progenitor of the Alfonso-Mádan branch of the magnate family. Triumvirato was decommissioned in 1918, and its cane sent to be ground at nearby Central Limones, where my great-great-grandfather had been cooked alive by an exploding vat in 1875.[4]

Like so many obsolete old Cuban ingenios, Triumvirato fell to ruin. There was nothing remarkable about the site when I first came across it on one of my bike journeys: a caved-in roof here, a wall there, an old rusty boiler, once filled with bubbling cane juice, slowly decaying amidst the weeds and vines. No one would have guessed what consequential events had taken place there exactly one century before I was born, when the slaveholders' vague fears of the day of reckoning became a scare about its imminence.

The Triumvirato residence has since been restored. The old highway has been widened and sealed, and many of the old trees are gone. An impressive monument commemorates the slave rebellion of 1843 and its protagonists: Carlota, a Lucumí woman, and her companions, Eduardo, a Fula; Narciso and Felipe, also Lucumís; Carmita and Juliana, both criollas; and Manuel, a Gangá. Their actions would resonate in an extraordinary fashion in the affairs of remote posterity. Cuban military operations in Angola beginning in the 1970s were known by the code name "Operation Carlota."

All that lay in the unfathomable future, of course, when Carlota and her fellow rebels paid with their lives for their love of liberty. We shall come back to them, but first let us consider what the "peculiar institution" meant for Cuba and Matanzas four decades into the nineteenth century. Slavery in the Americas was in retreat by 1843. It survived in the United States, Cuba, Puerto Rico, and the Empire of Brazil. As long as slaves could be brought across the ocean, slavery had a future. When Great Britain adopted the global end of slavery as national policy on the threshold of the nineteenth century, the end of the trade became a top priority. In 1807 Great Britain and the United States enacted legislation banning the slave trade. Ten years later the British pressured

Spain into a treaty binding the latter to terminate the infamous commerce by 1820. The treaty provided for verification in the form of a Mixed Commission to reside in Havana.[5]

Enforcement was difficult, however. Colonial authorities in Cuba were often in cahoots with slave merchants and smugglers. Reportedly, the captain-general's share of the bribes doled out by slave smugglers was in the neighborhood of $100,000 per year, a whopping sum.[6] The network of corruption went beyond the palace and enlisted the complicity of many others, from the harbor master and the commandant of the Havana naval garrison all the way down the food chain. Their nemesis was the intrepid David Turnbull, a combative, dyed-in-the-wool abolitionist who arrived in Havana as British consul and chief treaty inspector in 1840.[7] Turnbull was in no sense a diplomat. A feisty advocate of the rights of *emancipados* (slaves freed by treaty regulations), he would go as far as necessary to protect their interests. The clashes between Turnbull and Spanish authorities were legendary, and he was declared persona non grata in 1842.[8] Shortly after his expulsion he landed near Gibara with a group of free Bahamian blacks, supposedly to rescue illegally held emancipados. He was lucky the Spanish did not shoot him.

Fed by a constant stream of newcomers from Africa, Matanzas' slaves were anything but docile. *Cimarronaje* or, in English use, marronage (the condition of a runaway) was common, and numerous *palenques* (runaway communities) existed. Marronage and rebellion were visible and dramatic but, as Manuel Barcia has demonstrated in an elegant study, they were not the only forms of resistance. Resistance was woven into the everyday life of the slaves. Robbed of their honor and forced into a degrading existence, slaves rebelled not for abstract ideas like Liberty or Abolition. Resistance flowed from the existential predicaments of slavery: how to regain a sense of honor, avenge abuse, or relieve an unbearable work burden.[9]

Again, as Barcia points out, rebellions were not necessarily conspiracies except at the most basic level of organization. The pressing, immediate issues of a slave rebellion were how to get hold of machetes, break the locks of the barracón, and then survive. Conspiracies are much more complicated. They imply conspirators, forethought, secrecy, in short, a plan. They are not spontaneous.

At least since 1812, when the so-called Aponte conspiracy, a true and remarkable plot, resulted in the burning of several mills in the Yumurí Valley, slave rebellions were as predictable as hurricanes.[10] In 1825, a major slave uprising at Sumidero and Sabanazo was severely repressed. It left a momentous legacy in the unique slave code promulgated by Governor Cecilio Ayllón that year.

Sumidero and Sabanazo were not isolated incidents. In 1830 a rebellion was aborted by the authorities in Guamacaro. The following year, a slave named Trinidad attempted a rebellion at the Jesús María mill near Sabanilla. Between 1832 and 1839, rebellions were aborted at the Magdalena mill (Santa Ana) and the Conchita mill (Macuriges). In July of 1841 and again in July of the following year, a serious revolt occurred at Arratía mill, also in Macuriges. Led by Gregorio, a Lucumí, forty-two members of the slave crew burned most of the batey. They were brought under control after a brave resistance, and the rebellion brutally suppressed. Such news was unnerving to the slave masters, especially after a demographically disturbing fact was revealed by the census of 1841. For the first time ever, Cuba's colored population, both slave and free, surpassed the whites.

The year 1843 opened amidst turmoil. In January the slave crew at Triángulo sugar mill in Guamacaro rose in revolt. They hacked their *mayoral* to pieces and marched on nearby plantations. In a matter of a few days more than three hundred slaves armed with spears and machetes were on the warpath in the region. Bringing them under control required an unprecedented mobilization of military force. Their example spread rapidly. In March a major uprising at the Alcancía sugar mill in the Cárdenas district took the lives of three whites and resulted in the destruction of three mills and one cafetal. Almost simultaneously, rebellion flared up among the slave crews of the Cárdenas railroad. It was savagely repressed but not before a number of slaves escaped to the interior. In May there were serious uprisings at two other mills, Santa Rosa (an Aldama mill) and Majagua (an Alfonso mill), both near Unión de Reyes. As the tense, wet summer turned into the dreaded harvest season, another rebellion took place at the Acana sugar mill near Sabanilla on June 2.

On November 5, Carlota and her companions took control of Triumvirato, killed the *mayoral* and his assistant, and set the buildings on fire. Led by the brave lady, a ragtag force moved on to Acana, where they were greeted by Evaristo and Fermina, who had been secretly preparing for the day. Fermina was in shackles for her participation in the Acana event in June. She was freed and Acana laid waste. Their force, increased by fresh recruits, moved on to the San Miguel sugar mill. There they met resistance when the owners and loyal members of the crew put up a fight. They had to content themselves with sacking the batey and burning what they could. Next they attacked and destroyed

San Lorenzo mill, and moved on to San Rafael, where they met their match: a superior Spanish regular force dispatched by Matanzas Governor Antonio García Oña. Carlota was captured and quartered, and the rebellion suffocated. Fermina, four Lucumís, and three Gangás were shot in Matanzas in March of the following year.

Could all this unrest have been merely coincidental? Or had the line been crossed from a series of unrelated, sporadic rebellions to some coordinated effort far more worrisome from the authorities' perspective? Cuba's Comisión Militar Ejecutiva y Permanente investigated numerous instances of slave uprisings throughout the island. They did a thorough job, and indeed found reason for concern. David Turnbull emerged as a prime suspect and conspirator. The feisty British agent loomed large in the Spanish authorities' demonology, but he was now beyond reach. There was little that could be done about him except trying him in absentia, which, not surprisingly, was done.

Were the free blacks and mulattoes go-betweens between the slave crews

Fig. 18. Memorial to slave rebels and restored vivienda at Triumvirato. *Below:* barracks at Central Progreso in 1916.

and the mysterious masterminds of the conspiracy? Plausibly. If the large slave population was a security concern to the authorities by virtue of their sheer numbers, the free people of color were no less so by virtue of their position. Haitian freedmen had been the instigators of the slave rebellion there, and Aponte, the leader of the brilliantly organized if unsuccessful 1812 conspiracy, was a mulatto and a freedman.

While a minority in comparison with the overall colored population, the free colored cohort was ubiquitous and growing, for Spanish law allowed slaves to buy their freedom in a relatively straightforward fashion. Manumission was mandatory if slaves could produce their value in cash as compensation to their owners, a process called *coartación*. This they could do because slaves in Cuba, especially urban slaves, were allowed modest opportunities to earn income outside of the bondage relationship. This, and the support of cabildos de nación, enabled many a slave to obtain manumission. Others might be freed by testamentary disposition of their white fathers—sexual relations between masters and slave women were common. The importance of free people of color was not based on their numbers alone. Overwhelmingly urban, they were the backbone of Cuba's artisan class and held a virtual monopoly on some occupations, such as musicians. They were Cuba's shoemakers and carpenters, furniture makers and plumbers, blacksmiths and phlebotomists, midwives and seamstresses and, as such, indispensable.

Perhaps the old ways whereby slaves were kept docile did not work anymore. It was standard practice among slave owners to attempt to prevent communications between their crews. Barcia has shown this was easier said than done. In any case, the Triumvirato rebels were said to have communicated through drums. What seemed like innocent amusement to the unsuspecting ears of the masters was the voice of freedom sounding. That was new and unnerving news. If Carlota and her companions had been able to circumvent isolation and make common cause with slaves kilometers away, anything seemed possible. Moreover, the rebel columns were nothing if not diverse: Lucumís, Fulas, Gangás, and Mandingas had fought shoulder-to-shoulder. If they could do that once, they could do it again. As 1844 dawned, a single and therefore invincible movement seemed not only possible; it might already be under way.

On top of that, slave unrest in Cuba became an international issue. A successful slave revolt on the island was the worst possible scenario for the United States. Neither a second black republic like Haiti nor, conceivably, a British protectorate was an outcome acceptable to Washington. Consequently, the Tyler administration sent a squadron to Havana under the command of J. S. Chauncey with orders to report to the new captain-general and offer military support if matters ever came to that. General Leopoldo O'Donnell had taken office on October 20. Two weeks later Triumvirato exploded. Chauncey's squadron entered Havana on November 8. O'Donnell had hardly unpacked when he found himself confronted by a major emergency. Before we return to him, however, we need to consider another key component of the situation: the slaveholders themselves, especially the criollos.

Alarmed by the Triumvirato events, ninety-three Matanzas planters addressed a memorandum to the captain-general requesting military protection. They asked him to authorize a militia and urged an end to the illegal slave trade. The trade, in their view, was the root of the evil, a chief source of unrest as it continually pumped dangerous, unassimilated African elements into the slave population. They presented their memorandum to García Oña, who not only refused to forward it to the captain-general but tore it to shreds in their presence. Benigno Gener, however, a prominent member of the Matanzas criollo elite, decided to convey the document to O'Donnell on his own responsibility.

García Oña knew his boss better than the local patricians did. As he had predicted, the captain-general gave the document a jaundiced reading. O'Donnell was no fan of the criollo sugar planters' elite and had much to gain in kickbacks from the continuance of the surreptitious slave trade. The idea of arming a militia controlled by potentially disaffected criollos was prima facie preposterous. No Spanish colonial government could afford to arm the very people that, given time, could become Cuba's insurgents.

What historian Manuel Moreno Fraginals has called the Cuban "saccharo-cracy" was closely knit and interbred at the top, but the Cuban planters were not a monolithic group. At one extreme were the happy-go-lucky beneficiaries of a social system which, though unfair, had its rewards for those who could find them. Esteban Santa Cruz de Oviedo, a criollo blueblood and owner of La Santísima Trinidad mill near Matanzas, was an exemplary case. Endowed with a robust sexual appetite and a predilection for dark skin, he gathered about him a harem of slave women who bore him a small army of children. A superb novel by Marta Rojas, *El harén de Oviedo*, follows the adventures of his mixed offspring in a thoroughly racist society.

At the other end of the criollo slaveholding cohort was a learned intelligentsia whose members and satellites tried to deal with the social, economic, and ethical dilemmas of slavery as best they could, an insurmountable challenge if one held simultaneously the ideas of a nineteenth-century liberal and the vested interests of a master of slaves—what we might call the Thomas Jefferson dilemma, although the Cubans were not exactly Jeffersonians. This group viewed the continued expansion of the slave population through illegal imports (all imports were illegal after 1820, remember) as profoundly destabilizing and potentially lethal to the colony's continued existence. The memorandum to O'Donnell made that very clear.

They were not abolitionists. Their fortunes were heavily invested in slaves. Abolition made sense only if compensation was involved. Racist to the core, they viewed the increasing Africanization of Cuba—for which, of course, they as a class were ultimately responsible—with alarm, if not outright horror. They subscribed to a kind of soft nativism that delighted in evoking preconquest idylls, a position known as *siboneyismo* in its literary expression. They were not nationalists in the modern sense, and independence was not an objective. The argument could be made—as the criollo intellectual Domingo del Monte did—that the continued influx of slaves, patently harmful to Cuba, served the devious purpose of a guarantee against Cuban independence.[11]

As regards independence the criollo slaveholding class were the heirs of what, in retrospect, was a Faustian pact that had put them on the wrong side of history. Between 1810 and 1824, the Spanish colonies on the mainland had opted for independence and fought long and hard to secure it. Cuba and Puerto Rico did not. What accounts for their exceptionality?

Simón Bolívar, in his famous 1815 *Carta de Jamaica*, attributed Spain's "tranquil possession" of the two strategic islands to the criollos' "lack of contact with the independents." "But," Bolívar went on, "are those insulars not American? Are they not insulted? Do they not wish to improve their lot?" The question marks are notable in a document remarkable for its prophetic tone and detailed assertiveness about Latin America's future. Prudently, the Liberator does not touch again on the future of the islands.

The exceptionality of Puerto Rico and Cuba had nothing to do with their elites' lack of contact with the patriots, of course. It had everything to do with the huge numbers of slaves on the islands, particularly in Cuba. Cuban criollos understood all too well that slavery and revolution did not mix. That being the case, they could live without independence. In 1810, in fact, Cuban criollos did not pine for independence at all, for they exerted a remarkable if precarious hold on the colony's administration. Their entrepreneurial dynamism gave them clout, and we have seen how they were able to bend policy and the law to their end of transforming Cuba into one vast cane field. The Cuban criollos' deal with the devil was not a naive transaction. It was as adroit and calculating a move as was ever made by a social group in the history of the Americas.

The devil delivered, to be sure, as he always does. But he delivered on his terms. The fabulous profits of sugar were tainted by the blood of slaves. The price of prosperity was an uneasy conscience; that of wealth, anxiety. Racism, one of Cuba's central neuroses, was the product of both with a generous helping of fear thrown in for good measure. The karma was very bad.

The natural base for this group in Matanzas was the tertulia gathered about a prominent intellectual, Domingo del Monte y Aponte (the surname is also rendered as Delmonte). The cultural history of Matanzas in its heyday cannot be told without reference to del Monte, so we need to know a bit more about him.[12] Born in Venezuela, he was brought to Cuba as an infant and grew up on the island. A lawyer by profession, he married into the prominent Aldamas. His wife, Rosa Aldama y Alfonso, was the daughter of Domingo Aldama and a niece of Gonzalo Alfonso of Sabanilla Railways fame. Miguel Aldama, the head of the Aldama clan at the time of its greatest influence, was del Monte's brother-in-law. The Aldamas had large sugar estates in Matanzas but lived in Havana. The Aldama Palace, one of Havana's most important nineteenth-century buildings, still bears witness to the princely lifestyle of this family whose members played a major role in Cuba's economic and political history. The palace was initially designed by a Venezuelan architect, Manuel Antonio Carrerá,

Fig. 19. The criollo intellectual del Monte *(left)*. The mulatto poet Plácido *(right)*, an occasional visitor at del Monte's tertulias, was executed in 1844 as a sympathizer with the slave rebellion.

but it seems likely that the completion was the work of the French-Matanzan architect Jules Sagebién.[13]

In 1834, del Monte visited Matanzas for the first time and ended up living there for six months. It was a business trip; he had been hired as a lawyer, did very well professionally, and fell in love with the place. Quick to realize its potential, he became the leader of a group of like-minded individuals attracted by the booming city's prospects.

A born organizer and indefatigable letter writer, the young lawyer hosted a tertulia (salon).[14] Meeting every Wednesday at the home of another Matanzas booster, Pedro Guiteras—the house still stands on Calle del Río No. 9—the weekly gatherings attracted loyal participants, some of them peninsular but most of them criollos. Among the latter were the Milanés brothers, Federico and José Jacinto, both poets. Del Monte was especially impressed with José Jacinto's talent, encouraged him to write, and put his extraordinary gifts to good use. Also attracted to the weekly discussions and readings were poet Ramón Palma and *costumbrista* writer Cirilo Villaverde, whose *Cecilia Valdés ó la loma del ángel* is Cuba's best-loved nineteenth-century novel. Both Palma and Villaverde were in Matanzas as hired faculty for La Empresa School. Pedro Antonio Alfonso, Matanzas' pioneering historian and author of *Memorias de un matancero*, was another habitué.

Among the tertulia's signal accomplishments was the discovery of Juan Francisco Manzano. The future poet was born in bondage at the Havana mansion of the Marquis of Jústiz de Santa Ana, whose surname, recall, was Manzano. It was customary for slaves to take the surname of their owners. Juan Francisco was spoiled by the old marchioness, doña Beatriz de Jústiz Zayas Bazán, the same intrepid poet who had let Charles III of Spain have a piece of her mind in 1762. The marchioness took a special interest in the little boy, who was said to spend more time in her arms than in his mother's. Apparently she had resolved to grant him his freedom, but her death in 1807, when he was ten years old, complicated things immensely and Juan Francisco ended up as the personal slave of the Marchioness of Prado Ameno. He lived to rue the day, for he would suffer abuse and what would be referred to today as psychological torture at the hands of his sadistic mistress.

The Prado Amenos—their family name was Zayas Bazán—kept an elegant home in Matanzas where Juan Francisco would spend a good deal of his time. Manzano, who learned to read and write, was a poet of no mean talent. In 1836, he was invited by del Monte to address the tertulia. His reading of his moving sonnet "Thirty Years," in which he reviewed his life in servitude and despaired at what lay ahead, so moved del Monte and his friends that they bought his freedom. Manzano's autobiography, written at del Monte's urging, was published in English by Richard Madden in 1840.[15]

O'Donnell had no liking at all for this group and what it stood for. As criollos they were inherently unreliable lest the bug of independence infest them. To the captain-general's no-nonsense military thinking, their inconsistencies must have seemed at best effete and at worst contemptible. The feelings were heartily reciprocated. O'Donnell, at any rate, has become one of the ogres of criollo historiography, a perch he shares with Miguel Tacón and Valeriano Weyler. This dim vision of him contrasts with his place in the history of nineteenth-century Spain. Three times head of the government and a war hero, he was a consequential figure and a responsible statesman. While we can infer from the record that he was implacable and even cruel, we cannot infer that he was irrational. For O'Donnell to have launched a wave of systematic and thorough repression, as he did on his arrival in Cuba, without compelling cause would have been not only irrational but, indeed, the height of folly given its economic and political cost.

Just who was the new captain-general? Leopoldo O'Donnell y Jorrís brought an unusual background to his office. He was born in Tenerife, in the Canary Islands. The scion of an Irish military family in the service of Spain, he enrolled in the army and enjoyed a swift rise due to his merits. The family never lost its Irishness. O'Donnell's great-great-grandson, Hugo O'Donnell, the current Duke of Tetuán and a distinguished historian, is also the current Tanáiste, or heir to the chieftainship of the Clan O'Donnell of Donegal. Leopoldo O'Donnell's distinguished service in the Carlist Wars, especially his defeat of the insurgents at Lucena, earned him the rank of general. He would eventually be ennobled as Count of Lucena and later on as Duke of Tetuán in recognition of his services in Morocco. He was appointed captain-general of Cuba at thirty-four years of age, the youngest Spanish viceroy ever on the island.

Despite his youth, O'Donnell, like virtually all Spanish military officers of his time, was immensely sensitive to the prospect of Cuban independence. Spanish military mandarins in Cuba, especially during the crucial second quarter of the century, brought to their position a visceral reaction to the loss of Spain's mainland empire between 1810 and 1824 and, consequently, a deep mistrust of the criollos. O'Donnell's immediate predecessors, Miguel Tacón and Jerónimo Valdés, were extreme cases of that implacable *desconfianza*. Both were members of the Spanish army faction known as the *ayacuchos*, the losers of the Latin American independence wars. (The battle of Ayacucho, which ended the wars, was won by Bolívar's army under the immediate command of Sucre on December 9, 1824.) As governor of Popayán in Nueva Granada, Tacón had had to surrender to Bolívar's officers. All the sugar in Cuba could not sweeten that bitter experience. O'Donnell fully shared that mentality. A successful criollo-led independence movement must not be repeated in Cuba no matter what. The solution was to keep the potentially disaffected on as short a leash as possible.

The Chauncey mission put O'Donnell in a very awkward position. As the highest Spanish authority in Cuba, he could not accept American intervention however difficult the slave situation might be. He therefore assured Chauncey that Cuba was under control. Having said that, he had to make sure that it remained so. He had plenty of reasons to worry, however. Triumvirato demonstrated that Cuba was a tinderbox. To prevent ignition O'Donnell was willing to pay any price, no matter how high. As it turned out, the price was awesome but so was O'Donnell's resolve.

On December 1, 1843, Esteban Santa Cruz de Oviedo—the same one notorious for keeping black women as sex slaves—showed up at the office of Matanzas Governor García Oña. He had urgent news and demanded an immediate audience. The news was disturbing. Oviedo, one of the largest planters in the Matanzas region, was a reliable informant as far as the governor was concerned. He had pointedly not signed the memorandum requesting a militia and end to the slave trade. He was also a disagreeable character: a slave smuggler, a brutal master, and a scandal because of his harem. As it transpired, one of his concubines, Polonia, had revealed to him a vast conspiracy involving the largest of his sugar mills, La Santísima Trinidad, as well as others in the region. The plan included a major landing of arms and military supplies at Caguama Bech (Varadero), to be arranged by none other than Turnbull. This was serious. García Oña immediately relayed the news to O'Donnell, who gave swift and unequivocal orders to break up the conspiracy by whatever means were necessary. García Oña complied and sent an army unit to Sabanilla, where sixteen slaves were summarily executed. This was the opening salvo of an orgy of repression that would swiftly grip the country. "The Year of the Lash" was under way.[16]

Fear crept up to the highest echelons of society. Renowned criollos, such as the educator José de la Luz y Caballero, were accused of complicity in the plot. Luz y Caballero, who was out of the country, was indicted but bravely returned to face the charges. He spent the better part of a year under house arrest. The government left no stone unturned; state-sponsored terror recognized no boundaries. Among the whites caught in the authorities' dragnet were a handful of British subjects at work in the mills and railroads. Britons were inherently suspect given the plausible connection with abolitionist circles and, concretely, with David Turnbull. A few Irish laborers on the railroads were also implicated.[17]

The "Escalera Conspiracy" of 1844 remains one of the most fascinating and polemical issues in the history of slavery. A debate has long raged as to whether there was a conspiracy at all. Was the "conspiracy" an invention concocted by the Spanish authorities with captain-general Leopoldo O'Donnell at the head to justify a preemptive strike? Historians have not found the proverbial "smoking gun," the kind of documentary evidence that would demonstrate the existence—or nonexistence—of a vast, well-organized plot (as opposed to a series of isolated and unrelated uprisings).

There may be no visible gun, but one chokes in smoke. One could indeed argue that the scope of the repression is itself evidence of the existence of a conspiracy. Was a well-planned, massive slave revolt a reasonable possibility? The answer is yes. With a bit of luck Aponte might have pulled off his revolt. A slave revolt powerful enough to put an end not only to slavery but also to colonialism—the case of Haiti—was a vividly remembered chapter of recent history. Were Cuba's slaves under reliable enough controls to guarantee that Cuba would never go the way of Haiti? The answer was no. Was there an actual conspiracy in Cuba involving not only the slaves but numerous other confederates? The answer for many years was perhaps (note that no one has been able to disprove its existence). A more accurate answer today would have to be almost certainly yes.

The captain-general found several all too willing executors of his repressive agenda. One was the Matanzas governor; another was an obscure officer named Ramón González, who relished his newfound vocation as flogger-in-chief. Since official jails were not large enough to contain the flood of the accused, the government rented a number of houses where prisoners were held and floggings administered. Notorious among those was Medio No. 80. In Cárdenas an improvised flogging station was set up at the Torrientes' Progreso sugar mill. Another flogging franchise was set up at the Matanzas Hospital de

Santa Isabel. Since all those who died under torture were officially said to have died of acute diarrhea, the hospital lent a convenient cover. There was no need to lie on that account, of course.

Flogging victims on a ladder was not O'Donnell's invention. Ladders were standard disciplinary equipment in the British armed forces. From a practical viewpoint a ladder makes sense. One thinks of blood and sweat in connection with flogging, but these were not the only effluvia involved. One of the most horrifying and humiliating consequences of severe flogging was a release of intestinal contents. A ladder served both as a rack and a stretcher, thus making the handling of restive victims both before and after the punishment convenient and expeditious.

O'Donnell would not stop at flogging, maiming, and executing African slaves. He meant to reach higher, into the free colored population, and higher still, into the criollo elite itself. Indictments of distinguished criollo intellectuals were entirely consistent with the captain-general's policy of far-reaching terror. No one should feel safe. In the end, however, no whites of consequence were flogged or executed. The socially prominent had ways either to escape or to minimize danger to themselves. Not so the freed blacks and mulattos, who were entirely at O'Donnell's mercy, and of that the young captain-general had a very short supply.

Among those who lost their lives was Gabriel de la Concepción Valdés, "Plácido," one of Cuba's top poets.[18] Plácido had the misfortune of being mulatto, talented, and highly visible. His literary fame had made him the most renowned freedman in Cuba, but he lived from hand to mouth. He wrote poems on commission and articles for *La Aurora*, and did odd jobs as a silversmith and carpenter. He also made the then-fashionable tortoiseshell combs, or *peinetas,* that women wore in their hair to support their mantillas. He was said to deliver each of his combs with a poem honoring the client.

His complete name, Gabriel de la Concepción Valdés, though euphonious and even high-sounding, was a dead giveaway to Cubans sensitive to the subtle cues of social status and race. Valdés was the name given to foundlings in Cuba. It was his mother's surname. He bore it because he was born out of wedlock, the progeny of a Spanish dancer and a mulatto woman who earned her living as a hairdresser.

Plácido's first claim to fame came in 1834, when he won a poetry contest honoring Spanish statesman Francisco Martínez de la Rosa, prevailing over twelve white opponents, some of whom were established writers. The aristocracy took a liking to the handsome young mulatto who could write with such panache. He ghost-wrote poems for birthdays, baptisms, and weddings. His gifts caught del Monte's attention, and the poet became an occasional visitor to the former's fancy salons.

The Ximeno family knew him well. Lola María de Ximeno Cruz (1866–1934), Matanzas' indefatigable cultivator of the *chronique intime*, wrote memorable pages about the unfortunate poet based on family sources.[19] A daughter of privilege, the wife of legendary book collector José Augusto Escoto, and a writer in her own right, Lola María knew everybody. Her mother, Dolores Cruz de Ximeno, known as "Lola Cruz," was a legendary beauty.

Although Plácido was executed some twenty-two years before she was born, Lola María had access to unique information about the unfortunate bard. Her husband had a lifelong research interest in the Escalera Conspiracy events. Mindful of social distances, Plácido was a family acquaintance. Lola María's maternal grandfather, in fact, was Plácido's client in a manner of speaking. An inveterate philanderer, he would commission poems to woo his prey.[20]

As I did with my own Aunt Ñiquita, Lola Maria would sit down with her grandmother, Mamá Quinita, who died in 1899, and enjoy her stories of old times. One day the topic of conversation was Plácido. "Tell me, Mamá Quinita, about Plácido," asked the granddaughter. Lola María carefully wrote down the older woman's tale:

> I met Plácido towards the end of his life, when I was young. . . . He would accept invitations to parties but we never got him to sit at the table, although we certainly tried. He would arrive for dessert and, standing up, would easily improvise lovely poems. I will never forget this detail: he would be offered a cup of coffee, a must of Cuban hospitality. He would take it but never, ever agree to sit down. Once we managed to convince him, and he gulped it down, barely touching the chair.[21]

It would be unfair to Plácido's memory to say that he was an innocent victim. There is evidence that he was a sympathizer, perhaps even an active conspirator. He was certainly alive to the libertarian ideas of the time and expressed in good romantic fashion his support for the independence movements of Greece and Poland. But he was no martyr.[22] Martyrs accept their deaths as a consequence of their beliefs or actions. Such, indeed, is the essence of martyrdom. Plácido did not, proclaiming his innocence to the end. Perhaps he was hoping for a last-minute reprieve. Perhaps he truly was innocent, which makes his death all the more tragic. Or perhaps he really was implicated and his protestations of innocence were his way of protecting sensitive information. Probably. In the end, he chose to die, ostensibly at least, a victim, but one must admire the sangfroid with which he faced his end.

The star-crossed poet was executed on the esplanade between the new army barracks and the start of Cristina Boulevard in Versalles. A monument marks the spot. He was shot with a handful of others, including José Miguel Román (a noted violinist and composer José White's first music teacher), Jorge López, Pedro de la Torre (also a music teacher), Manuel Quiñones (a second sergeant of the Matanzas colored militia), Miguel Naranjo, and Antonio Abad.[23] They sat on a bench facing the Bay of Slaughters. When the noise and smoke of the shots died out, all the other victims were dead but Plácido was unhurt. He solemnly stood up and, turning to Ramón González, said in a calm and loud voice: "Señor don Ramón González, future centuries will say who were the true conspirators here." He then pointed to his heart and said: "Fire here." The next round got him.

Plácido understood the awesome power of drama. He was determined not to let Matanzas forget him—as if matanceros ever could. Poet to the end, he is famously said to have declaimed his "Prayer to God," composed while he was on death row, while walking the bitter stones of his Calvary:

> Almighty Being of endless charity,
> To you I turn, in pain dismayed.
> Extend your mighty arm, I pray,
> Tear up the odious veil of calumny,
> Erase the dreadful mark of infamy
> With which the world my brow would stain.
>
> . . . .
>
> But, if it is, O Lord, Thy will divine
> That I may perish like an impious knave
> And men my cold and lifeless corpse profane
> With malign joy by hatred blinded,
> Thy voice be heard; my life be ended.
> Thy will be done, O God of mine.[24]

When the corpses of Plácido and his companions in misfortune were taken to be buried, the poet's head dangled over the side of the wagon. Pieces of his brains were dripping on the pavement. A friend of his who happened to be standing on the sidewalk as the wagon went by took a hoe and respectfully covered the bloody mess with dirt.[25]

Was Plácido's death as dramatic, as hopelessly romantic, as all of that? Did he actually recite his last composition on the way to his execution? One could think of numerous practical reasons that render such an undoubtedly touching scenario unlikely, but that is the way posterity has chosen to remember him. It's the least we can do.

The implications of the terror unleashed by O'Donnell were profound. Whether or not there was actually a generalized, coherent, well-organized conspiracy,[26] the events of 1844 ensured that none would ever succeed. For the slaves, their already miserable existence was made even more so. Vigilance increased, and so did security. In 1847 Chinese coolies began to arrive, presumed to be a more manageable population than the Africans.[27]

O'Donnell's term of office ended in 1848. He was not a modest man: he was playing for posterity. In 1846, a catastrophic hurricane hit Havana, killing hundreds of people and toppling El Morro's lighthouse.[28] It was promptly rebuilt with "O'Donnell" inscribed in big block letters on the side. He just would not let Cuba forget him. It hasn't.

7   Tyre of the Western Seas

RAFAEL DEL VILLAR, a Matanzas booster, once suggested that the city of the two rivers be known as *el Tiro de los mares de Occidente*, that is, "the Tyre of the Western Seas."[1] The allusion to the ancient Phoenician city would have gone over the heads of most of his neighbors. To them a *tiro* was a shot, what happened when you pulled a trigger, but the comparison was apt. Like the Tyre of antiquity, nineteenth-century Matanzas was busy, maritime, and commercial. It was, in fact, a boomtown until the price of sugar entered a period of chronic decline in the 1870s.[2]

Growth translated into urban refinement and an expansion of infrastructure. Change went beyond the normal metrics of development into the intangible realm of attitude and mentality. For the matanceros of 1800 the foremost civic issue was the maintenance of their modest timber bridges. Those of 1860 were concerned that the majestic neoclassic theater going up at Vigía Square be the best on the island, and proud that La Empresa, the town's foremost school, was authoritatively ranked as the best in Spain and her dominions. An exuberant civic pride and a muscular urban competitiveness were very much part of the tissue of boomtown Matanzas. In this chapter I explore urban growth and change between 1800 and the 1880s from a material perspective—how Matanzas was put together. The next will consider cultural developments during the same period. Matanzas may be Cuba's Athens, but before becoming Athens she was Tyre.

The quickening pace of economic development during the nineteenth century meant better transportation. Options for the traveler of 1800 were limited to unpredictable sailings or an arduous overland journey from Havana.[3] To the south and east—the "Inland," or Tierradentro—there was very little worth traveling to. Neither Cienfuegos nor Cárdenas existed in 1800, and the older settlements of Santa Clara, Sancti Spiritus, and Trinidad were remote and served by poor roads.

On February 7, 1818, a clever Catalonian named Josep Coll began weekly stagecoach runs from Havana, establishing the first regularly scheduled ground transportation service between the two cities.[4] Coaches left Guanabacoa early Friday morning and arrived in Matanzas around noon on Sunday. Passengers had to endure rough highways, the awkward intimacies of the cabin, and the occasional scare about robbers or runaways, but now at least they knew when they might reasonably expect to depart and arrive.

Not quite a year later, a paddle wheeler made in the United States steamed past Havana's Morro Castle.[5] Onlookers marveled at the tall, smoking chimneys and the noisy contraptions that propelled the thing forward, like waterfalls in motion. The boat could do without the winds, an amazing feature that must have perplexed the port pilots.

Named after Neptune, the ancient sea god, the strange vessel belonged to

Fig. 20. Vigía fortress, Matanzas city, and harbor by Mialhe, ca. 1840. Note the boxes and *bocoyes* (hogsheads) in the foreground. (Courtesy of Prints and Photographs Division, Library of Congress)

Juan Manuel O'Farrill y Arredondo, a visionary Havana entrepreneur and Matanzas booster with a government concession to offer scheduled steamboat service between the two towns. In the early morning of July 18, 1819, *Neptuno* cleared the harbor channel on her inaugural run. At a safe distance from the rocky shore, the engine was revved up. The Havana coast receded to starboard as the vessel reached a breakneck speed of five knots (approximately six miles per hour). She arrived in Matanzas safely in the late afternoon. Speeches were delivered and salvos fired. The occasion was truly historic: the first steamship run in the Spanish Empire and Latin America.

The Havana-Matanzas run soon became routine, a true measure of its success, and competitors entered the lucrative market. Travelers now had a choice between backache and seasickness. If they could afford the fare, the choice was clear: the stagecoach carried six passengers in cramped quarters; steamboats carried many more in relative comfort, and a trip of almost three days was reduced to a few hours.

Creature comforts were initially few. Passengers had to board from lighters since no adequate docking facilities existed in either Havana or Matanzas. We have no reliable visual record of *Neptuno*[6] but a plate in the *Paseo pintoresco por la isla de Cuba*, an album of lithographs of island landscapes that began publication in 1841, gives us an idea of what she must have looked like. It shows the *Almendares*, a sister ship on the route, proudly berthed at the then brand-new Havana docks.[7] The Matanzas' terminal, the Muelle Real, was finished by then and was featured on another lithograph in the series.[8]

Growth brought much-needed improvement in a public service essential to modernity: the delivery of mail. In 1791 a system of mounted overland postal relays had been established for Cuba. It operated once a month between Havana and Santiago. Matanzas was on the route, naturally, and the town's first postmaster, José Antonio Noriega, was consequently appointed. The frequency and reliability of the postal service improved dramatically as the new century dawned. The advent of railroads made daily service routine as early as the 1840s.[9]

The first locomotive chugged into Matanzas not long thereafter, when the venerable La Junta de Fomento made her first run to nearby Guanábana. Cuban railways may have been designed to serve the sugar industry, but they inevitably had a massive impact on the movement of people. When Samuel Hazard visited Matanzas in the 1860s, rail passengers coming from Havana had two options. The long route started at Villanueva Station downtown, and the short one across the bay at Regla. The train from Regla left three times a day: at 6:00 and 10:40 in the morning and 3:30 in the afternoon. It offered two classes of service and ran smoothly on very good tracks, "the engineers being mostly American," as Hazard gingerly volunteered.[10]

As the nineteenth century unfolded, Matanzas was on a roll.[11] From its origins as a village of modest, mostly thatched buildings in 1800, the town by the Yumurí became a handsome provincial city in a very short time.[12] At the turn of the century, the only structures of any consequence were San Severino Castle, Vigía Fortress, and the parish church.[13] By the eve of the 1895 war, the situation was dramatically different. By then La Vigía had been demolished and two new splendid parish churches built. Both the loss of the fortress and the gain of the churches had profound significance. The former was immolated on the altar of modernization and urban redesign. The latter were built to anchor the two new suburbs that, with the old city, constituted the mature town's tripartite urbanity.

Matanzas, like Caesar's Gaul is divided in three parts: Old Town, or Matanzas proper; Pueblo Nuevo; and Versalles. As the nineteenth century closed, the census of Cuba conducted by U.S. authorities recorded respective populations of 22,438 inhabitants for the city core, 8,420 for Pueblo Nuevo, and 4,812 for Versalles.[14] To local folks, whether you are from Matanzas, Pueblo Nuevo, or Versalles matters: it defines you. Each of the core barrios has its own distinctive personality. In my day Matanzas, the urban core, was mainline, old-fashioned, and Afro-Cuban. The formerly chic Versalles was hardworking and middle class. Pueblo Nuevo was fun and proletarian. Such neighborhoods claim fierce loyalties. As Carilda Oliver Labra expresses in her "Chant to Matanzas," the most solemn oath would not require God's witness:

> I swear it by Pueblo Nuevo,
> Which is like swearing on one's knees.

The city of Matanzas rises on three salients defined by her two rivers. Old Town Matanzas takes up the tiny Mesopotamia between the San Juan and Yumurí rivers. This is essentially the town founded by Manzaneda in 1693, which grew over time within its fluvial confines. Pueblo Nuevo del San Juan was built south of the San Juan River, essentially to serve the export needs of the sugar complex. Versalles was built to the north and east of the Yumurí as a residential and service neighborhood. The city's military garrison was headquartered in Versalles, which was also the home of the town's two substantial hospitals, Santa Isabel and San Nicolás, both built in the course of the nine-teenth century.

The Pueblo Nuevo church, named after St. John the Baptist, was begun in 1828 and finished in 1832. It was meant to assist the expected new settlers to heaven, and the suburb's developers to profits. The graceful church rose on land donated by Rita Sotolongo, who had a substantial real estate interest in the "New Town."[15] The Versalles church was built in three short years between 1867 and 1870. The work of Daniele Dal'Allio, it rises upon a high platform, or *altozano,* and has a commanding presence over the surrounding urban fabric. Like the Pueblo Nuevo church, it was tied to a real estate scheme. The land was donated by Versalles developer Eloy Navia, whose philanthropic activi-ties included land donations to the nearby Hospital de Santa Isabel and the Cristina Barracks. A cash gift of $100,000 by Josefa Santa Cruz de Oviedo, a member of the local sugar oligarchy, provided the financial resources for the actual construction.[16]

Dal'Allio is both a key protagonist of Matanzas' architectural history and a bit of a mystery. He designed two of the most significant buildings in town, but we know little about him. A Roman by birth, he visited Cuba as a young man, left, and came back to settle permanently. Although a foreigner, he landed Matanzas' plum commission of the century: the Esteban Theater. Built on a marshy flat between Vigía Square and the bay, it was Cuba's second theater in size and appointments, comparable only to the Tacón in Havana. Its majestic presence more than compensated for the historic square's demotion from the city's de facto formal center to the category of a secondary urban space during the 1800s.

Vigía Square was Matanzas' birthplace. It grew haphazardly and served for more than a century as the town's makeshift plaza de armas but not to everybody's satisfaction. Bordering the sea and the San Juan, and close to the Yumurí, the square was prone to flooding. The sloping ground helped the flooding problem but made military drills difficult.[17] Towards the middle of the eighteenth century, a site for a new main square was designated on the traza: the city block defined by present-day Santa Teresa, Ayuntamiento, Contreras, and Milanés streets. The street profiles of the new plaza, however, would not be in place until well into the nineteenth century.

Notwithstanding her demotion, the venerable Vigía Square, renamed Plaza de Colón, received much improvement and updating during the second half of the 1800s. The obsolete, termite-infested fortress of San José de la Vigía

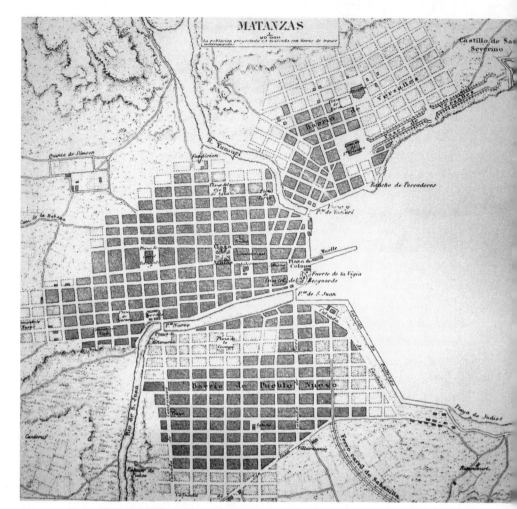

Fig. 21. The tripartite boomtown of Matanzas, ca. 1860.

had become an eyesore and was demolished in the 1850s. The lot was turned into a park honoring Miguel de Cervantes. The park was a derelict by 1896, and was razed to clear the way for the Fire Department Headquarters, one of Matanzas' architectural gems. The elegant classical structure by Bernardo de Grandas y Callejas was finished in 1900 under the American occupation.

Diagonally across the square, on Magdalena Street between Medio and Milanés, an elegant colonnaded customshouse was built in the 1820s to handle the port's dramatic expansion. The refined classicizing design was by Julio Sagebién. Redesigned in the early twentieth century to serve as the home for the provincial courts (Audiencia), the singled-storied customshouse was given an additional floor and a modestly monumental aspect that is nevertheless agreeable to the site's scale and proportions.

The Arechavaleta building with its Havana-style *portales*[18] was built in the 1850s farther along Magdalena Street (between Medio and Río streets) to house the hardware emporium of Bea, Bellido, and Company.[19] The Palacio de Junco occupies the shortest side of the irregular Vigía Square at a right angle from the Audiencia building. The mansion, begun by Bernardo Junco in the 1790s, was finished sometime in the first decade of the nineteenth century. It was damaged by the great fire of 1845 that leveled much of the adjoining Marina neighborhood, but was promptly rebuilt. Squat and heavy, it lacks the elegance and lightness of Havana's best urban noble houses like those of the counts of Casa Bayona or the marquises of Arcos. It is, however, a member of the genus: a criollo palatial home with a portal, balcony, and *entresuelo*, a malapropism for *entrepiso,* to secure the domestic slaves.[20]

The undoubted jewel of Vigía Square's monumental ensemble is its grand theater, opened to the public in 1863. It is one of about six surviving nineteenth-century opera houses on the island. Santiago de Cuba was the first city in the interior of Cuba to have a proper theater, the Teatro de la Marina, inaugurated in 1823. Matanzas was the second with the Principal (it opened in 1829 and will be discussed in the following chapter). Pinar del Río inaugurated the Milanés, chivalrously named after Matanzas' poet laureate, in 1837; Trinidad opened the Brunet in 1840, and Camaguey its own Principal ten years later. The curtain went up at Santa Clara's Teatro de la Caridad in 1885, and at Cienfuegos' opulent Teatro Tomás Terry in 1890.

Dal'Allio's sober neoclassic façade is an eye-catcher. It was articulated above a porch where quality theatergoers could gracefully alight from their carriages, even under driving rain. Cast iron chairs made in Pittsburgh and caned, not upholstered, offered solidity and a respite from the heat of summer nights, when the swish of the ladies' fans created a soft, pervasive, and certainly refreshing background noise. The surrounding loggias were a practical and visually pleasing solution allowing for exceptional cross-ventilation. Designed to serve a dance-crazed public, the floor could be raised for grand balls, just like the floor of the Tacón Theater in Havana. A gifted painter, Dal'Allio also executed the ceiling murals.

The theater's original name, Esteban, honored the Matanzas governor of the day. Its current name, Sauto, is a salute to the colorful Dr. Ambrosio Sauto i Noda, a successful businessman of Catalonian origin and the town's preeminent pharmacist. Sauto is said to have cured Queen Isabella II of "a very bothersome herpes." (The queen notoriously enjoyed men but she took such awful risks!) The royal cure earned the elfish-looking Dr. Sauto an appointment as a royal apothecary. More to the point, he also cured the theater project of a crippling cash-flow crisis and is credited with arranging the financial package that saved the day.[21]

The San Juan was first bridged in the early eighteenth century, but the 1730 hurricane washed that ramshackle bridge away. Several others followed, including the hardwood span commissioned by the Marquis de la Torre. Julio Sagebién's entry, known as the "Puente de Bailén," opened to traffic in 1849 but was destroyed by the catastrophic hurricane of 1870.[22] A prefabricated steel bridge made by Baume, Marpent, and Company in Belgium has connected Vigía Square with Pueblo Nuevo since 1896.

In the early days, Pueblo Nuevo was not considered part of the city at all. It was, strictly speaking, an *arrabal,* an outlying barrio. Writing in 1830, Cirilo Villaverde, the eminent novelist and a temporary resident of Matanzas, tells us that crossing the bridge from Pueblo Nuevo to Matanzas or vice versa was tantamount to entering or leaving "the city." Entering Pueblo Nuevo "from the city," don Cirilo goes on, one was greeted by two miserable taverns, one on either side of the street. The tiny taverns were "ramshackle but proud because they fell directly under the jurisdiction of the bridge guard."[23]

Villaverde's quaint reading of a pedestrian crossing the bridge almost as if he were passing through the gate of a walled city is at odds with the sprit and functionality of Pueblo Nuevo. There was nothing quaint about the eminently practical "New Town." Shortly after Villaverde's narrative, the Sabanilla rail line was laid exactly over where the two ramshackle taverns had been so that locomotives could reach the riverside docks and the sugar warehouses that lined it.

The San Juan River shore defined one of Pueblo Nuevo's sides. Three *calzadas,* Tirry, Esteban, and Campuzano (San Luis), completed the perimeter. The riverfront was a service area for sugar transshipment and storage. Rows of identically gabled façades of huge warehouses, now mostly in ruins, dominated the skyline. The riverfront functioned essentially as a quay. Cranes (*machinas*) would be used to load the heavy boxes and bocoyes onto the lighters that ferried them to the waiting ships in the harbor.

The largest warehouse complex, built by the de la Torriente family in the 1860s at a cost in excess of 600,000 pesos, rivaled Havana's mammoth Almacenes de Regla and could hold 80,000 boxes of sugar and 20,000 hogsheads of molasses.[24] The operation of this integrated system required vast slave labor resources. The barracks for the port's slave crews, known popularly as the "Matasiete," were near the river's mouth.

Pueblo Nuevo's design as a transportation hub is evident. The city's three successive railroad depots were located there. Fortunately, all three survive, almost miraculously in the case of the San Luis Station, whose platforms are gone but graceful timber depot still stands. The Sabanilla Railway Station on the Calzada de Tirry, designed by Carrerá, the Aldamas' Venezuelan architect, boasts a sober colonnaded façade one block in length. Its nearness to the San Juan River transshipment area attests to the close partnership that bound railroads and sugar together in times gone by.

The main railway station, completed in the 1870s, was built where Tirry intersected the Calzada de Esteban. In the best tradition of architectural eclecticism proper to railroad stations, it is an English Jacobean folly complete with a cast iron statue of Britannia in the front yard. The Calzada de Esteban runs from the little square in front of the railroad station past the 1870s city jail to the Palmar de Junco, where Cuba's first recorded baseball game was played in 1874 and the grand Matanzas International Exhibition of 1881 headquartered.[25]

Past the Palmar de Junco, Esteban intersects the Calzada de San Luis. The latter completes Pueblo Nuevo's perimeter roundabout. A hardwood bridge, also designed by Sagebién and opened to traffic in 1834, spanned the San Juan again at the city market and Dos de Mayo Street. The current armed concrete span dates to 1916 and is named Sánchez Figueras after a local hero. Sagebién's bridge was simply the Puente de la Carnicería, or "Slaughterhouse Bridge." What visitors thought as they crossed the Slaughterhouse Bridge in the City of Slaughters we can only imagine.

In the direction opposite Pueblo Nuevo, the Calzada de Esteban led to what was popularly called "La Playa de Judíos," Matanzas' first beach resort. (Jews' Beach is a misnomer born of colonial prejudice: Dutch buccaneers who happened to die while in Matanzas were buried there; for local colonial folks, heretics and Jews were much the same.) Conceived from the beginning as a prestige residential address, Calzada de Esteban was lined with fine homes by the 1870s. The half-dozen or so quintas built to the design of Catalonian architect José Borrell by 1860 are identical and have become local icons.

Fancy Versalles stood in sharp contrast to the utilitarian Pueblo Nuevo. Developed by financier Eloy Navia and originally called San Alejandro, the suburb was renamed to reflect its aspirations to cachet and residential elegance. Versalles was surrounded by a ring of luxury villas rising on La Cumbre Heights. The suburb's backbone was the Paseo Nuevo or Paseo de Cristina (presently Paseo de Martí), a true boulevard with broad sidewalks planted with a row of pines. The paseo ran from the Cristina Barracks to a monumental rotunda. With the sea on one side and a row of quality homes on the other, it was suitably upmarket when it was essentially completed by mid-century.

With Vigía Square upstaged as the town's definitive plaza de armas, the provision of a suitable civic center became a major concern. An important symbolic step was the installation of Ferdinand VII's statue at the center of the designated but as yet undeveloped space in 1828. The statue was the price the king exacted for granting Matanzas a proper city charter and arms. The Matanzas city council of the day ordered a first-rate piece of sculpture from the Genoese artist Antonio Peschieri. To keep up with the matanceros, Havanans ordered their own statue of the king from the Spanish sculptor Antonio Solá. The Matanzas statue was taken down when the Bourbons were deposed in 1868 and installed at the rotunda on the Paseo de Cristina in Versalles. After independence, Cuban nationalists demanded that it be taken down altogether but it was instead bricked up in situ—such a Matanzas thing to do! It was finally removed in 1947 and consigned, first, to the Matanzas Academy of Fine Arts, and eventually to the Provincial Museum, where it is a major exhibit today. Regardless of Ferdinand's bad historical press, the sculpture is superb. It shows the monarch in classic attire and regal ermine mantle. One barely notices the missing Bourbon nose.

The vile perimeter of the new plaza de armas (now Liberty Square) did not become a worthy ensemble until the third quarter of the nineteenth century. A survivor and memento of the square's earlier aspect is La Viña, a former tavern on the corner of Milanés and Santa Teresa streets. A few steps along Milanés—then Gelabert—Street, the future Louvre Hotel was built by architect Bartolomé Borrell in 1859 as a private residence for Isabel Polleschi, widow of former Governor Antonio García Oña. The clubhouses for the Liceo (founded in 1860) and the original one-story building for the Casino Español (founded in 1864) rose across the square on Contreras Street. Between them stood the luxury home of the Sánchez family (ca. 1865). The Instituto building (corner of Milanés and Santa Teresa) and Triolet's French Apothecary also date to that period. After being family-owned for generations, Triolet's is now Cuba's Pharmaceutical Museum. The imposing Government House, designed by Antonio Montenegro, took up an entire side of the grand civic space along Ayuntamiento Street.

Perhaps most important of all, the city's residential tissue was woven during the years of the sugar bonanza. There was a great deal of domestic building, ranging from opulent mansions to countless vernacular dwellings. The city's original traza expanded naturally towards the swampy banks of the Yumurí, drained to become the neighborhoods of La Marina and Ojo de Agua, and up towards the hills surrounding the old city. By the 1860s, the uplands, known as the Alturas de Simpson after a well-known American resident, had been colonized by the well-to-do in search of breezes and a view. The elegant Foundlings' Asylum was built there in the 1870s.

Matanzas was blessed with excellent building materials. City streets were paved with granite cobblestones from New Hampshire and Massachusetts. Brought to Cuba as ballast, they could be had for very reasonable prices. The city had an abundant supply of the limestone aggregate known as coquina extracted from nearby quarries along the Yumurí. Cirilo Villaverde found the material excessively friable and consequently not appropriate for sidewalks, but it stood up well enough in walls. Being soft it was easy to cut and work. Stone from the Yumurí ended up in some of the most important buildings.[26] Rubble masonry, however, was the preferred technique for walls.

When timber balloon framing construction techniques were developed in the United States, Cuba and Matanzas followed suit. As early as 1805, Baron von Humboldt reported that numerous prefabricated homes were "ordered from the United States just as one would order furniture."[27] Demand for North American timber grew exponentially as the nineteenth century progressed and Cuban forests disappeared. The traditional timber summer homes of Varadero and San Miguel de los Baños are balloon frame construction done in southern pine. So indeed is La Panchita, a distinguished surviving exemplar of the genre in the La Playa district of Matanzas city. The stone lion at the front gate was the delight of kids when I was one myself and La Panchita belonged to the Urréchaga family.

By 1827, the Rev. Abiel Abbot reported that most houses were single-storied, although some could be as tall as twenty feet. Roofs were either tiled or thatched with palm fronds in rural fashion. Abbot attended services at the parish church and could not have missed—but was obviously not impressed by—the two-story neoclassic mansion built by José Ramón Cabrera (*alarife*, or municipal architect, since 1802) for town notary Joaquín de la Fuente. The structure (finished 1822) still stands across the alley from the church. The distinguished architectural historian Alicia García Santana calls it "a notable testimony of the early presence of Andalusian 'stone' neoclassicism in Cuba."[28]

Towards mid-century, when the British traveler Amelia M. Murray came calling, the houses of Matanzas, "like those of Havana, were almost all low, some of them with one, or at most two stories, some of them with flat roofs, and others heavily tiled with circular-shaped tiles as if rows of chimney pots were strung together and laid in rows half a foot apart."[29] In other words, they followed the rhythm of flat *azoteas* and *tejados* that is so characteristic of colonial Cuban cities.

Unlike Havana, Matanzas had no city ordinance for portales to shade the sidewalks, so façades ended flush with the inner edge of the pathway. As in Havana, *medios puntos* and *vitrales* (fanlights and stained glass) were common, lending to interiors extraordinary daylight effects that must be experienced to be fully appreciated.

There were vast differences between the haves and the have-nots. Well-to-do matanceros could afford a life of elegance and ease. The better houses would be equipped with furniture of fine Cuban manufacture, gilded mirrors in the *salas* (living rooms), and chandeliers brought over from Europe (or gasoliers from the United States after gas lighting was introduced in Matanzas in the 1850s). Heavy beds and the ubiquitous armoires and chests (*armarios* and *arcones*) would make up the furnishings of bedrooms, invariably laid en suite and opening to a courtyard verdant with potted or planted arecas and vines. A large *pajarera,* or aviary, would often grace one corner. Carved *portieles* or *mamparas* with colored glass inserts separated the rooms and provided minimal privacy. Normally, the dining room would be located at the rear of the patio or courtyard, with the kitchen and servants' quarters behind.

The dead were not forgotten in Matanzas' explosive development. The city's first cemetery, blessed in 1811, was insufficient in a few years. The cholera epidemic of 1833 saw to that. A second cemetery opened in 1840, the result of a civic movement led by the vicar of St. Charles Parish Church, Father Manuel Francisco García, with the resolute support of Governor Garcia Oña.[30]

The new burial ground had capacity for four thousand graves and was solemnly blessed on November 1, 1840. A carriage with the remains of prominent matanceros in lead boxes made its way to the new facility in solemn procession amidst clouds of incense, chants, responsories, and the *Dies Irae*, the sequence for the dead. Plácido dedicated two poetic compositions to the enterprising vicar, whom he compared to "the great [Bishop] Espada and [Félix] Varela," the latter a telling detail since Varela was then an exile more or less openly advocating Cuban independence.[31]

The cemetery filled up before you could say "libera me Domine de morte aeterna." The third, consecrated to St. Charles Borromeus, was blessed in 1872 and was state-of-the-art.[32] Located in the suburban neighborhood of Naranjal, it is still in use. It has an elegant colonnaded portal, a domed chapel, and an enceinte wall. An important design feature was the subterranean galleries reminiscent of a Roman *columbarium*.

With two rivers and several natural springs near at hand, good water had always been plentiful. That did not prevent the city from being ravaged by cholera's visitations. Dormant in India for centuries, the dreadful disease surged back to life in 1817 and spread to all corners of the globe. It devastated Cuba in 1833.[33] There would be further serious outbreaks in 1850–56, 1865, and 1867–70. In 1833, cholera carried off approximately three thousand lives in Matanzas and decimated the slave crews, considerably more exposed than the rest of the population.

Many left the city for Havana in the hope of escaping (vain hope: Havana was just as deadly). Given that cholera is transmitted by Koch's bacillus, an organism that thrives in water, it is possible that Matanzas' abundant streams may have contributed to mortality as they became contaminated. José Antonio Saco describes scenes of utter horror in the face of a scourge that defied all medical ministrations then available.[34]

In 1871 the franchise to build and operate a much-needed aqueduct was granted to a German entrepreneur, Ferdinand Heydrich (1827–1903). A native of Barmen, near Düsseldorf, Heydrich was a heavy machinery salesman. He went to Cuba, did well selling equipment to sugar mills undergoing modernization, and returned to Germany a rich man, intending to grow cotton in the southern part of the country. The scheme failed, so back to Cuba he went. The aqueduct venture succeeded beyond anyone's expectations. In 1887, the Empresa del Acueducto de Matanzas was further granted a permit to draw water from the Río de Cañas by means of a reservoir. Heydrich, who had met and married a Valencian and was now the father of six Cuban-born children, built a mansion in the then-exclusive neighborhood of Alturas de Simpson and named it "Bismarck" after the Iron Chancellor.[35]

Ferdinand Heydrich's career suggests the extent to which the prosperity of nineteenth-century Matanzas had attracted an international, multicultural population. (Another prominent German in nineteenth-century Matanzas was the eminent naturalist Juan Gundlach, about whom more in the next chapter.) Ironically, the largest segment of Matanzas' international and multicultural population—the Africans—had not come freely. Chinese coolies were in a parallel category. (Curiously, it was a Colombian with strong links to Matanzas, Nicolás Tanco Armero, who pioneered the business of supplying Chinese labor to the Cuban plantation economy.)[36] Yucatec Mayas, prisoners of the bloody Caste Wars, were also transported in virtual bondage.

To further pursue classical comparisons, Matanzas at her apogee may well have been Cuba's Corinth—a place of meeting. A handful of foreign powers had consulates in town. The town's elite included German Heydrichs and Uhrbachs, English Drakes, Italian Yarinis, Irish Mádans, American Schweyers, Venezuelan del Montes, and Colombian Tancos. Foreign artists, such as the Frenchman Guillermo Colson, the Belgian Henry Cleenewerck, and the Americans Charles DeWolf Brownell and Eliab Metcalf, were admired and patronized. An Italian, Daniele Dal'Allio left a lasting mark on the city's skyline.[37] One could even have one's watch repaired by a genuine Swiss watchmaker at Au Bon Marché on Gelabert Street.

Richard Henry Dana, an American visitor in the 1850s, described this cosmopolitan ambiance. He was a guest at one of the city's best hotels, the Ensor House, run by an American catering to the city's many overseas visitors. His last day in town he spent visiting La Victoria, a sugar estate in the Yumurí Valley owned by William Jencks Updike, an American married to a Ximeno. "On the way up from the city" he had been impressed by the villas "all of one story, usually in the Roman or Grecian style, surrounded by gardens and shade trees, and with every appearance of taste and wealth."[38]

He had one last obligation to fulfill before leaving: bid farewell to the Chartrands, a distinguished local family of sugar mill owners and visual artists. The Chartrands had an extraordinary family history. After a harrowing escape from rebel Saint-Domingue in the care of Samedi, a slave, the brothers Philippe and Juan Matías Chartrand ended up in Charleston, South Carolina. Juan Matías eventually moved to Matanzas with Samedi and married Luisa Juliana Carlota Dubois, an American of French origin. He successfully developed a coffee plantation, El Laberinto, and a sugar mill poetically named Ariadne in the Limonar district.

The Chartrands were impeccable hosts. "Mr. Chartrand," wrote Dana, "lives in a part of the suburbs called Versailles [*sic*], near the barracks, in a large and handsome house, built after the style of the country." The Yankee visitor spent the evening amidst the extended Chartrand family and was impressed by their cosmopolitan ways, "where are found French origin, Spanish and American intermarriage, education in Europe or the United States, home and property in Cuba, friendships and half a residence in Boston, New York or Charleston, and three languages at command."[39] Sugar was not all about the cracking of the whip and the infernal noise of a grinding mill. It was also about profits and how they were spent. If you could somehow sublimate the horror at the base, life at the top could be rewarding, and the Chartrands were trend-setters. Like perfume spray, art and beauty could help hide the stench of blood and sweat rising from below.

José Jacinto Milanés pondered such issues in one of Matanzas' quintessential poems, *De codos en el puente*. His elbows resting on the balustrade of the San Juan bridge, the poet contemplated his surroundings. Prosperity was evident but to what end? Was his beloved city destined to be a crass entrepôt, or was there hope for something better? Milanés the aesthete is not concerned with the ethics of the situation, merely with its aesthetics. He does not ask whether Matanzas can ever produce justice, a fair question given the circumstances. Rather, can Matanzas gain *cultura* and, consequently, art and beauty? Asking for no more, let us join him at the bridge as he confides to the breeze his hope that Matanzas would become a suitable home for "the beautiful arts that now go a-begging, their childhood polluted by vice." For otherwise,

> What good are your waters, o gentle San Juan,
> Your shimmering currents that placid go by,
> Your lighters highlighted in black and in red
> Now nimbly arriving at the sugar docks
> To the harsh-sounding chanties of the slave crews
> that row in close lockstep while standing erect,
> and cleave with their oars your surface moiré.[40]

8   Athens of Cuba

IN 1860, THE MATANZAS of sugar, sweat, and floggings proclaimed
that it would henceforth be known as "the Athens of Cuba." How that decision was made and by whom I will tell later on. To be taken seriously, however,
so presumptuous a claim by so improbable a place required a justification. The
metamorphosis that changed the hardscrabble frontier town of 1800 into the
island's third largest city and a major cultural center in half a century was justification enough to the would-be Athenians of 1860. If anyone else was lis-
tening, let alone cared, nobody seemed to mind, so Athens it was. To be fair,
Matanzas-as-Athens was a work in progress. The proponents of the idea may
have been naive and provincial but they were not foolish. Rather, calling their
city "Athens" implied a program for a future to be achieved, not necessarily a
description of the present.[1]

Like every myth, that of Matanzas as a nest of culture vultures has a kernel
of truth at its core. Obviously, it is an important component of local identity
and pride. Matanceros like to think of themselves as cultivated people—who
would not? Matanceros, however, believe they can prove it. Every matancero
has in the back of his or her mind a list of local Athenians who have made
exceptional contributions, from the fragile Romantic poet Milanés to the ex-
troverted mambo king Dámaso Pérez Prado.

The erudite might cite the work of Carlos M. Trelles y Govín, Cuba's amazing bibliographer, who catalogued and described almost 70,000 books and
wrote—as if he did not have enough—quite a few of his own. Every matancero

worth his or her salt is aware that Carlos de la Torre y Huerta, the eminent naturalist and compatriot, was Cuba's towering scientific figure of the twentieth century. He looked the part, with his sage's mane and his august professorial aura.

Art lovers might argue that the modern Cuban tradition began with the academic Matanzas landscapes of the Chartrand brothers. Or insist that Juan José Sicre was Cuba's greatest sculptor. Or remind us of the work of another member of that talented family, the immensely influential art critic and promoter José Gómez Sicre. Others might mention the work of Matanzas classicist Antonio Guiteras y Font and his translation of the *Aeneid,* the fact that brother Pedro José produced Cuba's first modern history, or that Cuba's very first historian, Antonio José Valdés, was born in Matanzas. One could boast that the city had Cuba's first public library, the first children's library, and the first circulating library. There is seemingly a poet in every matancero (not necessarily a good thing), but there have been great poets in Matanzas.

Some of Cuba's great literary figures have had significant ties to the city—suffice it to mention José María Heredia and Cintio Vitier, both adoptive mantanceros, and Ramón Palma and Cirilo Villaverde, both faculty members at the city's famed La Empresa School. In Matanzas, talent has come in all sizes. Espiridiona Cenda, known as "Chiquita" (she was twenty-six inches tall), was a top international vaudeville star in the 1890s. When it comes to arguing about music, matanceros smile. They know they have been pitched an easy ball and are about to score a home run. You will come across a chapter on Matanzas music as you read on. Home runs? That too. Like Athens, Matanzas cherishes athletics. To baseball fans, Matanzas is simply the place where Cuban baseball began. Boxing fans will remind you that Ultiminio "Sugar" Ramos, was from Matanzas. He died in exile in Miami. These lists can be long.

Most of those accomplishments lay in the inscrutable future in 1860, of course, but city boosters at the time could gauge their hometown's progress in their lifetimes and take from it pride and hope. In 1827 Matanzas received an important civic accolade when the Sociedad Patriótica, the local branch of the Royal Economic Society of Friends of the Country began functioning.[2] A year later the elegant Peschieri statue of Ferdinand VII, that least elegant of kings, was erected on the still threadbare main plaza to mark the onset of civic maturity, and Matanzas passed its first public lighting code. It stipulated the *vecinos'* obligations, the location of the lamps, and the routines for their maintenance. Though the light was dim, the idea was bright. Matanzas was the second Cuban city to enjoy dependable public illumination. Another bright local initiative also took shape that memorable year: *La Aurora de Matanzas* began publication as the official organ of the Sociedad Patriótica.[3] Matanceros, it seemed, were ready for more enlightenment than that which came from tapers or oil lamps.

The printing press had been introduced to Matanzas in 1813, the fourth one on the island after Havana (1720), Santiago (1793), and Puerto Príncipe (1812). A number of ephemeral publications followed, including the *Diario de Matanzas* and *El Lucero*, the latter the predecessor of Havana's *El Noticioso y Lucero de La Habana*, later the renowned *Diario de la Marina*. Founded by, among others, a colorful Canary Islander writer, Francisco Guerra Bethencourt,[4] *La Aurora de Matanzas* (later renamed *La Aurora del Yumurí*) opened a chapter in the history of Cuban journalism. It was no ephemeral gazette but an effort of a far more ambitious scope. Called "the prince of Cuban newspapers," it was published without interruption until the end of the nineteenth century.

By 1886 *La Aurora* had a run of three thousand copies for the Matanzas market alone, an impressive achievement for Cuban provincial papers of the age. Yet it could not compete successfully for readership with large Havana dailies such as the *Diario de la Marina*, which enjoyed a much larger demographic base, economies of scale, easier access to talent and to the news, and much better positioning relative to island-wide distribution networks. *La Aurora* would not survive into the 1900s.[5]

Impeccable in its large format and exhaustive in its coverage, *La Aurora* made a lasting contribution though. The history of nineteenth-century Matanzas simply cannot be written without it. *La Aurora* was in good company. More than eighty journals and periodicals saw the light in Matanzas between 1813 and 1900, including Cuba's first women's and children's reviews.[6] The latter, *El Periquito*, was a creation of the habanero Ildefonso Estrada y Zenea during a period of residence in Matanzas. It had an unexpected international diffusion when Estrada introduced it to Mexico while in exile.[7]

In 1833, Matanzas scored an important Cuban first when the island's first public library was established. It was the beginning of a lasting bibliophile tradition. Writing in 1955, future Dominican President Juan Bosch noted the city's apparent decay from its former opulence but also "the loving care with which the people look after their old libraries and their love of letters."[8]

Population growth meant an expanded audience. Signs of the city's cultural

Fig. 22. The front page of the *Aurora de Matanzas* in an 1830s format.

promise were everywhere, especially in the performing arts offerings, which grew exponentially and culminated with the opening of the Esteban, later Sauto, Theater in 1863. The first theatrical performance in Matanzas had taken place in 1746 but without repeat. By 1800, however, several improvised stages existed. One functioned at the home of José Matías de Ximeno y Uzaola, a Basque immigrant who did well and raised a family noted for its devotion to the arts and letters. He was Lola María de Ximeno's great-grandfather (Lola Maria's connection with the poet Plácido has been explored in chapter 6). Another had been set up by Vicente Junco y Sardiñas at the then still-unfinished Palacio de Junco. In 1814, a dedicated space with a stage suitable for drama was erected at the home of Rafael Caraballo on Contreras Street, facing the new plaza de armas. It was there that José María Heredia's play *Eduardo VI* was staged in 1819, with Heredia himself in the cast.

In 1829, the town's first proper theater, the Principal, opened on Manzano Street between Ayuntamiento and Jovellanos. It could seat 250 persons on the orchestra level and had a few balconies. Unfortunately, the building has been lost. In the 1950s it was a parking space and auto-repair business. Only parts of the façade remained, including the pediment and a few pilasters. Dal'Allio's Sauto represented a quantum leap and established the Matanzas stage as a must for touring Cuban performances.

Matanzas in her apogee was of critical importance to the development of Cuban art. Frenchman Guillermo Colson was inspired by the Yumurí Valley to paint Cuba's first known landscape. The work's excellence earned him the directorship of Havana's San Alejandro Art Academy, where he succeeded Jean Baptiste Vermay.[9] In addition to Colson, foreign artists like the Americans Eliab Metcalf and Charles DeWolf Brownell, and the Belgian Henry Cleenewerck, worked in Matanzas in the 1800s.

The most remarkable contribution to nineteenth-century Cuban painting, however, was homegrown: the brothers Esteban, Augusto, and Philippe Chartrand. Esteban and Philippe were born at Ariadne, the family's sugar mill; Augusto in South Carolina. Their estates in the country and their home in Versalles hosted many an illustrious visitor. Richard Henry Dana had warmed up to the family, and U.S. Vice President William Rufus King literally made history in their living room, as we shall see later on. All three brothers produced important work, but Esteban led the pack. Educated in France, he fell under the influence of the Barbizon school. While a student in Boston he got to know the work of the Hudson Valley painters. He began painting in 1857, and by the time of his death had recorded 106 works, the vast majority of which portrayed Matanzas. The brothers' collective oeuvre is the earliest corpus of landscapes produced by Cubans.[10]

Fully aware of its cultural significance, the Matanzas elite of the sugar-frosted nineteenth century appreciated, collected, studied, and bragged about art, especially that with a local flavor. The home of the patrician Ximenos on fashionable Contreras Street contained notable European art, but the family's pride and joy was the work of artists connected to the city. Metcalf, Cleenewerck, and the Chartrands were all represented there with major works and pride of place.[11]

Matanceros' civic pride went to the sky in 1830. Aerostatic flight had its Cuban debut in 1828 when a Frenchman named Robert ascended in a Montgolfier aerostat to mark the inauguration of Havana's Templete. Two years later, matanceros had their own lift when another Frenchman, Adolphe Theodore, effected two flights in a balloon, one on August 15 in honor of Queen María Cristina de Borbón, and the other on October 4, to mark Ferdinand VII's birthday. Matanzas thus became the second Cuban city to witness a balloon ascension. The pamphlet printed as a record of the ascent is among the very first Latin American publications about aeronautics.[12]

The Athens of Cuba in its heyday was a good place to get sick, if that was in the cards. All things considered, Hippocrates himself might have been pleased with the Cuban Athens' clinical environment. In the decade of the 1860s, Matanzas boasted more medical practitioners than any other Cuban city save Havana and Santiago de Cuba, and a ratio of surgeons to other physicians higher even than Havana's. As early as 1847 Matanzas was one of two cities outside of Havana to have a certified midwife.[13] Matanzas not only had more; it had better, for most of Matanzas' medical elite had attended the Sorbonne.

Dr. Juan Guiteras y Gener, one of Cuba's great scientific luminaries, was one who did not. He did his medical studies at the University of Pennsylvania when virtually his entire family was in exile there during the Ten Years' War. He received his MD in 1873. The son of Eusebio (one the "Guiteras brothers" of scholarly fame) and Josefina Gener y Puñales, he was born in Matanzas in 1852 and died in 1925. He did notable research on yellow fever and parasitology.

If one preferred Chinese medicine to the still notoriously unsafe western practices, that could be accommodated too. Dr. Chan-Bom-Biá, Cuba's fabled *médico chino,* practiced for years in Matanzas and trained apprentices there, before dying in Cárdenas in 1872. A legendary figure in his day and since, his seemingly miraculous cures earned him folk immortality. To this day, the phrase "a ese no lo cura ni el médico chino" (not even the Chinese physician can cure him) indicates a terminal prognosis.[14]

From very modest beginnings, the education sector made rapid and dramatic progress. To their credit, Matanzas' municipal authorities promoted public education from very early on, despite limited means, and proved adapt-

Fig. 23. *Above:* The Chartrands' Ariadne sugar mill. *Below:* Esteban Sebastian Chartrand Dubois, "View of the Pan of Matanzas" (oil on canvas, 30 × 47¾ inches, 1882). Courtesy of Cernuda Arte, Miami. The somber palette bespeaks European influences but the thread-bare bush, the lonely surviving tall tree on the right and the encroaching palm groves reveal Chartrand's keen direct observation of a landscape in transition.

able as circumstances changed. In 1805 the only formal schooling available in Matanzas was imparted by José Antonio Urbista for ten pesos a month, plus room and board, paid out of the municipal account. Six years later city hall paid three hundred pesos a year to Agustín de la Lastra for like services. His classroom included twenty-five pupils, all of them "poor." The affluent were educated at home by tutors or preceptors, with predictably uneven results. In 1818, however, the city council raised the compensation for teachers to 1,400 pesos yearly and was able to attract a remarkable educator, Ambrosio José González. He taught, among others, poets José Jacinto and Federico Milanés and the Guiteras brothers. In the 1830s, four free schools for boys following the Lancasterian method were established in the town.[15] By 1842 there were twenty-three schools with more than one thousand pupils.[16]

In 1840, Matanzas' legendary private school, La Empresa, welcomed its first students. Founded by a group of prominent liberal criollo intellectuals, its entrepreneurial name (The Enterprise) gave away its modernizing educational philosophy.[17] The first headmaster was José Antonio Echevarría, a Havana publicist. La Empresa recruited a star-quality faculty, including Ramón Palma and Cirilo Villaverde, Cuba's preeminent nineteenth-century novelist. Originally a primary school, it was authorized to offer a secondary curriculum in 1855.[18] In its glory days it was one of the top schools in Cuba, competing with the best Havana had to offer. José de la Luz y Caballero, the dean of the criollo intelligentsia of the day did not hesitate to call it "the best in Spain and her dominions." Its criollo ambiance and liberal agenda, however, made it vulnerable, and it was closed in 1869, when the Ten Years' War broke out.

An *instituto* (secondary school) was established in 1867, suppressed in 1872, and thoroughly reorganized in 1883.[19] Like La Empresa, the instituto was inherently suspect as a focus of juvenile opposition to the colonial regime. The collapse of secondary education in Matanzas meant that many local young men would be sent to the United States for their education, with incalculable consequences, one of them being the eventual popularity of baseball in Cuba.

University education secured a toehold in Matanzas when the vicar of the main parochial church, Father Manuel Francisco García, applied for an appointment as *catedrático* (i.e., full professor) of philosophy and mathematics within the University of Havana. Father García was a remarkable character. He held his post as vicar between 1822 and 1853, a time long enough to complete the detailing of the church building, from the Carrara marble floors to a colonnaded portico that shows up in contemporary images but has since disappeared. His application for the professorship sailed through the colonial bureaucracy with the resolute endorsement of his superiors and the rector of the University of Havana. As catedrático, Father García, who was a noted mathematician, could teach classes that earned full university credit. He had his first student intake on September 14, 1839.

Nineteenth-century Matanzas was notably open to the education of women. In 1839, Governor Antonio García Oña—the same who would later achieve notoriety during the Escalera affair—requested authorization to establish a free school for "poor girls" in addition to the four public schools for boys then existing, and proposed that it be funded by a tax on bocoyes of molasses. He noted that there lived in the city some five hundred "poor" girls from five to fifteen years old whose education was much neglected because of their families' penury.[20]

García Oña's school opened the following year. Known as the Santa Cristina School for Girls, it lasted until the end of the colonial period. Its stated mission was to become a "moralizing" force in society. (The implied meaning, "save the girls from the whorehouse," was all too clear.) Its curriculum consisted of "Christian doctrine, sewing, reading, writing, and the four rules of Arithmetic." A private school for girls, Nuestra Señora de Covadonga, opened in 1872 under the direction of Francisca de Cárdenas Tió. Members of the staff operated the San Francisco School for colored children on the side, a remarkable feature.

One cannot discuss the intellectual life of nineteenth-century Matanzas without a reference to the Guiteras family.[21] They have become emblematic of the city's commitment to learning, although a definitive study of their contributions awaits an author. The family's robust genealogy is nothing if not complicated. The founders of the family in Matanzas were Ramón Guiteras i Molins, a Catalan merchant from Canet de Mar, and his Barcelonese wife, Gertrudis Font i Xiqués. They had a daughter, Gertrudis, and four sons: Pedro José, Antonio, Eusebio, and Ramón Guiteras y Font. Ramón, the youngest, eventually settled in Bristol, Rhode Island, where he married Elizabeth Manchester Wardwell. This branch of the family later on donated the funds for the Ramón Guiteras Public Library, Cuba's most technically advanced library during the 1950s.

The three older sons, Pedro José, Antonio, and Eusebio, married women of the Gener family, another important local gens, and begat a generation of cousins sharing both parental surnames. One of those cousins, the son of Eusebio

Guiteras and Josephina Gener was the physician and scientist Juan Guiteras Gener. Another, the son of Antonio Guiteras and Teresa Gener, was Calixto Guiteras Gener, who was in turn the father of Antonio Guiteras Holmes, the tragic 1930s revolutionist about whom more is to follow in due time.

Antonio was a distinguished classicist and Eusebio a poet of note. Both got to run La Empresa School. Among Antonio's many accomplishments was a translation of Virgil's *Aeneid* from the Latin, published in part in Matanzas and in its entirety in Barcelona in 1885.[22] Pedro José was the first Cuban historian to practice a modern historiography based on documentary research and sound criticism.[23] His main works are a monograph on the fall of Havana in 1762 (published in Philadelphia in 1856) and the first synoptic history of Cuba, published in two volumes in New York in 1865–66.

Domingo del Monte's influential tertulia initially met at the Guiteras home at Calle del Río No. 9. Del Monte was a superb talent scout and quite adept at mobilizing others in the service of his complicated intellectual and political chess games. He had done so quite adroitly with the slave Manzano and would do so somewhat more tactfully with his other great "discovery," José Jacinto Milanés.

The Milanés family was originally from Bayamo. The bard's maternal kin, the Fuentes, were from Matanzas, where he was born in 1814. His maternal aunt, Isabel Fuentes y Rodríguez, had married into the powerful Ximeno clan. A brother, Federico, was also a poet of some note. The family was by all accounts caring, loving, and close but their circumstances were modest and José Jacinto's schooling extremely deficient. He developed an interest in the theater because of books his father gave him. When he started writing little plays, they would be performed at home on an improvised stage. Milanés had an inquisitive mind and was a voracious reader. A gifted autodidact, he taught himself French and Italian. As a young man he worked as a clerk at a hardware store and seemed headed for the serene mediocrity of a provincial writer when he met del Monte in 1834. The tertulia was the perfect incubator for the fragile poet's unique talent.

In all probability, Milanés would not have been Milanés without del Monte. The latter's friendship gave the poet access to a stimulating intellectual milieu and a vast library. Del Monte developed an almost paternal solicitude for Milanés, encouraging him to write, making sure that he got published, and resolving the problem of subsistence by arranging for an easy but lucrative job at the Sabanilla Railroad. Del Monte was the corporate secretary of the railroad; Milanés did all his routine work. It was a symbiosis. The poet served in that capacity until his career was cut short by mental illness in 1843. He had seven years to write. That was all.

There was a pathetic dimension to Milanés' life beside the tragic one of his illness. He fell deeply in love with his rich cousin, Isabel Ximeno Fuentes, to the point of breaking off a ten-year engagement. "Isa" Ximeno brushed him off. Her family thought the whole matter rather silly, which caused him deep anguish. This may have been a contributing cause in his coming mentally unhinged when he was barely twenty-nine.

So much to do and so little time, but his seven productive years were amazingly so. Of a Romantic sensibility, he took nature and historicist themes for his métier and a liberal literary nationalism as a key point of reference. His best poems are excellent, on the same level as the best Spanish-language poetry of his day. The less said about his not-so-good ones the better.[24] The perennially popular—and often parodied—"La fuga de la tórtola" (The Flight of the Turtledove) lives on as a brilliant exemplar of what Cintio Vitier called "lo cubano en la poesía."[25] Into an otherwise trivial tale of a tame turtledove that flies away Milanés weaves moving references to Cuba's lush landscape. Freedom—a "blessed passion"—is expressed in the context of the slave world that he knew. *Cimarrón,* a word that specifically denotes a runaway slave becomes *cimarronzuela* as applied to the runaway turtledove. The italics are the poet's, the translation mine.

> My turtledove without a cage;
> Used to my bed, used to my ways;
> To one kiss now, one later on.
> Red-footed *little runaway,*
> What flight is this? Why are you gone?
>
> . . . .
>
> I see it now, in flight you strove,
> To gain the liberty that you love.
> That has my blessing despite my pain.
> Alas, my darling, my turtledove,
> Gone to the hills, there to remain!

Milanés the playwright made a big splash with *El conde Alarcos,* a runaway success when it opened at the then brand-new Tacón Theater in Havana in 1838. Del Monte saw to it that the work was properly staged. The plot, set in medieval Spain, was an encoded manifesto against the Mother Country's ingratitude for the loyal support the Cubans had given her during the South American wars for independence. Concretely, it was a barb aimed at the captain-general of the day, Miguel Tacón y Rosique, whose name the theater bore and whose antipathy towards criollos was well known—and heartily reciprocated. Traditional nationalist historiography, in fact, has demonized Tacón as "the governor that ruled by kicking with his heels" (*tacón* means "heel" in Spanish).

To write a play with an ulterior political message was one thing. To have it staged at the island's best theater before a select audience that included, no doubt, members of the authorities alluded to, may have caused more stress than the fragile Milanés could cope with. At any rate, he refused to attend the opening or any subsequent performance. It may have triggered his first nervous breakdown.

As the nineteenth century reached midpoint, local criollo bourgeois culture became institutionalized with the foundation of the Liceo Artístico y Literario and the Ateneo. Both had American prototypes. The modern lyceum movement had begun at Millbury, Massachusetts, where Josiah Holbrook (1788–1854) founded a program of adult education in 1826.[26] The movement found eager followers in Cuba. A Havana chapter was founded in 1844 by, among others, the Catalonian businessman Ramón Pintó.[27] Pintó was thoroughly criollized. He was executed in 1854 for his leadership of a separatist plot. Flourishing lyceums were established in Guanabacoa, Regla, and Santa Clara, in addition to the one at Matanzas. The Liceo de Guanabacoa, founded in 1861 by the reformist lawyer Nicolás Azcárate, had none other than José Martí briefly as its secretary.[28]

Matanzas' Liceo was incorporated in 1859 and formally inaugurated in February 1860 with poetry readings, recitals, and the performance of the second act of *El conde Alarcos*. The institution proved its mettle, however, with the brilliant *Juegos florales* of 1861, when Gertrudis Gómez de Avellaneda, Cuba's reigning writer, was feted and presented with a laurel crown. "La Tula," who was then living in Cárdenas—her permanent home was in Madrid—gave a memorable speech and offered a reading of her works.[29]

The other criollo bastion was the Ateneo de Matanzas, founded in Pueblo Nuevo in 1874 as the Sociedad Talía and renamed the Ateneo in 1879.[30] Historian Mireya Cabrera Galán mentions the Ateneo de Madrid as a possible antecedent.[31] Clearly, the Matanzas founders were well aware of the illustrious

Madrid institute, founded in 1820 and revived in 1835. The Madrid Ateneo itself, however, had sprung from Anglo-Saxon roots. The first Athenaeum was established in Liverpool in 1707. One hundred years later, in 1807, the ever-cultured Boston followed the Liverpool example and established its own Athenaeum, likewise dedicated to the diffusion of knowledge.

The local Ateneo's climax during the nineteenth century was not poetic, literary, artistic, or even pedagogic. It was downright mercantile: the organization of Matanzas' memorable 1881 International Exhibition, the first effort of its kind in Latin America. The exhibition was so successful that it almost bankrupted its patron.

The nineteenth century was the heyday of international exhibitions, natural showplaces for the mature Industrial Revolution and powerful combinations of mart and museum. Beginning with London's immensely successful 1851 venture of Crystal Palace fame and an 1862 encore, many other major cities followed suit: Paris (1867, 1878), Vienna (1873), Philadelphia (1876), and Chicago with the enormously influential Columbian Exhibition of 1892.

Matanzas' version of a world's fair was not—how could it be?—of the same scope as such enormous undertakings. It was, however, completely out of proportion to the size and possibilities of its host city. The exhibit organizers spared no expense, from plates and tableware imprinted with a view of the exhibit grounds to commemorative medals and awards. Gilded sterling silver souvenir spoons were ordered from the famed Towle Silversmiths of Newbury, Massachusetts. The exhibition had a superb venue in Pedro Celestino del Pandal's building, designed for the purpose and built at the Palmar de Junco. Mostly made of timber dressed to simulate stone, it was roofed with galvanized iron and was the first building in Cuba wired for electricity.

The exhibits were remarkable. Of particular significance was the display of Cuban zoological specimens presented by that luminary of Cuban natural science, the German-born but thoroughly *aplatanado* (Cubanized) Juan Cristóbal Gundlach.[32] A native of Marburg, Gundlach arrived in Cuba in 1839 after several visits to Puerto Rico. An encyclopedic naturalist, he settled first on a farm on the banks of the Canímar and subsequently at a cafetal near Cárdenas. In 1864 he moved to La Fermina, a plantation near Bemba, where he remained until 1884, relentlessly collecting and classifying his adoptive land's fauna. He spent the last decade of his amazing career in Havana.

If the creature wore feathers, hair, scales, or a shell; flashed a bare skin; flew; crawled; burrowed; or ran on two legs or all fours, he was interested in it. His

Fig. 24. *Left:* Exhibition building designed by Pedro Celestino del Pandal for the 1881 Matanzas Exhibition. *Right:* Souvenir plate and spoon from the exhibition. The plate featured a view of the exhibition building; the spoon (gold plate on sterling silver) was made by Towle Silversmiths of Newbury, Massachusetts.

published contributions and well-preserved collections are to this day internationally recognized monuments to precision and cornerstones of Cuban science. One can imagine his delight when visitors to the exhibition came across one of his most spectacular discoveries, *Calypte helenae,* Cuba's unique bee-sized hummingbird and the world's smallest bird.

Voltaic arcs generated with appropriate apparatuses were certain attention-getters, no less than the plethora of industrial goods, agricultural products, and consumer goods displayed.[33] Even verdín tobacco made an appearance for old time's sake. The Matanzas cigarette factories El Sol de Matanzas and El Rayo Verde displayed their potent wares next to carved timber statues of an American Indian man and his female companion like they did in the United States.[34] The grand Matanzas exhibit deserves the thorough study it has yet to receive. One cannot avoid the impression that, coming at a time of profound economic depression, the exhibit, more than a triumphal statement of Matanzas' progress was an effort to arrest the city's decline.

For all the material advances of the nineteenth century's first half, genteel matanceros would have insisted that their city was not so much a commercial as a cultural happening, hence "the Athens of Cuba." The Attic conceit was the fabrication of a group of boosters affiliated to the brand-new Liceo. Their self-appointed task was to find a label to express the city's values and aspirations. Like the Liceo itself, the Athenization of Matanzas may owe much more to the contemporary American experience than is commonly recognized. In all likelihood the inspiration for "the Athens of Cuba" came down from New England, like the hard granite cobblestones that paved the streets. It was part of the intellectual ballast of the sugar trade.

Boston had been called "the American Athens" for decades when the statue of Aristides was unveiled in Louisburg Park on Beacon Hill in 1852. This caused considerable enthusiasm for things Athenian, and Boston took ownership of its nickname. The New England metropolis was not alone. Nashville, Tennessee, also went Greek and became the "Athens of the South" in the 1850s. This chronology fits hand-in-glove with the timing of the Liceo's initiative. But U.S.–Spanish relations being delicate, criollo affinities for Cuba's northern neighbor demanded circumspection and discretion, so one would not expect such linkages to be made explicit. Connections between Matanzas and Boston were particularly close, however, as the most cursory inspection of movements at the port will reveal.[35] Whatever the source of Matanzas' Attic appellation, it is only fair to note that the original New World Athens was not Boston, Nashville, nor Matanzas but Bogotá, Colombia, which was so designated by no less than Humboldt as early as 1803.[36]

Finding the right label for Matanzas was not easy. The debate that ensued among city leaders reveals a profound ambivalence between the merits of a successful commercial identity and an imagined destiny as an elegant home for the Muses. In the end "the Athens of Cuba" won, but there were alternatives like "the Naples of the Americas" (Matanzas simply looks like Naples) and, of course, "the Tyre of the Western Seas." "The Venice of Cuba" emerged as a compromise that combined mercantile prowess with cultural panache.

Comparing Matanzas to Venice was not new. Cirilo Villaverde, among others, had waxed lyrical about the perceived similarities in 1840. Venice partisans from Villaverde onwards argued that the San Juan in its course through the city suggested the Grand Canal, and sugar lighters brought to mind romantic gondolas. Traveler Samuel Hazard drew a highly Venetian-inspired view of the river. All that, of course, was at best a mighty leap of the imagination. (One is reminded of a delightful Cuban movie, *Cartas del Parque,* based on a short story by Gabriel García Márquez. The action takes place in Matanzas during the first decade of the twentieth century. At one point there is a magic lantern presentation. In the darkened room, a commentator is explaining the scenes that flash successively on the screen. Suddenly, a view of Venice appears and the commentator deadpans: "This is Venice, the Matanzas of Europe.")

This layering of the cultural and the mercantile reinforces Boston as the clandestine inspiration. Boston-as-Athens had Harvard and the Athenaeum, but it was also a successful Tyre of the Western Seas that bought a lot of Cuban sugar and molasses and sent to Matanzas a lot of salted cod. If Boston could successfully mix cod and culture, Matanzas could do cane and culture just as well. Tyre, yes, but Athens first. That was the challenge, the ideal. Tyre was easy: to immerse themselves in ancient Phoenicia, slaves included, all white Matanzans had to do was to walk a few blocks to the riverfront.

Fig. 25. In the 1860s Samuel Hazard caught Matanzas in a Venetian mood with the San Juan River as the Grand Canal and sugar lighters as gondolas.

The vast majority of Afro-Matanzans had never heard of Athens. Clandestinely, however, Matanzas was to them fast becoming like unto another legendary ancient city, Ilé-Ifé of the Yoruba, the seat of godly wisdom and the holy oracles. More about that in the next chapter. Nobody would have thought in 1860 that Matanzas might be called "the Ilé-Ifé of Cuba." Indeed, no one has made such a proposal but, were it to be made today, many Matanzans would applaud. All would certainly understand.

The Liceo moved to a new home on the plaza de armas in 1863, just in time to bury Milanés, who had been essentially catatonic for the last twenty years of his life. His mother would bring him out from time to time for a ride in their volanta, his gaze lost in a space comprehensible—if at all—only to him.

When he died on November 14, 1863, there must have been some relief, no doubt tactfully expressed, that his zombie-like existence was at last mercifully over. The brand-new Liceo offered to arrange Matanzas' solemn farewell to her star-crossed bard. It was Milanés' apotheosis and, indirectly, the Liceo's consecration as Matanzas' Parthenon. The new plaza was still an uncouth and raggedy place. Not exactly the Acropolis, but it would have to do.

The poet was buried on a gray and rainy Sunday. At four o'clock in the afternoon, a procession of sixty dignitaries dressed in strict mourning left the Liceo. Arranged in rows of three, the cortege solemnly crossed the square and proceeded down Gelabert Street (now Milanés Street) to the poet's home three blocks away. The sidewalks were packed with onlookers and mourners.

As the rosewood casket left the poet's house, Gelabert No. 38—two doors away from where the Casa Cabañas would rise half a century later—a pause was made in the *zaguán,* the breezeway. A poem was read and a crown of laurel placed on the casket on behalf of the Liceo by Emilio Blanchet, the dean of the town's intelligentsia. As the casket left the house it had to be tipped somewhat upright in order to clear the high rise of the entrance step above the street level (the sidewalks are still exceedingly narrow along that stretch of the street). That must have been an awkward moment. I vividly remember a similarly awkward moment when a friend of my family was buried from an adjoining home in 1957. When the casket was maneuvered out of the house in much the same fashion as the poet's, it appeared for an instant as if the pallbearers might lose control with ghastly results. Everyone gasped but fortunately nothing untoward happened.

The cortege wound its way slowly along Gelabert Street, flowers raining down from the balconies as it went by. At every corner a new company of pallbearers would put their shoulders to the casket while the previous one moved to the rear and held the ribbons dangling behind. After ten blocks of this routine a hard rain began—real water, not flowers—and the casket had to be placed on a hearse for the rest of the procession. A large crowd waited at the cemetery, where the cortege arrived at dusk to the customary eulogies before internment in the Ximenos vault.[37]

The Liceo's golden age was short-lived. Liceos throughout Cuba were closed during the Ten Years' War. The Matanzas one reopened after the war as the Club de Matanzas. Then, as the local sugar industry declined, and along with it, the city itself, the Liceo reflected the slide into a lethargic complacency. Maturin Ballou, a visitor in the 1880s, commented on the city's intense club life and on the "excellence of the appointments" of the Liceo and the Casino Español. "Club life prevails in Matanzas," Ballou went on, "just as it does in Havana, as usual at the expense of domestic life, being very much like London in this respect."[38] Mercifully, Ballou's observation came too late for anyone to come up with "Matanzas, the London of Cuba."

Tyre and Athens are ultimately myths. They represent expressive choices for defining Matanzas criollo group identity. In 1860 Matanzas was on the cusp of its days as an economic powerhouse. She was so obviously Tyre that this metaphor needed no reinforcement. In fact, the elite were a bit embarrassed to admit the parallels. Milanés had expressed their sentiments poetically, his elbows resting on that long-vanished balustrade. Economic prowess was fine but it was not enough. The flour of success needed culture's leavening. Athens thus sublimated Tyre.

By the 1870s and 1880s, however, Matanzas' economic soufflé had deflated. Tyre had gone bust. The 1881 exhibition, as I have suggested earlier, may well have been an attempt to revive the city's flagging economy, but it did not work. Nobody could wish away beet sugar or the ruinous economics of slavery. "The Athens of Cuba" thus moved on to an uncertain future as a fossil. What had been a credible boast in the halcyon days of prosperity became a slightly ridiculous provincial conceit. Absent the entrepreneurial dynamism of yore, however, the slogan was more important than ever before, not so much to reinforce success as to sublimate failure.

9　Disguises and Holy Spaces

THE IDEA OF ATHENS as home of the Muses and citadel of learning is well established in the western imagination. Calling Matanzas "the Athens of Cuba" required no explanation; it was a clear message. That half the population of this "Athens" happened to be African, tribal, illiterate, and in bondage was not considered. Like the ancient Spartan helots, the servile did not count. (But, of course, they do.)

Matanzas might be Athens but mid-nineteenth-century local criollos knew all too well that they were not Athenians. Their government was no *demokratía*, and they lacked *politéia*, the rights of citizenship. At the turn of the century their grandparents had co-opted captains-general and all but imposed their own agendas, from opening up new ports to cutting down old trees. That was over. Since the conclusion of the Latin American independence wars, the political disempowerment of Cuban criollos was a fact of life.[1]

Before 1810 Spain had half a world to romp in and could well afford to cut some slack to a peripheral island colony like Cuba. After 1824, only Cuba, Puerto Rico, the Philippines, and the tiny Marianas could possibly accommodate the aspirations of *peninsulares* to plum colonial postings. A legacy of the wars for independence—which must include Spain's own bloody struggle against Napoleon—was a large military establishment. The Carlist Wars and sundry colonial conflicts from Mexico to Morocco further nourished Spanish militarism for the rest of the century. In consequence, the administration of

Cuba was not only peninsularized but also militarized during the 1800s, in both cases to the detriment of the criollos.

In 1825, a Spain nervous about sedition and slave rebellions placed Cuba under a permanent state of siege and installed the captain-general as a military dictator. Censorship was severe. Cubans faced a keen identity dilemma under this arrangement. A popular phrase nailed it on the head: "a Spaniard can have whatever he wants in Cuba except Spanish children."[2] The children were fatally Cuban, but the existing colonial regime had no use for an assertive Cuban identity; expressing it meant trouble.

One of the coping mechanisms of the oppressed is to deal in the oblique, to wear disguises. The prevalence of masked balls in nineteenth-century Cuba was amazing. Samuel Hazard attended one at Matanzas and left a memorable description. Cubans, like eighteenth-century Venetians, another creative but very stressed society, were seemingly always ready to don a mask and pretend to be somebody else. It is at the very least suggestive that when they were not imagining themselves as Athenians, the Matanzas elite of the Victorian age fancied themselves as Venetians. Disguises can be quite revealing in their own way.[3]

Towards the middle of the century, festivals known as *bandos* were held in a handful of locations in Cuba. They were citywide pageants in which white folks—criollo society for the most part—imagined themselves to be, for a few days at least, citizens and courtiers of a fictitious realm with a queen, a court, and all the accouterments of the real sovereignty they so conspicuously lacked.

The most extravagant of such pageants was held in Matanzas in 1855. Lola María de Ximeno dedicated quite a bit of space to it in her memoirs. Her mother, the famed beauty "Lola Cruz," was Queen of the Bando Punzó, one of the two rival "realms" of the 1855 festival. (*Punzó* is a Gallicism for "deep red.") Lola María, ever mindful of proprieties, laid aside her first-person perspective and ceded the floor to the reporters of the *Aurora de Matanzas*, citing extensively from their coverage. Being the chronicler of an event in which her mother was a star was simply not good form.

Lola Cruz was a legendary figure in her day. She is one of the handful of Romantic-era Cuban women captured in zarzuelas, along with Rosa la China, Cecilia Valdés, and María la O. "Lola Cruz" is possibly Ernesto Lecuona's least known zarzuela, but it features one of his most popular lyrics, *Damisela en-*

cantadora, composed especially for diva Esther Borja and inserted into the libretto for her sake. Although an afterthought, the piece captures an essential facet of Lola Cruz. She was truly a "charming damsel," famed for her looks and elegance but gifted also with a probing mind and a trenchant intellect. Like cousin José Jacinto Milanés she was a brilliant autodidact with a great library at her disposal and time on her hands.

A polyglot, she acquired several languages by sheer persistence and ingenuity. Once, after a lengthy conversation with visiting actor Joaquín Arjona, the latter expressed his admiration at the breadth of her travels, so vividly had she evoked faraway places. He was stunned to learn that Lola had never left Cuba, and only rarely Matanzas. She never wrote. Her learning was, at least for the most part, neither practical nor philosophical but merely ornamental.

Lola Cruz was born in 1840 to a member of the lesser planter oligarchy but entered social eminence through the wide door of marriage to José Manuel de Ximeno y Fuentes, the head of the then fabulously rich Ximenos. Their wedding was the social event of the year 1862: beauty in great measure joined money in vast quantity. As mistress of the Ximeno household, she could entertain lavishly, collect art enthusiastically, and indulge in what for the society of her day was eccentric behavior, such as—according to her daughter's tender recollections, of course—strictly forbidding corporal punishment of slaves and delighting in lending her trusted servants her own jewels to wear at their festivals.

In 1855, when she was elected Queen of the Bando Punzó, Lola Cruz was barely fifteen and a stunning beauty. We shall follow Her Punzó Majesty into the fun and merriment of the festivities. First, let us peek briefly indoors, into the charmed, faux-antique, self-consciously precious, dilettantish, and pretentiously aristocratic world of nineteenth-century grand bourgeois Matanzas. This prissy cocoon—*prissy* in its dictionary sense of excessively proper and affectedly correct—emerges in Lola María's prose imaginatively remembered (or, perhaps more accurately, invented). It was a world of noble ancient *casonas* and palatial dwellings luxuriously appointed. Gilded mirrors reflected the light of Bohemian crystal chandeliers, paintings lined the walls and, of course, books lined the dark mahogany shelves—do not forget this is Matanzas. Lola María's vivid re-creation is also a lamentation for a lost world. The Ximenos lost their own casona and much of their fortune in the economic crises of the late 1800s.

According to Lola María, the denizens of her charmed citadel of good taste were prim and proper patricians, witty, clannish, well read, worldly, exacting performers of the most complex quadrille steps, and engaging conversationalists. They were fashionable, chivalrous, and elegantly conventional, yet amusing and fun-loving. They lounged on Louis XV–style furniture—caned, not upholstered, in deference to the heat—and were surrounded by small armies of liveried servants. (Domestic slave crews were notoriously numerous in nineteenth-century Cuba, but our Lola María gets a bit carried away in her gentrifying Matanzas patriotism: "not even in Europe's most opulent courts would there have been as many lackeys.")[4]

Lola María de Ximeno seeks to represent the Matanzas elite, the "old and distinguished families" that were known collectively as the Señorío, as an aristocracy with plenty of *abolengo*, unimpeachable pedigree. But there was a problem: the Matanzas sector of Cuba's nineteenth-century high society was conspicuously nouveau. The city itself was mostly new construction. Undeterred, Lola María lays a patina of age and seigneurial cachet on what she had to work with. Let her vivid prose take us into a reception for violinist José White hosted by her parents in 1875. "The grand house," she wrote, "looked at its best . . . all the refinements reserved for great events being on display that evening. . . . In the cabinet, the Steinway was open, showing its beautiful interior . . . and that intimate, ineffable, occult, mysterious something musical instruments have, especially the very costly ones." Lola María would not want us to overlook that the piano was a Steinway—and very expensive, too—sounding a dissonant note of bourgeois materialism. Then she goes on:

> My father was in love with the past and tradition and never altered in the least, not even a stone, the slightest detail of [our] dwelling—only the dining room was modernized. The rest remained just as it had been during the lifetime of the modest Basque [great-grandfather Jose Matías de Ximeno y Uzaola (d. 1839)]. My father's friends . . . followed the natural trend and built themselves beautiful and sumptuous mansions, true palaces with exquisite features, marbles, crystals, and gilded reliefs. . . . Only my father remained anchored to the past . . . in the solid, vaulted, enormous house . . . full of shadows and trellises, arches and pillars . . . keeping within its walls, as if in an old safe, a world of art, books, and the components of a dear, priceless, exquisite civilization.

In truth, of course, the house, though no doubt a magnificent exemplar of Cuba's criollo vernacular, was barely built when her father was born. "The past" was just all too close at hand. A coat of antiquing was in order, and Lola María's prose again rises to the task with clever implications and allusions to "primitive" austerity, "feudal" grandeur, "centuries old" materials, "very old" techniques, and manorial pretensions, tracing the house's pedigree, though not the house itself, to the time of the conquest.

> Flagstone floors, some colored like slate; fire-red bricks, strong, primitive, indestructible; big, dark, hard maroon-hued clay shingles. . . . Big, solid-hinged mahogany doors, some folding into wall recesses and running on floor tracks of gilded bronze. The main door had iron bosses and an enormous key, like a feudal castle. . . . Thick beams of centuries-old cedar revealed the roof's primitive technique without a ceiling or paintings of any kind. . . . Such roofing schemes are characteristic of the country, very old, very provincial, and proper to manor houses [*casas solariegas*], and can be seen in paintings of the age of the [Spanish] conquest.

The Matanzas Señorío's vintage antiquity thus implied, Lola María moves on to the palatial houses of more recent vintage, the homes of the newly rich whom her father is said to have disdained with the hauteur of a grandee. What does she make of them? Are they incongruous with the Matanzas elite's ideals? Far from it. Just as the big, feudal parental home suggested the criollismo of Matanzas' patricians, the new palatial ones revealed their chic, au currant good taste, worldliness, and sophistication. A good example was the home of Rafael Lucas Sánchez on the main plaza, now Liberty Square. It was "one of the handsomest in town, with exquisite refinements, vast spaces, beauty, the height of a cathedral, rich ceilings, windows, chandeliers, and crystal especially ordered from the factories in Bohemia; brass marquees guarding and sheltering doors and windows. . . . [The house] was furnished with sober luxury . . . [with] enormous mirrors . . . marble floors and stairs . . . and so much distinction and grandeur throughout!"

How appropriate for her mother, the darling of this charmed world, to become Queen of the Bando Punzó. Lola Cruz' counterpart reigning over the opposing Bando Azul was another Matanzas belle, Juana Páez. Lola I and Juana I were elected amidst the kind of anticipation, secrecy, and rumors that surround a papal conclave. Socialites divided their allegiances among the Reds and the Blues with all the intensity of Capulets and Montagus. Each bando became a make-believe "kingdom" with a monarch's court, her ministry, officers, ladies-in-waiting, ambassadors, chamberlains, generals, armies, and navy—boat owners eagerly joined the charade. There were proper, official, and luxuriously printed gazettes. The Blue royal standard was so exquisite in its many-hued tones of azure embroidery that the *Aurora* reporter wondered what it could possibly have been dyed with. For days on end, matanceros lived in a fantasy of seemingly endless seaside fetes, with the Playa de Judíos hamlet transformed into make-believe royal citadel, ceremonious receptions, luxuriously outfitted cavalcades, royal progresses to and from the "palaces" on Contreras and Zaragoza streets, and balls in the royal presences, where the "queens" would be greeted with the Spanish *Marcha Real*, the national anthem! In truly regal fashion, Juana I cut the official ribbon opening the Matanzas gasworks. Unlike during Carnival, license, mockery, and fun were not the objectives; there was a serious vein underlying the amusement and frivolity. To all appearances, at least for a few days and innocently enough, Isabella II of Spain, the real queen, was rendered quite superfluous. Nobody, of course, would have said so quite so bluntly but that may well have been the point.

Defining identity was by no means confined to rich, light-turquoise, blue-blooded criollos. When a committee of the Liceo convened to find an alternative identity for Matanzas in 1860, another group of Matanceros was also dealing with identity and its expression at Daoiz Street No. 182, not quite four blocks away. They were trying to make sense of an imagined place from the past and its meaning to them. Not, to be sure, from a position of power and privilege but from one of bondage and hardship. Unlike the nouveau Liceo, the institution they represented had an established history in the town. The African cabildo of Santa Teresa de Jesús had been founded in 1809, possibly earlier, antedating the Liceo by at least a couple of generations. It was the first of many such organizations recorded in Matanzas.[5]

Lucumís had been brought to the island in bondage as early as the sixteenth century. The conquest of the Yoruba empire of Oyo by the Islamic Fulani and the destruction of its capital in 1835 meant that Yoruba-Lucumí slaves were brought in large numbers to Cuba, mostly to the Havana and Matanzas districts. Athens would have meant nothing to them but Ilé-Ifé, the sacred city of the Yoruba, certainly would. At the end of the day, Matanzas as the Ilé-Ifé of Cuba makes so much more sense than Athens.

Many a Yoruba Matanzan in the mid-nineteenth century would have remembered the splendor of Ilé-Ifé rituals and the awesome power of her oracles. It was from Yorubaland that the first sacred *batá* drum ensemble had been introduced to Matanzas, a story I will unfold in greater detail in a following chapter. The same ancestral memories sustained, *mutatis mutandis*, the other African nations: theArarás, Carabalíes, Congos, Gangás, Iyesás, Mandingas, Minas, and other peoples represented in the Matanzas African population. Their cabildos were disguised as Christian mutual-assistance brotherhoods and as such were tolerated by the colonial authorities. They were in reality an escape valve and so much more: a framework where the hierarchies of their lost homes were preserved, the ancient deities of Africa clandestinely worshipped, and a sense of identity maintained. The key to cabildo membership was not status—both freedmen and slaves participated—but ethnicity. The African "nation" of origin was the determining factor. Not all "nations" were African, however. At least three cabildos in Matanzas between 1816 and the 1870s were said to be "of the French nation," that is, immigrants from Saint-Domingue.[6] The apparent generosity of the masters had an obvious Machiavellian underside. Segregation by *naciones* made it harder for slaves to make common cause.

The Abakuá, a secret male society originating in Calabar, was a departure from the traditional cabildo setup. An Abakuá branch, or *potencia,* was launched in Matanzas on December 24, 1862. The Abakuá, or ñáñigos, enjoy great prestige among Afro-Cuban organizations, and the Matanzas branch was especially well regarded throughout the island. Abakuá initiates would play a major role in organizing Matanzas' stevedores during the labor struggles of the twentieth century, when the port was seething with radical social ideas.

Cabildos were active and quite visible in looking after community needs. They were often quite audible also. From time to time, they would gather to play the drums. Each *toque* required a municipal clearance. In the year 1864 alone, a total of 1,269 toques were authorized to the thirty-six cabildos then legally recognized in Matanzas. On the Feast of the Epiphany, January 6, slaves were allowed their freedom and Cuban cities such as Havana and Matanzas would become Africa for a day. The festival was not a carnival, although there were superficial similarities. The point was not merriment and release, but a re-encounter with an amputated sense of self. The public projection of belief involved the imaginary re-creation of ancient divine and profane orders embedded in the social tissue of the community.

There are extraordinary written and visual testimonies and a remarkable body of scholarship about the slaves' day of freedom, the feast of the Día de Reyes. Lola María de Ximeno wrote down striking reminiscences of her childhood, when she was awed yet fascinated by what was to her a barbarous spectacle. Between the lines she lets us in on what was no doubt girl talk at a prudent distance from nosy nannies and sharp-eared chaperones: the allure of African women and the athletic, well muscled, no doubt strangely attractive African young men—"tall, and Herculean (*de flor*, they used to call them) with their buff physique, and sturdy muscles better defined than those of criollo blacks."[7] She even ventures into body smells, the product, she argues, not of lack of hygiene among the Africans, but of the trying routines of the dance.

Most of the testimonies deal with Havana. There seems not to have been that much difference between the proceedings in the capital and those in Matanzas, both being home to an extraordinary diversity of African cultures and tribal groups. The Countess of Merlin was amazed by what she saw; so indeed was Frederic Mialhe, whose extraordinary, definitive lithograph captures in vivid detail a climactic moment of the event at Havana's San Francisco Square. (Lola María's eyewitness accounts from Matanzas bear striking parallels to Miahle's images, revealing their source in a commonly observed reality, although Lola María was certainly aware of the great lithographer's work.) Xavier Marmier, writing in 1852, left us what Leví Marrero calls a "hallucinating" description that might have been written in Matanzas. Its reach and details deserve some space:

> The Day of the Kings is here the feast of the blacks . . . that day they are exempt of all duty. . . . From one corner of the city to another, artisans, peons, and servants gather in different cohorts around the Head of the tribe because, even though they are under the same yoke, African groups preserve their distinctive aspect and customs. . . . Before me, within the walls of one city, I had a sampler of all the costumes of Africa. . . . The Chiefs are superb. Some appear on stilts, like the Basque, and, when they tire of that aerial journey, they collapse in the arms of their retainers, who gladly carry them while a third gets hold of the stilts and carries them with the same respect as ladies-in-waiting once carried the trains of great ladies. Some are covered by a mantle of straws that looks like a bearskin. Others carry a castle on their heads . . . [or] a thick mask revealing a pair of sparkling eyes. Some have made themselves up to look like birds of prey or wild animals. Many are bare-chested, their cheeks tattooed, and their backs and chests painted. Some are smeared with ochre, others with white chalk; still others, not deeming themselves black enough, have painted lines on their faces with pitch.[8]

The cabildos came under increasing pressure from the authorities as emancipation loomed in the 1870s and 1880s. They disappeared altogether from Havana's and Matanzas' streets at the time of the U.S. occupation. Sadly, some of the key proponents of their passing were members of the black bourgeoisie, such as Juan Gualberto Gómez and Martín Morúa Delgado, who were likely embarrassed by the barbaric intensity and explicit Africanness of the proceedings. Thus, while white Matanzas created a fictitious Athens, the combination of Cuban and American racism and Afro-Cuban alienation dismantled the public expression of a vital tradition that lay at the core of the city's soul. Those cabildos that survived the suppression fell victim to outright persecution in the early twentieth century and the horrific witch hunts of 1919, about which more in a following chapter. Only three of the historic cabildos survive, the venerable Cabildo de Santa Teresa (Lucumí or Yoruba), the Cabildo de San Juan Bautista (Iyesá), and the Cabildo del Espíritu Santo (Arará).

Hard as it is to admit that anything good came out of the slave trade, in at least one sense the constant replenishment of Cuba's workforce with native Africans was an important factor in the preservation of African culture. This phenomenon, evident throughout the island, is particularly significant in Matanzas. The Arará cultural and religious tradition, for example, is preserved better in Matanzas than anywhere else in Cuba. Lydia Cabrera conducted some of her most important work in Matanzas, researching the ways of the Orisha community and the Abakuá secret society. People from all over the world go to Matanzas in search of the living charisma of her African roots.

An African cultural and religious complex that has survived with remarkable integrity in the city of the two rivers is the Yoruba-based worship of the orishas, what today is commonly known as Santería or, properly, Regla de Ocha. Orisha theology is rich and complex and its pantheon of deities as extraordinary as its Greco-Roman counterpart, to which it is often compared.[9] Belief holds that the universe was created by a supreme being, Olodumare, who, being remote from His creation, deputized a group of intermediaries, the Orishas, to deal with nature and humankind. Yemayá Olokún, one of the deity's caminos, or manifestations (syncretized as the Virgin of Regla, patroness of Havana's harbor), presides over oceanic depths and is especially venerated in Matanzas. That seems fitting, given the harbor's enormous marine depths, more than eight hundred meters off Rubalcava Point at the entrance.[10]

Some of the most important figures in the development of Cuban Santería hailed from Matanzas province. Eulogio Gutiérrez, a former slave from

Calimete, returned to Africa around 1880 to reconnect with the sources of his spirituality. While there he visited Ilé-Ifé and was initiated as a son of Orulá, the patron of divination (although he had earlier been initiated as a son of Obatalá in Matanzas). In obedience to a command from Orulá he returned to Calimete, where he ordained Bernabé Menocal, Bernardo Rojas, and Tata Gaytán, Cuba's pioneer babalawos, or priests of the Regla de Ocha.

According to Natalia Bolívar, towards the end of the nineteenth century, Lorenzo Samá, a Matanzas initiate, moved to Regla, where he met Tata Gaytán and others, who did not recognize the validity of his Matanzas initiation. Samá began a reform movement within Santería, took the African name of Obadimeyi (meaning twice crowned),[11] and joined forces with Latuán, a Yoruba woman who had sailed to Cuba freely in 1887. Obadimeyi's insistence on the uniformity of form, substance, and efficacy of the liturgy throughout Cuba became the modern Regla de Ocha, the rich and compelling Cuban Orisha worship.

Monserrate is one of Matanzas' sacred spaces. The lovely hermitage (the Catalonian Montserrat pointedly Castilianized to Monserrate) has dominated the city's hilly surroundings since it was consecrated in 1875. From the esplanade in front of the sanctuary the view is breathtaking. To those who return after many years, the sense of place is intense and the experience overwhelming. Come close, however, and your heart sank, for the *ermita* at the time of my last visit was a complete ruin. The four statues that once stood for the four Catalonian provinces, Barcelona, Lleida, Tarragona and Girona, were gone. So was the holy image; the famed cork *retablo*, a folk masterpiece; and all the furniture. One thought with sadness of the tender *Virolai* by Jacint Verdaguer, a frequent visitor to Cuba, with which two generations of Matanzas Catalonians greeted their patroness during their annual *romerías:*

> April rose, dark maiden from the hills,
> Star of Montserrat
> Illuminate the land of Catalonia
> And guide us to Heaven.[12]

The ermita is key to Matanzas' sense of self. It is also a testimonial to Cuba's close cultural and spiritual ties to Spain, which uniquely mark her among Latin American nations, with the possible exception of Puerto Rico. One is entitled

Fig. 26. The hermitage at Monserrate in 1898. The statues representing the four Catalonian provinces disappeared in the 1980s.

at the very least to certain reservations about a regime that tolerates—and a society that endures—such pointless and needless ruination, regardless of doctrine or ideology. Even as a straightforward tourist attraction—just for the view—the ermita was worth caring for.[13]

Matanzas' modest but moving version of Catalonia's Holy Mountain is evidence of the need of yet one more group of nineteenth-century matanceros, those born in Spain, to reconnect with their roots. There was, of course—there always seems to be—a political motivation behind the sublimation of nostalgia that such a monument represents: namely, the reaffirmation of peninsular hegemony versus the criollos' search for identity and, ultimately, independence. That the ermita of Monserrate was an artifact of *integrismo*, however, in no way diminishes its monumental importance.

Peninsular Spanish immigration to Cuba was massive during the nineteenth century and the early decades of the twentieth. It was one of the key building blocks of Cuba's population.[14] Between 1868 and 1898 about a million immigrants entered Cuba from Spain and the Canaries. Especially after the outbreak of the Ten Years' War, emigration to Cuba became a policy tool: a mechanism to Hispanicize the island's population as a deterrent to potential insurrections. This vast, regionally diverse, and disproportionately male cohort tended to take root in cities. A large proportion of migrants were military personnel who simply stayed. Some 535,495 immigrants were originally in uniform, 464,503 were civilians.[15] Many absconded in order not to be sent back to Spain in 1899.[16]

Migration to Cuba during the first four decades of the nineteenth century was led by the Catalonians (58 percent) followed by the Asturians (13.7 percent), with the Galicians coming in at a very modest 2.75 percent.[17] In later years the trend reversed, with more immigrants coming from the Cantabrian-Atlantic (Galicians and Asturians) than from the Mediterranean (mostly Catalonians). A strong Canary Islander component became dominant at mid-century. By 1859, some 46 percent of the migration was drawn from the Canary Islands, with Catalonia, Asturias, and Galicia ticking in at a fraction over 10 percent each. By 1900 Catalonian migrants to Cuba represented a paltry 5 percent of the total, with the proportion of Galicians and Asturians rising dramatically, to 28.57 percent for the former and 23.73 percent for the latter. That Galicians and Asturians formed the bulk of Spanish immigration to Cuba in the early twentieth century is dramatized architecturally by the splendid palaces of the Muy Ilustres Centro Gallego and Centro Asturiano de La Habana.[18] Many Spanish immigrants made a living as *dependientes del comercio,* that is, store clerks. Between 1850 and 1930 some 73 percent of all Asturian immigrants to Havana were classified as *comerciantes,* encompassing both store owners and clerks, with the latter, of course, in an overwhelming majority.

How did this migratory stream integrate into the Cuban population, and how did Matanzas figure in its distribution? As to the former, the answer is that Spanish migrants integrated at every level of the society, from the most exclusive ranks of the criollo aristocracy to the poorest sectors. Relationships between down-at-the-heel Spanish males (especially gallegos) and Cuban women were common, indeed, they are folkloric. The pairing of the gallego and the mulata is a quintessentially Cuban theme. Marriages of Spaniards with criollo women were common, and remained so for a very long time. The marriage of Ramón Bretós and Bárbara Almirante was a case in point; my grandfather Tomás Cabañas and my grandmother Dolores Batista another.

Matanzas' Canary Islander past seems to have made it an attractive destination for *isleños*. At any rate, the census of 1893 shows Canary Islanders as the dominant peninsular strain in the Matanzas immigrant population, with 36.5 percent of the total; Asturians represented 14.6 percent, Galicians 10.3 percent, and Catalonians 8.4 percent.[19]

Although a minority, the Catalonians were the most influential sector of the Matanzas Spanish colony. It was natural, not to mention advantageous, for them to take the initiative in local reaffirmations of peninsular identity. What they eventually achieved was remarkable: no less than a re-creation of the Holy Mountain of Montserrat above Matanzas. There, all sorts of cherished Catalonian rituals and traditions found a home, from the grand romerías of the 1880s—Matanzas' famous Fiestas Catalanas—to the dancing of the *sardana* on Sunday outings.

In his excellent monograph about the fiestas, Ernesto Chávez Alvarez makes it clear that Matanzas' Catalonian leadership did not sell its project as an expression of mere Catalanism, but of *hispanidad*. All were welcome to celebrate their identity under the welcoming mantle of the Black Madonna: the Asturians with their own vernacular language (Bable) and their devotion to the Virgin of Covadonga, the gallegos with their bagpipes and their *murriña* (homesickness), the Canary Islanders with their numbers and their subtropical ways, and even the criollos if they cared to come. Many did.

The Matanzas Catalonians enjoyed the advantages of entrepreneurship and group cohesion. As early as 1840 the local Catalonians had organized themselves as a branch of Havana's Sociedad de Beneficencia de Naturales de Cataluña.[20] In 1850, the matanceros seceded, forming their own Sociedad de Socorros. Unlike other region-based Spanish social organizations in Cuba, the Sociedad opened itself to all Spaniards regardless of regional origin.

This spirit of pan-hispanismo was reflected in the foundation of Matanzas' main Spanish club, the Casino Príncipe Alfonso, later the Casino Español, in 1864. The original casino building, at the corner of Contreras and Santa Teresa streets, had one story and was completed by 1880. A second story with a large Spanish coat of arms on the parapet, a Matanzas landmark, was built later. It now houses the Gener y del Monte Library.

The Casino Español differed markedly from its neighbor, the Liceo, a short walk away with the Sánchez mansion in between. Liceos promoted culture and the arts, thereby celebrating the supposedly cultivated and artistic criollos, whereas the Spanish social clubs' fundamental mission was to keep alive sentimental and practical links to Spain and its many regions. Where the liceos organized recitals and *juegos florales* (literary contests), the Spanish clubs sponsored picnics (romerías) vibrant with patriotic sentimentality; colorful with Spanish regional song, dance, and typical costumes; and redolent of the longing and homesickness captured in that untranslatable Galician word, *murriña*—the sadness of the uprooted. They provided social services; medical insurance; and a place to feel at home, meet compatriots, and speak *eúskera*, *galego, valencià, català*, or *asturianu*.

The soundness of the integrationist approach was demonstrated when the first Cuban insurrection broke out in 1868. With half the island up in arms demanding independence, it was only natural for Spanish immigrants to rally around their identity and loyalty to their country, not their region. The Matanzas Catalonian community took aggressive advantage of the opportunity. They proposed to stimulate a feeling of Spanishness through traditional devotion to the Virgin Mary and participation in the festivals and pageants that characterized Spain.

To assume responsibility for this program, the Sociedad Catalana y Balear de Beneficencia was created in 1870. The first of Matanzas' Fiestas Catalanas began on September 8, 1871, the feast day of Our Lady of Montserrat. Promotion of the event was spectacular. A luxurious carriage decorated in the Catalonian fashion and pulled by a team of five richly caparisoned mules made the rounds of the city announcing the great event and tolling a thousand-pound bell.

At last the great day arrived. Historian José Mauricio Quintero was there and wrote a vivid description:

> At four in the morning of the eighth of September 1871, nine bands from the Corps of Volunteers called muster and a Mass was celebrated in front of Government House, whereupon the bands scattered to every corner of the city, calling the pilgrims who, full of enthusiasm and not having slept at all, awaited the signal to take part in the great festival. Meanwhile, a provisional chapel had been built at Alturas de Simpson. Around the chapel there were countless spacious tents covered with wildflowers, banners, and allegories, not to mention an abundance of drinks and pastries in honor of the pilgrims. To the right of the sanctuary was the kitchen, where they had cooked for five thousand persons.[21]

Food was an important incentive. The promise of a nice lunch was a potent attractor to the young and isolated Spaniards who were the community's core. *La Aurora de Matanzas* reported that at the 1894 fiesta were consumed 506 legs of ham, 700 jumbo sausages, 2,000 chickens, 500 arrobas of rice (an arroba is 25 pounds), 150 arrobas of lard, 10 barrels of wine, 3,000 bottles of beer, 300 bottles of brandy, 1,000 canisters of gin, and 200 hogs. "If the sausages were strung one after the other," wrote the *Aurora* reporter, "one could lay a telegraph line between Matanzas and Mocha."[22]

The solemn dedication of the lovely ermita was the centerpiece of 1875's fiesta. The Catalonian feasts were interrupted by the War for Independence. Although they went on for a few years after 1902, the steam had gone out of them. By the mid-twentieth century the ermita was barely used at all. I entered it once or twice. There was an aura of mystery about it, with its hieratic image of the Black Madonna and Child looking down from their medieval throne, probably missing the crowds of pilgrims that no longer came.[23] Now even they are gone.

Stephan Palmié, writing specifically of the Afro-Cuban context, has brilliantly shown—and thrown much light upon—the complex interaction of the old and the new, the remembered and the imagined, the discarded and the invented, and the often unintended but efficacious complicities that contributed to the formation of Cuba's modernity.[24] Looking back to this bygone Matanzas, I am impressed by the extent to which city life was a constant mise-en-scène. The year began with the spectacular African Día de Reyes, progressed through the very public solemnities of the Catholic tradition, to the grand celebration of the Catalonians, and finally to the feast of the city's holy patron, Saint Charles Borromeus, on November 4, celebrated with a grand public procession until processions were suppressed in the 1960s. Of course, by then we were all Cubans . . .

10 The Tyranny of Nearness

IN THE SPRING OF 1977 I was appointed to the faculty of the University of New South Wales in Sydney. Two years later I was tenured and spent eight very happy years in that lovely Australian city. One of the many books I read in anticipation of my move there was Geoffrey Blainey's *The Tyranny of Distance*, where the author brilliantly argues that vast distances from just about everywhere shaped modern Australia. If, as Professor Blainey suggests, mileage means destiny, Cuba's has been shaped by the exact opposite, close proximity. That Havana was, from a practical seafaring perspective, the closest to Spain of all the ports of the Indies was a key to Cuba's early colonial experience. Later on, what General Porfirio Díaz is said to have remarked about Mexico—"so far from God and so close to the United States"—applies equally to Cuba. That Key West is ninety miles away from a point on the Matanzas shore has weighed heavily on the island's history.

The relationship has not been as lopsided as one might imagine. For such a small nation, Cuba's imprint on American history has been considerable. Thomas Jefferson wanted to buy Cuba—he had a good eye for real estate and was in a buying mood—but it did not work. The United States has had to deal with a "Cuban problem" at least since the days of John Quincy Adams. It eventually went to war over Cuba, was launched as a world empire because of Cuba, and came to the brink of a global conflict in 1962 as a result of events there. For half a century Cuba has haunted the United States in its relations with Latin America. Cuban Americans represent a tiny fraction of 1 percent of the U.S. population but, as of this writing, fully 1 percent of the U.S. Senate and almost 1 percent of the House of Representatives. They also have gotten to run the corporations that make such iconic American products as Coca-Cola and Kellogg's Corn Flakes. No need to mention subtler influences from Desi Arnaz to Latin jazz.

Since at least the second half of the eighteenth century, Cuba's relationship to the thirteen British colonies and subsequently to the United States of America has been a key to the island's history, and to that of Matanzas in particular. For the better part of a century, Matanzas was deeply linked to American ports from New Orleans to Boston. Americans played a key role in the development of the region's sugar complex and kept a high profile in the local economy until the revolution. The largest industrial plant in twentieth-century Matanzas was a rayon factory developed by the Hedges family, originally of Long Island, New York, but thoroughly Cubanized by the 1950s. The province's other important seaport and urban center, Cárdenas, was also the recipient of heavy American influences.

The brief occupation of Havana by the British in 1762–63 bound Cuba to North America. In the few months the occupation lasted, forces that would fundamentally shape the future were suddenly set in motion. Inasmuch as was possible, Spain had kept Cuba formally insulated from the outside world. Suddenly, that changed. From North American ports came long-coveted goods at decent prices. The genie was out of the bottle. After independence, when sugar from the British Caribbean was no longer available, the thirteen former colonies developed a sweet tooth for the Cuban product.

Cuba remained loyal to Spain during the Latin American wars for independence (1810–1824). As the Spanish Empire shrank and the American domain expanded, the island became a front-line issue in Spanish-American relations. Spain ceded its Florida colony to the United States in 1819. Was Cuba next? Some thought so, famously John Quincy Adams, who compared the island to a ripe apple ready for the American basket.[1] Cuba became in effect a southern extension of Manifest Destiny. In the end, history proved Adams wrong. The Cuban apple—if it was an apple at all—never ripened as expected. It remained resolutely green and tough—the stuff of bellyaches, not apple pies.

Several offers to buy Cuba outright were made between 1808 and the 1860s, all of which failed.[2] In the United States, the annexation of Cuba became an issue again in 1898. The Teller Amendment of that year, which renounced

American designs to annex Cuba as a condition for Congress to declare war on Spain, put a definitive end to the annexation option as a U.S. initiative.

Manifest Destiny had a counterpart in the Cuban annexationist movement. Just as some Americans would have welcomed a Cuban star in the national constellation, some Cubans thought that Cuba would be better off as an American state—a slave one, of course. The movement had a life of its own. It reached its apex in the late 1840s and early 1850s for a very good reason: the American capture of half of Mexico's territory dramatically validated the idea of Manifest Destiny. The neighbor to the north was a winner, and Cuban annexationists were betting on it.

If one accepted as a good thing the premise that Cubans would all have to learn English and become Americans in the fullness of time, annexation made eminent sense. To its critics—there were many, of course, but none more articulate than José Antonio Saco—annexation meant the eventual loss of Cuba's identity and culture. (Ironically, many Cubans in remote posterity, myself included, ended up learning English and becoming Americans after all. The Cuban American population today, in fact, is larger than the entire population of Cuba in 1850. Cuban identity and culture thrive in the diaspora.) Virtually all annexationists were liberals who thought Spain was a backward country mismanaging an obsolete colonial operation. They also tended to be invested in sugar and slaves, and figured out that annexation would simultaneously guarantee privileged access by Cuban sugar to the U.S. market and the continuance of slavery in Cuba, at least for as long as it held out in the north.

President James K. Polk tried to buy Cuba at the close of the Mexican War, but failed.[3] American presidents interested in a deal never quite understood that buying out Cuba, cash on the counter, while sensible from the perspective of Washington, was a political impossibility from that of Madrid. But what if a Cuba seceding from Spain knocked at the gates of the American Union, as Texas had done after seceding from Mexico?

Annexationist cabals in Cuba and the United States seeking to repeat the Texas scenario went on conspiring. The most important was the group gathered about Narciso López. Like Domingo del Monte, López was a Cubanized Venezuelan. A native of Caracas, he had fought with the Spanish in the wars for independence. He went to Cuba at the end of the conflict and, like his compatriot del Monte, married into the Cuban aristocracy. His brother-in-law was Francisco de Frías y Jacott, Count of Pozos Dulces, a reformist leader, journalist, and criollo intellectual luminary.

The Matanzas region, near to the United States and full of Americans, loomed large in annexationist agendas. López had a plan: invade Cuba and secure the island's independence. How? Land in Cárdenas, hold the city, move on to Matanzas, take it, and then, with covert freelance American support, march on to Havana itself.

To do that he needed allies and resources in the United States. He could count on both, so off to the north he went to plan his invasion. His chief accomplice was Mississippi Governor John Quitman, who sought Cuba's eventual entry into the Union as a means to expand the number of slave states beyond the boundaries of the Missouri Compromise. With Quitman's resolute—and quite illegal—backing, López recruited 610 men, overwhelmingly Americans from the southern states. There were more Irish than Cubans in the filibustering army, and more Kentuckians than any other variety of North American Caucasians. There were only five Cubans if you counted the Venezuelan López as one, four if otherwise, all from Matanzas.

This improbable legion met off Cozumel Island and embarked on the *Creole*, bound for Cárdenas in May 1850. On Sunday, May 19, López landed under cover of darkness and briefly occupied the city—long enough to unfurl the tricolor with a red triangle that he had brought along, which would become Cuba's flag. Cárdenas, settled earlier in the century by Spanish loyalists from the mainland, was not likely to support treason. There would be no poorer choice for a landing in Cuba until the Bay of Pigs fiasco in 1961. "I made a mistake," López is said to have remarked as he clambered back aboard the *Creole*. "We should have started at Matanzas."[4] The crestfallen filibusters were lucky to make it safely to Key West. A year later López tried again, but was captured and executed in Havana. He was dispatched via the *garrote*, the gruesome Spanish instrument of capital punishment. The victim, strapped to a chair, had his head secured by a metal collar and his cervical vertebrae crushed by the quick turn of a screw. Cárdenas got something out of Narciso López' misfortune. It became "Ciudad Bandera" (Flag City)—the first place in Cuba where the flag waved.[5]

Launching the national standard was the most consequential result of López' 1850 fiasco.[6] The flag was designed by a true-blue matancero, Miguel Teurbe Tolón y de la Guardia with the help of his cousin-wife, Emilia, Cuba's version of Betsy Ross, the flag's seamstress. The Teurbe Tolón family had settled in Matanzas during the second half of the eighteenth century.[7] Miguel was born there in 1829. Educated in his hometown, he became a teacher. A poet and playwright, he served as chief editor of *La Aurora*.[8] He got in trouble with the authorities on account of his annexationist politics and had to go into exile in New York.

Every Cuban schoolchild knows that Miguel Teurbe Tolón designed the flag and Emilia made it, but little credit is given them for their unique vexillological achievement. The Teurbe Tolón team is to flags what Pierre and Marie Curie are to physics: true creative geniuses. The Cuban flag is a coherent and rigorous synthesis of historical precedents, political objectives, and aesthetics.

The annexationist movement sought an encore of the Texas experience. First independence, then annexation. The Texas Lone Star flag was therefore a natural model. López was adamant about that. He wanted to stay on message: as Texas went so would Cuba. It is no coincidence that the Cuban flag is called La Bandera de la Estrella Solitaria. Yes, the "Lone Star" Flag. It was hoisted publicly for the first time at Gracie Mansion, the official residence of the mayor of New York, in 1849.

What Miguel Teurbe Tolón as designer was given to work with was stripes; the republican tricolor of red, white, and blue (originally a Dutch idea, of course); and a lone star. There was only so much he could do with that. His genius is revealed in what he cooked up with those ingredients and what he added to the stew. First, he reversed the colors. The Cuban star would shine against a red, not a blue, background. Here he moved one important step from naturalism to abstraction. Stars make sense against a blue background for obvious reasons—the sky is blue. Stars against a red background are rarer. Then he went for broke and laid his colors on a new template: the Masonic apron. The apron's mystic triangle became the setting for the star, thereby conflating the politics of annexationism with the rich symbolism and heritage of Masonry.

Fig. 27. Miguel and Emilia Teurbe Tolón, with the Cuban flag they created.

Cirilo Villaverde, a novelist and a party to these discussions, had important input as well.

Visually stunning, the Cuban flag was the first national flag to feature a triangle. It has served as the inspiration for some sixteen national flags the world over, from the Comoros to the Philippines, and from Puerto Rico to Zimbabwe, including the spectacular Senyera Estrelada of Catalonia. The power and originality of the design overcame its annexationist karma to become the flag of Martí's resolutely nationalistic movement. No one could have come up with anything better.

Teurbe Tolón had a gift for visual synthesis, which he proved again in his design for the coat of arms, another inspired performance. He used an ogee for a shield, no doubt an influence of nineteenth-century neo-Gothicism. All three quarters of the shield are rich with explicit and implied annexationist messages, but the chief was a tour de force. Teurbe Tolón represented Cuba as a key between two headlands—namely, Florida and Yucatan—indicating Cuba's proverbial position as the "key to the Gulf." A sun rises on the horizon. In his choice of motif Teurbe Tolón may have been influenced by Matanzas' own coat of arms, which was also a visual expression of place.

The annexationist aims of the movement are clearly expressed in the language of heraldry. The coat of arms featured on the López expedition's official stationery is revealing. The stripes originally shown at base dexter are those of the U.S., not the Cuban, flag. By the same token, the thirteen stars surrounding the Cuban palm tree on base sinister are a clear allusion to the original thirteen U.S. colonies. Moreover, the shield was supported by an American and a Cuban flag—but Old Glory was in the position of honor. There is another intriguing possibility. The inclusion of Yucatan in the chief quarter may be an oblique allusion to Cuba's potential as a bridge for an eventual U.S. expansion into Central America. Yucatan, in fact, was seeking to secede from Mexico and enter the American Union at about this time.

One of the reasons the United States was so keen to acquire Cuba was the island's thorough integration into the American economy by the middle of the nineteenth century. Matanzas' links were particularly dramatic. By 1823, out of 197 ships entering the harbor, 191 were U.S.-owned. In 1826, the figure was 209 out of 226. That year 91.3 percent of all Cuban imports (by value) came from the United States. This situation would remain essentially unchanged—with oscillations this way or that, of course—for the better part of a century.

Northbound ships carried sugar and molasses. Southbound ones carried all sorts of merchandise, but heavy cargoes were especially appropriate: they were both freight and ballast. As Cuba's noble timber resources became depleted, a market opened in Cuba for southern pine. Many a Matanzas timber building was built with it. One of the earliest exports from New England to Cuba was ice, which was harvested from lakes in the frigid northern winter and shipped to Cuba packed in straw. A lot melted away, but enough was left for the ice merchants to make a tidy profit in Cuba's hot weather. The availability of locally manufactured ice ended that trade. (Matanzas, ever progressive, had one of Cuba's first ice factories, built at Los Molinos in the 1870s.) Granite from Massachusetts and New Hampshire made excellent ballast also and was exported to Cuba cut into cobblestones. Matanzas' main streets were paved with them until the 1950s. Much of that exotic pavement was dumped in the harbor as fill, but some still lies under the city's streets, entombed in asphalt.

Its proximity to the United States meant that Matanzas was the recipient of Yankee influences well in advance of the rest of Cuba. Cuban criollos were more often than not the conduits. Such influences range from O'Farrill and his *Neptuno* to sugar mill machinery and rolling stock (La Junta, Matanzas' first locomotive, was made in Paterson, New Jersey), Louis Moreau Gottschalk recitals, the Matanzas tramways (made in Philadelphia), the cast iron seats at the Sauto, polished by the backsides of generations of Matanceros (made in Pittsburgh), and the Liceo and the Ateneo, based on American prototypes.

Many of the ships from the United States bound for the Pearl of the Antilles brought visitors. Cuba became one of America's top foreign tourist destinations during the nineteenth century. Matanzas figured prominently in most visitors' itineraries. "Of all the towns in Cuba visited by travelers," wrote Samuel Hazard, author of a best-selling Cuba travel guide first published in 1871, "Matanzas is the one that, to my knowledge, gives entire satisfaction to the generality of visitors."[9] There was the city, of course, an attractive and well-laid-out town adjoining a beautiful bay. The Yumurí Valley never ceased to enchant. In 1861, a new and important incentive joined the city's offerings: Bellamar Caves. Discovered when a Chinese laborer lost a pickax down a crack in the ground, they were developed by the landowner, Manuel Santos Parga, an immigrant from Galicia.[10] Mr. Santos had bought the property, known as "La Alcancía," for three thousand pesos two years before. The land was rocky and quite useless for agriculture. He knew about mining, however, and may have suspected there was something below ground. Or he may have planned to develop the land for residential purposes. *Alcancía* is the Spanish word for "piggy bank," and Santos Parga surely knew how to stuff one. Realizing that he had a saleable product in his hands, he built a splendid visitors' center over the caverns' entrance. One entered the fascinating underworld as one would a palace, down a grand Carrara marble staircase. To this day the Bellamar Caves remain as Cuba's oldest consciously developed tourist attraction in continuous operation.

Santos Parga, the astute businessman, had a romantic streak. According to Dr. Ercilio Vento Canosa, a brilliant matancero and president of Cuba's justly famed National Speleological Society, to Santos goes the glory of having been Matanzas' first serious spelunker after the native Taínos. An intrepid explorer of his underworld kingdom, he was zealous about its wonders and ready to defend them at gunpoint if necessary. This he literally did when a group of drunken British marines vandalized the caverns in March of 1872. At any rate, his marketing savvy turned his windfall into a world-class attraction. Hazard visited the caves and described the unique experience in his terse prose. Part of the cavern was lit by gas, but most of the journey was done by the flickering light of a taper—Hazard advised his readers to insist that the guides carry more than one. Compared to other famous caves, "this cave is like fairies keeping gay reverie to soft music. . . . Who has not seen the Caves of Bellamar has not seen Cuba."[11]

In Hazard's day—the late 1860s—Matanzas offered quite a menu of amenities, most of them aboveground, of course. The city was accessible from Havana by boat and railroad. The Havana-Matanzas Railways (also called Ferrocarril de la Bahía and Cuba's first trunk line in the modern sense) had its first run on May 4, 1863.[12] Matanzas offered quite an array of lodgings, from the French-run Hotel Ferrocarril ("recommended if all else failed") right across from the new train station, to the American-run Endsor House ("quite good"), to the León de Oro at Jovellanos Street No. 6. In Hazard's experienced judgment, this was, with one possible exception, the best hotel in all of Cuba.

The best rooms at the León de Oro had high ceilings with tall windows and transoms in the Cuban style. From the balconies one had a panoramic view of the city. (And, of course, of the ladies across the street; ladies were never far from Hazard's roving eye.) The walls were gaily painted with murals "representing Flora, Venus and other charming nymphs, evidently, from the scarcity of their clothing, trying principally to stay cool." The beds had "neat little bedsteads" with simple sacking bottoms and mosquito nets.[13]

Hazard had plenty of opportunities to enjoy the Cuban table, which he discussed extensively from the Matanzas perspective. He was impressed by the diversity of the menu and the sheer quantity of it. There was much on the table then that Cubans of today would recognize. "Boiled rice is served with eggs at every meal" (the invariable lunch, or *almuerzo,* which, with the addition of beef hash, or *picadillo,* I partook of with more frequency than I care to remember when I was growing up in Matanzas).

The stupendous breakfasts that Hazard polished off included fried fish, shrimp boiled with *salsa blanca* or *salsa picante,* stewed or broiled liver, mutton chops, veal, stewed kidneys, steak—"very poor as is nearly all the beef on the island"—sausages, potatoes, fried or boiled plantain, lettuce salad, scrumptious watercress, and guava paste and jellies. Cuba's "national dish," Hazard noted sarcastically, was *bacalao* (cod) imported from Boston and Providence.

Matanzas took advantage of easy accessibility, an equable climate, a first-rate gastronomy, and unique attractions to sell its offer as a tourist destination. It was the first Cuban city outside of Havana to promote itself consciously as a place folks would like to visit. Manuel Santos Parga understood that perfectly well when he developed his visitor-friendly caverns. Consequently, the "Athens of Cuba" received significant attention in Cuba's exceptionally rich travel literature of the age. Visitors came from just about everywhere, although Americans were by far the largest contingent.

During the nineteenth century Matanzas developed a reputation as a place where the sick were cured, attracting some remarkable visitors from the north. The Massachusetts cleric Abiel Abbot—who was not cured—went to Matanzas in the 1820s to recover from tuberculosis. He was one of the first to mention the remarkable sulfurous waters of San Miguel de los Baños. Equally enthusiastic about Cuba's therapeutic aura was the South Carolina physician J. G. F. Wurdemann, another tuberculosis patient who spent a considerable time in the City of the Two Rivers in the 1830s.[14] Lamentably, he was not cured either. In all fairness to Matanzas, little could be done about tuberculosis before the advent of antibiotics.

The most illustrious American health-seeker in Matanzas was William Rufus King, the thirteenth vice president of the United States. King was born in North Carolina in 1786, attended the University of North Carolina at Chapel Hill, and became a lawyer. Elected to the U.S. Senate from the newly admitted state of Alabama in 1819, he served four full terms. In 1846 he was appointed Minister to France and, in 1852, ran for the vice presidency on the Democratic ticket headed by Franklin Pierce.

When the results came in, King found himself vice president elect, but by then he was in a sorry shape. Tuberculosis, which he claimed to have contracted in France, was killing him and, on his physicians' advice, he sought Cuba's warmer climate as a last hope for recovery. A special dispensation of Congress allowed him to take the oath of office in Matanzas on March 18, 1853, which he did at the Chartrand family's Ariadne sugar mill near Limonar with the American consul in Matanzas administering the oath. He returned home right away, but death caught up with him at his Alabama plantation one month later. The only vice president sworn in abroad turned out also to be the shortest-serving.

Fig. 28. Florida's Joseph Marion Hernandez *(left)*, the first Hispanic in Congress, died a Matanzas planter in 1857; Alabama's William Rufus King was sworn in as U.S. vice president at the Chartrands' Ariadne sugar mill in 1853. (Courtesy of Prints and Photographs Division, Library of Congress)

A large number of Americans went to Cuba as investors, mechanics, and engineers in the province's booming sugar industry. Notable among American expatriates who sought the sun of the Pearl of the Antilles and a new career in Cuba was the first U.S. delegate to Congress elected from Florida and a William Rufus King contemporary, Joseph Marion Hernandez. A native of St. Augustine, Hernandez was the son of Majorcans who had settled in Florida during the period of British occupation (1763–1782). Born José Mariano Hernández Gomila, he dropped the accent on his surname and changed his given names to Joseph Marion when the Americans took over from the Spanish in 1821. He was ready to make a mark under the new regime, and he did. In 1822 he was elected as Florida's nonvoting territorial delegate, serving one full term in Washington. This gave him the distinction of having been the first Latino elected to Congress; a century would elapse before the feat was repeated.

Hernandez made a bid for the U.S. Senate as a Whig candidate when Florida became a state in 1845. He would have been the first Latino to serve in the Senate but lost to David Yulee Levy, who became the first Jew instead. Florida would have made congressional history either way but Hernandez, naturally, would have preferred a different outcome. Disenchanted with politics, he became a sugar planter in Matanzas. He died at his plantation, Audaz, in the Coliseo district, on June 8, 1857.

Nothing remains of Audaz. A road sign indicates its former location, but the next estate up the road toward Cárdenas, Santa Amalia, retains a charming mid-nineteenth-century main house that, but for the colonnaded porch, could well be in Maryland or Pennsylvania. It is a legacy of the mill's Yankee developer, a physician from Philadelphia. From the upper story, a Cuban landscape of palm trees and cane fields could once be seen through U.S.-made double-hung glazed windows. A pitched roof has been waiting for the first snow for the past century and a half. My father, who grew up in the house, reported that it was evacuated in advance of the 1926 hurricane because everybody expected the apparently flimsy glass windows to burst and the house to fly away. No such thing happened.

Evangelical Christianity also entered the island from the United States, and Matanzas was a major port of entry, though not the only one. Cuba, hitherto a hardship situation for Protestant missionaries and proselytizers, opened up dramatically under the American occupation (1899–1902) and the Estrada Palma administration (1902–1906). The dominant Roman Catholic Church was in crisis, having lost its established position under the Spanish Patronato. American authorities, and subsequently President Estrada Palma, a longtime resident of the United States and a Quaker convert, were especially friendly towards Protestant activities. American occupation officials had to deal with Protestant missionary groups as constituents; Estrada Palma saw them as allies and fellow modernizers. It is not coincidental that Baptist and Methodist congregations were established in Matanzas around 1900. The Methodists also opened a school, the Colegio Irene Toland, possibly the best such institution in Matanzas.

The American black church also made a bid for Cuban souls at the turn of the twentieth century, although this story is less well known. The African Methodist Episcopal Church set up missions in Oriente. The turbulent racial situation in that sector of Cuba made its ministry difficult, however.[15] There is evidence of, although considerably less research and information about, the activities of the African American churches in Matanzas. One wishes more were known, for example, about careers such as that of the Rev. W. McHenry Winters. Rev. Winters, who claimed to be Matanzas-born and -based, preached at churches in the United States. In the summer of 1910 he led a revival at Great Bethel AME church in Atlanta. He billed himself as a graduate of universities in Spain, an Oxford alumnus, a polyglot in full command of seven languages, and—to top it all off—a nephew of General Antonio Maceo.[16] Whether he did that tongue-in-cheek or took himself seriously is a mystery.

In a curious fashion, the Catholic Church in Matanzas was especially affected by the American connection. The scarcity of worthy Cuban clergy was such that, when the Diocese of Matanzas was created in 1912, a U.S. citizen, Charles Warren Currier, was named its first bishop.[17] Bishop Currier, a distinguished Latin Americanist scholar, lasted but a year as Matanzas' first prelate before he succumbed to mental illness. He retired to Baltimore, where he died in 1918.

In the 1950s Protestantism was very much a component of Matanzas life. Catholics in those days were not entirely at ease with them, however. That was before the modern ecumenical movement and commonsense revealed the absurdity of hatred and mistrust among supposedly fraternal communities. Catholics were not to enter Protestant temples. Never "churches"; only Catholics had churches, Protestants had "temples," like the heathen. Serious discussions would come up from time to time in my Catholic school as to whether it was actually a sin to cross the threshold of a Protestant "temple." "Not, for example," argued Father Tito Hernández, a brilliant mathematics instructor and our spiritual director, "if you are a tradesman doing your job, like a carpenter." Jesus would have appreciated that.

The reason why we worried about the implications of crossing a temple threshold was not theoretical. Matanzas had quite a few such thresholds. By the 1950s, in fact, Matanzas was an important center for Protestant missionary activity in Cuba and, in a larger sense, Latin America. It was the home of an eminent institution, the Matanzas Evangelical Seminary, founded in the 1940s. Cárdenas, like Matanzas, was an important center for Protestant irradiation. It was the home of the Colegio Presbiteriano La Progresiva, a top-notch institution. No wonder the Matanzas Catholic Church—besieged and fragile—felt threatened by the Lutheran cohorts closing in on it.

Matanzas had the honor of having the first Protestant church in Cuba (that is, the first building specifically designed and built as a place of worship serving a Protestant congregation). Matanzas also had the first Protestant cemetery and the first Protestant school on the island. They were the work of a tireless matancero, Pedro Duarte.

Unusually for Latin America, the Protestant cause in Cuba only prospered when the Cubans themselves assumed evangelical and pastoral responsibilities. Before the Ten Years' War, the tenuous Protestant presence in Cuba was limited to private services for foreigners and sporadic efforts to disseminate the Bible. Public worship other than the Roman Catholic cult was absolutely forbidden by law. In the wake of the Ten Years' war, however, many Cuban exiles returned home having experienced conversion in the United States and took upon themselves the task of proselytizing. Protestantism had a political angle, to be sure. It represented freedom and progress—the antithesis of the backwardness and oppression associated with Spanish colonialism.

Duarte was a case in point. Born in Matanzas in 1855, he went to the United States, where his family had sought exile during the Ten Years' War. While there he became an ardent Episcopalian. Back in Cuba at the end of the war, he became a committed missionary. His church succeeded where earlier efforts to seed Protestantism in Cuba by American missionaries had yielded little fruit.

The year 1883 was especially fruitful for the Protestant cause. That year the Florida pastor F. W. Wood and the Cuban Eduardo Díaz founded the island's first Baptist congregation, while Arturo Someillán and Aurelio Silvera pioneered Methodist services in Havana. In 1883 also, Duarte founded an Episcopal congregation in Matanzas known as "Faithful to Jesus," which still exists.

None of Cuba's Protestant apostles had Duarte's feistiness and determination. In 1896 he was thrown in jail by island authorities who argued that the freedom of private worship that the Spanish constitution guaranteed in Spain did not extend to the colonies. Undaunted, Duarte appealed to the crown and, as a result of his appeal, the right to freedom of private worship—only the

Catholic Church could conduct public worship—was guaranteed for Cuba as well as metropolitan Spain. The history of civil rights in Cuba owes much to this unsung hero.[18]

As the history of early Cuban Protestantism showed, if distance be fate it need not be an adverse fate. Actually, it might be fun. In 1866, the crew of an American warship docked in Matanzas decided to go ashore to play baseball. They played in front of a fascinated and amused audience of dockhands. Whatever virus they carried must have been at a very infectious stage, for baseball soon entered Cuba's bloodstream and became a chronic condition, an incurable obsession of the national soul. The zealous defenders of Cuba's Spanishness saw the danger right away. As early as 1868, Captain-General Francisco Lersundi outright prohibited the game which, to him, embodied a profound anti-Spanish spirit.

Baseball became popular among Cuban émigré communities during the wars for independence. Cubans gave themselves to the game with gusto in Tampa, Key West, New York, and elsewhere. The number of Cuban students at American schools and universities had vastly increased as a consequence of Spain's repression during the Ten Years' War (1868–1878). They brought the game back to Cuba in the early 1870s in a more or less organized fashion. Matanceros Nemesio Guillo, José Dolores Amieva, and José's brothers Ricardo and Manuel got the bug in the United States and formed a team in Matanzas early on. It was Cuba's first organized *novena*. Guillo, the team's captain, is rightfully considered the founder of Cuba's baseball on that account. The need for a proper playing field soon became apparent, however. Fortunately, Dr. Martín Junco, a member of the wealthy Matanzas family and an amateur *pelotero* (he played pitcher) found a solution. A tract on the edge of Pueblo Nuevo called "el Palmar de Junco" became a stadium with the addition of bleachers, a canopy and, of course, a diamond. It was the first baseball stadium in Latin America.

Baseball in Cuba provided an early meeting place for the great linguistic miscegenation that has given us Spanglish. The Latino baseball argot, largely a Cuban creation, is a sort of proto-Spanglish—an exercise in borrowing, mixing up, and inventing.

From that day in 1866 all the way down to "El Duque" Hernández, Cubans have been at the forefront of baseball history. They adopted it, giving it a colorful language and more. Cubans introduced the game to Mexico—the first game there was allegedly played in Mérida, Yucatan, although Saltillo,

Coahuila, has a competing claim. They also made history in Mecca itself. In 1871, Esteban Bellán, who had learned the game at Fordham University, played third base, second base, and outfield for the Troy, New York, Haymakers—the first Latin American to play professionally in what became the National League. Actually, Bellán played in the league's first official game. It would be forty years before another Latino played in the big leagues: Alberto Marsáns and Rafael Almeida, both of whom played for the Reds in the 1911 season. The cardenense José de la Caridad Méndez was one of the stars—the first of many—in the great Cuban constellation within the Negro Leagues. He also enjoys the distinction of being the first professional on record wearing a number on his flannel.

If the locus of first contagion was Matanzas, the honor of official primacy—the first recorded and written-about baseball game in Cuba—also belongs indisputably to the fair city by the Yumurí. Matanceros are fiercely proud of that, although, truth be told, the home team was severely trounced on that historic Sunday, December 27, 1874. The opposing teams were Club Matanzas and Club Havana. The game took place at the Palmar de Junco, which has remained hallowed ground to Cuban baseball to this very day.[19] Matanzas' claim to baseball fame, however, rests on firmer ground than fortuitous facts of primacy. The city was also the hometown of some of Cuban baseball's greats, such as Martín Dihigo, José Cardenal, and Leo Cárdenas. Dihigo, in particular, has become a legend in baseball history. Born Martín Magdaleno Dihigo y Llanos in the suburban town of Cidra, he grew up, appropriately enough, in Pueblo Nuevo, within walking distance of the Palmar. A star in the Negro Leagues, he is widely recognized as the most versatile player that ever lived.[20]

That epic first game began in the early afternoon and went on until dusk. Ricardo Mora pitched for the Havanans and scored a home run. But it was the participation of Bellán and Emilio Sabourin (another young Cuban who organized Cuba's first baseball league and died in a Spanish prison during the Cuban War for Independence) that carried the game decisively for the elegantly uniformed Havanans. The score? I wish you hadn't asked. It was 51 to 9. The Palmar has another important first on its records. In 1877, the first international game between a Cuban and a U.S. team took place there also.

My grandfather, Miguel Bretos del Pino, was captivated—and almost literally ensnared—by the American national pastime. He attended Rollins College in Winter Park, Florida. A gifted athlete, he played third base on the varsity team. In 1908 and again in 1909, Rollins won the "Best in Florida"

Fig. 29. *Above:* Matancero Martín Dihigo, the most versatile player in baseball history, on a philatelic item commemorating the Latin American baseball centennial. *Below:* the Rollins College varsity baseball team, 1909. Bretos is in the first row, second from right. (Courtesy Department of College Archives and Special Collections, Olin Library, Rollins College, Winter Park, Florida)

pennant. A photo of the 1909 lineup shows Grandfather in his Rollins flannels. Champions get noticed, and Grandfather was: he was approached by the Cincinnati Reds. Beside himself with joy, he dutifully cabled his father in Matanzas, asking for permission to sign up. The answer was no, so Grandfather went back home, chagrined at not having been among the first Cubans in the big leagues. That honor belonged to Marsáns and Almeida, who played for the Reds two years later. Of course, had my grandfather been able to follow his dream, I would not be here to tell the story.

Nearness to the United States has meant much to Cuba. It has been the source of good and bad things. Some of the good things—Protestantism, advanced technology, investment capital, and baseball—have been very good. Some of the bad things—Guantánamo, Meyer Lansky, and the Platt Amendment (more to follow on that subject)—have been very bad. By the same token, the challenge of nearness has been met by the wisest and the basest responses of the Cuban imagination. Among the wisest is the well-known aphorism of Cuban diplomat and statesman Manuel Márquez Sterling: *a la ingerencia extraña, la virtud doméstica* (to foreign intrusion oppose domestic virtue). Among the basest is the corrosive anti-Yankeeism that has been the cornerstone of Cuba's U.S. policy for half a century, nourished by the equally mindless U.S. embargo.

The distance between Cuba and the United States is not likely to change anytime soon. To ensure both countries' happiness in each other's company, the relationship therefore must. For constructive change to occur, however, one cannot ignore the weight of history, underestimate the power of inertia, or lay aside the Cuban people's aspirations some day to be citizens of a free and democratic society, in the words of José Martí, "with all and for the good of all."

As the nineteenth century drew to a close, the forces of political gravitation John Quincy Adams had talked about suddenly intensified, and the ripe Cuban fruit finally fell into the American basket. Adams had been wrong, however. What looked like an apple to him was in fact a guava. Strange-looking, partially worm-eaten, and redolent of the sharp smells of ripening tropical fruit, the Cuban guava proved unappetizing to the American palate. Cuba might as well make a go of it on her own. Unfortunately, when the time came for the Cubans to make their own guava pastries, the Americans insisted on a recipe for apple pie. It did not work out quite as expected. The events of 1895–1902 and what the new century brought to Cuba and Matanzas will be discussed in chapter 12. But first, some music.

11   Las Alturas de Simpson

YOU COULD READ THIS CHAPTER NOW, immersing yourself in a musical interlude before moving on to the destruction wrought by the independence war of 1895–98, or you could leave this chapter for the end. The choice is yours: in Matanzas you run into music at every turn. (Or, better still if you have a command of Spanish and an interest in the subject, acquaint yourself with the work of the dean of Cuban music scholars, Cristóbal Díaz Ayala. That Dr. Díaz Ayala, an habanero, considers himself a "matancero-maniac"[1] is as serious an accolade to Matanzas' musical prowess as one can imagine.)

Throughout history, the gentle hills of Matanzas have been alive with the sound of music. Indeed, the city of the two rivers is to Cuban music what Bordeaux is to French wines. When maestro Miguel Faílde composed the first danzón, he named it after one of the city's neighborhoods, Las Alturas de Simpson. Aniceto Díaz reminds us in the first stanza of his *danzonete* that it was created *allá en Matanzas*. La Sonora Matancera and the Muñequitos, Cuba's foremost African ensemble, are "de Matanzas." So is Afro-Cuba. I could go on and on, but you get the drift. Like a Michelin star on a restaurant door, an *appellation contrôlée* notice on a bottle of Saint-Émilion, or a Royal Appointment on a bolt of prime-grade Scottish tweed, a "Made in Matanzas" label is well worth displaying when it comes to Cuban music.

Fredrika Bremer discovered the local obsession to her delight in the spring of 1850. While visiting, the Swedish writer was enchanted by the seemingly constant cascade of music all around her. "Nowhere does one hear so much music," she wrote, "the whole day through . . . Cuban dances may be heard from four or five pianos in the neighborhood; and in the evening, a couple of gentlemen come out upon a piazza [porch?] nearly opposite ours, and sing Spanish songs, and accompany themselves on the guitar; a skillful harp-player goes about from door to door, twanging upon the strings as he carries his harp about." Bremer's last evening in town was made unforgettable by a recital en famille. She heard her hostess play the Aragonese *jota* for the last time and enjoyed her host's spirited rendering of "Adeste Fideles" at the organ, even though Christmas was long past. "Never more," she lamented, "shall I feel such an atmosphere . . . never again hear such a flood of joyous music."[2]

Local musicality was evident as far back as 1778, when the town was still in its infancy and the titillating story of the town's first recorded murder was told in classic décima format by an anonymous folk composer. The décima originated in medieval Spain. It went to the Antilles via the Canary Islands and became an essential genre in Cuba and Puerto Rico.[3] A décima may have one or several stanzas of ten eight-syllable lines and diverse rhyming schemes. It is spontaneous and improvisational. The Spanish word that describes it, *repentista*, indicates something that happens or is done suddenly, on impulse. Clever lyrics are strung together on the go and are by their nature evanescent.

Those of Matanzas' first composition have survived because José Rodríguez, a *regidor* (city councilman) wrote down the seventeen stanzas that tell the story of Antonia María Unsiga Gálvez and her lover. The tale of an adulterous couple's plot to do away with a cuckolded husband was just too juicy to let go in a gossipy village. Matanceros must have talked about it for years on end. Pedro Antonio Alfonso, one of Matanzas' first historians, published the Rodríguez transcript in 1854. It is among the earliest décimas recorded in Cuba. The very first date to the time of the British occupation.

The Iberian décima, with Cuban strings and bongos thrown in for good measure, gave rise to one of Cuba's great musical streams. Known as *punto guajiro* or *punto cubano*, it is present from one end of the island to the other, although it is most associated with the central provinces of Matanzas, Las Villas, and Camagüey. In its diverse regional variants, it is Cuba's true "country music." Its never-ending enchantment derives from on-the-spot versification. It is a marvelous mélange of music and poetry seasoned by predictable vocalization. It enlivens communal celebrations with much merriment and hearty applause for clever improvisations on the *laúd* or a few memorable lines convincingly delivered by often competing vocalists.

Matanzas has been fertile soil for punto guajiro. It produced the all-time queen of the genre, Celina González. Born in 1928, she is still going strong as a national icon and one of Cuba's most revered performing artists. The future star first attained national recognition in the late 1940s and 1950s as one half of a duet with her late husband, Reutilio Domínguez, who died in 1971. Known as "Celina y Reutilio," they became one of Cuba's supreme interpreters of the genre. One of their greatest hits was not based on a traditional guajiro theme at all. It was a salute to Changó, the powerful African orisha. Remember, Matanzas is Cuba's Ilé-Ifé.

After performing on her own for a while, she teamed up with her son, also named Reutilio. She has done much to maintain and preserve one of Cuba's essential musical treasures and introduce guajiro music to younger audiences. The vitality of the genre is evident by the currency it is enjoying in, of all places, the mostly urban Cuban American community of South Florida.[4]

The hybrid music of Spain is one of the parents of a large Cuban family. As it was making its way to the Pearl of the Antilles, so too was its eventual consort: the music of Africa. When I finally visited Cuba in 2003, I heard the dim sounds of batá drums in the still air one evening. That night, for the first time, I truly felt I was home again. As a child growing up on the edge of the Barrio de la Marina, I had heard those sounds often. It was always at night, when the air that carried them was redolent of molasses from the Yucayo Rum distillery across the San Juan. Sheltered within a mosquito net, I would lay my head on the pillows and listen to the barely audible sounds of a world nearby yet—to me—deeply mysterious and remote. Over the many years of my exile hearing Afro-Cuban drumming, more than anything else, has always somehow evoked Matanzas.

The batá are the sacred drums of the Yoruba.[5] They are hourglass-shaped and double-headed, meaning that they are played on both ends. Because the heads are asymmetrical—one larger than the other—each produces a different sound. The large head (*enú*) yields more melodic tones; the smaller (*chachá*) has a more rhythmic function. Like most African ritual drums, the batá ensemble is said to be a "family" consisting of a "mother," known as the *iyá*; a "father," known as the *itótele*; and a "child," the *okónkolo*. Duly consecrated batá drums are said to possess a sacred power, *añá*, and may be played only by ordained drummers, known as *olubatá*, subject to strict liturgical rubrics and demanding protocols. The drumming invites the holy orishas into the gathering of the faithful. In a secular guise, the batá ensemble has taken its place among the instruments of Cuban folk and popular music.

According to Fernando Ortiz, the first duly consecrated batás in Cuba—unconsecrated drums already existed—were made by two Yoruba slaves, Atandá and Añabí, who had the proper ritual credentials. Several of the handful of ritual batás made by them or attributed to them ended up in Matanzas. One came into the possession of Miguel Faílde's father, a santero and a noted musician in his own right. At least one was still being played liturgically when Fernando Ortiz published *Los instrumentos de la música afrocubana* in 1952.[6]

Many visitors to Matanzas are attracted by the city's rich Afro-Cuban musical offerings and its reputation as a major center of Afro-Cuban culture. Matanzas is not only one of the handful of places where the sacred drums of the Yoruba were first introduced to Cuba. It is also a major base of the Abakuá secret society—the legendary ñáñigos. Like the Yoruba batá, the ñáñigo drum ensemble is a "family" of drums. Its members are known as Ekué, Ekueñón, Empegó, Bríkamo, and Seseribó.[7] Matanzas is said to be the only place in Cuba where the Arará liturgy has been essentially preserved.[8] It was there also that the late Cuban ethnographer Lydia Cabrera did most of her research and recordings of sacred music in the 1940s and 1950s.[9]

People flock to Matanzas from all over the world to listen to the city's justly famed African ensembles, learn percussion, and polish their skill as *rumberos* in one of the places where the rumba was born. Others are on a spiritual quest and seek initiation into the sacred mysteries of Regla de Ocha or another of the Afro-Cuban religious disciplines. To be initiated in Matanzas is to Santería what being confirmed at Canterbury is to Anglicanism. The efficacy of the sacrament is the same but the venue does make a difference. The Matanzas priesthood zealously guard the holy secrets they alone possess in all of Cuba. For certain rituals, in fact, only Matanzas will do.

Nurtured by a community where drumming is, literally, the language of the gods, neighborhoods such as La Marina–Ojo de Agua and Pueblo Nuevo have been fertile breeding grounds for Matanzas percussionists. The Afro-Cuban musical tradition has found a major vehicle in two contemporary ensembles, Afro-Cuba de Matanzas and Los Muñequitos de Matanzas. Both were founded in Pueblo Nuevo in the 1950s. Afro-Cuba's original name, in fact, was Guaguancó Neopoblano. Some of the all-time master drummers of Cuba, such as the great Francisco Aguabella, were nurtured by that rich soil.

La Marina and Pueblo Nuevo represented concentrations but by no means monopolies of excellence. José Rosario Oviedo, the legendary "Malanga," was from exurban Unión de Reyes. The death of Cuba's timbero mayor in 1923 is famously lamented, of course, in a rumba: "Unión de Reyes llora porque Malanga murió."

> Unión de Reyes mourns
> the greatest of drummers
> Who covered the way with flowers
> From Matanzas to Morón.[10]

Unión had Malanga and Pueblo Nuevo the energy, but La Marina had the character. The neighborhood was built in a slight basin next to where the Yumurí River debouched into the bay (a mangrove swamp at the time of the city's founding in 1693). White matanceros of my day used to refer to La Marina as "allá abajo," literally "down there below," a reference not only to its terrain but also to its place in white matanceros' imagination. At night La Marina became an animated potpourri: sailors looking for action and ladies inviting customers with a "psst, psst" from red-lit windows, an occasional drunken brawl here and there, and, from time to time, the drums from some toque or *bembé*. Even uneducated ears like mine could recognize the presence of virtuoso drumming and out-of-this-world rumberos. The rumba, after all, was invented in places like La Marina.

The rumba did not emerge in complete form in one location. It is a great collective achievement, the end product of an entire culture or, rather, of a mixture of cultures. It has rural as well as urban components. Matanzas shares with Havana the invention of the rumba, which emerged in the western part of the island, just as *son* emerged in the east. There will always be a debate as to details, but one thing is certain: Matanzas yields to no other locale as a primary matrix for the genre.

The word *rumba* itself is derived from *rumbo*, which means "direction," and its verbal form *rumbear*, which implies to go out and about or, if you prefer, to go out and have fun. The African pedigree of the rumba is obvious enough in its instrumentation and highly rhythmic nature. Less evident is its indebtedness to the Spanish tradition, but it is there nonetheless.

There are at least three kinds of rumba: the *yambú*, the *columbia*, and the *guaguancó*. Of the three routines within the so-called rumba complex—all pantomimes of sorts—yambú is the most sedate. The choreography of the yambú re-creates the slow movements of old age, and it is almost always a female dance. It is devoid of the aggressive sensuality that characterizes the other two forms. Columbia derives from the countryside of Matanzas province, where it was created. It is a male—actually, a *macho*—dance that suggests the movements of animals and those of all sorts of daily activities, such as playing ball or cutting cane. Like all manifestations of the rumba, it involves highly competitive performance. A first-rate rumbero has the opportunity to show off (*lucirse*) in the fast and complex but precise stream of movement of this marvelously expressive form of the classic rumba. At its most exciting, columbia involves swift maneuvers with cutting weapons, such as machetes. Dancers receiving gashes and cuts in the heat of the dance is not unheard of.

And then there is the guaguancó. Mongo Santamaría, the eminent Cuban percussionist, once compared guaguancó to "a Cuban black trying to sing flamenco."[11] As Cristóbal Díaz Ayala points out, the guaguancó is proud of its urban origins. It emerged in Matanzas' docks amidst the bitter struggles for fair labor conditions for the port stevedores. That guaguancó is erotic is an understatement. "Sexually explicit" better captures its genius, for it is essentially a mating dance. Its theme is seduction and its ultimate objective copulation and sexual surrender. It is consequently danced by a male-female couple, with the man enticing the woman, who variously responds to and draws away from his advances. In the end, she gives in. The climax of the dance is the *vacunao*, a series of steps in which the man thrusts his pelvis at the woman in an undisguised allusion to penetration. After the vacunao takes place, the now-tame woman goes through the motions of homemaking and taking care of her man; in other words, subordination.[12]

"Rhumba," a derivative of Cuban rhythms, became an established ballroom dance in the United States in the 1930s. The intermediate *h* is anathema to rumba purists, who view it as Yankee nonsense. Son, rather than rumba, seems to be the likelier source of Cuban musical DNA for the hybrid genre, which soon found a niche in Hollywood and popular magazines. In 1935, George Raft, not yet typecast as Hollywood's ultimate mobster, danced his way to the lady's heart in the feature film *Rhumba*. Raft was sighted in Matanzas from time to time during the 1950s. He was a Cuba fan and kept a home in Havana.

Being Cuban, matanceros make music with everything and anything. The instruments of Cuban percussion, in particular, betray their birth and survival amidst the hardships of slavery and poverty. They are a combination of ancient wisdom and magnificent improvisation. The clave, literally the "key" to Cuban rhythm, is basically two hardwood sticks. But careful, matters are not that simple: one is male and the other female, and their protocols are quite different. One is cradled in the hand and gets beaten; the other does the beating—you can guess which is which.

The clave, which according to Fernando Ortiz originated in Cuba, is the main carrier of the *cinquillo*, the building block of virtually all Cuban music.[13] It consists of either three short knocks of the claves followed by two long ones, or two long ones followed by three short ones, depending on the genre. Expressed in musical notation, the cinquillo looks like this:

The *cencerro* is a cow bell. The *quijada de burro*, as its name reveals, is but a donkey's jaw—the loose teeth rattling against their bony sockets produce the sound. The classic rumba is played with *cajones*, that is, empty wooden crates, and with *cucharas* (spoons)—you name it. At the other end of the spectrum, José White, Matanzas' amazing violin prodigy, made music with a Stradivarius on the world's most exclusive stages.

Sometime in 1830, when the city's population was pushing thirty thousand and the sugar boom was on, *La Aurora de Matanzas* ran a classified ad offering a Stradivarius for sale. "One would not expect to come across such an offer in an obscure Spanish American provincial city," wrote city historian Raúl Ruiz, who reported the unusual offer, "but then Matanzas was not just any place." At the very least, the sale of so fine an instrument in Matanzas implied a certain level of musical finesse: the presence of folks who could do more than just fiddle around.

In 1828 the Philharmonic Society was established, the second on the island after Havana's. It would become the city's main booster and patron of classical music, although its bread and butter was organizing the balls that the dance-crazed Cubans of the day demanded.[14] After many years of a virtual monopoly on music by free *pardos* and *morenos* (people of color), the first European teacher of music hung out his shingle in 1829. Named Mariano Berga i Valart, he was a Catalonian from Mataró who offered tuition in "music, piano, guitar, viola, cello, flute, clarinet, fagot and oboe" at a clothing shop named Las Ninfas on Medio Street. By 1835 two music schools, Santa Matilde and Santa Cecilia, were functioning.[15] The Philharmonic Academy was established in 1841.

Matanzas' paramount classical musician of the nineteenth century was José

Silvestre White y Laffite.[16] A world-class violinist and inspired composer, he wrote the habanera *La bella cubana*, one of Cuba's essential and most evocative pieces of music. White was born in Matanzas on December 31, 1835. His mother, María Escolástica Laffite, bore him out of wedlock. It was not until 1855 that his father, Carlos White, recognized him. The house where he was born still stands and served for many years as a convent for the Servants of Mary, an order of nuns. It is located across the street from the legendary Sauto Theater, where White would play later on as a famous violinist. The elder White had a grocery shop called La Armonía at No. 56 Gelabert Street. He was also a musician and his precocious son's first music instructor. As a child, young "Joseíto" would play at the shop, delighting customers with his talent. He received his first violin lessons from José Miguel Román, a victim of the wave of terror of 1844.

White's great career break came when Louis Moreau Gottschalk visited Matanzas in May 1854. The American pianist and composer habitually shared billing with local artists wherever he performed, and asked for nominations. Somebody recommended White, and Gottschalk invited the then nineteen-year-old Cuban to perform with him. By then White had already composed a mass for two voices and orchestra, and was locally recognized as a prodigy.

Gottschalk's tour was ill-timed. President Franklin Pierce was plotting to annex Cuba and pressuring the Spanish government to sell it to the United States. Gottschalk ran into trouble, almost went broke, and at one point even offered his Pléyel piano for sale. Fortunately, he was able to line up enough gigs to make his venture worthwhile if not lucrative. The trip, his first visit to Cuba, was enriching in other ways: it thoroughly immersed him in Cuba's musical ambiance. Pity that his farewell piece, *Adiós a Cuba*, is lost.

Gottschalk's visit to Matanzas reveals much about the town's social milieu of the day. Matanzas in the 1850s was at the climax of the sugar boom. Enriched by sugar though still somewhat rough around the edges, Matanzas was then the Dallas of Cuba. Whatever habaneros had, matanceros just had to have as well, and if that meant Louis Moreau Gottschalk, then so be it. Gottschalk's presence in Matanzas, moreover, furthered the interests of two important social and economic cliques: the small but influential foreign, mostly American, community of sugar planters and entrepreneurs, and the increasingly powerful criollo sugar sector. The former resonated to the fact that Gottschalk was American; the latter to the fact that he was world-class.

S. Frederick Starr, Gottschalk's biographer, reports that the main recital in Matanzas was "a mess." Three recitals were offered for early in May, but it was not until May 21 that Gottschalk and his young protégé were able to perform at the Principal on the Calle de Manzano. Despite Gottschalk's fame and White's locally known virtuosity, their recital was no competition for the alternative entertainments available to audiences that evening: Robreño's zarzuela troupe and Barnum's Swiss Bell-Ringers. The recital failed to draw a full house. The *La Aurora* concert reviewer bemoaned the fact that Matanzas' supposedly cultured audience went for "trained dog shows and monkeys" to the detriment of an outstanding classical program.

Starr offers an explanation for this apparently inexplicable indifference by what was assumed to be an eager audience facing a unique opportunity. The problem, argues Starr, was that matanceros considered piano fantasies based on William Tell or the Carnival of Venice to be alien works.[17] Perhaps, but more likely Gottschalk's choice of White, a mulatto, to share the billing with him may have been a bit too much for the thoroughly racist matanceros of 1854. Because these things lay in the realm of the unspeakable, one would not expect to see them reported.

The encounter between White and Gottschalk was fateful. Impressed by the young man's virtuosity, Gottschalk sponsored his application to the Paris Conservatory, where he was accepted in 1855. The next year he won first prize in violin. The rest is music history. White was an amazing interpreter who mastered sixteen instruments. He was renowned as one of the world's top violinists of his time, an honor he shares with a contemporary and fellow Afro-Cuban, Claudio Brindis de Salas.[18] In 1875 he returned to Cuba after years of residence in Europe but, suspected by the authorities of separatist activities, he had to leave again. He served for a while as director of the Imperial Conservatory in Rio de Janeiro and died in Paris on March 12, 1918.

Fig. 30. Racism at work: José White in a photograph (*left*) and on a 1955 postage stamp. With a nose job and a new hairdo courtesy of the postal artist, voilà, White becomes whiter.

The Haitian revolution, a key event in the history of Cuba's economy, was no less so in that of Cuban music. Many members of the French planter class who escaped with their lives made it to Cuba, in many cases with their slaves. Their musical heritage determined the way future Cuban music would sound and dancers would move. At the heart of that heritage was the French *contredanse*. A corruption of the English "country dance," contredanse was rooted in the Anglo-Celtic tradition. It was a figure dance, a collective experience involving easily learned steps and the exchange of partners. A descendant on the Anglo side of the family is American square dancing, with its promenades and its do-si-dos.

Although derived originally from English prototypes, the French contredanse that arrived in Cuba had gone through a remarkable evolution. As a dance form favored by the petty nobility and the emerging middle classes, it was Baroque-ized during the seventeenth century in France and thoroughly creolized in Saint-Domingue itself. In the words of Alejo Carpentier:

> In essence, it responded—although with more reserve and rules—to a mechanism analogous to the *calenda*, the *congó*, and other rumbas created by blacks and mestizos in the Americas. This action-filled choreography took greater license as it grew more popular. The black musicians of Saint-Domingue adopted it with enthusiasm, imbuing it with a rhythmic vivacity overlooked by the original model.[19]

What came to Cuba in the exiles' baggage was thoroughly processed, predigested for rapid absorption by Cuba's eager dancers and musicians. Most of all, the Saint-Domingue exiles came to stay, in numbers large enough to be influential, and they settled throughout the island, notably in Santiago de Cuba and Matanzas. And so the French, formerly English, formerly Celtic, and now creolized country dance became the thoroughly Cuban *contradanza*.

By the late 1870s the Cuban contradanza had enjoyed half a century of undisputed hegemony on the dance floor. Called also—quite incorrectly—simply *danza* and at times *habanera*, the lively contradanza reached extraordinary heights and found sustained public favor at the hands of Manuel Saumell and Ignacio Cervantes. (The danza proper was a distinct genre that did not long survive, possibly because of its strong European flavor.) Contradanza became, in fact, the sturdy trunk from which successive generations of popular Cuban music sprouted.

As the nineteenth century entered its last third, the venerable genre was showing signs of fatigue. A renewal was needed, and a brilliant mulatto cornetist, Miguel Faílde Pérez, a remarkable musician, was ready for the task. Faílde's father, Cándido, was a santero of legendary piety and an accomplished musician. Matancero through and through, Faílde was born at Caobas sugar mill near Limonar in 1852 and lived his entire life in Matanzas.[20] He died in 1922 at his home on Velarde Street, which is today a memorial to him. Faílde himself described the setting in which the classic danzón was born:

> Back in those days, square dancing . . . was very popular in Matanzas. It was executed by up to twenty couples carrying arches and floral bouquets. It was really a figure dance and its steps were tied to the rhythm of the habanera. . . . The director of this figure dance invited me to write music ad hoc for, until then, the couples executed the figures singing viva voce. So, as I wrote, the idea of what we now call danzón occurred to me, so I jotted it down and rehearsed it. Musicians and dancers loved it, so it became popular in short order.[21]

The rehearsals took place at the Quinta Luna, one of the luxury villas perched on the hills surrounding the city, so it was there that the first danzón was actually played. The credit of being the official birthplace of the danzón, however, rightly belongs to the Liceo Artístico y Literario (then known as Club de Matanzas). The first danzón, "Las Alturas de Simpson," music and choreography by Miguel Faílde, debuted under the maestro's baton at the New Year's Eve ball of 1878–79.

The ball was the high point of the social season. Samuel Hazard, who attended a Liceo ball in the late 1860s, has left us a marvelous description of the party. The elegant crowd danced and sipped refreshments in the brilliantly lit interior while a mass of people crowded against the open windows and danced in the street. The format was much the same and the setting little changed when I attended my one and only New Year's ball as a young man eighty years later in 1959. It was a memorable occasion: not only did I get to dance with a gorgeous young lady formally in public for the first time, it was also the Liceo's own centennial and the ball was billed as historic. Fidel Castro had been in power for a year and passions were running high. Some Liceo members were fervent Fidelistas and wanted to open the doors to "the people," which caused palpable trepidation. The conservatives won, however, and "the people" stayed out, dancing in the streets as always. In hindsight the ball was historic in unanticipated ways. The Castro government confiscated all private clubs in 1960, so the 1959–60 ball turned out to be the last.

All of that, of course, lay in the unfathomable future when Faílde raised his hand and the orchestra launched into a spirited performance of "Las Alturas de Simpson." Guests at the ball immediately realized they were in the presence of a winner. The new genre was strictly instrumental—no vocalist and no lyrics. This was music to dance to. No more quadrilles or figure dancing: the danzón involves a couple caught in a sensuous pas de deux with a premium on virtual intimacy. The best *danzoneros,* in fact, should be able to go through the motions of the dance *en un ladrillo* (on a brick). There's no exchange of partners either. The dance steps amount to an exquisitely sublimated mating dance that carries the couple through the motions of courtship and surrender in a way sensuous enough to be exciting yet decorous enough to be danced in front of a jaundice-eyed chaperone.

Aniceto Díaz's danzonete, a popular Matanzas spin-off of the danzón, was launched at the Casino Español's New Year's ball in 1929. It was a very formal affair with men in black ties and women in furs—mercifully Cuba can be fairly cool at that time of the year. Family tradition has it that Aniceto was initially hesitant to play his first danzonete, "Rompiendo la rutina," at that time and place, but my grandfather, Miguel Bretos del Pino, who was on the Casino's board of directors, twisted his arm. Neither regretted it, for the ball made music history and "Rompiendo la rutina" became wildly popular.

My grandmother Consuelo, who was in her early thirties then, had vivid memories of that evening. "Aquello fue el acabóse," she used to recount. "We went wild." Aniceto's band had to play several encores while his appreciative audience delighted in the rhythm and the lyrics' explicit accolade to the city:

> There in Matanzas has been born
> A new ballroom dance.[22]

Although the invention of the danzonete may seem relatively inconsequential, it marked a milestone in the development of Cuban popular music. Music historian Francisco Ojeda notes its critical importance as a fusion between the danzón, by then declining in popularity, and the increasingly popular son. He writes,

> The huge popularity of the son caused a division of the Cuban dancing public into competing factions: soneros and danzoneros. Aniceto Díaz, a

young clarinetist deeply troubled by the situation, set out to create a style that would lure back lost audiences, or at least satisfy both sides of the divided dancing public.[23]

The presence of lyrics and a vocalist was among the most popular features of the son, so Díaz' solution was to simplify the danzón format and introduce a vocalist. The formula proved effective and lasting, and led, among other things, to the modern danzón that was the trademark of Barbarito Diez and the Antonio María Romeu Orchestra.

A remarkable Matanzas-born musical figure of fin de siècle fame was Juan Francisco "Tata" Pereira. Trained as a flutist in Havana, Pereira joined the Cuban insurgent army in 1896 at age twenty-two after a brief career in sundry orchestras. As a soldier he saw combat, but his main contribution was musical. Jointly with "Chencho" Cruz, he formed an insurgent military band that well served the *mambí,* or insurgent, forces until the end of the war. In peacetime he founded Havana's Police Band, precursor to the renowned Municipal Band. He crowned his colorful career manufacturing pianola rolls.[24]

The twentieth-century pop ensemble was the brainchild of yet another matancero, Valentín Cané. Under his guidance, La Sonora Matancera made Cuban music history. The fabled ensemble celebrated its eightieth anniversary not too long ago, an achievement comparable only to the Cienfuegos-based Orquesta Aragón, founded in 1930. Over the years, the ensemble's vocalists—among them Bienvenido Granda, Bobby Capó, Daniel Santos, and Leo Marini—have become legendary figures, especially a slender young woman from Havana gifted with a voice that could ring like a trumpet or flow like molasses: the future "Queen of Salsa," the late, legendary Celia Cruz. Indeed, for the better part of the 1940s and 1950s, the orchestra's billing was "Celia Cruz y la Sonora Matancera" in recognition of her unique charisma and talent. Celia met the love of her life, Pedro Knight, in the Sonora. Knight was an accomplished musician in his own right. They left Cuba in 1960, never to return.

Nothing in La Sonora's modest origins betrayed its future greatness. On January 12, 1924, a group of young performers met at 21 Salamanca Street between Ayuntamiento and Jovellanos, in the classic Matanzas barrio of Ojo de Agua. The neighborhood's name harked back to the source that had supplied drinking water to the early settlement.[25] The springs still run under the streets, producing slippery, slimy sidewalks when they overflow. In 1924, as now, the neighborhood was predominantly Afro-Cuban. Unlike the adjacent, pictur-

Fig. 31. La Sonora Matancera and Celia Cruz in the golden age of radio, ca. 1950. Pedro Knight, Celia's future husband, stands immediately behind the diva.

esque La Marina, it was the abode of Matanzas' hard-working, struggling black middle class.

Valentín Cané was the meeting's host. He played the *tres cubano*, a kind of guitar with three double strings. His aim was to launch a sonero ensemble. The group was at various times called Tuna Liberal; Septeto Soprano; and Estudiantina Sonora Matancera, shortened to La Sonora Matancera in 1932. The founding members were Pablo "Babu" Vásquez (bass); Eugenio Pérez (vocalist); Manuel "Jimagua" Sánchez (timbal); Ismael Goberna (trumpet); and Domingo Medina, José Manuel Valera, Julio Gobín, and Juan Bautista Llopis (guitarists).

La Sonora—which, as its name indicates, was proudly matancera—has remained a protean ensemble, always open to innovation yet the possessors of a unique style and a remarkable capacity to cross Cuba's racial divides and appeal to a general audience. It was the first Cuban ensemble invited to play in Cuba's presidential palace. La Sonora's extraordinary popularity was to some extent based on its ability to exploit the new mass media of radio (beginning in the 1930s) and film (beginning in the 1940s).

Classical music lived on in Matanzas. My own childhood would have been immeasurably poorer without Matanzas' excellent chamber orchestra led by maestro Mario Argenter. Taught music by an aunt, he went on to become a cellist and, in 1949, founded the chamber orchestra. It was not easy. Such ventures never are, but at least the sometimes philistine but tolerant Matanzas society of his day paid little heed to allegations that he was a card-carrying

Communist. A true believer in the power of music in a society, Argenter, who made a living as an electrician, was a one-man crusader for good music in the community. In 1962 he became the founding director of Matanzas' symphony orchestra.[26]

Also significant in local twentieth-century music history was the work of Rafael Somavilla. Born in Matanzas in 1899, Somavilla was a trumpeter by training. A memorable teacher, he made a remarkable contribution as director of the José White Conservatory in his hometown. His public impact, however, was as leader of his own Orquesta Rafael Somavilla, which he founded in 1923.[27]

Matanceros have made distinguished contributions to the bolero, the Latin American romantic song. Frank Domínguez' "Tu me acostumbraste . . ." (You Got Me Used to . . .) was an immediate success and has become a classic in the canon of boleros. Its encoded celebration of homoeroticism resonates today in ways it could not when it was composed in the 1950s. Leaving no doubt as to where his heart lay, Domínguez also wrote "Luna sobre Matanzas" (Moon over Matanzas).

Another world-famous Matanzas bolero, Nilo Meléndez' "Aquellos ojos verdes" (Green Eyes) has been recorded by numerous interpreters in countless languages but most famously and unforgettably by Nat King Cole. Cole's silky interpretation, diction-perfect but delivered in the tonality of his American English may well be the greatest global hit in the history of the genre. Meléndez himself pursued an international career arranging scores for Hollywood movies. He died in Burbank, California, in 1987.

Music is deeply imprinted on Matanzas' DNA. On December 11, 1916, a child was born there who would in time revolutionize popular music and dance worldwide. His name was Dámaso Pérez Prado. His father was a journalist, his mother a schoolteacher. Growing up in a modest but loving and secure environment, young Dámaso was a child prodigy. He studied music and piano in his native city and soon was playing piano and organ in local clubs. He began to arrange music for La Sonora Matancera. In 1940, he moved definitively to Havana.

Two years earlier, the brothers Orestes and Israel López of the Arcaño y sus Maravillas ensemble had created an innovative arrangement based on the danzón's third segment, into which they incorporated a syncopated *estribillo* or *montuno*. Pérez Prado took this core and developed it into the dance and rhythm creation that became the rage in the 1950s: the mambo. He died in exile in Mexico, a country that adopted him as much as he embraced it.

As city historian Raúl Ruiz reminds us, an obscure Spanish colonial city dealing in Stradivari was no ordinary place. A provincial city that cultivated Spanish and western music with educated appreciation while preserving the instruments and sounds of the African tradition with faith, devotion, and skill is no ordinary place either. No ordinary city could have produced White, Faílde, Aniceto, Cané, and Pérez Prado; world-class boleros, danzones and danzonetes, mambo, rumba, and guaguancó; Afro-Cuba and Muñequitos, not to mention the multitude of forgotten or little-known musicians and dancers whose contributions live on embedded in the music itself and its choreography. Without Matanzas, Cuba's musical score would be missing too many chords.

12   Forget the *Maine*!

THE USS *MAINE* ENTERED HAVANA HARBOR on January 25, 1898. She docked near the spot from where the *Neptuno* had left for Matanzas one sunny morning of 1819 on the first scheduled steamboat run in the Spanish-speaking world. The mood, festive then, was somber now. A rebellion raged from one end of the island to the other, threatening American lives and property. President William McKinley had sent the *Maine* to Havana to show the flag. On February 15, a huge explosion sent her steaming into legend with more than 250 casualties. "Remember the *Maine*!" became the battle cry for an all-but-inevitable conflict.

The blast was heard around the world. It rattled windows in faraway Melbourne, where the premiers from the six disparate Australian colonies were busy drafting a federal charter. When they learned of the *Maine*'s loss, the Australian premiers did something unprecedented and unique. Anticipating federation by almost two years, they cabled official condolences to President McKinley on behalf of Australia and "in the name of the Australian people." Historians cite their message as the first exercise of Australian sovereignty, and the president's response as its first formal, if oblique acknowledgment.[1] Curiously, Australia (1900) and Cuba (1902) were the first two decolonialized nations of the twentieth century. Where Cuba had lagged behind she now led the pack. In any case, Cuba's exceptionalism and penchant for global notoriety long antedate the Castro revolution.

The *Maine* tragedy led to the so-called Spanish-American War and the

United States' debut as a Johnny-come-lately colonial power. Whether one cheers America's new role to the stirring tunes of a John Philip Sousa march or deplores it as a loss of American purpose, 1898 was a watershed. For Spaniards, it stands as *el Desastre* (the Disaster). For Cubans it is a deeply ambivalent moment. The *Maine* explosion has resonated in Cuban history down to our own day, its adverse consequences relentlessly amplified by the Castro regime's propaganda.

The *Maine* memorial, commissioned to Matanzas architect Félix Cabarrocas in 1925, is one of Havana's best-known landmarks. It stands near the former American Embassy, built in 1953 in an elegant design by the Chicago firm of Harrison and Abramovitz. The *Maine* memorial is a stunning composition. Until it was sent crashing down by a demolition crane on January 18, 1961, a bronze American eagle perched on two slender marble columns flanked by cannons from the star-crossed vessel.

The eagle's demise was not an accident but a purposeful act of grand vandalism, the climax of an auto-da-fé broadcast on radio and television to the entire country. The moment was critical. President Eisenhower had just severed diplomatic relations with Cuba and President Kennedy was hours away from the White House. Fidel Castro officiated and delivered an oration about Yankee imperialism and its dark legacy in Cuba. To leave no doubt as to the monster's evil ways, years later Castro had an explanation of the *Maine*'s true significance inserted on the monument itself. Summarized, it states that the U.S. government knowingly sent her and her crew to their doom in a perverse search for a pretext to intervene and prevent a Cuban victory in the rebellion.

What thoughts crossed the mind of this son of a Galician veteran of the *guerra de Cuba* we shall never know, but Fidel's popularity in Spain has always been high. The desecration of the Maine memorial was an important symbolic event and a significant milestone in the ideological itinerary of the Castro revolution. The falling eagle dramatically asserted that, having defeated the tyranny of Batista, Cuba's Maximum Leader was now ready to take on the far more intractable tyranny of nearness.

One could but should not read Freud into this event. A simpler explanation is that Castro, though perhaps contemptuous of geography, knew his Cuban history well. He knew that historical grievances, if properly harnessed, conferred power. Next morning, a copycat Matanzas mob smashed a plaque near Liberty Square commemorating Vice President King's accession. It was open season on American eagles in public places from one end of the country to the other. (Except on quarters, of course; many people were feverishly hoarding whatever American currency was left in Cuba, just in case.)

One could with equal certainty speak of Cuban affinity and love or of Cuban resentment towards the United States. The relationship is truly of the love-hate kind, as only family relationships can be. To understand the resentment, however, it would be helpful to revisit one of its sources, the "Spanish-American" War and its aftermath, and see it as many Cubans do. This may seem to take us away from Matanzas, but it doesn't really. Matanceros are an important, if often unremarked, part of that story.

What Cubans call the War for Independence—the War of '95, if you wish—had already made history before the U.S. intervened. It uncannily presaged things we associate with the fast-approaching twentieth century. Long before the Vietcong made this lesson painfully evident to the French at Dien Bien Phu, and to the Americans later, the Cuban war of '95 demonstrated that a determined and capable guerrilla army could bring a much larger regular force to grief. The concentration camp also had its first dress rehearsal in Cuba in 1897. Spanish *trochas* anticipated the Maginot Line and, in a sense, the Berlin Wall.

Forget the *Maine*. The war did not begin in Washington or Madrid in April 1898. It began at Ibarra, a hamlet near Matanzas, on the morning of February 24, 1895. When the USS *Maine* called at Havana three years later, Spain was broke and Cuba devastated. The United States declared war on Spain in April 1898. Spain sued for peace in August. American forces saw little combat, unless mosquitoes count as belligerents.

One of the positive outcomes of the war, in fact, was the effective prophylaxis of yellow fever based on the work of a Cuban physician, Carlos J. Finlay, an effort to which Matanzas' own Dr. Juan Guiteras y Gener contributed significantly. Dr. Finlay, a graduate of Jefferson Medical College in Philadelphia, Pennsylvania, was the first ever to postulate that insects, such as mosquitoes, might be vectors of disease. His hypothesis turned out to be correct. It held the key to the prevention of the disease, albeit not yet to a cure. The thoroughness with which Finlay was excised from the U.S.-sponsored narrative of the conquest of the disease never fails to rankle Cubans regardless of race, class, or political views.[2]

Swift victory in Cuba had nothing to do with muscular America encountering effete, degenerate Spain, a racist theme popularized by the yellow press of the time. Many American generals of Spanish-American War vintage were cholesterol-challenged. William Shafter, the commandant of U.S. forces in Cuba, was grossly obese. His Spanish and Cuban counterparts were svelte by comparison. The war had farcical elements. Teddy Roosevelt's charge up San Juan Hill, a stunt tinged with epic colors by wartime and electoral propaganda, was no more a charge than San Juan is a hill.

"From beginning to end," admitted U.S. envoy to Britain John Hay to Roosevelt with unbecoming cynicism, "it has been a splendid little war."[3] It was consequential, to be sure. The United States, tempted by the easy fare, helped itself to a bellyful of indigestible morsels like the Philippines and Puerto Rico, but that is another story.

What should have been an exemplary case of collaboration between a free-dom-loving power and a small nation in pursuit of its own liberty—or three nations if you count the Philippines and Puerto Rico, where pro-independence feelings were also strong—was awkwardly played out as a crude exercise in raw military expansionism. By 1898, all the Americans had to do after witnessing the suicide of the Spanish fleet at Santiago and Manila, was to accept the Spanish army's surrender. In Cuba they did so with no grace whatsoever. General Calixto García's troops had kept the Spanish army bottled up in the city of Santiago virtually for the duration, but he, like other Cuban officers throughout the island, was pointedly excluded from the surrender ceremony by American military authorities as a palliative to Spanish pride.

To Cubans the war was not little, and it was far from splendid. For Matanzas, in particular, it was a scourge of biblical proportions, as I will discuss. Most important, the war of '95 was but the third act of a drama that spanned two generations. Let us therefore set our time machine to October 10, 1868. That is the day the Ten Years' War, Cuba's first struggle for independence, formally began at La Demajagua, a tiny sugar mill near Manzanillo. The city of Manzanillo then was part of what became Oriente province ten years later and is now a provincial capital in its own right.[4] The mill's owner, Carlos Manuel de Céspedes y Quesada, proclaimed the island to be free from Spain and became the first president of the Cuban Republic in Arms. All Cubans honor him as the Padre de la Patria, the Father of the Fatherland.

Céspedes freed his own slaves and gave his movement an abolitionist cast. Slavery was not important in eastern Cuba. There was very little sugar made there and, consequently, few slaves. That in no way diminishes the nobility or significance of the gesture, however. Céspedes decreed abolition knowing full well that in so doing he would lose support for national independence in the slaveholding west. But he also understood the profound contradiction of a free nation full of enslaved people. When given the choice between the expedient and the principled, he chose the latter.

After scoring a few initial victories, the Cuban insurgents occupied Bayamo, a key communications center in the Cauto River valley. Unable to defend it from Spanish regulars, they withdrew and burned the city. The Bayamo episode was a heroic moment, no doubt, but a tactical blunder that demonstrated at the outset and in the most dramatic of ways the rebels' inability to hold a town. Céspedes died by his own hand while surrounded by Spanish troops at San Lorenzo, his estate in the Sierra Maestra, in February 1874.

Spain managed to keep the insurgency confined to the eastern part of the island. A handful of uprisings in the Matanzas region between late 1868 and early 1869 were swiftly and severely repressed. On Christmas Eve 1869 José Eleuterio "Tello" Lamar, a brilliant young man and a member of one of Matanzas' most elite families, was shot by a firing squad. His execution had a chilling effect on would-be rebels. A major city street was renamed after him following independence. Toward the end of the conflict, insurgent troops under Brigadier Henry "el Inglesito" Reeves and Lieutenant Carlos Agüero roamed the countryside torching a handful of sugar mills and many cane fields. This was a preview of what the next stage of the long conflict would bring.

Exemplary terror was Spain's prescription for western Cuba. In 1871, seven students of medicine at the University of Havana were charged with desecrating the tomb of a Spanish loyalist writer, summarily tried by a kangaroo military court, and shot. One of the defendants, Carlos Verdugo, was home in Matanzas on the day the alleged desecration took place. The colonial authorities did not let such trifles bother them: he was shot with the others, and damn them all. The incident resonates in Cuban history to this day. The anniversary of their execution is a Memorial Day of sorts for Cuba's schools.

State-condoned terrorism was the preserve of a paramilitary corps known as the Real Cuerpo de Nobles Vecinos, or Voluntarios for short. The "Volunteers," a vigilante militia, were recruited from the ranks of the uprooted and the scared: young Spaniards hoping to make it in Cuba and far away from their homes, villages, and families. To them, terrorizing those who would cut Cuba away from Mother Spain was a patriotic duty. It could be fun, too. They got to wear a uniform, and membership was a source of identity and reassurance in a world full of uncertainty and menace.

The Voluntarios could be silly when they were not being brutal, and often they were both. In Cuba circa 1868, Spaniards were called *gorriones* (sparrows). One day a Voluntario found a dead sparrow on a street. Could it have been murdered by some evil separatist cat? (A cat was actually tried, convicted, and shot near Havana for such an offense.) The sparrow was buried with full honors due to a captain-general killed in combat. In Matanzas, the bird lay in state with an honor guard and all the trimmings, including military bands and flags flying at half-staff.[5]

All in all, repression might well have been unnecessary in western Cuba, where independence was at best a hard sell. Unlike in the Oriente region, where sugar was of relatively little consequence, the west had much to lose from any harm to the sugar economy. In addition, slavery and the large black population gave pause to the landed, educated criollo elites such as Matanzas' Señorío, presumably those most likely to lead an effort to secede from Spain.

In the east, a combination of the insurgents' chronic inability to overcome factionalism and bloody-minded regionalism coupled with a shrewd application of counterinsurgency tactics by the Spanish regular army stalemated the patriot effort soon enough. The Spanish controlled the cities and towns, and the patriots roamed the countryside while their Republic in Arms government managed to stay one step ahead of the Spanish army.

When it came in 1878, the negotiated end of the conflict was by all accounts welcome in Matanzas. The truce was commemorated with the dedication of Concordia Bridge over the Yumurí, an elegant span that has become the city's logo. *Autonomismo*, the movement for home rule, a middle position between colonial status and complete independence, gained considerable popularity in Cuba during the truce years that followed the Ten Years' War. Matanzas, ever moderate and pragmatic, was one of the sturdiest political bases of home rule. "Autonomist" thought found expression through newspapers such as the old *Aurora*, and political mobilization was articulated around institutions such as the Matanzas Club (formerly the Liceo Artístico y Literario). Autonomismo was ready-made for the Matanzas temperament: it was genteel, conciliatory, verbal, and peaceful. It placed a premium on the power to persuade and the ability to compromise. Speeches, not guns, were its weapons.

Matanzas contributed impressive human resources to the cause of home rule. One-half of the thirteen signatories of the Autonomist Liberal Party's Manifesto of 1878 were matanceros like Miguel Figueroa, José Antonio

Cortina, and Eliseo Giberga. All three were gifted communicators who played distinguished roles in the politics of late colonial Cuba. So indeed was the party's first president, José María de la Cruz Gálvez.

The heroic but ultimately unsuccessful Ten Years' War had two important consequences. First, it spawned a remarkably capable cadre of guerrilla leaders: Máximo Gómez, Antonio Maceo, Calixto García, and many others, both black and white, who learned in the school of hard knocks the skills that would make them legendary years later. Second, Spanish repression generated Cuba's first historic exodus, when thousands of Cuban separatists sought refuge in Tampa, Key West, and New York.

José Martí's great contribution was that he picked up the pieces of the failed 1868–78 movement and reconstituted them into a formidable effort that culminated in the 1895 war. This he accomplished by sheer talent, perseverance, and a remarkable vision of a future free Cuba. He disseminated that vision masterfully through his charisma as a public speaker, his gifts as a writer, and his remarkable organizational skills.

Mindful of the flaws and errors of the Ten Years' War, Martí and his associates were determined not to fall into the same traps. Hostilities would commence simultaneously in the east and the west on February 24, 1895. Ibarra, a hamlet not far from Matanzas, and Baire, near Santiago de Cuba, were the localities chosen for the pronouncements. The official national holiday is known as the "Grito de Baire." Why not Ibarra? I will discuss that later.

The well-laid plans for the Ibarra uprising deflated when key conspirators failed to show up at the appointed site early in the morning of the twenty-fourth. Juan Gualberto Gómez, the brilliant mulatto revolutionist, was one who did. He was born in 1854 at Vellocino, a sugar mill near Sabanilla del Encomendador, a few miles from the epicenter of the slave revolts of 1843. Juan Gualberto's parents, Fermín Gómez and Serafina Ferrer, bought his freedom when he was still in his mother's womb. As a young man he was sent by his parents to Paris to learn carpentry and coach making. They were aiming high and wanted their son to be at the very top of the colored artisan class. Juan Gualberto's wings were big enough to carry him much higher, however. He had a keen intellect, a thirst for learning, and an indomitable will. Instead of becoming a crack coach maker, he became a journalist, a radical advocate of Cuban independence, and Martí's closest confidant and collaborator.

When news of the Ibarra pronouncement reached Matanzas, a train full of Spanish troops was dispatched immediately to put down the rebellion. The few would-be insurgents on the scene had to scatter, losing in the process a large Cuban flag that was subsequently exhibited to the populace from the balcony of the Palace of the Captains-General in Havana.

Some separatists were killed, most prominently the local patriot Domingo Mujica Carratalá. Mujica, an inveterate conspirator, was not a particularly notable figure, but he enjoys a posthumous fame of sorts as the first casualty of the war. He was dispatched by firing squad shortly after Ibarra, which prompted Matanzas poet Bonifacio Byrne to write a memorable sonnet that lives on in Cuban patriotic lore:

> He died bravely, facing the sea,
> Bathed in the glow of new daylight
> Noble, serene, and strong his sight;
> His head held high, his heart at peace.[6]

The sonnet, posted anonymously on the wall of City Hall, was promptly copied and disseminated. The authorship did not long remain a secret in gossipy Matanzas, and Byrne had to seek the safety of exile. The protomartyr's honor accruing to Mujica might have gone instead to the Matanzas patriot Antonio de Jesús López Coloma, another of Juan Gualberto Gómez' co-conspirators. López Coloma was captured four days after Ibarra but the Spanish delayed his execution by months to the detriment of his posthumous fame. (Matancero to the core, he was lost when he chivalrously decided to stay with his betrothed, Amparo Orbe del Valle. They married while he was on death row.)[7]

The crucial role of women in the Cuban struggles for independence was neglected until the advent of feminist historiography. The stories of Mariana Grajales and Lucía Iñiguez are secure in Cuban lore, their role as Spartan mothers firmly anchored in posterity's imagination.[8] The considerably less famous, such as Ana Betancourt, deserve as much credit. What did Ana Betancourt do? She asked to address the Guáimaro Constitutional Assembly on behalf of her absent husband, Ignacio Mora. The framers expected a polite salutation and a smile but what did she say? She let them have a fiery speech asking them to recognize the absolute equality of women in the new constitution for the future republic. That may seem humdrum but for the date: April 10, 1869.[9]

Most of those brave women are unknown, as are my great-grandmother América del Pino Valdés and her sister Dulce. As is true of many other women, their contribution was just as essential as soldiering—and often just as risky.

I have heard many times how one day, shortly before the Ibarra uprising, América and Dulce returned from one of their trips to Havana with two very heavy bags. Seeing the two ladies struggling with their luggage at the train station, a young Spanish lieutenant came over, saluted smartly, and barked orders to a couple of underlings. The bags swiftly disappeared into the carriage hold. The two women thanked him, no doubt profusely, as the carriage headed for home with two bags of ammunition, supplies, and sensitive papers. Later on, when her husband joined the rebel army, América went into exile in Tampa with her mother-in-law and her four children. She survived on her own and pulled her family through years of great material want driven by a sense of hope and purpose.

Ibarra undone, Juan Gualberto Gómez and a handful of his fellow insurgents were spared the ultimate penalty and banished instead to Spain's African outpost of Ceuta. They were probably expected to die there anyway, sparing the government the bullets and the embarrassment. Gómez survived and went on to become a key political figure in early republican Cuba.[10] A related uprising near Jagüey Grande was equally unsuccessful. The rebels there, however, managed to exchange a few shots with the Spanish at a farm called La Yuca. (Yuca is a tuber, *Manihot esculenta*, but *yuca* in the Cuban vernacular stands for the male member.) Perhaps what happened was for the best. "Grito de la Yuca" would not have been particularly elegant as a national holiday.

As the abortive rebellions at Ibarra and Jagüey Grande proved, Matanzas was not nearly as safe for would-be insurgents in February 1895 as was faraway Oriente, where the Baire rebellion did indeed succeed and take root. (The same was true during the fight against Batista in the 1950s. The rebels in rugged Oriente were, ironically, in one of the safest places in Cuba. Those in the cities were the ones who risked their lives.)

Nothing much happened at Baire that long-ago February Sunday. A group of men, mostly relatives of Saturnino Lora, a subaltern officer, gathered around a flag, declared their solemn intent, cried "Long live Free Cuba," and slipped into the bush. Nobody got killed. Baire went unchallenged: the nearest Spanish soldier was nowhere near. Baire, in fact, was but one of several local uprisings in Oriente, not one of them immediately challenged by authorities or having other than symbolic significance.[11] For unclear reasons, the Baire event occupies a place of honor in Cuba's mythology while its Matanzas counterpart receives nary a mention.

When it comes to heroics, Matanzas definitely has an image problem.

Let Matanzas nurture martyr-bards like Plácido and exquisite, fragile poets like Milanés. Matanzas may be Cuba's Athens, but Oriente is Cuba's Sparta. Hatuey, the symbol of native resistance to the Spanish Conquest, died heroically in what is now Oriente. He wasn't even Cuban. He came from Kiskeya (later Hispaniola) but, like his compatriot Máximo Gómez, he is one of the quintessential heroes of Cuba's imagination.

In fact, the only victory achieved by the aboriginal Cubans against the Spanish invasion was the capture and massacre of the Spanish ship's crew that gave name to the Bay of Slaughters. There is more to that event than the picturesque source of an improbable place-name: it is an important milestone in the history of native resistance. The most consequential slave rebellion in the island's history took place in Matanzas as well, at Triumvirato in November 1843. Matanzas' native defenders and heroic slave rebels, however, do not enjoy the fame of their Oriente peers.

A tenacious Cuban mythology holds that, like the morning sun, Cuba's freedom rises in the east. The Castro brothers, themselves from Oriente, did not originate this reading of Cuban history but they surely like being seen as the ultimate agents of Cuba's heroic destiny.

Oriente fits the part. The legendary cradle of liberty is Ur-Cuba: an epic land of mountains, primeval forests, and wild shores. Sweet Ochún, the Afro-Cuban Venus, has her throne there amidst the hills, but it is Ogún, the Afro-Cuban Mars, who has the run of the place. Oriente is Ogún country, a land drenched in blood and testosterone. That is where the first, epic War for Independence began in 1868. As Bayamo burned the national anthem was supposedly composed on horseback (lyrics by Pedro Figueredo, theme an arrangement of "Non Più Andrai," an aria from *The Marriage of Figaro* by Wolfgang Amadeus Mozart). The famous Cuban machete cavalry charge, the *carga al machete*, was invented in Oriente. It was there as well that Mariana Grajales, mother of the great Afro-Cuban General Antonio Maceo, made him and his brothers swear the Cuban version of the Oath of the Horatii.

Martí, the Zeus of Cuba's patriotic Olympus, was no son of Oriente, to be sure. The future Apostle was born in petit bourgeois Havana in 1853. He lived a good bit of his adult life in exile, mainly in New York, where he was what we would call today a Latino community organizer. But it was in Oriente that he achieved martyrdom. He was shot dead during his first and only visit there as the War of 1895 was getting underway. He was not supposed to die, but he did.

He was killed on May 19, 1895, while embedded in a column commanded by

Máximo Gómez. When shots were heard, Gómez asked Martí to lie low. The seasoned generalissimo was concerned. He might have wondered how Martí, an urbanite and a pedestrian in the best sense of the word, would handle his mount in an emergency. But Martí was an Apostle. Apostles do not just sit by. So the short man in his black suit mounted his white horse and rode on to meet the bullet that bore his name. He lived a poet's life but died a warrior's death. The Spanish recovered the corpse, to their credit rendering it honors after proper forensic routines.

Martí was denied the supreme grace heaven grants to successful great nation builders from Moses to Mandela: not to die in a dark dungeon or "facing the sun," as Martí once wrote in one of his many lapses into messianic immodesty, but to survive and organize the transition team. Fatally, once you are dead others will make the arrangements. Cuban schoolchildren today learn that Martí was the "intellectual author" of Castro's revolution. Martí might take some exception to that statement. A civilian to the core, he might not be entirely at ease with the daily military honors at his mausoleum in Santiago's Santa Ifigenia cemetery. At the changing of the guard, martial young men and women in spit-and-polish military trim smartly goose-step to the Apostle's resting place. The drill, impeccably performed, would more likely gladden the heart of Frederick the Great than that of Martí. One might think the soldiers Russians or Germans but for the unmistakably Cuban way they move their hips and shoulders.

Matanzas earned a wartime honor, fair and square. It was one of three Cuban objectives shelled by the Yankees during the Spanish-American War. In April 1898, the USS *New York* lodged several projectiles into the city. An eight-inch shell hit a bakery, La Pamplonesa, on Gelabert Street; another killed a mule near the Peñas Altas battery. There were no biped casualties. The shell that hit the bakery was exhibited at Bea, Bellido, and Company, Matanzas' hardware emporium on Vigía Square. Many came to see it. Some cried themselves hoarse denouncing Yankee barbarism while others, no doubt, sought secret reassurance that—at long last!—the Yankees were on their way.[12]

Despite its triviality, the "Bombardment of Matanzas" incident was treated by the U.S. press as a major turning point in a war that was disappointingly boring. The *New York Herald Tribune* editorialized that the bombardment had put a major strategic target out of action. War illustrations by Russell White show the USS *New York* as she delivers the blasts, her hull gracefully turning on the surf like a ballerina. There is plenty of smoke. A movie was made, *The*

Bombardment of Matanzas (1898), one of the first war movies in history and the first with a naval theme.[13] The producer and director was Edward H. Amet, the inventor of the first practical movie projector. As it turned out, the true impact of the shells the USS *New York* fired off at Matanzas was on the history of cinema and that of wartime propaganda.

My father's side of my family was solidly placed on both sides of the 1895 conflict. In the Cuban corner were my great-grandfather Américo Bretos Pérez and his wife, América del Pino Valdés, the gunrunner. My great-grand-

Fig. 32. *The Bombardment of Matanzas,* by Russell White, 1898. The only known casualty was a mule, but the event inspired the first naval war movie, one of many farces of the "splendid little war."

father, a fourth-generation Cuban and an accountant by trade, served in the Fifth Corps of the Cuban Ejército Libertador (Liberation Army), operating in Matanzas under the command of General Pedro Betancourt. After the war he had a brief stint in politics and chaired the Matanzas City Council. He was for many years involved with the war veterans' organization in Matanzas province, which evolved as a powerful lobby in early republican Cuba. The veterans delivered a lot of votes. He died in 1917.

My other great-grandfather, Laurentino García Alonso, was an immigrant from Asturias who made a huge fortune as the Matanzas sugar industry rapidly recovered during the first decade of the twentieth century. His wife, Isabel Amechazurra Gómez, was born in Cuba of proudly Basque stock. Laurentino was born at Illas, near Avilés, and arrived in Matanzas almost penniless. His brother, Francisco José, had preceded him in a highly familiar migration pattern in Cuba, where uncles or older brothers would migrate first and then facilitate the migration of other family members. That is also how my maternal grandfather, Tomás Cabañas Vallín, likewise an Asturian, got to Cuba.

Young Laurentino got a job at a Matanzas shop ironing hats. He was a strong supporter of colonial rule and believed Cuban independence to be a *disparate* (a crass mistake), but he was too busy making money to waste his time burying sparrows with the Volunteers. He managed to get a horse. On Sundays, he would go out into the country towns peddling trinkets. With his profits he bought land at Sumidero near the town of Limonar, the first of several acquisitions. He was on his way up. Taking advantage of the depressed real estate values postwar, he greatly expanded his acreage. Never one to miss a good business opportunity, he correctly calculated that the Russo-Japanese war of 1903 would dry up the supply of Russia's beet sugar. Coupled with the collapse of Cuba's production, this was certain to drive sugar prices upwards for several years to come. So, he plowed everything he had into the acquisition and rehabilitation of productive capacity. In 1903 he teamed up with a fellow Asturian; formed a holding company, Bango y García, S.A.; and purchased Progreso sugar mill from the heirs of José Ramón de la Torriente. The following year they bought Santa Amalia from the Taylor family heirs. In 1911 he bought out Bango and emerged as sole owner of the firm. At the height of his career he owned two substantial centrales outright and controlled a large acreage of Matanzas' best land in the environs of Cárdenas and Coliseo. In his heyday don Laurentino could rightfully boast that he would ride on horseback from one mill to the other, a distance of about twenty kilometers, without stepping on land that was not his. He had come a long way from his earlier riding days. Américo and Laurentino were strong personalities and respected each other—but from a distance.

What war had divided peace brought together in new configurations. Américo's son, Miguel, married Laurentino's daughter, Consuelo, in 1912. In 1909, before they met, my grandfather and my grandmother had their pictures taken in settings that were well-nigh allegorical of the cultural values they brought to their marriage: he in his baseball flannel at Rollins College, she dressed as a Moorish princess in Seville. Their relationship was ideologically charged and culturally conflictive but in the end successful, like that of most Hispano-Cuban families after the war. Indeed, one of the salient sociological facts of postwar Cuba was the speed of reconciliation, even in the presence of a vast Spanish immigrant cohort between 1902 and the 1920s.

To get to reconciliation, of course, we must first end the shooting phase. Generalissimo Máximo Gómez, affectionately known to his men as "el Chino Viejo" (the Old Chinaman), once said that his top generals were June, July, and August. The Spanish soldiery, sweltering in the merciless heat of summer and stung by countless fever-bearing mosquitoes understood him all too well. The astute Old Chinaman also knew that the surest way to lose the war was to fight it following the failed strategy of the last one. All it takes to realize why the Cuban War of Independence of 1868–1878 went sour is a look at the map. The rebellion brewed in eastern Cuba but the capital, the bulk of the population, and the colony's economic engine were on the island's western half. Whoever controlled Havana and the west controlled Cuba. The strategic objective of the War of 1895, therefore, was to export the conflict to the rump and tail of the Cuban crocodile. In other words: put the torch to the mills and cane fields of western Cuba.[14]

The Spanish understood that very well. During the Ten Years' War they built a chain of fortifications across the width of the island from Júcaro to Morón, on the border of Camagüey province. A predecessor of the Maginot Line and the Berlin Wall, the so-called *trocha* was supposed to insulate Havana and the island's sugar-producing districts from the eastern infection. The trocha scheme worked very well during the Ten Years' War, helping to contain the war in the east. Matters would be different the next time around.

On November 30, 1895, a column of 2,600 men left Oriente under the command of Antonio Maceo. Their mission: to reach the western tip of Cuba, burning mills and cane fields as they went. The order to march was issued at

Fig. 33. Families divided in war, united in peace. Américo Bretos and América del Pino (*left*) shared a commitment to Cuba's freedom. Laurentino García Alonso, a Spanish immigrant, and Isabel Amechazurra, his wife, partnered in amassing a vast sugar fortune.

Baraguá, the exact spot where Maceo had formally denounced the armistice that ended the Ten Years' War in 1878. To accomplish their mission the insurgents had to traverse the length of the island across hundreds of kilometers of enemy territory.

As Maceo's "invading column" prepared to ride into the sunset, Spanish propaganda was spreading the allegation that "el mulato" Maceo was at the head of a barbarous colored horde from which little should be expected save rape and rapine. Spanish propaganda originally referred to them as *mambises*, a derogatory term of Congo origin. The allegation was all too true in one fundamental sense. The rape and rapine were pure propaganda, but one is left with the fact that many of Maceo's tightly disciplined troops were indeed proudly black.[15] Afro-Cuban fighters—the Cubans transformed *mambí* into a badge of honor that included all partisans of independence regardless of race—were not merely line troops. What was true of the infantry was true also of the officer corps. Antonio Maceo and his brother, José, were neither alone nor exceptional. Several key generals in the mambí army were black, including Guillermo Moncada (the namesake of the Moncada Barracks), Quintín Banderas, and Jesús Rabí.

The last surviving Afro-Cuban mambí general, Generoso Campos Marquetti, "el General Generoso," died in exile in the United States in the 1960s. The general, one of Juan Gualberto Gómez' close co-conspirators in Matanzas, was elected to the Cuban Congress after independence, representing several constituencies over many years. In the 1950s he was a Batista ally, in fact, a minister without portfolio in Batista's government. He died in Washington, D.C. Although frail and in his nineties, he had agreed to testify before the House of Representatives about the situation in Cuba. He died in his hotel room shortly after leaving Speaker John McCormack's office. It was May 20, 1966, Cuba's independence day.[16] We just need to keep in mind the substantially African component of the mambí army to understand some key problems that plagued early republican Cuba later on.

Crossing the trocha in broad daylight amidst a carga al machete would have been suicidal. Maceo knew better than that, so the column slipped by the trocha at night in complete silence. By the next morning they were safely on the other side. They reached the provincial border of Matanzas in December 1895. Halfway into Matanzas province, Maceo's column ran into a superior enemy force at Coliseo on December 23. Maceo feigned a retreat and rode back towards neighboring Las Villas province with the Spanish army in hot pursuit. Near Manacas the Cubans turned around and swiftly headed back towards Matanzas, leaving their pursuers thoroughly confounded. Combat, such as there was, took place in the environs of Santa Amalia sugar mill. It was a mere skirmish but Maceo almost lost his life; his horse was shot from under him. A monument on the central highway not quite a kilometer away from the batey commemorates the encounter. Matanzas province was ground zero. The devastation of the countryside, especially the sugar industrial plant, was spectacularly thorough. What Maceo's invading column did not torch, the local insurgents did.

In January 1896, Valeriano Weyler y Nicolau became captain-general of Cuba. Like O'Donnell, he was born in Tenerife, in the Canaries. Weyler was not a nice man, but he was a very good general. He had seen service in Cuba under the Count of Valmaseda during the Ten Years' War and in Spain's failed attempt to reannex the Dominican Republic in the 1860s. There, Spain's smart regular army was roundly defeated by the tropical environment and the Dominican irregulars, mostly mulattoes, who brought the latter-day conquistadores to grief. He understood perfectly well the nature of combat in Cuba and was well ahead of his time. Weyler saw that the main source of support for the mambises was in the countryside and sought to counter it. His tool was "reconcentration," the forcible evacuation of the countryside in order to deny support and intelligence to the enemy.

On February 17, Weyler decreed his infamous Bando de Reconcentración.[17] Rural folks were to remove themselves to designated urban areas. Those who remained could be shot on sight. Matanzas and Havana provinces, relatively small, flat, and thoroughly interconnected by railroad were a perfect stage for enforcing Weyler's draconian edict. How to feed and care for the tens of thousands thus displaced was left to God's mercy.

What Weyler did not reckon on was that the militarily expedient turned out to be politically disastrous. The boomerang he had thrown at his target would soon head back straight towards his spiked helmet. It was in response to the deteriorating situation in Cuba that President McKinley sent the USS *Maine* to Havana.

The cumulative effect of the hostilities was calamitous for those caught in the middle. At the end of the war, U.S. occupation authorities reported that out of 271 sugar mills grinding in Matanzas province in 1895, only twenty remained intact. In the environs of Matanzas city, including the neighboring towns of Arcos de Canasí, Cidra, and Sabanilla del Encomendador, all twenty-six mills grinding at the beginning of the war were either torched or demolished. The countryside was deserted and productive land went to weed. Matanzas' herd was wiped out. The fifty thousand beasts of draft and burden living in the province before the war had shrunk to five thousand in 1899, mostly hide and bones.

This was a catastrophe of unprecedented scope but what happened to the people was worse still.[18] American occupation authorities reported that no less than sixty thousand persons died in the province between 1895 and 1898—between 25 and 30 percent of the province's population in absolute terms. One is reminded of the Black Death of medieval Europe. In Matanzas city, the number of annual deaths was, on average, 1,290 between 1889 and 1895. In 1896 it climbed to 2,327, and in 1897 to a whopping 6,729. In 1898, Matanzas city reported 5,972 deaths. These frightening figures correlate with an equally dramatic decline in births. To keep these figures in perspective, bear in mind that Matanzas city had a population of 38,000 in 1895, and the province some 160,000.

What killed all those people was the lethal combination of starvation and disease. The mambí invasion and Weyler's reconcentration meant that Matanzas city's population climbed from 38,000 to 60,000 in a matter of months. The city's facilities were simply insufficient to care for so many in such dire straits. With the fields abandoned, there was no food. The dead could not be buried fast enough.[19]

Bandits had infested the roads connecting Havana and Matanzas for many years. The collapse of social order gave them a field day, a free-for-all. Traditional bandits now proclaimed themselves *insurrectos*, perhaps hoping for a meal ticket in a future independent Cuba. From the Yumurí Valley to Madruga and Catalina de Güines in Havana province the realm of Cuba's most legendary outlaw extended: Manuel García, *el rey de los campos de Cuba*.[20]

My grandaunt Ñiquita, she of the quilts, was thirty-something at the time. She spent the entire war in Matanzas. Many years later, she remembered vividly the misery and suffering of those days. Virtually no family in town was untouched by death or disease. She lost her first husband to typhoid. Hers and her neighbors' homes were full of refugees from Unión de Reyes, Bemba, Ceiba Mocha, Sabanilla del Encomendador, Arcos de Canasí, Guamutas, and other localities in the interior—family, friends, and friends of friends who had nowhere else to go. She nursed many, helped others to die, and came close to death herself from drinking contaminated water. "In Matanzas there were not

Fig. 34. Starving Cubans at Matanzas from a stereo view by Griffith & Griffith, 1899. (Courtesy of Prints and Photographs Division, Library of Congress)

many shots," she used to say, "but there were many dead. I know because I saw them . . ." and she would pause for effect, ever the storyteller. "They died of hunger. You could count their *huesitos* ("little bones"; my grandaunt was fond of the diminutive that is so characteristic of Cuba's vernacular). "And every morning they came down to pick up the dead in wheelbarrows." She paused again for effect: "In wheelbarrows! I know because I saw it when I could still see."

And then it all ended. The official transfer of authority took place on January 1, 1899—the first of January is definitely a day to watch out for in Cuba's history. At ten minutes before noon, Lt. Col. M. Edgar Padwin, Commandant, Third Battalion, Third Regiment, USV, marched to the courtyard of San Severino Castle at the head of a military detail. At noon sharp, cannon boomed and the Spanish flag began to come down the mast slowly and solemnly. Tears came to the eyes of toughened soldiers as the flag was ceremoniously folded and delivered to the Spanish commanding officer. Minutes later cannon boomed again as the Stars and Stripes was hoisted up the mast. Similar ceremonies were simultaneously held across town at City Hall and, indeed, throughout the island. Four centuries of Spanish rule were at an end.[21]

When the U.S. and Cuban armies entered the city, they found a population in shock. Still, liberation brought tremendous jubilation and the party lasted for the better part of a week. War-weary matanceros found the strength to erect an elaborate triumphal arch in Vigía Square. "Hurrah for the U.S.!" proclaimed the signs amidst Cuban and American flags.[22]

Spain was out, but was this necessarily a good thing? The range of Cubans' emotions between elation at the end of the colonial regime and depression at the ambiguity of the present was probably best captured by Bonifacio Byrne. When the ship on which he was returning from exile entered Havana harbor, he saw the U.S. Stars and Stripes flying in the position of honor above Morro Castle next to the Cuban Lone Star. "I did anxiously search for my flag," wrote Byrne,

> But another beside her was waving.
> Where, O where, is my dear Cuban flag
> The most beautiful flag that can be?
>
> . . . .
>
> With the faith of convictions austere,
> I proclaim with a voice firm and strong
> That two flags should not fly over where
> Only one is sufficient: my own!

The *Maine* is well enough remembered, and so is Baire. Is Ibarra worth the same honor? At the very least, rising up in arms in the flat countryside of Matanzas, near a main railway, and within a couple of hours' march of a major Spanish military garrison required mettle. It incurred casualties. It was noted. Shortly after the "Viva Cuba Libres!" were shouted and formalities taken care of, a small Cuban contingent led by López Coloma was crossing the rail lines when the train carrying Spanish troops approached. The Cubans carried the Lone Star flag that was later captured and exhibited in Havana. As the train sped by, the wheels clickety-clacking on the rails, each side looked at the other in silence, as if mesmerized by the unreality of the moment.[23]

One who did remember Ibarra was Juan Gualberto Gómez. In February 1933, Gómez, a legendary cigar smoker, was dying of terminal lung cancer. On the eve of the twenty-fourth, he gathered his family and recounted, lest they be forgotten, the events of Ibarra. The effort much weakened him. Next morning, with the courage and determination that had carried him through a remarkable career, he painfully shuffled to the front door and personally hoisted the Cuban flag. He then asked for a chair and sat under the flag's shadow for as long as his condition permitted. He could barely breathe. The moving mise-en-scène with which he saluted the great day was watched by the entire neighborhood. There were few dry eyes.[24]

He died on March 5. He had refused a state funeral. He would just as soon keep the then dictator, Gerardo Machado, out of it. Cuba was in a profound crisis then, and the danger of yet another American intervention was palpable. His last words, deliriously uttered before he lapsed into a coma were: "Roosevelt is president. Cuba is safe." It would be hard to imagine a more ironic finale to the life of this stubborn and principled Cuban nationalist. Or a more profound statement of the frustrations of the Cuba that was born from the ashes of the war and, like him, died in that extraordinary year of 1933.

13   The City Sleeps

THE WAR FOR INDEPENDENCE devastated Matanzas seemingly in vain, for its immediate result was foreign military occupation. Independence did come on May 20, 1902, but with sovereignty amputated and territorial integrity under an ominous threat. The Platt Amendment, presented by the McKinley administration to the framers of Cuba's 1901 Constitution with all the finesse of a don Vito Corleone, placed limits on what the new Cuban state could do and authorized direct U.S. intervention in Cuban affairs under certain circumstances. It was the proverbial offer you can't refuse: no amendment, no end to the occupation. A key Platt Amendment issue with immediate practical implications was the status of the Isle of Pines. The large island south of the Cuban mainland had been subject to Havana since the sixteenth century but it was mischievously left in limbo by members of the U.S. Congress scheming to annex it. The Isle of Pines question was resolved diplomatically in Cuba's favor in 1924.[1]

The Platt Amendment, a matter of great pith and moment to Cuban nationalists, lapsed in 1934, when Cuba ceased to consider it binding with the tacit agreement of the recently inaugurated Franklin D. Roosevelt administration. That it ever existed, however, is a severe irritant to Cuban nationalist sensibilities. The amendment's most gallant foe within Cuba's 1901 Constituent Assembly was Juan Gualberto Gómez. Joining forces with the Camagüey patrician Julio Sanguily, the son of Matanzas slaves mounted a scathing and cogently reasoned attack against what was a de facto protectorate.[2] The Platt

Amendment was like a spoonful of foul-tasting medicine. Nobody liked it but in the end a majority of the framers held their noses and swallowed. Gómez and Sanguily held their noses and voted no.

In retrospect, the Platt Amendment was a bad idea for almost all concerned.[3] It was bad for Cuba for obvious reasons of national morale, but it was bad also for the United States because it made the U.S. administration of the day a hostage to Cuban events. That is exactly what happened in 1906, when the first Cuban president, Tomás Estrada Palma, reached the end of his term with a rebellion on his hands and the crucial matter of succession unresolved. Don Tomás, who enjoys the reputation of being Cuba's only honest president, simply packed his bags, boarded a train, and moved to Matanzas. The state of near anarchy on the island precipitated a second American intervention nobody wanted, least of all President Theodore Roosevelt. Ironically, the only net Platt Amendment winners were the Spanish in Cuba, who were thereby insulated against reprisals and confiscations. Cuba, though perhaps reluctantly, gained much by the continued presence of Spanish capital and the guaranteed flow of Spanish immigration.

For Matanzas, in particular, there was some cause for rejoicing as the new century made its debut. The Athens of Cuba had been one of three Cuban sites actually shelled during the war. It was clearly a stretcher case when peace came, quite possibly the single most distressed Cuban city as a consequence of the hostilities. After the calamities of the conflict, it was only natural for the desperate matanceros to be well disposed toward American authorities, whence cometh relief.

They were especially fortunate in Brig. Gen. James H. Wilson, the military governor of Matanzas and Santa Clara provinces.[4] An Honors West Point graduate and a Civil War legend, Wilson was enlightened, intelligent, and well meaning. He developed a genuine affection for Cuba and Cubans, as is evident from his reports, the best of any produced by occupation authorities, but even more so from his actions. An annexationist—he would have welcomed a Cuban star on the American flag—Wilson wanted to impress Cubans under his authority with the virtues of an American affiliation. We can perceive his concern in the big things that he did, but more poignantly in the little ones. Aware of Matanzas' bookishness, he took a special interest in stocking local libraries with English-language books. His personal intervention attracted gifts from the Smithsonian and Andrew Carnegie. The latter contributed 2,079 books, the standard reference booklist for a Carnegie library, to the Matanzas counterpart. Not content with stocking the shelves, Wilson also improved access to books. Unfortunately, his short tour of duty on the island was marked by personal tragedy when his wife lost her life in a freak accident. Mrs. Wilson was alighting from a carriage when she stepped on a match, igniting it. Her dress caught fire and she later died of her burns.[5]

Wilson developed an excellent rapport with the Cuban patriots, whom he saw as the country's true leaders, particularly General Pedro Betancourt, who became a personal friend. The first free and democratic municipal elections in Cuban history took place in June 1900. General Domingo Lecuona y Mádan was elected mayor of Matanzas. Among those elected to the city council was my great-grandfather Américo, who became its chairman.

The municipal inauguration was captured by Robert Miles in a magnificent photo showing City Hall bedecked in bunting, the original main balcony still in place. Another photo of his, possibly taken at the same time, shows a joyous crowd in their Sunday best at Vigía Square. In the middle of the square, the triumphal arch erected the preceding year to salute the arrival of U.S. and mambí troops into the city still stands. "Viva Cuba Libre" and "Hurrah for the U.S.," read the side panels.

Matanzas was on its way up again, or so it seemed, and important improvements followed. Methodists and Baptists placed their bets on the city's new era, opening their first churches in town in 1899 and 1900, respectively. Not to be outdone, the followers of Allan Kardec's variety of spiritualism busied themselves developing communities throughout Cuba. The first Kardecian spiritualist organization in Matanzas was founded as early as 1882. The city became an important center of Cuban *espiritismo*, a further component of the colorful local mixture of religion and mysticism. In 1935 Matanzas wrote a notable page in the history of Cuban spiritualism as well as Cuban radio: the first *espiritista* radio broadcast. It was known as "La hora espírita" (The Spirits' Hour). The format included placing a glass full of water on a little table at the studio. The water supposedly aided the medium, that is, the person serving as a conduit to the spirits' world to "connect" with supernatural entities. This format became a runaway radio success in the 1940s.[6]

In 1903, the first automobile in the city took the full measure of Matanzas' legendary potholes.[7] The following year matanceros celebrated the completion of the swiveling railroad bridge over the San Juan, a unique addition to the city's fabled bridge inventory.[8] In 1905, long-distance phone service to Havana was inaugurated and, in 1906, Matanzas' up-to-date new city market opened

Fig. 35. Vigía Square (*above*) and City Hall on June 1, 1900, the day the first modern Matanzas city government was inaugurated. Photo by Robert Miles. (Courtesy of National Anthropological Archives, Smithsonian Institution)

in the old Plaza de la Verdura. The magnificent statue of Martí on Liberty Square was dedicated in 1909, a major civic effort and the second statue to the Apostle of Independence to be erected in all of Cuba.[9]

In 1916, Matanzas became the first Cuban city to have electric streetcars.[10] Five years later, the Hershey Cuban Railroad began operating regularly scheduled electric passenger trains between Havana and Matanzas via the Hershey sugar mill and refinery in northern Havana province. This meant that interurban as well as suburban public transportation between Havana and Matanzas was virtually integrated using modern transportation technology.

The Hershey train—"el tren de Jersi" to true-blue matanceros—still runs. Streetcars were discontinued in the 1950s, though not without a fight. Matanzas, in fact, was the last Cuban city to operate *tranvías*. The streetcars of my childhood were enclosed but seemed designed for the tropics. Huge windows let in the air, and cane seats remained cool despite the heat. The cars had their own unique smell of seasoned wood, old iron, and electric spark. They added immeasurably to the amenity of the Matanzas in which I grew up. The streetcar lines connected the entire city, running all the way from Peñas Altas in the La Playa district to the top of Matanzas proper and the very ends of Pueblo Nuevo and Versalles.

Matanceros generally loved their streetcars, but the quaint tranvías found a determined foe in motorists. The overhead wires, motorists argued, interfered with car radios, and the vibration of moving streetcars dislodged the cobblestones, creating potholes. In response, the streetcars were retired in the mid-1950s. Their passing brought about a great deal of collateral damage. Removing the tracks meant that the hardy New England granite cobblestones that had covered the town's main thoroughfares since the first half of the nineteenth century had to go as well. Most were dumped in the bay as landfill, although quite a few remained under the city streets, entombed in asphalt.

This display of material progress only disguised Matanzas' chronic decline. From being the island's third city in population and importance during the nineteenth century, Matanzas dropped to the fourth, then the fifth, and the sixth. In the 1953 census it came in seventh behind Havana, Santiago de Cuba, Camagüey, Santa Clara, Holguín, and Cienfuegos. During the first half of the twentieth century, Matanzas was a place living off former glories. It already had a great past to look back on when it added one more to its lengthening list of nicknames. The new sobriquet suggested neither culture nor progress but paralysis: "la Ciudad Dormida" (the Sleeping City). Carilda Oliver Labra—

one of Matanzas', and Cuba's, great contemporary poets—captured something of the place's has-been, down-at-the-heels charm in her affectionate "Chant to Matanzas" (1954), the city's emblematic poem. "Slow Matanzas," it begins,

> I love you because you are
> As sad as sadness might be,
> And I love your poverty
> Of canary without feed.
> I love you because you bear
> Green laurels upon your head,
> For your Pan always asleep,
> And your small future
> Of matches and henequen.[11]

Matanzas became the butt of jokes. There is a well-known folk story of a circus owner who went to Matanzas with his show during the Depression. The people of the city were so impoverished that the circus almost went broke. He lost his monkey. The tent burned down. The lion escaped. The circus man left town swearing never to return, but not before casting his departing curse upon the threadbare Athens of Cuba. He did it in a clever ditty that lives on in numerous folk versions. The unchanging opening lines are lacerating:

> Matanzas, I shit on thee,
> I shit on your fucking Pan,
> On your damned old San Juan
> And your slimy Yumurí.[12]

Matanzas' basic problems were twofold. The first was location. Close enough to Havana to preclude its becoming an important regional hub, it was still far enough from the center of the action to entice enterprising matanceros to move to the capital altogether in search of opportunity. The second, intimately connected to the first, was economics. Matanzas was no longer the commanding sugar producer it had once been. Leadership passed to Camagüey's and Oriente's mammoth mills, built for the most part during the heady speculative days of the Menocal administration (1913–1921). President Menocal himself, although a matancero from Jagüey Grande, built his own mill, Chaparra, in Oriente.

The decline of sugar brought in its wake the decline of the port. The militancy of the stevedores' union, heavily influenced by the Afro-Cuban Abakuá society, became legendary, as did strikes and labor stoppages. The port languished for years, caught between declining traffic and strained labor relations that often culminated in severe strikes and stoppages.

In an attempt to inject dynamism into the local economy, presidential decree number 490 of September 14, 1934, created the Matanzas Free Trade Zone adjacent the port.[13] Modestly successful economically, the main legacy of the Zona Franca was aesthetic: a lovely monumental gate by Matanzas architect Enrique Marcet inspired by Trier's famous Porta Nigra and a fancy stamp issue that is a landmark of Cuban philately. The gate elegantly defines the end of Versalles' Paseo de Martí. The stamp issue, printed by London's legendary Waterlow and Sons, is a salute to the harbor and the city's natural and cultural environment. Airplanes and dirigibles fly over stunning aerial views of the town, the valley, and well-known landmarks, while ocean liners project the port's anticipated but elusive rebirth.[14]

The 1936 stamp series was both retro- and proactive; a celebration of the city's past and an anticipation of a modern, dynamic future that never quite arrived. It seemed like a good idea but like the postal rocket, another project of the age, it did not quite work out. On October 15, 1939, a rocket launched from Havana was supposed to reach Matanzas with a load of mail. The missile, no Wernher von Braun creation, was launched as scheduled. It achieved ignition—did it ever—but no liftoff. Although the experiment bombed out, literally, the postal surcharge issued to mark the event is the first to celebrate rocketry anywhere in the world and is consequently valued by stamp collectors as the philatelic starting point of the space age. The charred and twisted remains of the rocket are a prized exhibit of Havana's small but excellent Postal Museum.

With the exception of the prosperous World War I years, when war-induced demand revived sugar briefly and spectacularly, economic liftoff was not easy for Matanzas. A promising venture was large-scale cordage manufacturing. The pioneer of cordage making in Cuba was Alfredo Heydrich, the son of aqueduct founder Ferdinand Heydrich. In the 1890s Alfredo set up a plant in Havana that used Yucatec fiber, but it soon became evident that growing henequen on marginal Matanzas land could be profitable.

At the turn of the century, Heydrich joined forces with Ernst Roeffler, a German entrepreneur, and secured overseas venture capital. Henequen fields began to be planted as early as 1903; however, it takes several years for the plants to become productive. In 1911, with sufficient local supply secured, the

Heydrich Havana plant was moved to Matanzas. The Compañía de Jarcia de Matanzas (Matanzas Cordage Company) began operations that year.[15]

Henequen was a natural fit for Matanzas. The rocky terrain south of the bay offered growing conditions not unlike those of the Yucatan Peninsula, the world's main source of henequen fiber at the time. Uncertainty about Yucatan supplies of the fiber during the Mexican Revolution gave a competitive edge to Matanzas cordages.

Matanzas' henequen episode attracted to the region a remarkable immigrant group: the Koreans.[16] Matanzas' Koreans did not come directly from their Asian homeland but from the nearby Yucatan, where they had been lured by the promise of good jobs in the booming henequen economy. By 1921, however, disenchanted by the arduous working conditions in Mexico, about one thousand Koreans moved to neighboring Cuba. Their point of entry was Manatí, in Oriente province. The Cuban Korean diaspora spread out from there to such places as Cárdenas, Havana, and Matanzas. Many ended up in the last, a poor choice as it turned out, for both the Yucatan and Matanzas henequen industries were done in by the emergence of synthetic fibers as the century progressed. Matanzas' Koreans settled in a village named El Bolo; adapted to Cuba's rural economy; and became, like so many other immigrant groups, hyphenated Cubans. A few did very well, as did Ramón Pack, who owned by 1957 two optical stores, a hardware store, a ladies' fashion boutique, and La Casa Ultramar, one of the city's largest appliance shops.[17] Descendants of the original settlers live in Matanzas today.[18]

The advent of synthetics was not all bad news for Matanzas, however. The Rayonera, a large rayon manufacturing plant, was built in the 1940s on the hills above Versalles. The Rayonera was an offshoot of Textilera Ariguanabo, S.A., a manufacturing complex developed by a remarkable entrepreneur, Dayton Hedges, of Long Island, New York.[19] Hedges arrived in Cuba in the early 1920s with his wife and children, a car, $5,000 in cash, and a lifetime of experience building steel armatures for skyscrapers. Once in Cuba, he convinced the First National Bank of Boston to let him assume the debt of a derelict hydroelectric plant in Bauta, a town in Havana province. In a few years Hedges had turned the plant around, helped electrify Havana province, and sold it for three million pesos.

Synthetic fibers were a new frontier after World War II. Hedges, with the help of his two sons, James and Burke, moved aggressively into the field. By then the family had become thoroughly Cubanized, spoke Spanish at home, and moved easily in Cuba's social circles. The Rayonera was a modern plant, its products well reputed, and its research and development effort strong—James was a Georgia Tech engineer. Its fibers went into all kinds of applications, from women's dresses to racing car tires. In 1958 the elder Hedges' contributions to Cuba were honored with a stamp issue.

Rayon and fertilizers were the city's manufacturing base at mid-century. In the 1950s, CUBANITRO, a plant producing nitrogen pellets, was built near Punta Gorda. Everyone wondered about the plume of yellow smoke the smokestack belched forth. There were some lesser industrial activities, of course. Ice had been made in Matanzas since the 1870s. Matanzas made a significant contribution to the national production of tennis shoes and galvanized iron buckets. The firm of Altuna y Obias was a significant source of hydraulic tile ("Cuban" tile), the cement-based flooring that was universally used in Cuba and, for a while, in historicist Miami suburbs such as Coral Gables. The Yucayo distillery turned out a pretty decent rum, and a lot of alcohol was distilled in Matanzas. Alcohol would play an important role in the city's economy, especially during World War II.

The food and drink industry, though limited in scope, undercapitalized, and lagging in marketing savvy, enjoyed a reputation for quality. Ortiz & Arnaiz in Pueblo Nuevo was a source of pasta, and the De Casas Company produced highly regarded fruit preserves for the national market. La Bella Matancera, S.A., was the source of Matanzas' own drink, Sidra Achampañada—neither cider nor champagne, but a carbonated soda. With exemplary civic panache, De Casas' preserve cans prominently featured a large Matanzas coat of arms where one would expect the image of a ripe guava or a bowl full of marmalade. Not to be outdone, the manufacturers of Sidra Achampañada insisted that their firm was "Matancera," like the Sonora.

Most of Cuba's matches—rest in peace, Mrs. Wilson—were made in Matanzas. The Chesterfield match factory near the riverfront burned down spectacularly while we lived at the Casa Cabañas, two blocks away. For an hour or so it seemed as if the strong wind might spread the fire and a whole swath of Matanzas burn, as had happened at La Marina in 1845. The wind cooperated, however, and the firefighters were able to put out the conflagration.

Undoubtedly with an eye on sales, Chesterfield matchboxes mimicked the design and graphics on the packs of the then very popular Chesterfield cigarettes. Casas, Rabelo y Compañía, the manufacturer, was nevertheless a 100 percent Matanzas firm. The other large match factory in town—Matanzas was

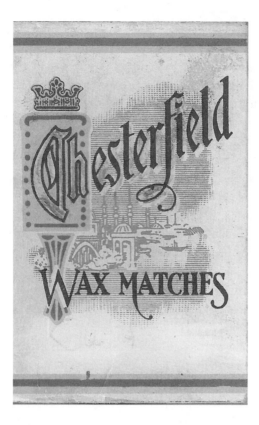

Fig. 36. Chesterfield matchbox from the 1950s.

the match capital of Cuba—was El Crisol on San Juan Bautista Street. Its match-boxes featured pop singers and movie stars. Musical and artistic, Matanzas was also highly combustible, perhaps a reason why the Fire Department occupied one of the city's architectural gems, Bernardo de Grandas y Callejas' elegant neoclassic firehouse on Vigía Square.

Notwithstanding Carilda Oliver Labra's "small future of matches and henequen," Matanzas attracted considerable immigration, resulting in remarkable demographic diversity for a provincial town. Spanish immigrants gravitated to the retail trade. As in the rest of Cuba, the Spanish bodega, or grocery, was a social institution, much like the Jewish delicatessen might be in New York City. The Lebanese began trickling into the city during the first quarter of the twentieth century, and Lebanese families such as the Rohaidys, Bechilys, and Hadeds were well established by the mid-1900s.

The Jews came also. In the beginning they were mostly Sephardim. About forty Sephardic families made their home at Unión de Reyes.[20] The community became more diverse as time went on, enriched by new arrivals such as Samuel Szwec, a Russian Jew, and his wife, Raquel, who settled in 1923.[21] Through sheer effort and persistence, the Szwecs established a successful shoe factory, La Estrella Cubana. By 1925 Matanzas boasted an organized Colonia Israelita.[22] My circle of school and neighborhood friends in the 1940s and 1950s included children with surnames like Rosenblatt, Esquenazi, Egozi, and Ashman. An overwhelming majority of the pre-Castro Cuban Jewish community—matanceros included—opted for exile.

Americans, at home in Matanzas since the nineteenth century, continued to be very much in evidence. John B. Skidmore, a U.S. veteran of the 1898 war, fell in love with Matanzas and went on to become the city's first car dealer. La Casa Skidmore continued to sell Chevrolets, Oldsmobiles, Cadillacs, Vauxhalls, and Opels until it was confiscated by the Castro government. In 1958 it began selling Toyota jeeps as well. Toyotas were the object of much scorn. They were derided as *juguetes*—toys—by a Cuban buying public besotted with Detroit's finned behemoths of the age. My father, a lawyer by training, opened Matanzas' first Pontiac dealership in 1951 and had a financial interest in La Casa Skidmore as well. He had a gift for closing the deal, loved cars, and enjoyed nothing more than finding them new owners.

The Chinese had come to Cuba under circumstances that can only be described as brutal, as indentured substitutes for African slaves. By the twentieth century, however, the industrious Chinese held a niche position in the laundry business and the small commerce of fruits and vegetables. By 1925, Matanzas city boasted its own branch office of the Kuo-Ming-Tang, the Chinese Nationalist Party, with its offices at the Calzada de Tirry.

Lacking its former level of energy, however, the city languished on the verge of an economic takeoff that never seemed to get actually airborne. A bright spot during the depressed 1920s and turbulent 1930s was the work of a daughter of the old Matanzas ruling class, Hortensia Lamar y Delmonte. Born to privilege, Hortensia was also a born crusader. Her causes were women's suffrage, women's rights, and fighting the exploitation of women through prostitution. She was one of the forces behind Cuba's historic feminist congress of 1923 and, a decade later, a key participant in the overthrow of dictator Gerardo Machado. I vividly remember her in the Matanzas of the 1950s, still a formidable presence in her old age. She died in 1967.

Impacted by war, economic decline, and the indescribable malaise of the have-beens, cultural initiative was drained from the Athens of Cuba, and its cultural institutions declined. Sauto Theater became a movie house in the 1920s. In all fairness, it was not the only one among Cuba's grand old theaters to undergo such a reversal of fortune. The Terry in Cienfuegos and the Caridad in Santa Clara were likewise downgraded.

No more Sarah Bernhardt or Italian opera. The stage—pardon, screen—now belonged to Greta Garbo, Rodolfo Valentino, and King Kong. The last, one of the first talkies shown in Cuba, had its Matanzas debut at the formerly elegant theater in January 1934. The mighty ape made a contribution to Cuban political folklore. In January 1934, the provisional Ramón Grau San Martín presidency was facing its terminal crisis. Renowned for their commitment to radical social reform, Grau and his firebrand minister of the interior, Antonio Guiteras, had failed to obtain U.S. recognition or put an end to the nation's economic chaos. Government employees went unpaid and city streets unlit because the government simply had no cash. A folk wit came up with the street slogan that became the administration's political epitaph:

> King Kong, go home, Ramón,
> Kong King, go home, San Martín.

Gone With the Wind debuted in 1939 at the old theater, a fitting locale for a tale about the vanished South of cotton, slavery, and social pretensions. Even as a cinema the Sauto was in trouble. What had made it a grand opera house made it a very poor movie theater. The metal columns supporting the second and third rows of balconies were a nuisance to moviegoers.

Hot and increasingly seedy, the Sauto lost out to the more modern Velasco Cinema on Liberty Square and to the Matanzas and the Abril in Pueblo Nuevo. The Moderno on Río Street showed only Mexican movies. The Matanzas bourgeoisie pooh-poohed it, calling it the cinema for domestics, and ferocious bugs were said to inhabit the seats. (Not true: my friends and I sneaked into the Moderno whenever a new Cantinflas movie or one of those outrageous Mexican wrestling sagas came to town.)

When the next big technical innovation after Technicolor came around, the Sauto wasn't even in the running. CinemaScope's first release, the epic *Quo Vadis* starring Robert Taylor, Deborah Kerr, and Peter (later Sir Peter) Ustinov as an unforgettable Nero, had its local debut at the Matanzas in 1952. VistaVision debuted at the Abril Theater in 1954 with Bing Crosby, Danny Kaye, and Rosemary Clooney in *White Christmas*. To promote it, the managers must have exhausted the local supply of first-aid cotton to stand in for snow. By then the Sauto was good only for B-grade movies and reruns, and for such things as local school pageants and occasional recitals by the Chamber Orchestra. The machines once used to lift the floor for the grand balls of yesteryear rusted away for lack of use. Today, however, the old theater, beautifully restored, is once again put to the use for which it was intended.

The Liceo, where Matanzas' claim to Athenian identity was forged, lost its original penchant for culture and its diffusion and retreated behind the frivolities of an ostensibly aristocratic social club. In 1913, the servants were dressed in fancy livery as behooved such a place. One year later, important and rare Cuban imprints—the Liceo's very own heritage and métier—were exchanged for a collection of Alexandre Dumas' novels without anyone protesting.[23] By mid-century, there was talk of selling the downtown site and moving the entire Liceo to a beachside location. Fortunately, enough old-timers viscerally understood the outrageousness of the notion to guarantee its blockage at least for a generation.

Like virtually all the social clubs in Cuba, the Liceo was thoroughly segregated. Ironically, the current name of the Liceo's building—Sala White—honors somebody who would never have been admitted to membership at any time in the Liceo's history. José White was not white. Matanzas' Afro-Cuban community supported their own equally exclusive club, La Unión. Younger than the Liceo by a few years, the club was founded on the initiative of Antonio Maceo, a fact of which the institution was justifiably proud. Of course, in terms of age or continuity, the oldest social organizations in town continue to be the surviving cabildos de nación, a handful of which have adapted and subsisted to this day.

Though economically depressed and sometimes aggressively philistine, twentieth-century Matanzas would not entirely let go of its Athenian agenda. In this regard, a player was the organization Amigos de la Cultura Cubana, founded in 1935 by a group of local intellectuals. Music continued to flourish as well, and Matanzas simply would not yield an inch as Cuba's poetic capital. To prove it, it produced two giants of modern Cuban poetry, Agustín Acosta Bello and Carilda Oliver Labra. Acosta opted for exile. Carilda cast her lot with the Castro revolution and is a revered grande dame of Cuban letters. She is also a Matanzas legend.

Carilda—she has achieved the glory of not needing a surname—was born in Matanzas in 1922. She has lived her entire life in her hometown, which is very much a presence in her oeuvre. She has had to live down her reputation as an "erotic" poet. Her gift for erotic imagery is remarkable, as evidenced by her early (1946) popular sonnet "Me desordeno, amor, me desordeno":

> I lose composure, love, I lose composure
> when I linger, unhurried, on your mouth,
> and not meaning to, almost by chance,
> I touch you with the nipple of my breast.[24]

Anyone writing in this vein could hardly escape the accusation of eroticism, especially in a conservative social context like Matanzas. Carilda, however, thoroughly enjoyed her fame as Matanzas' naughty girl of the 1950s, when some important and lasting works of hers appeared. I have never met her personally but remember seeing her many times in the street, a woman of remarkable presence and appeal. I, like many of my schoolmates, found her immensely alluring.

There is a great deal more to this remarkable poet than eroticism. The mystery of relationships, the pain of loss, the pride of identity, and a vibrant joie de vivre have memorably marked her poetics. Her steadfast devotion to her hometown is famous, yet she has more than transcended the boundaries of the province to become a national figure and a universal voice.

Acosta was born in 1886. Educated at Matanzas and later at the University of Havana, he led a distinguished career as a public intellectual and politician. He served as senator and minister. In 1955 the Cuban Congress honored him as Cuba's National Poet. Observing the formalities of the generation gap—I was a teenager then and he a vigorous retiree—I had the privilege of meeting him as a family friend. I vividly remember a memorable tribute given to him at the Matanzas Tennis Club in 1955, when he was named National Poet. Although a modest and unassuming man, Acosta had a tremendous public persona, and hearing him recite some of his poems in that setting was unforgettable, even for a thirteen-year-old. He died in exile in Miami in 1979.

The future National Poet's mentor was another renowned Matanzas bard, Federico Uhrbach.[25] Acosta's early poetry was influenced by Uhrbach's modernism, the prevailing aesthetic of late-nineteenth-century Latin American poetics. His mature work, however, fully belongs in the twentieth century. He was a pioneer of Cuba's nationalist, socially charged poetry. Like his fellow matancero and predecessor as National Poet, Bonifacio Byrne, he wrote a memorable poem to the Cuban flag.

Sugar and its corollary, slavery, marked Matanzas' soul indelibly. It is fitting that Agustín Acosta, a true-blue matancero, should have written the most moving reflection of what sugar has meant to Cuba in what most critics consider to be his most influential collection of poems, *La zafra*, published in 1926.[26] "Carretas en la Noche," with its vivid, almost palpable imagery of cane carts en route to the nearby American mill, is the best known. It is especially poignant as a response to the sugar price catastrophe of 1920, which led to a drastic denationalization of the Cuban sugar industry and which I discuss in the next chapter:

> While slowly the oxen plod as they may
> The old cane carts creak away, creak away.
> In ponderous queues they bear heavy loads
> Alongside cane fields, down old country roads,
> Crossing rivers and mountains and plains,
> Carrying the future of Cuba in the canes.
>
> . . . .
>
> They go to the mighty colossus of steel;
> They go to the nearby American mill
> And, as if complaining nearing the batey,
> O'erloaded, exhausted, dismayed,
> With what Cuban reasons the cane carts
> Go on creaking and creaking away!

14   Nightmares and Cold Sweats

MATANZAS' SLUMBER WAS NOT ALWAYS RESTFUL. Every now and then it was broken by nightmares and cold sweats. In early republican Cuba, race, sugar, and the United States caused the indispositions that led to bad sleep. The Platt Amendment and all it portended was the cause of much stress, and the price of sugar a perennial worry. Race, a deep-seated national neurosis, troubled the Cubans' sense of who they were and how they related to one another.

A key issue in the Cuban racial politics of the early twentieth century was the nature of Afro-Cuban identity and how it played out in the public arena. Were all those in whose veins flowed African blood defined by that essential genetic fact, regardless of proportion? Or, conversely, was the Afro-Cuban experience a layering of gradations where being a mulatto—neither entirely black nor entirely white—was a defining category? The great debate found champions in Juan Gualberto Gómez and another brilliant Afro-Matanzan, Martín Morúa Delgado.[1] Gómez held the view that all Cubans bearing African blood, whether pure or mixed, were united in a single community, if for no other reason than because they were all discriminated against.

Another issue of fundamental importance was the nature of a common citizenship and its philosophical foundations in a racially divided society such as Cuba. In other words, did the exercise of full and equal citizenship by all Cubans of whatever color derive ultimately from the *ius gentium*, as argued by both Gómez and Morúa (not to mention other distinguished members of

Fig. 37. An ongoing debate: a 1954 stamp honored Gómez' centennial, then a strikingly similar one saluted Morúa's in 1956, hailing him as "the champion of confraternity."

the Afro-Cuban community, such as Rafael Serra y Montalvo and Generoso Campos Marquetti). Or was full citizenship fundamentally earned by Afro-Cubans on the battlefield, the promise that white Cubans dangled before them? There is, of course, no contradiction between the two principles, except perhaps in their politics.

One thing was certain: Afro-Cubans had fought bravely and well for independence but found out soon enough that promises of fairness and justice rang hollow. When the war cries ceased and the dust settled on the battlefields, white Cuban society closed ranks and resolutely denied dark-skinned Cubans their dignity and the fullness of their hard-earned rights.[2] True, the likes of Gómez and Morúa were honored citizens. Both served in Congress, Gómez in the House, and Morúa in the Senate. There were other Afro-Cubans in positions of eminence as well, but they were notable for their exceptionality.

This was tragic and led to violence culminating in the so-called Race War of 1912. That deplorable episode was no war, of course, but a ruthless move by the government to prevent the formation of Afro-Cuban political parties, an entirely congruent and logical response to systematic discrimination. A bill sponsored by Morúa Delgado—the "Morúa Law"—forbade them. It was enforced with brutal efficiency and with the active but covert support of the United States.[3]

Mass immigration of black Caribbean folks into eastern Cuba exacerbated the Cuban racial hornets' nest during the opening decades of the twentieth century. Ravenous for cheap labor, the booming sugar economies of Oriente and Camagüey attracted large numbers of Haitians and Jamaicans to Cuba's cane fields. Their demographic impact was substantial. As before, their presence fattened the bank accounts of the few and stirred the nightmares of the many in the white Cuban community.

The *negros brujos* (black sorcerers) scare that gripped the island during the first decades of the twentieth century was a salient feature of Cuba's racial landscape. Matanzas was the stage of some of its worst excesses, due to the legacy of slavery exacerbated by the systematic defamation and fear-mongering that are essential components of racism. The brujos were the bogeymen of white Cuban kids well into the days of my childhood. The ñáñigos were especially feared.[4] Growing up in the Matanzas of the 1940s and 1950s, my sister Raquel and I were sternly forbidden to go outside when the feast days of St. Lazarus, St. Barbara, or St. John approached. There were no ifs, ands, or buts. There was to be no standing outside at all or playing with the other neighborhood kids, who were every bit as spooked as we were.[5]

Stories circulated of white children, the fairer the better, whom the brujos had sacrificed to their bloodthirsty gods. There was talk of torture and even cannibalism. We heard about the niña Zoila, kidnapped and sacrificed in Havana at the turn of the century, and many other niños and niñas that had ended up as offerings on the brujos' altars.[6] I was a rather cute kid with famously blue eyes, and these harrowing stories scared me out of my pants. Filet mignon that I was, I worried a lot about the brujos. How could you tell when you were in their evil presence?

Our nanny, Antonia, had it all figured out: any old black man with a sack was suspect. Old black men with sacks were probably brujos. What they carried in the sack was a white child ready to be sacrificed and eaten. Maybe the kid in the sack was already roasted, his brain fried like the *seso* fritters my grandmother loved to make and we loved to eat with lemon and a bit of salt.

One day something embarrassing and, in retrospect, quite shameful happened. I was old enough to remember vaguely but I have heard the story many times, so pathetic and memorable my fright must have been. Peña, the electrician, had come over to my grandparents' house to do some wiring. He was black and in his fifties then, which made him look ancient to me. He showed up carrying a sack. When I saw him, I froze and began to weep inconsolably. I ran to my grandmother Consuelo. "He's a brujo," I said, "and he is carrying a dead child in his sack."

"You are wrong," she answered as she tried to calm me down. "Peña is a very good man. Come with me and let's ask him to show you his sack." Peña graciously obliged. Where I expected to see a roasted baby there was naught but wires and tools. Grandmother was embarrassed and apologized profusely to Peña, who graciously took the incident in stride. But I wonder how he really felt.

During the first quarter of the twentieth century, the brujo issue was front-page news. Stories of brujo misdeeds popped up with dismal frequency in places like Regla, Guanabacoa, and Matanzas, where African culture was deeply rooted. Alejandra Bronfman offers a clear analysis of the terms of the debate on *brujería* and its participants as a component of Cuba's larger concern with race.[7] The brujo debate was the platform that launched the career of Fernando Ortiz, Cuba's eminent humanist and undisputed founder of Afro-Cuban studies.

Ortiz' *Los negros brujos* was published in Madrid in 1906. The book was exemplary in its pioneering research but unfortunate in some of its implications. Ortiz' premise was that some Afro-Cuban religious practices were tantamount to a criminal lowlife—*hampa*. However, certain patterns of "criminal" behavior associated with Cuba's black population were determined by culture and had not to be so much condemned as understood.[8] The book's detailed discussions of Afro-Cuban religious praxis gave the public, for the first time ever, a sense of what happened in African religious services. Scholar Ernesto Chávez Alvarez points out the irony that the "eyewitness accounts" of many an accuser of the brujos seemed to have derived from a reading of Ortiz rather than a personal observation.[9]

Matanzas has a notorious racial skeleton in its closet. It is a small skeleton—that of a child, in fact. It was not kept in a closet at all but, quite appropriately, at a tomb at San Carlos Cemetery. The tomb—a shared space—bears an unusual epitaph.

> Here lies the little girl Cecilia Dalcourt
> murdered by the brujos
> on June 22, 1919, at age 3
> and the brave young men
> who demanded a condign punishment
> for her murderers
> José Guerra and Armando Arbelo
> 23 and 25 years old, respectively.
> who covered themselves with glory
> when shot by the garrison
> of San Severino Castle
> on the dreadful evening of June 29, 1919
> Glory to the Heroes!

The alleged ritual murder of the niña Cecilia, a case that rocked Matanzas and all of Cuba in 1919, is full of mysteries.[10] Dr. Ercilio Vento Canosa, an eminent scholar and forensic physician, exhumed the remains said to be of Cecilia Dalcourt a few years ago. When Dr. Vento and his colleagues opened the vault they found that it was secured by two rails intended to discourage access and that the vault cavity was filled with dirt, an unusual case in vault burials. Even more intriguing, the infantile skeleton inside was no match for that of a three-year-old, a mystery that only deepens the fascination of the strange story of little Cecilia.[11] Tragic and sordid, it is a tale of racism and chicanery and the lasting heritage of fear. It is the story of Matanzas' very own witch hunt, not in some dark and distant past, but well into the twentieth century. It resonated down to the brujo stories that populated my childhood nightmares.

On June 22, 1919, Cecilia Dalcourt Jaruco disappeared from her grandparents' home near the corner of Río and Ayuntamiento streets. Her parents, Regino Dalcourt and Adelina Jaruco, were both light-skinned mulattoes who all but "passed" for white. Regino was a shoemaker, by all accounts a hardworking, respected member of the community. Little Cecilia was blonde and fair.

She was last seen around ten in the evening. Her parents were preparing to return to their own home after a day's visit. It was a Sunday, the traditional day to visit family and friends. Little Cecilia had been catnapping in a rocking chair. Somebody awoke her. She must have stepped outside while her parents bid their farewells. When they looked for her, she was gone. A frantic search was conducted, neighbors knocked on doors and shouted her name up and down the street, but to no avail. She had well and truly vanished. Next morning her distraught parents went to the police.

Another version of Cecilia's mysterious disappearance circulated among Matanzas' black community as the event's consequences became painfully obvious in the next few days. According to this tale, Cecilia was the fruit of an illicit relationship between Adelina and a Spanish shopkeeper, Manuel Alvarez. Regino suspected something—little Cecilia was just too blonde and too fair. When Adelina admitted to the girl's true paternity, an agreement was reached between the mother, the real father, and the putative one. The Spaniard, who was returning to his own country after several years in Cuba, would take the child with him. The mysterious disappearance was a charade. This story, as Chávez Alvarez demonstrates, has no merit.[12]

Enter Captain Tomás Curtis of the army secret police and journalist Ovidio

Santana of *El Imparcial*, one of the town's two newspapers. Curtis was the officer who took down the complaint and conducted the investigation. They came to the conclusion that this could be the case that proved once and for all the existence of the brujo menace. That little Cecilia, a mulatto however light-skinned, did not fit the key requirement for brujo sacrificial hosts was glossed over. It was dark, after all, and one would hardly expect kidnappers of such an obviously fair and lovely child to concern themselves with pedigree.

To Curtis and Santana, Cecilia's disappearance smacked of brujo chicanery. It was their duty, therefore, to expose the facts, discover the guilty, and see that justice was done. That doing so could dramatically enhance an officer's career and sell newspapers might have occurred to them. Be that as it may, *El Imparcial* broke the story on June 24. "All the inhabitants of this city," Santana wrote, "are justly alarmed and fearful that this might be a tremendous crime committed by the brujos, since Matanzas is a good lair for that unworthy rabble."[13]

This put the town on tenterhooks. Amidst the general alarm, Captain Curtis turned up a lead, then a witness, and then a handful of suspects. His star witness was a Chinese known as Goyo, who had overheard certain things. The suspects were José Claro Reyes, Marcos "Pasamajá" Rodríguez Cárdenas, Benito "Chacho" Oliva, Francisco "Parra" Pereira, Luis Gálvez, and Ricardo Villegas. They were all arrested over the next few days and held at the castle. For good measure, José Claro's aunt and grandmother were also arrested and held incommunicado.

According to one story, Luis Gálvez, said to be the chief brujo of Bolondrón, had required a human sacrifice to cure his *comadre*. One of his followers had kidnapped the girl, put her inside a sack, and taken her to the place of sacrifice, where she was stripped naked, killed, eviscerated, and her organs marinated with onion, garlic, and sesame seeds. The coven had then offered the ghastly meal. Claro was said to be directly responsible for the actual kidnapping. After the monstrous deed, the girl's carcass was handed down to Ricardo Villegas for burial. Villegas was a bootblack who had a little stand in the City Hall's portals. Gálvez was indeed a *babalawo*, a Santería priest. That did not automatically damn him, let alone make him the celebrant of such an evil eucharist, but Captain Curtis would not stop at such details.

The next few days were bleak ones for the Matanzas Afro-Cuban communities of faith. One by one, Curtis arrested the leaders of every African cult group he could lay his hands on and confiscated their cherished ritual artifacts. The prisoners, eighteen in total, were sent to the castle. Only a handful of Matanzas' African organizations would ever recover from the blow.

On June 28, news from the castle rocked the city. Ricardo Villegas, one of the prisoners, had committed suicide, hanging himself with his belt. That evening, José Claro had agreed under torture to reveal the location of Cecilia's remains. It was dark, so the search had to be postponed until morning. At daybreak they dug up the remains of a child at the cemetery. They were in an advanced state of putrefaction, but Cecilia's father identified them as those of his daughter. The corpse was examined by Dr. Antonio Font, who reported that the victim had been eviscerated and her brain extracted.

On the night of June 29, a lynch mob of several hundred gathered and marched on San Severino. They demanded the immediate execution of the culprits. Two young men, José Guerra and Armando Arbelo, climbed the wall and were shot dead by the garrison. The mob became even more incensed and, carrying the two bodies aloft, moved downtown, where another mob had begun to gather demanding "justice." The popular mayor, Dr. Armando Carnot y Veulens, appealed for peace, concord, and reflection but the mob wanted none of that.[14] They wanted blood.

Meanwhile, the army, fearing a frontal assault by an out-of-control mob— and perhaps basically in sympathy with the mutineers—applied the *ley de fuga* to five of the prisoners. That is, they were shot while supposedly attempting to escape. When the mob appeared again at the castle gates, the garrison's commandant invited the people, eight at a time, to enter and view the corpses of the brujos. The corpses could not be buried, reported Havana's *Diario de la Marina* on July 1, because a mob of one thousand awaited with cans of gasoline outside the gates, ready to incinerate them.

The tragic niña Cecilia affair clearly had a racist motive. It also had—or developed—a political one as well. In the end its objectives went beyond harassing the city's black population and eradicating the fearsome "brujería." It became the perfect tool to derail the career of Matanzas' progressive mayor.

Dr. Carnot had been elected mayor by an overwhelming majority in 1916 on the Liberal Party ticket. Young, eloquent, handsome, and intensely charismatic, he had the bearing of a prince, which doubtless endeared him to the city's elite. The fact that he was scrupulously honest—a rare virtue in Cuban politics—also helped. He was just as popular on the other side of the tracks, where he was known as "the Physician to the Poor" because of his extensive pro-bono practice. Pampered by the town's high society, who saw him as *gente decente*, and popular among the city's poor and black folks for his charity work, he was expected to win reelection by a landslide, and who knows what life might hold for a young politician so gifted.

The plot against Carnot was very simple: implicate him somehow with the dark forces that populated the nightmares of white Matanzas and he was a goner. The mayor had a resolute enemy in the chief of the army regiment, Colonel Emiliano Amiell, a dyed-in-the-wool Conservative Party hack. The Liberals—Curtis was one—had been useful in the early move against brujería but could not reasonably be expected to move against Carnot. So Amiell had Curtis retired from the army. The retirement decree came directly from President Mario García Menocal.

Carnot unwittingly helped his would-be defamers just by being himself: by refusing to rush to judgment and seeking to defend the civil rights of the accused. As tempers rose in connection with the disappearance of little Cecilia, and later around the alleged circumstances of her death, the mayor became a voice, seemingly the only voice, advocating calm, fairness, and reason. When it became clear that the crisis was getting out of hand, Carnot called on the national government to put Matanzas under martial law and military supervision. That played right into the hands of his enemies and further isolated

Fig. 38. *Left:* Memorial plaque on Armando Carnot's birthplace at Manzano and Jovellanos Streets, now in ruins. *Right:* Carnot during his term as mayor (1919).

Armando Carnot. The last thing the witch hunters wanted was order and the army. They wanted blood, fire, and lynchings. White matanceros demanded a Grand Inquisitor, not a peacemaker, and that Carnot steadfastly refused to be, however much it might have advanced his political career. By going against the grain of the irate mob, the mayor made himself vulnerable. With luck, his enemies calculated, they might yet have his head on a platter.

When the remains said to be of little Cecilia were exhumed, the corpse was found to be wrapped in a handkerchief bearing the initials JC. That was it! The horrendous ritual had been meant to cure the mayor's sister, Juana, of a dreadful and unspeakable disease. The rumor spread like wildfire. The story explained everything. Carnot was unwilling to confront Evil because he was complicit![15] Moreover, one of the accused brujos was a municipal employee, and José Claro was said to be the mayor's coachman—it was not true but who cared. That was evidence! Carnot, frustrated, resigned under a cloud. As tempers cooled, many of his fellow citizens came to realize how deeply he had been wronged. The survivors among those arrested were, in fact, tried in a court of law and acquitted. When Carnot died in 1926, his burial was the largest ever in Matanzas' history. It was as if his neighbors wished to atone for their shameful behavior, but the damage had been done.

Carnot and the little child whose bones are said to be Cecilia's lie not far from each other at San Carlos Cemetery. Captain Curtis disappeared from the scene. Ovidio Santana's paper survived until its confiscation by the Castro government in 1960. Regino and Adelina spent the rest of their lives in obscurity. Matanzas' cabildos de nación were decimated; her shame was beyond outliving or erasing.

If the brujos had wished to cast a curse on Matanzas as their revenge for racism and persecution, they could not have come up with anything worse than what actually happened the following year. Nineteen twenty will always be remembered as the year of the great sugar "Crack." The spectacular drop in sugar prices after years of consistent bonanza has been called a turning point in the history of capitalism.[16] The price collapse bankrupted many a mill owner and dramatically denationalized the sugar industry. It brought Cuban banks low and left a residue of bitterness that would last a generation. It affected Matanzas directly and dramatically.

Sugar prices had been at all-time highs during the Great War, enriching

Cuba. In fact, the period was called "las vacas gordas" (the Fat Cows). The dislocations brought about by the war in the beet-producing areas of Europe generated a tremendous demand for Cuban sugar. This led to high prices and easy credit. Mill owners assumed heavy debt burdens to increase their productive capacity, or simply to spend on luxuries such as homes in Havana's palatial Miramar neighborhood. It also led to the development of vast new sugar mills in the island's eastern districts. Cuba reacted to the extraordinary circumstances of the war years as if they were to last forever. Of course, they could not.

During the war the price of sugar had been capped at a very lucrative five to six cents per pound by the U.S. Sugar Stabilization Board. When the war ended, price controls were eased, leading to a remarkable upwards surge known in Cuba as the "Dance of the Millions." Ultimately, however, the bonanza was based on the erroneous assumption that wartime-induced scarcities would outlast the war. This was not to be, and it is remarkable with the benefit of hindsight that so many smart people could have been so delusional, but such is the intoxicating power of avarice.

Assuming that they had God by the beard, as the old Spanish proverb goes, many of Cuba's mill owners created a cartel designed to control supply in order to keep the upward price spiral energized.[17] They would not sell their product until the price of sugar per pound reached the hitherto inconceivable threshold of twenty-five cents. My great-grandfather Laurentino García was an enthusiastic speculator. He was offered a whopping $16,000,000 for his business at the height of the boom, but he decided to come down to the wire.[18] Truth be told, his decision was not all cupidity. He had made his two mills, Progreso and Santa Amalia, virtually new from a technical point of view and was heavily mortgaged to the tune of several million, principally to the First National City Bank of New York.

So, don Laurentino dispatched his son, Laurentino Jr., to New York in April 1920 to await his instructions to sell. While in New York, Junior was a house guest of Manuel Rionda, whose firm, Czarnikow-Rionda, handled Laurentino García's account. In its heyday it was the largest sugar trader in the world, so he had access to the best market information.[19]

Rionda, who knew the ins and outs of the world sugar market and had great esteem for the old man, a fellow Asturian, told Junior that holding on to their inventory was a great risk. Sugar stocks existed which, when dumped on the market, were certain to depress prices, conceivably to catastrophic levels. "Tell your father," Rionda would advise Junior over lunch, "to sell, and soon." Junior would cable his father back in Cuba, but the answer was always wait. He had given his word of honor to stand firm.

Meanwhile, the price of sugar continued its upwards waltz. Don Laurentino might have fantasized about his retirement. Maybe to Spain, to his village near Avilés, to live the opulent life of an *indiano*; or maybe to Matanzas, by the sea. He commissioned a palatial villa to be built across from the Malecón near Peñas Altas. The foundations were dug and a floor actually built before the project was abandoned. The walls had a lead damp course, and people digging out the lead did substantial damage to what there was of the structure over the years. Stone mullions and the vines growing over cornices and carved surrounds gave the appearance of a ruined medieval fortress. As a child I loved to visit "the ruins," which were inhabited by a couple of families that, due to negligence or a misguided sense of generosity, seemed to have acquired squatters' rights. The case was perennially in court.

Up, up, and away, sugar prices skyrocketed during that memorable spring of 1920, and then the music suddenly stopped, as it had to. The Dance of the Millions was over. From a height of 22.5 cents per pound on May 19, 1920, sugar prices began heading south. The story of those exhilarating, then depressing weeks in New York lived on in Junior's dramatic retelling. When the downward price spiral began, Junior dreaded opening the morning's financial pages. He would take long strolls in Central Park to ease his nerves. But there was nothing he could do. It was now a buyers' market, and there were no buyers. Notch by dramatic notch, the family's dreams of vast wealth visibly trickled through their fingers. When the downward curve hit rock bottom at 3.75 cents per pound, it became obvious that the old man had made a mistake by delaying, and the family firm was confronting a severe cash flow crisis. With no cash on hand, it might not even be possible to bring in the 1921 zafra.

In January of 1921, Laurentino Sr. applied to Rionda for an advance of $100,000 to bring in the 1921 harvest. It was rather dramatic. My grandfather Miguel recounted how he and his father-in-law made a special trip to the Havana docks literally to await Rionda's arrival from New York and press the case personally. With two mills shipshape and enough actual and potential sugar stocks at the close of the 1921 harvest to clear expenses and service the debt even in a severely depressed commodities market, Laurentino García, S.A., was worth the risk. Rionda saw that immediately and agreed to the emergency loan but, confronted with the financial disintegration of many of his

Fig. 39. Vivienda (*above*) and factory of Laurentino García's Progreso mill (*below*) at the heyday of the wartime sugar bonanza, 1916. The house (1911) featured classical elements and a *portal*.

other clients, he decided he could not make exceptions and backed off on the bailout. The family fortunes would never recover.

Progreso went into foreclosure proceedings. Grandfather's advice to his father-in-law was simple: Let us get some rifles, circle the wagons, and say "come and get us." But the old man was too much of an old-fashioned Spanish gentleman to even consider that. Others actually did it, notably the Marzol family of Matanzas, owners of Triunfo sugar mill. Adolfo Marzol, the family patriarch, let it be known that they would never get him out of his mill alive and, true to his word, distributed arms among his loyal employees. The bankers got the message and held off long enough for don Adolfo to save his mill. To don Laurentino, however, a debt was a debt, and he surrendered Progreso. It must have been painful to have the Yankee accountants poring over the books. Had he managed to survive a few more weeks, he would have benefited from the Moratorium Law of 1921, but by then it was all over.

He was not alone. His was but one in National City's portfolio of $35 million in bad Cuban loans. As the notes were called in, National City ended up with more than sixty centrales in receivership.[20] The New York banking giant therefore became the single largest stakeholder ever in the history of the Cuban sugar industry, in both absolute and relative terms. Progreso was gone, decisions concerning its fate to be made for the time being in New York, not Matanzas. The mill passed to Cuban hands eventually. In 1943 it was purchased by José Arechabala, S.A., the Cárdenas-based manufacturer of Havana Club rum.[21]

The family, now incorporated as Sucesión de Laurentino García, S.A., let go of Santa Amalia a few years later and got out of the sugar-making business altogether. The Sucesión was left holding a vast amount of land—some 650 caballerías (8,800 hectares)—a rail network used for the transportation of cane to the mills, and a number of *chuchos* and *trasbordadoras,* or loading stations. Had the family firm decided to operate this strategic estate directly, it would have been a very lucrative enterprise. It contained some of the best agricultural land in the country. However, the decision was made in the early 1930s to lease out most of the land. The old man had died in 1925 and, chastised by recent history, his heirs had grown risk-adverse. The timing of their decision could not have been worse. In 1937, a comprehensive Law of Sugar Coordination guaranteed tenancy to renters virtually in perpetuity. This meant in effect that Sucesión de Laurentino García lost the usufruct of most of its landholdings.

My grandparents' predicament was not unlike that of the owners of rent-controlled apartments in New York. In theory they were big landowners, presumably comfortably rich; in practice they were modestly solvent. They kept up appearances, to be sure. They had inherited finery, but the Limoges china and the Baccarat cups had to be handled with great care because, if they broke, there was no replacing them. Surprisingly for such a dyed-in-the-wool conservative, my grandfather Miguel welcomed the 1959 Agrarian Reform Law enthusiastically as a way to break the logjam, provided adequate compensation was involved. It did not work out that way. He died in 1960, a victim of mild dementia, hallucinating that Fidel and Raúl Castro were armed at the door, waiting for him.

15   Kilowatts and Revolution

Salitre, the salty residue of sea spray, is everywhere. It coats surfaces, clings to nostrils, and floats in the midday breeze. The brine is a constant reminder to the people of what they owe to the bay: a truculent name and rusty lampposts, to be sure, but a measure of celebrity as well. The Bay of Slaughters scored another fifteen minutes of international fame almost exactly three hundred years after Piet Heyn's escapade. One October day of 1930, Matanzas became the first place where electrical energy was drawn from the sea. What Kitty Hawk is to aviation, Matanzas Bay could be some day to ocean thermal energy conversion (OTEC), potentially one of the twenty-first century's transformational technologies.[1]

If the advocates of OTEC have their way—and that includes a remarkable working group at the University of Matanzas Faculty of Engineering[2]—the planet's oceans could join wind and the sun as key alternative, nonpolluting global sources of energy. With a bonus: OTEC yields vast amounts of fresh water as a by-product. Futurists envision "energy islands" in the world's tropical oceans where a combination of the three technologies could supply virtually all of the world's energy and freshwater needs.[3]

OTEC was the brainchild of Georges Claude, a prolific French inventor. Without him there would be no Las Vegas—one of his many inventions was neon lighting. His patents made him a millionaire, and he would be famous as France's Edison if he had not become infamous first. Georges Claude was tried as a Nazi collaborator at the end of World War II and served four years of a life sentence. He died in 1960 at ninety years of age.[4]

Claude's idea rested on principles postulated by his professor, Jacques Arsene d'Arsonval, in 1881 (coincidentally, the same year the great Matanzas Exhibit opened). A large enough temperature differential between the surface and the bottom layers of seawater make a "heat engine" possible. Warm surf water (as much as 29°C in the tropics) would be brought to a boil in a vacuum chamber by the rays of the sun. The resulting steam would be forced into a turbine to generate electricity. Cooled by water from the bottom of the ocean (as low as 5°C at a depth of one kilometer), the steam would condense into desalinated water to be recovered and used. The main practical problems: how to bring a stream of water upwards from the bottom of the ocean while keeping it cold enough and, naturally, the weather.

In 1927 Claude set out to prove that the theory could be engineered. With the support of the French Academy of Sciences, he raised substantial research funds. Cuba was chosen as an ideal locale for an experiment. It had the main ingredients: sunshine, warm surf, and great oceanic depths offshore.

Gerardo Machado y Morales had been sworn in as president two years before the French inventor showed up in Havana aboard his luxury yacht, the *Jamaica*. Entrepreneurial and businesslike, Machado had a reputation for getting things done. He was at the height of his popularity then, which he was about to gamble away in a dubious gambit to extend his term of office. Machado's endorsement was essential, not in terms of money—Claude had enough—but in logistical backing. The Cuban president was impressed and pledged his government's support.

The next step was to find a proper site. The French soon discovered what Matanzas Olokún devotees just knew and Captain-General Manzaneda had figured out in 1693, feeding *braza* upon endless braza of line into the murky depths: Matanzas Bay was *deep*. The choice was electrifying to the local citizenry. For the next few months, Claude's operations were the talk of the town and a great free show. Matanceros opened their homes to the French, who were feted and lionized.

By early 1928 the French team was ready to begin. The project required two components, a shore plant with a vacuum chamber, turbine, and condenser, and a pipe long enough to clear the insular platform and reach the required abyssal depths. Constructing the shore plant was easy enough, but assembling and deploying the pipe was not. It was to be constructed of sections made of "deeply corrugated" stainless steel. Each section was 2 meters long with a diameter of 1.5 meters—large enough for an adult to stand inside.

Splicing the sections proved difficult, floating them out challenging, and sinking them adequately so daunting that it almost sank the project itself. Fabrication of the pipe began at the new customshouse on Ayllón Street. When the first seven hundred meters of pipe had been spliced together they were floated and towed to the middle of the harbor. Bad timing: a storm blew in and the pipe just sank.

Undaunted, Claude launched a second attempt. This time he decided to assemble the entire pipe length along the meandering Canímar. The pipe would grow while afloat, saving one labor-intensive intermediate step. In July, the pipe, an awe-inspiring steel sausage almost two kilometers long, was tugged across the harbor with deeply tanned Cuban divers hanging from the flotation tanks. Matanzas seethed with excitement. Would it sink? Could it be connected to shore? Some, no doubt, wondered whether anybody had bothered to propitiate Olokún before trespassing into his cold and dark realm.

When one end of the pipe was successfully attached to the shore plant, the entire town sighed with relief. Efforts to sink the other end began in earnest. At first everything seemed to go well but then, unexpectedly, one of the cables securing the long pipe to the shore plant snapped. Possibly, the downwards pressure of the descending pipe exceeded calculations, the underwater currents were stronger than expected, or divers along the line had filled the floaters much too soon—or not soon enough. Perhaps Olokún was just fed up with the intrusion. We will never know, although none other than the great Jacques-Yves Cousteau tried to find out.[5] The shiny metal snake popped free, lurched to one side, and plunged to join its sister in the cold darkness below.

The situation was now critical. His budget was depleted, but Claude was not one to give up. Even though he was now digging into his own pocket, he decided to go for broke. At this point the Cuban observers came up with a sensible suggestion. Why not—the Cubans argued—transport the sections to the shore plant by train? (The rail lines ran close by.) The team could then assemble the long snake outwards from the shore plant, two manageable sections at a time. The plan worked, and soon sufficient pipe had been committed to the deep to justify a demonstration.

On October 30, 1930, before a gathered audience of engineers and notables,

Claude proceeded. The inventor threw a switch and, slowly at first, steam began to build up in the vacuum chamber. Leisurely, the turbine began to spin. A *Time* magazine reporter described the moment:

> When the visitors saw the turbine gathering speed at a rate of several thousand revolutions per minute they stopped their whispers and stared. Then Georges Claude turned on the electric generators. Forty large bulbs began to glow dully but soon lit up and shone bright for minutes. Cuban scientists nodded their heads.[6]

Claude had succeeded. His machine did what it was supposed to do.[7] He had also failed because it did not produce net energy, that is, energy in excess of that needed to run it, let alone the projected commercial output of 12,000 kilowatts Claude had promised. A few weeks later a storm did away with the sea power machine, lending credibility to the argument that the proposed plants' extreme vulnerability to the elements made them impractical. Of course, in 1928 nobody had yet anchored a drilling platform to an ocean floor and hurricanes were no more predictable than adultery.

The following year Claude repeated his experiment off the coast of Brazil, this time from a boat. It worked. Claude, in fact, was even able to make some ice from desalinated water. Unfortunately, another storm sent his equipment to the bottom before he could achieve payoff. The Great Depression poured a cascade of ice water on any further experimentation with OTEC. Interest in the technology's promise, however, is dramatically rising in our own day, now that solutions exist for some of the practical problems Claude could not overcome. His was simply a good idea whose time had not yet come. Matanzas—a pleasant surprise—is a household word in the environmental, scientific, and technological circles surrounding OTEC.

Another idea tried out with partial success in the Cuba of that time was revolution. To understand how that happened we must return to Machado and introduce two improbable figures that became immensely consequential in Cuban history: Fulgencio Batista Zaldívar and Antonio "Tony" Guiteras Holmes.

Batista was from Oriente. He must have been related, though in no way anybody would guess, to the more illustrious Cuban lineage of that name, one of whose members is the reigning Grand Duchess of Luxemburg. Batista (Fulgencio) was racially mixed and came from the humblest of backgrounds.

Nobody would have guessed what lay ahead for the former railway line-man when Georges Claude was tinkering with cold water and hot cables in Matanzas.

Guiteras' lineage, on the other hand, was illustrious indeed. Tony Guiteras' grandfather was Antonio Guiteras Font, the eminent educator and cofounder of La Empresa School. Pedro José the historian and Eusebio the poet were his great-uncles. Juan, the eminent physician, was a cousin. During the Ten Years' War the family had lived in exile in Philadelphia and developed lasting links to the United States.

Guiteras' father, Calixto Guiteras y Gener, was one of Antonio's thir-teen children. A civil engineer, he worked for a while in Latin America be-fore settling down in suburban Philadelphia and marrying a local woman, Marie Therese Holmes. The couple had three children, Calixta, Antonio, and Margarita.

Maybe it was the tug of the Guiteras genes, or perhaps a midlife crisis, that prompted Calixto Guiteras to abandon his engineering practice and devote himself to teaching. He landed a job in Girard College's Foreign Languages Department in 1912. Along with the lure of a new career, Guiteras felt another pull, that of Cuba itself. The family moved back to Matanzas in 1914 and took up residence at the old family home, No. 9 Río Street, where the del Monte tertulias had met three-quarters of a century before.

Their only son was a restless kid and somewhat accident-prone. When he was about five he fell while playing and as a consequence experienced severe motor disorders on the right side of his body. He had to learn to write with his left hand. He also lost muscular control of one of his eyes, which affected both his eyesight and his appearance. To compound his woes, he developed a growth on the sole of his left foot that affected his gait. Walking was painful but, pain or no pain, he became an avid hiker.

Calixto, Marie Therese, and their brood lived in Matanzas for almost two years, until the head of the family received a teaching appointment effective with the 1915–1916 academic year at the Instituto de Pinar del Río, the capi-tal city of Cuba's westernmost province. During their brief Matanzas stay, the Philadelphia Guiterases befriended the bishop, the Most Reverend Charles Warren Currier. The prelate must have welcomed the arrival of this vibrant family with whom he could converse in English, stay in touch with home, and perhaps talk about his problems. Bishop Currier was fighting a losing battle with mental illness. The figure of the tall and stately man in his purple robes must have impressed young Guiteras, who expressed his desire to be a bishop when he grew up.

That was not to be. Instead of the seminary, Tony Guiteras enrolled in the School of Pharmacy at the University of Havana and began attending classes in the fall of 1924. He hoped to go for a medical degree after he had completed one in pharmacy. Instead he got involved in radical university politics.[8] In the

Fig. 40. Charles Warren Currier in 1912. (Photo by Cav. G. Felici, Rome; courtesy of Department of Special Collections and University Archives, Marquette University Libraries).

1920s, Cuban university students had been influenced by what was called the Córdoba Movement. Begun at Argentina's University of Córdoba, it held that students were Latin America's unpolluted avant-garde. Their role was to serve as a moral force for the regeneration of society and a progressive impulse in national politics.[9]

The year following Guiteras' matriculation, Machado was inaugurated as the fifth president of the Cuban Republic. Cuba had had indifferent luck with the first four. Tomás Estrada Palma, dour and straight-laced, was honest financially but politically inept. José Miguel Gómez—Liberal, endomorphic, and a jolly good fellow by all accounts—was Cuba's version of Boss Tweed. The third president, Mario García Menocal, was Conservative, handsome, and a Matanzan from the town of Jagüey Grande. A Cornell engineer, he was the darling of the business community. With his carefully trimmed beard he looked a bit like Tsar Nicholas II. His successor, Alfredo Zayas y Alfonso, skinny, ungainly, and lantern-faced, had a sharp intellect and a talent for political maneuver. He was also vain and encouraged the dedication of a statue to himself with his right arm stretched high. Somebody wrote on the plinth "la mierda llegó hasta aquí" (shit reached this high), a reference to the state of the republic. All Havana laughed. To his credit, so did Zayas.

Machado was the son of a butcher from Santa Clara and a protégé of former President José Miguel Gómez. Sullen like Estrada Palma, he was efficient and entrepreneurial like Menocal but lacked either the populist instincts of his mentor or Zayas' flexibility. Cuba, not to mention his own interests, would have been better served if he had had his scholarly predecessor's sense of humor, but the fifth president had a thin skin. He had a hard time taking criticism or tolerating dissent. Jokes about him soon circulated. One had Machado asking his aide-de-camp for the time of day. The aide-de-camp's answer: "whichever you like, Mr. President." The radical poet Rubén Martínez Villena memorably called the stubborn, vindictive Machado "a jackass with claws."

Machado had a rival for the Liberal nomination, Colonel Carlos Mendieta y Montefur, who was as aloof in the pursuit of voters as Machado was diligent. The nomination was decided when Zayas and former Matanzas Governor Carlos de la Rosa endorsed Machado, the latter in exchange for the vice-presidential nomination.

The new administration was received enthusiastically. During the first part of his term Machado presided over a vast program of public works. Some, like the luxurious new capitol, were fatuous. Others were farsighted and strategic, such as the Central Highway, a landscaped, paved road with wide shoulders linking all provincial capitals.

This was the Gerardo Machado that Georges Claude had met in 1927, but there was another side to Machado. Relatively honest but prone to flattery and disdainful of rivals, he was afflicted by the authoritarian style often found in those who view themselves as somehow providential. Buoyed by his initial successes, Machado forced a constitutional amendment extending the presidential term of office from four to six years. Beginning the count in 1928, he was to be—or so it seemed—solidly in office until 1935.

He overplayed his hand, and drew two jokers. The first was the wave of popular revulsion that met his fraudulent maneuver. The second was the Depression's massive impact on Cuba. The nation, not yet recovered from the sugar bust of 1920, watched in dismay as sugar prices dropped to an unprecedented 0.57 cents per pound by 1932. The opposition and the government resorted to terror. In this heady atmosphere the young Guiteras found his métier and became a fearless anti-Machado revolutionist. At some point he and a group of commandoes attacked an army barracks, something that Fidel Castro would do later on. Such actions—whether by Guiteras or Castro—had nil military value but yielded a stupendous psychological payoff. He became a hero, somebody his fellow students could and did look up to. Elected delegate to the Student Directorate from the School of Pharmacy, he had a loud voice at student cabals.

He did not have a commanding physical presence but was charismatic in his own way. He was skinny—what Cubans call *flaco*—and had a slight limp as a result of his foot problems. His hair was quaintly parted at the middle. Crossed eyes and a slightly deviated septum accounted for a distracted expression. Tony Guiteras may have looked inoffensive, a bit like Franz Kafka, but he had resolve, principles, and clear ideas that he expressed forcefully. Above all, he had mettle—what Cubans call *cojones*. [10]

Machado was deposed on August 12, 1933, as the result of an underhanded intervention by the American ambassador, Benjamin Sumner Welles. *Mister* Welles had been instructed by the new Franklin Roosevelt administration to resolve the Cuban crisis—meaning get rid of Machado without marines or battleships—and that is exactly what he accomplished. His tools were truculent maneuvering, astute subornation, and the threat of consequences. Carlos Manuel de Céspedes, the anodyne son of the 1868 hero and Machado's secretary of state, was elevated to the presidency. He lasted less than a month in of-

Fig. 41. A Cuban for all seasons. Antonio Guiteras commemorative stamp issue, 1950.

fice. On September 4, to Welles' consternation, a group of noncommissioned officers led by Sergeant Fulgencio Batista overthrew Céspedes. The coup was not only unexpected but stunning as well. Nay, unprecedented. In Latin America generals did such things, not sergeants like this Batista. Who the heck was he, anyway?

The entire officer corps committed political suicide when they abandoned their posts in protest. Honor first. They then went as a group to the National Hotel, Ambassador Welles' temporary residence, to make a stand. What followed was embarrassing for everybody except perhaps Batista, who smoked them out with artillery.

Sensing that he had caught a tiger by the tail, Batista turned to the students. This bizarre alliance crafted a collegiate executive to rule the country provisionally. It was elegantly called "the Pentarchy." It was Greek to Batista but the sergeant, suddenly promoted to colonel, was a quick study. He had a sharp intelligence; a gift for politics; and a nose for power, where it lay, and how to get it. Meanwhile, in Matanzas, future national poet Agustín Acosta became provisional governor and Manuel Labra, a respected mathematician, took over the mayoralty.

A few days after the coup, a popular professor of medicine, Dr. Ramón Grau San Martín, was acclaimed as sole president. Guiteras became his minister of the interior. What followed was a comprehensive program of nationalistic social reforms. In his first public speech, Grau dramatically denounced the Platt Amendment, but it was Guiteras who held the government together and infused it with a burning reformist zeal. A minimum wage and the eight-hour workday were enacted, professional licensing regulated, the basis for an agrarian reform laid out, and a Ministry of Labor created. Guiteras dealt with kilowatts also, though not in a fashion the conservative Georges Claude would have approved of: he slashed electrical tariffs and nationalized the U.S.-owned Cuban Electric Company. In response to the tendency among Spanish businesses to hire only Spaniards to the detriment of Cubans, a decree mandated that private employers hire at least 50 percent of their payroll from the pool of Cuban citizens. Thus, Cuba merrily invented affirmative action.

Alarmed by the revolutionary fervor south of Key West, Washington withheld recognition of the Grau-Guiteras government. In late 1933, Sumner Welles was recalled and Jefferson Caffery sent down as his successor. By then a number of sugar mills were being occupied by "Soviets." The entire Cuban situation was seemingly getting out of hand. Meanwhile, Batista had been solidifying his position by the day. As chief of staff he strategically distributed brass among his NCO close allies—not much, just enough. He was good at identifying talent and knew how to command loyalty from the improvised officer corps. He pampered the troops at one end and opened channels of communication with Welles, and later on with Caffery, at the other. Caffery was resolved to put the brakes on Cuba's revolutionary frenzy, but his instructions were clear: no battleships and no marines. The old approach was a no-no in the new era of the "Good Neighbor." The shrewd Batista sensed an opportunity. His ragamuffin army was no U.S. Marine Corps, but it would do. It was all there was. It had the weapons, and Batista controlled it. His work was cut out for him.

On January 15, 1934, Grau resigned and was succeeded by Secretary of State Carlos Hevia. Grau quit with a record as a reformist thwarted by the United States—a windfall in political credibility that was to make him president again, this time by a landslide, in 1944. Hevia was expected to make only one substantive decision: select a secretary of state to whom he would immediately relinquish the presidency. Guiteras earnestly hoped to be the choice. He was sorely disappointed when Hevia, no radical, chose the old-fashioned Mendieta instead.

The new provisional president proved himself unequal to the moment. It took no time for Batista to reduce him to the status of a wall decoration. If social peace was the requirement for U.S. diplomatic recognition, Batista was all too willing to do the dirty work in the hope of eventually gathering the harvest. Guiteras went underground and founded Joven Cuba, an organization pledged to carry out the interrupted revolution. Middle class in membership, nationalistic in tone, and suffused with socialist ideas, Joven Cuba rejected Marxian Communism. Its essential characteristic was its willingness—indeed, eagerness—to promote violent action if deemed necessary to bring about social change.

Where the main concern of Grau-Guiteras had been social reform, the task of Batista-Mendieta was to preserve public order and prevent things from going too far. In stark, simplistic terms, if Grau-Guiteras was the Revolution, Batista-Mendieta represented the Reaction. Which side would prevail was decided in March 1935, when a revolutionary general strike supported by Guiteras was aborted by the army. The young firebrand had to go into hiding.

Two months later he was to have been spirited out of Cuba by boat. His destination: Mexico, there to plan a comeback. The rendezvous with his rescuers was to be at the Morrillo, the old Spanish fort on the mouth of the Canímar. Remnants of Claude's piping and paraphernalia were still to be found strewn about. The canal dug by the French at the sandbar in the river's mouth was still open when Guiteras and his companions arrived. They included Carlos Aponte, a Venezuelan Marxist; José Antonio Casariego and his wife, Conchita Valdivieso; Xiomara O'Halloran, and others.

Someone was a snitch. In fact, by the time the army set out to get Guiteras, gossipy Matanzas was abuzz with the news that he was hiding at the Morrillo. Guiteras was resting on the roof when he heard a commotion. It was not rescue but the army: truckloads of soldiers armed to the teeth. There was no escape with the army in front and the deep blue Bay of Slaughters behind. Shots were heard. Some said Aponte was the first to open fire. An army corporal named Man Hernández was shot dead. Some more shots, and now it was Guiteras and Aponte who fell. Their end reminds one of Butch Cassidy and the Sundance Kid.

Antonio Guiteras' death put the last nail in the coffin of the Revolution of 1933. Not all was lost, of course. The laws enacted from the trenches in 1933–34 became a body of social legislation that profoundly changed Cuban society in the decade and a half that was to follow. Guiteras, the luminary of Cuba's reform movement, lived on as a hero of Cuba's democratic left honored for his achievements as a social reformer. His persona as a gun-toting man of action and dedicated militant revolutionist faded away, either attributed to the spirit of the times or sublimated in the electoral politics of the 1940s and 1950s.

The idea of revolution as the root of progress, however, remained safely at the forefront of Cuban public discourse, especially now that revolution itself was in remission and asymptomatic. The great Martí, after all, had named his organization the Cuban Revolutionary Party. The party Grau created and that carried him to power in 1944 was also the Cuban Revolutionary Party. As a courtesy to Martí's brand, the party's revolutionary authenticity was decently expressed in parentheses as Partido Revolucionario Cubano (Auténtico), or PRC(A). With commendable modesty, its members did not call themselves Revolucionarios, as logic would dictate, but merely Auténticos. The idea that revolution in the abstract was a good thing was honored even by Batista, who referred to the predatory coup that brought him back to power in 1952 as a "revolution without cruelty."

The Auténticos' claim to Martí's mantle was subtle. Their reclaiming of Guiteras' legacy—it helped that he was dead, of course—was anything but. On the day following Grau's inauguration in 1944, Eduardo R. "Eddy" Chibás, newly elected senator on the Auténtico Party ticket, personally demolished a small monument erected to Corporal Man Hernández' memory near the Morrillo. To leave no doubt of Guiteras' redemption, the enormous bridge planned to span the Canímar was named after him. It opened to traffic in 1951.

Eddy Chibás, a wildly popular politician and hands-down favorite to win the presidency in 1952, wrote an incredible page in Cuba's history by shooting himself during a radio broadcast in August 1951. Chibás had positioned himself in Congress as the *malleus maleficarum,* the hammer of corruption and terror of evildoers. He broke away from the Auténticos and formed his own party, the Ortodoxos. (Fidel Castro was a member and a candidate for office in 1952.) His message touched a nerve, for the new party soon became by far the largest in the country. Cherubic-faced and severely myopic, he did not look like a charismatic leader of the masses behind his thick bottle-bottom eyeglasses. But he was a consummate radio demagogue. His broadcast was an exposé of the administrative malfeasance of the week. All went well until he picked on Aureliano Sánchez Arango, the minister of education. The minister must have been the proverbial just man in Sodom and Gomorrah, for Chibás could find nothing. Rather than apologizing, he shot himself in the thigh, calling his action the "last knock on Cuba's conscience." Alas, the bullet intended for his butt found its way to his abdomen, giving peritonitis a chance to vote. His death, perhaps unintended but all too consequential, opened the way for Batista II. It is extremely doubtful that Batista would have staged his March 1952 coup if Chibás had been alive. Chibás was seemingly invulnerable, except perhaps to himself; the sitting president, Carlos Prío Socarrás (1948–1952) was not.

Militant student activism remained, very much a legacy of the turbulent days of the struggle against Machado and its exciting revolutionary sequel. As legacies go, this was a very mixed one that could with equal ease produce sophomoric virtue and campus racketeering. Since the university campus was by law inviolable and hence off-bounds to the police, the latter abounded—always, of course, in the guise of patriotism.

Just like Grau and Chibás, Fidel Castro has laid claim to Guiteras' legacy. Not, indeed, as the leader of a revolution eventually accomplished (as Grau did) but as the mentor of a revolution tragically aborted. Correction: not *a* revolution but *the* one and only Revolution. In this scheme, Martí is also recognized as the "intellectual author" of the Revolution, an ongoing aspiration of the Cuban people it was Castro's destiny to accomplish.

Truth be told, there is an undeniable parallel between Castro and Guiteras. They are both bourgeois. They are both white (assuming that the only radical, truly transformational revolution for Cuba has to do with race and is yet to come). They were both formed as leaders by university politics. They were both quite willing to use violent means to further their objectives. They both planned to stage a comeback from Mexico after initial failures in Cuba. Nobody knows what Guiteras would have done had he managed to gain power. This much is certain about Castro: there is no Matanzas, and certainly no Philadelphia, in him.

Guiteras was buried at Matanzas' cemetery a few yards from where the corpse said to be of little Cecilia Dalcourt had been laid to rest in 1919, not far from Armando Carnot's grave, and a short walk away from Laurentino García's final resting place. Two years later, in the dark of night, somebody violated the tomb and stole Guiteras' mortal remains, allegedly to protect them from desecration.

It would be hard to imagine anyone whose interest would have been served by such a ghoulish extremity. The last thing Batista would have wanted was to put Guiteras back on the front page. In death, Guiteras had become a national hero. The Prío government honored him with a beautiful stamp issue in 1950. Guiteras' bones remained at large for almost thirty years, their location known only to a José M. García, one of the grave robbers. In 1966, García delivered the remains to the government and they were solemnly reburied at the Morrillo. Castro was on hand to render honor and deliver the eulogy of his honored predecessor and presumptive mentor.

Antonio Guiteras Holmes did not become a bishop after all. The same year that his remains were stolen from their place of rest, those of someone who did were interred nearby. He was Matanzas' second prelate, the Most Reverend Severiano Saínz y Bencomo. Bishop Saínz passed away on Sunday, March 14, 1937. The following Saturday, the terminals of the national lottery were 40 and 64. In the Chinese charade these numbers stood for *cura* (priest) and *muerto grande* (eminent deceased), respectively. Droves of matanceros bet on those two numbers in the numbers game that week and . . . bingo![11] Unable to meet the prize payments due, numbers game bankers absconded until they found financing. At one go, the good late bishop put bread on people's tables and dealt a blow to vice. Some thought him a saint. Saints do such things.

Those seeking to understand Cuban history in conventional ways are doomed to frustration. André Breton, the eminent French art critic and father of surrealism, was a visitor to Cuba in the late 1920s, and he knew better. "Truly," he famously wrote, "Cuba is too surrealistic a country to be livable."

16   Deus ex Machine Gun

IN A PART OF THE WORLD PRONE TO HURRICANES, Cuba's twentieth century seems like one big storm of capricious trajectory and wildly fluctuating intensity. The 1900s began in the wake of a devastating war that lasted almost four years. They ended amidst a category 5 revolution—in reality, a dynastic-charismatic dictatorship—that has endured for half a century.[1]

True to type, the Cuban storm had a stretch of calm at the center. The twelve-year-long eye of the hurricane settled on the Cuban archipelago precisely at noon on July 1, 1940. On that day, the Constitution for the new Cuban state emerging after four decades of turmoil was signed into existence.

The Constitution of 1940 was a creature of paradox: a result of the revolutionary ferment of the early 1930s made possible by the Batista-imposed peace that followed. The ferment brought forth the ideas; the peace secured the setting for them to crystallize into an exemplary constitutional document. Fulgencio Batista y Zaldívar had entered Cuban history in 1933 like the deus ex machina of ancient drama, where an actor impersonating a god was dropped to stage center by means of ropes and pulleys to provide the dramatic resolution. In 1940 he was rightfully the man of the hour. He would preside over Cuba's first four years in the calm of the eye.

That Batista, a man of color, was able to achieve power in a majority-white, thoroughly racist society is one of his genuine accomplishments. He had others, very significant ones. The early Batista was rather progressive. He was, in fact, the Communist Party's candidate for president in 1940, which brings to mind André Breton's dictum about Cuba and surrealism. He earned a great distinction when he left office four years later, confounding his critics by merely going home after leaving the Presidential Palace. The candidate he had backed lost, and that was that.

Ramón Grau San Martín won the presidency in an election so clean that election day 1944 went down as *la jornada gloriosa*—"the glorious day." Grau and his successor, Carlos Prío Socarrás, ran Cuba between 1944 and 1952.[2] Cuba had made remarkable progress in the fifty years since independence. Approximately 15 percent of Cubans could read and write in 1902; by 1953 that figure had increased to 76.4 percent of those ages ten and older. Cuba had become one of the healthiest tropical areas in the world, but not everyone had equal access to health care and grave inequities existed. Sugar remained the cornerstone of the economy.

Cuba in the 1940s and early 1950s was something else that neither politics nor economics can explain: an open, happy country with an intoxicating joie de vivre. Leftist Dominican President Juan Bosch—no Miami exile he—brilliantly captured the excitement and spirit of the prosperous Cuba of those days in his book *Cuba, la isla fascinante*, published in 1955. Tropicana, the high temple of a legendary nightclub scene, opened in 1939, and not for the benefit of gangsters or American tourists.[3] Cubans traveled overseas at least as often as foreign tourists entered Cuba. Without discussion, it was a golden age for Cuban music, to be sure, but there were serpents in the garden.

Administrative corruption was allowed to run rampant, a blight on the nation's public life. Cuba's problem during these years was neither inept government nor a supine subordination to Yankee interests. The Auténtico administrations, in fact, were intensely nationalistic. The people who ran Cuba, Batista included, were in some cases exceptionally competent, but many—by no means all—were compromised by pervasive corruption. Corruption bred cynicism but it also stimulated a deep civic longing for redemption. Chibás had tapped into that deep reservoir, and so would Castro.

The eye of the Cuban storm may have been calm, but one could hear thunder in the distance. The avant-garde, progressive Constitution of 1940 had given Cubans the practice of democracy without necessarily conferring the habit. Habits flow from practice over time, but time was cut dramatically short by one unpredictable event that changed the course of Cuban history. That was the day the eye completed its pass over the Cuban archipelago. We can be precise almost to the hour: around 4:30 in the morning of March 10, 1952, when

Batista entered Columbia Military Barracks in Havana through gate number 6, took over command, and mortally wounded the 1940 Constitution. Had the coup never happened, Fulgencio Batista would be a revered historical figure today: a military caudillo who fathered a stable, progressive, democratic republic. His tragedy is that he undid what was in substantial measure his accomplishment.

Matanzas had an indirect but important involvement in the 1952 coup. Under Grau's and most of Prío's regimes, the army had been the bailiwick of a matancero from Versalles, General Genovevo Pérez Dámera, the army chief of staff. Pérez Dámera was no martial fashion plate. He was grossly overweight and a notorious vulgarian, but he had accomplished his mission well: keeping Batista's partisans in the army—the sergeants and corporals of 1933, now colonels and generals—on a short leash. Then, under pressure from within the army itself, President Prío dismissed the fat general. Pérez Dámera's successor, the more presentable Ruperto Cabrera, lacked his backbone.

Winds reached hurricane force again soon enough. On July 26, 1953, Fidel Castro, an Orthodox Party candidate for Congress in the elections that the 1952 coup had aborted, led an attack on the Moncada Barracks in Santiago de Cuba. Castro and his resolute followers sought to depose Batista and reinstate the 1940 charter. They failed, but the brutality with which the army retaliated, the unpopularity of Batista's usurpation, and the youth and sincerity of the young rebels invested the event with a heroic aura.

Batista's post-coup discourse cast him once again as the savior of a country gone awry. The corrupt Auténticos had violated a sacred trust, and he was back to set things right again. He encapsulated this vision in a little fable that became the theme of his 1954 campaign for a full, legitimate term in office. A *grulla* (egret)—or so Batista told the story—had flown into his backyard with a broken leg. Batista took the wounded egret to his bosom, set and bandaged its leg, and nurtured the bird back to health. Did the inevitable comparison to the Birdman of Alcatraz ever cross his mind? An egret on crutches became the mascot of Batista's campaign.

He won, and might have gotten away with it if only he had managed visibly to curb corruption and convince Cubans that he would once again leave office at the end of his new, bastardized four years. Instead, it was more of the same. In Matanzas the most glaring Batistiano rags-to-riches story was that of Mayor Carmen Olga Taquechel de Pérez Coujil. The wife of one of Batista's coup accomplices, she came out of nowhere to capture the mayoralty in the 1954 elections. She could rightfully boast of being the first woman to run a major Cuban city but proved to be no different from the good old boys when it came to the basics. The new mayor did away with the streetcars and relandscaped Matanzas' historic Liberty Square, inserting a "luminous fountain" that looked like a cross between a henequen plant and a bunch of bananas. Promptly dubbed "the plantains," the fountain turned out to be a failure—either the illumination or the hydraulics worked but never in synch. It was soon turned off altogether, and its aggressively phallic protuberances became the landmark of a convenient trash repository. The mayor also proceeded to build a mansion on the bluffs of the Caním. Visible for kilometers around, "la casa de la alcaldesa" became a daily reminder of the frugality of public servants who could build so handsomely on their modest salaries.

The case of Carmen Olga Taquechel in Matanzas suggests a fascinating aspect of the former sergeant. Of all pre-Castro Cuban rulers, Batista seems to have been the one least troubled by the empowerment of women. Unlike his predecessor and his successor, both notorious womanizers, Batista was a devoted family man. Indeed, for a figure so often stereotyped, a militarist, and a politician who adroitly cultivated a macho image for public consumption, his personal life is at the very least remarkable.

The Auténticos had tainted their hands mostly with loot, not blood, and had managed to keep the army, originally a Batista creature, under control. After the 1952 coup, Batista, realizing that he owed his power to the military, cut the army a piece of the action. Where Genovevo Pérez Dámera had held a virtual monopoly, captains and lieutenants were now allowed a slice of the pie, and the army reverted to the predatory mode of the 1930s.

The Cuban public had a certain tolerance for old-fashioned shenanigans. However, when stories of disappearances, allegations of torture, and the pictures of corpses of government enemies began to appear in the media after the Moncada incident and with increasing frequency after 1956, that was too much. Matanzas was plagued with one of the miscreants who did the government's dirty work. He was an army lieutenant known as "Pocopelo" (Baldhead). A successful practitioner of *forrajeo* (foraging), the retail form of corruption involving pimping, extortion, and protection rackets that was the specialty of the army and police, Pocopelo had more serious crimes to answer for. Several murders were attributed to him. A widely circulated story had it that he had once pulled out his gun and wasted a poor devil who had dared call him "Baldhead." His own turn came in the first week of 1959, when he was tried by a kangaroo court and shot.

As Batista reached the second year of his "legal" presidency, it became increasingly evident that his followers were digging in for the duration. Batista began to be referred to as Fulgencio Batista y Pa'rato, where Batista's maternal surname, Zaldívar, became "Pa'rato" (For-a-long-time).

Matanzas took all of this in stride. Then, one day in April 1956, all hell broke loose. April 29 was not to be like any other Matanzas Sunday, but it began predictably enough. Around nine o'clock my aunt Nena Cabañas called. She was going to late-morning mass at the cathedral and wanted me to join her. I was her godson and she took my religious education seriously. She did not trust my mother, a polite anticlerical, in that regard. After mass Aunt Nena complained of *debilidad*, a quaint Cuban euphemism for hunger. It was customary then to observe the Eucharistic fast—no food before Communion—and neither of us had eaten breakfast.

In the bright sunshine we crossed the little park flanking the church with its iron fence and its tall Chilean araucarias and headed for La Crema, on the other side of Milanés Street. La Crema occupied the site where, a century before, José White had enchanted the customers at his father's grocery shop with his little violin. We sat down for café con leche and *roscas*, La Crema's delicious custard-filled, sugar-glazed doughnuts.

My aunt was a strong, independent woman. She loved baseball and was a fierce and loyal fan of the Almendares team. A chain smoker and a great conversationalist, she never married and ran her own business, a fabrics shop called La Época on Milanés Street. Her partner, Benigno García, was a cantankerous Asturian with a resolute contempt for what he took to be the Cubans' levity.

Aunt Nena and I were walking down Jovellanos Street when we heard a strange noise that sounded like the banging of timber boards being piled up on top of one another.

"What could that be?" asked Aunt Nena.

"I don't know. Sounds like boards being piled up."

The noise continued as heads began to pop out from doors and windows. When we turned the corner of Jovellanos and Contreras streets, the sounds became louder and much clearer: *Tac-tac-tac-tac-tac-tac. Tracka—tac-tac-tac-*

tack-tac. Crack-a-tracka-tracka-track. . . . They were coming from the direction of the Goicuría army barracks in Versalles.

> "Están atacando al cuartel," somebody said. "They are attacking
> the barracks."
> "Let's go home," said my aunt.

We walked briskly down to my grandmother Lola's house on Contreras Street. We had been safely inside for a few minutes when my parents called. Mother was beside herself, and Father demanded that I stay put. After waiting for a while, I decided to make a dash for my own home. I was dying to see what was happening.

The staccato had ceased and there was an eerie silence in the nearly empty streets. I ran into García. "A ver en que cagada os habéis metido," he shot at me. "Let's see what kind of shit you Cubans have gotten yourselves into." A military fighter roared by, almost grazing the rooftops. Would it strafe the lines of helpless refugees, as happened in the movies? Would they do that? There were no lines of helpless refugees, but I hugged close to the walls just in case. That day the Cuban Revolution began for me and Matanzas.[4]

The attack was a copycat operation inspired by the Moncada event. The attackers, however, belonged to the Organización Auténtica, a group financed by the deposed president Prío. Led by the ruthless commandant, Colonel Pilar D. García, the garrison wiped the attackers out without a single casualty among the soldiers. It was a rout. Colonel García was later photographed next to the bloodied corpse of Reynold García, the head of the Prío commandoes and no relation of his. Batista's henchmen had a fatal propensity for being caught on camera in truly despicable settings. The image of a smiling, uniformed Pilar García squatting amidst the gore like a hyena about to feed was truly shocking. Even more embarrassing for the regime was the photo of a prisoner being shot in cold blood which the Spanish edition of *Life* published shortly thereafter.[5]

There was no cure for the malaise caused by the regime's spurious origins. Its embarrassing illegitimacy afflicted the body politic like a chronic fever. Next to Batista's own persona, radioactive to many Cubans, usurpation was an original sin for which there was no possible redemption. And, to constantly remind the citizenry of Batista's evil ways, there was *Bohemia* magazine.

If William Randolph Hearst's yellow journalism was one of the causes of the Spanish-American War, *Bohemia*'s was without a doubt one of the causes of the Cuban Revolution. Castro had two big career breaks in the media.

Fig. 42. Batista's soldiers poke their fingers at bullet holes. Goicuría Barracks, April 29, 1956.

One was his key February 1957 interview in the Sierra Maestra with Herbert Matthews of the *New York Times*, which I will discuss later. The other was *Bohemia* magazine's relentless, vividly written and gruesomely illustrated reportage of the government's atrocities. (Batista, an inept dictator, allowed freedom of the press whenever he could get away with it.)

Bohemia, founded in 1908, was a bizarre amalgam of tabloid journalism and some of the best writing in the country. Girlie pinups—"the Chick of the Week"—shared space with articles by anthropologist Fernando Ortiz and Jorge Mañach, the unelected dean of Cuba's intelligentsia. In 1953, the centennial of José Martí's birth, one of *Bohemia's* contributions to the centennial's iconography was a photo of Martí's face in the early stages of putrefaction taken by the Spanish for purposes of identification. The apostle as *transi*. I remember recoiling when I saw it at age ten.

Government goons would rarely hit on those truly implicated in serious clandestine activities. Those who are operationally committed tend to be careful. More often than not, Batista's agents vented their anger on the small fry. Four students at my school were murdered by government goons. Each young life thus absurdly wasted made every parent fear for his or her offspring. My parents' eagerness to know my whereabouts whenever I arrived home slightly later than usual was not from concern about drug use—unknown in those days—or unsafe sex. It was about politics: you wouldn't be involved in some crazy juvenile conspiracy against the government, would you?

Fulgencio Batista would not be "Pa'rato," after all. Destiny reserved that for Fidel Castro. Like Batista, Castro entered the scene as another deus ex machina, although, in his case, he was more like deus ex machine gun. The Moncada putsch, a failure for the day, turned out to be a triumph for the ages. It has become an epic narrative, of course. Of immediate significance for its time, it established the obscure Fidel Castro as a key player and the prophet of the "insurrectional way" to get rid of Batista. The attack made Castro overnight a household word in Cuba. His trial defense, later released as *History Will Absolve Me,* made a major impact.

The court sentenced him to a long jail term. Curiously but tellingly, one of the sitting judges wrote a dissenting opinion upholding a citizen's duty to oppose usurpation by violence if necessary. In the end, Batista, seeking after popularity and convinced that Castro posed no danger, set him free in 1955. Castro went immediately to Mexico to plan a comeback. It was there that he met Ernesto Guevara, an Argentine ideological pilgrim in search of meaning. "Ché" was on his way.

With Batista almost halfway through his term, corruption was rampant. His military henchmen engaged in random and counterproductive brutality. The suicidal attack on the Matanzas garrison added to the turmoil, and then a vast plot was uncovered within the army, led by Colonel Ramón Barquín. The heart of the conspiracy was an army faction known as *los puros,* consisting of younger officers trained professionally since 1940. "The pure ones" proved no more successful in rolling back the coup than they had been in preventing it. Barquín and a handful of his fellow plotters ended up behind bars.

My uncle, Major Tomás Cabañas Batista—again, no relation to the dictator—was a member of the faction and a party to the plot. A respected athlete, he was well known as Cuba's foremost pistol marksman. He escaped imprisonment partly because of that, and possibly because Fulgencio Batista did not wish to irritate Carlos Núñez, his powerful father-in-law and president of Cuba's second largest bank. But my uncle had to leave the country immediately and, after a face-saving interval, the army as well. When Barquín took over the armed forces in the chaotic hours that followed Batista's departure in 1959, he appointed Major Cabañas commandant of the Matanzas Regiment.

When he got there the Batistianos had fled and there was nothing Cabañas could do but surrender the brand-new army headquarters to Guevara, which he did. (Since the Goicuría attack the army had moved to state-of-the-art barracks on the town's outskirts, which are still in use by the Cuban military.)

When Castro successfully landed in Oriente province on December 2, 1956, he scored no military success of any consequence. Barely surviving with a group of twelve followers—"los Doce," like Jesus' apostles[6]—he found his way into the rugged Sierra Maestra. Seemingly not much, and yet everything. It was a psychological triumph with vast ramifications. At first Batista tried to deny that Castro had made it alive, a bluff that was dramatically called by Herbert Matthews' now-famous *New York Times* interview of February 1957. Matthews' interview was worth at least another Moncada to Castro. It was, in fact, the turning point of his fortunes. Matthews gave the lie to Batista's misinformation about the rebel leader's fate: contrary to the official story, he was alive and well and smoking cigars in the Sierra. Unlike Martí, he was not about to go forward on a white stallion. To govern one must first survive.[7]

Castro's landing was not well received by all the groups opposing the Batista regime, among them the student organization at the University of Havana (Federación Estudiantil Universitaria—FEU). Led by José Antonio Echeverría, a matancero from Cárdenas, the students sought to beat Fidel at his own game. Their plan: attack the presidential palace, kill or capture Batista, call the people to the streets and the army to rebellion, and voilà. The attack took place on March 13, 1957. It failed, and many brave young men, Echeverría included, joined the gallery of bloodied corpses featured by *Bohemia*.

There was more excitement left in store for 1957, however. On September 5, a naval mutiny in the port city of Cienfuegos was repressed with great loss of life. Meanwhile, elements of the student directorate opened a "Second Front" in the Escambray Mountains of central Cuba. The year closed in an atmosphere of crisis and almost universal repudiation of Batista. In March 1958, the Eisenhower administration withdrew all military support from the Cuban government. Though weakened, the Batista regime had plenty of life left. The following month it successfully aborted a general revolutionary strike organized by Castro's 26th of July Movement.[8]

The insurrection had lighter moments. In the altogether exciting year of 1957, a new building for the Matanzas branch of the Ministry of Public Works was inaugurated in Pueblo Nuevo. Batista showed up for the ceremony, and picnic boxes were distributed among the three to four hundred guests. Some clever saboteur, however, had gained access to the catering service—the army catering service, no less—and managed to taint the sandwiches with some substance or toxin of highly purgative properties.

It is not known whether Batista himself suffered the indignity that befell the guests, some of whom had to drop their pants on the side of the building to answer nature's urgent call while ambulances wailed the worst cases to emergency rooms. A couple of days later, *Zig-zag*, the national humor magazine, ran a cover with a picture of the building and the first two lines of a classic Spanish scatological graffito often found on the walls of public toilets:

> In this sacred place, oh my,
> That the people visit lots
> The fainthearted bravely try
> And the bravest get the trots.[9]

Scenes of rebels moving into the outskirts of the capital as the evil dictator flees are romantic fictions at best. That was Saigon, not Havana. It took about a month and a half for the regime to unravel. Batista insisted on holding the elections scheduled for November 1958. He was not a candidate. He wanted out, but on his timetable. Carlos Márquez-Sterling, former president of the 1940 Constitutional Convention and a public figure of impeccable probity, offered his candidacy in opposition as a dignified way out for Batista, but 1958 was not 1944. Batista cheated, the Auténticos withdrew at the last moment, and many voters simply stayed home. The government's candidate won, but the day ultimately was Fidel Castro's.

The electoral outcome validated Castro's tenet that the only way to get rid of Batista was through violence. The victorious government candidate, Andrés Rivero Agüero, was to be inaugurated on February 24. With Batista out of office and almost certainly out of the country, Rivero Agüero might yet find a non-insurrectional endgame to the situation created in 1952. As the nation sank into despondency, Castro, realizing that a window of opportunity might soon close, made a brilliant tactical move: he sent Ernesto Guevara with his so-called Column 8 (Ciro Redondo) to Santa Clara. Whether Guevara conducted a heroic campaign or was the figurehead of a farce financed by rich Cubans is beside the point. What is important is that, as December came to a close, an overwhelming majority of Cubans were fed up with Batista to the point of despair, Guevara was in Santa Clara and had managed to derail an "armored train" carrying army troops and reinforcements to the east, all of

Cuba was glued to ham radios purporting to report seemingly massive rebel maneuvers on the ground, and Batista was increasingly unnerved by the fast pace of events.

Batista's flight in the early-morning hours of January 1, 1959, took even his followers by surprise, save for the handful who were chosen to depart with him or the exceptionally astute who smelled a rat and ran away discreetly in the knick of time. With Batista gone, the armed forces simply disintegrated. The top brass in Havana desperately sought a way to prevent a complete institutional collapse. Barquín was brought back from his Isle of Pines prison, but it was too late. By mid-morning on the first of January Castro had gotten hold of a microphone and broadcast to the Cuban people that any arrangement concocted in Havana was inherently spurious and would only prolong the war. In other words: "I am in charge."

Batista's departure on New Year's Day gave Jesús Orta Ruiz, a folk poet known as "el Indio Naborí," the powerful opening line of a poem, "Triumphal March of the Rebel Army," that became enormously popular. Orta Ruiz composed the first version of the poem in the morning and afternoon of January 1. The definitive version was ready for Castro's arrival in Havana on the eighth and was read that evening on national radio and television.

The poem is worth pondering not only on account of its clever, effective composition—it was simple and easy to remember, and culminates in a rousing antiphony. Its hyperbolic tone captures the intensity of those few days in January 1959 when the deal between Fidel Castro and the Cuban people was closed, when the overwhelming majority of Cubans concluded that they were in the presence of an extraordinary leader of epic stature. It was conspicuously featured in *Bohemia*.

> First of January!
> Brilliantly rises the sun.
> The shadows are gone!

The poet then goes on to describe Castro's triumphal progress from Oriente to Havana. In so doing he reveals to Cubans the revolutionary hierophants: Guevara, Camilo, Almeida.[10] Some ending!

> This, that bile has turned into *miel* (honey)
> It's called Fidel!
> This, that thorns became a *clavel* (carnation)

It's called Fidel!
This, that my country be not a *cuartel* (army barracks)
It's called Fidel!
This, that the Beast was beaten for the good of Man;
This, that darkness has turned into *luz* (light)
This has a name; only one name:
Fidel Castro Ruz!

Castro's achievement was not overthrowing Batista. Many people not necessarily connected to him did that, among them Dwight D. Eisenhower. Ultimately, Batista just threw in the towel. Castro must be credited—no doubt—with the establishment of a methodology that was honored in the emulation. Prío tried it at the Goicuría and failed. Echeverría tried it at the Presidential Palace and also bombed out. Acts of heroic derring-do were insufficient to overthrow the dictatorship, but they did succeed in creating a climate of chronic and ultimately irreversible unrest. Provided one survived them—Castro's forte—they were peerless political platforms. The 1953 Moncada attack, the prototype of those events, projected Castro's figure on to the center of the national stage. He is still there, the survivor.

Where Castro's genius aided by remarkable good luck emerges is in the way he claimed and took power. First, his beautifully choreographed, slow, eight-day progress to Havana gave him an opportunity to "connect" with a nation that knew little about him but could not do enough to express its gratitude, a nation mesmerized by the man and the drama of the moment. Relentless television coverage projected the weeklong royal progress into countless Cuban living rooms.

Second, the way he disposed of rivals. Armed students had independently taken possession of the University of Havana campus. "They have weapons," Castro said from the podium, surrounded by his own followers armed to the teeth: "Weapons, what for?" Next morning the students meekly surrendered the campus to Fidel's designates. There were hours-long speeches and even little details that subtly revealed Fidel's almost superhuman power. He ostentatiously wore two watches: he was so busy working for the people that he could not afford the time to rotate his arm. He took to using helicopters in the early days so that he could materialize anywhere, anytime. Untainted by the sewage of corruption, Fidel pledged to clean it up wherever he went, and people believed him. How could they not? They needed to believe, and Fidel was no

Fig. 43. Celebrating Batista's fall at Liberty Square. Matanzas, January 1959. (Courtesy of Prints and Photographs Division, Library of Congress)

ordinary man. It was Cuba's good luck that he was her "Maximum Leader," a title that just sprouted forth in those exciting few weeks.

The imagery was powerful. Shortly after entering Matanzas, a bearded rebel soldier climbed on the shoulders of the larger-than-life statue of Lady Liberty breaking her chains at the base of the Martí memorial. He wore an Australian-style slouch hat and held up his rifle in triumph as the UPI photographer aimed his camera. Surrounded by his comrades and an awed crowd, and seemingly blessed by the apostle himself, he became the central character of a grand baroque allegory. Carried on front pages throughout the world, the photograph conveyed a potent, exhilarating message.

Fidel Castro sensed that history had not only seemingly absolved him; it had also dealt him a winning hand. He could play his cards in many different ways. He knew that he was numerologically and mystically gifted. Cubans, always given to such speculations, wondered. Did he not come to power on the first of January? Is he not thirty-three—the age of Christ? Is his name not

Fidel (Faithful)? Aren't the colors of his 26th of July Movement—black and red—the same as those for Elegguá, the revered Afro-Cuban orisha who opens the ways? If any doubted that Cubans had been granted the proverbial Gratia Dei in their new ruler, that was when the doves flew in.

The night of Castro's first speech in Havana, on Thursday, January 8, 1959, a few doves were released, white as snow. Emblem of the Holy Ghost to Christians and sacred to santeros as the bird of the powerful Obatalá, the winged symbols of peace and might fluttered briefly overhead until one of them honed in on the podium and settled on the handrail. A second one followed suit. And then a third one incredibly, miraculously, gently landed on Fidel's shoulder. The Maximum Leader, now in full pontificals, went on with his speech without missing a beat. The dove remained there under the glare of TV lights for five, ten, fifteen minutes, seemingly forever. This was no egret on crutches. It wasn't even Martí's blessing but that of a higher authority. This was the hand of God visibly, dramatically, definitively touching the shoulder of his Anointed One. This was Pa'rato.[11]

Fidel was loved by his people deeply, overwhelmingly, unconditionally. It is good to be loved, wrote Machiavelli, but if the Prince has to choose between being loved and being feared, he must choose the latter. Fidel didn't have to choose but he prepared for that eventuality. The summary trials and swift execution of Batistianos were a good start. The trials were held at Havana's Palace of Sports and broadcast nationally; the dirty work was carried out at La Cabaña fortress under Guevara's supervision. True, most if not all of those indicted had blood on their hands, but their trials were travesties. They were also spectacular television, a medium for which Fidel was a natural and that reached every corner of the country. For those not blinded by the intensity of the moment, the trials and the sight of half a million people chanting "Pa-re-dón! Pa-re-dón!" ("To the shooting wall!") was frightening enough. Armed with authority, fortified with resolve, and secure in history's absolution and the adulation of a nation mesmerized, Fidel could do as he saw fit. That he did and called it a Revolution.

17   Nero's Cheer

IN MAY 1943, a Cuban submarine chaser sank German U-boat 176 in waters north and east of Matanzas. The operation was praised for the precision of its execution, but the Cuban public did not learn about it until the end of the war.[1] One more reason, no doubt, why Cubans took the seemingly faraway conflict in stride. The war was an inconvenience but, apart from a few brave volunteers, Cubans were not fighting on foreign battlefields.[2] Tires were hard to come by but fuel was reasonably available.

The Cuban people met fuel shortages with the same ingenuity that has kept the country's fleet of 1950s American gas guzzlers running. Long before ethanol was heard of, Cuba ventured into alternative motor fuels. Enormous amounts of alcohol were produced during the war years. Matanzas distilleries played a key role, and local production levels expanded notably.[3] Alcohol mixed with petroleum, a blend known as *mofuco*, fueled Cuba through the war emergency. Today a mofuco of sorts is available in developed nations under a fancy name.

My parents married in 1942. Being young and fashionable, they decided to marry at night like couples in Havana did. When Monsignor Jenaro Suárez, the feisty, old-fashioned dean of the cathedral, heard of it, he smelled a rat and fulminated against what had to be yet another Masonic plot to undermine cherished community values.

"Father Jenaro" was a Matanzas legend. A fierce polemicist, his combative articles in the parish bulletin ruffled many feathers. Revered by many for his dedication and learning, he was feared by all for his tongue. If it was a spade, that's what he called it, but he could get carried away. Castro expelled Cuba's Spanish-born clergy in 1960. Father Jenaro, who had been taken to Cuba as a toddler, went kicking and screaming, protesting that he was Cuban. As he later wrote in his memoirs, he had expected trouble the day of his arrest and wore a new cassock.[4] His beloved priestly garb would be his undoing. He had a death to match Isadora Duncan's. While getting off a bus in Spain, he caught his cassock on the bumper. The bus dragged him for several blocks.

My grandfather Miguel, a Mason and an aspiring politician, was furious at Father Jenaro's refusal to perform an evening ceremony. My grandmother Consuelo, a pious Catholic, was deeply hurt. They went to see Bishop Alberto Martín Villaverde, and a compromise was worked out. Father Jenaro would end his anathemas. My parents would not marry at the cathedral as planned but at Dal'Allio's beautiful Saint Peter's Church in Versalles. For the sake of peace, the ceremony was to begin a few minutes before sunset but Mother, a fierce contrarian, had the last word. She took a long time to get dressed. Like the bride of Dracula, she stirred to life only when the sun had safely set.

Travel was severely curtailed then. Civilian aviation was still in its infancy, and nobody wanted an encounter with a prowling German submarine. In consequence, my parents honeymooned in Varadero, where it was my great good fortune to be conceived—I was born exactly nine months later. They spent their fruitful honeymoon at the legendary Chez Roig, Varadero's pioneering hotel. The white-and-blue timber structure surrounded by Australian pines was built by my father's uncle, Santiago "Cuco" Roig Iduate. When the hotel was confiscated in the early 1960s, Uncle Cuco quipped, "I suppose they will rename it 'Chez Guevara.'" They did not. The old Chez Roig is gone, along with most of classic, timber-built Varadero.

When my parents married, Batista had been president for two years. The former sergeant had considerable popular support during the first phase of his career, although not in my family circle to be sure. Grandfather had run for governor of Matanzas on the Conservative Party ticket in 1940. He went to his grave convinced that he had won the vote but lost the election because of some chicanery attributable to the Batista camp. Grandmother Consuelo was traumatized. The word *contempt* might have been invented to describe her feelings towards that lowlife "Sergeant Batista." Ironically, Grandmother cast a vote for the Batistianos in the November 1958 elections. She had died two months earlier, but somehow her name appeared on the list of people who voted.

Batista's 1952 coup set in motion a chain of events that would soon enough radically change the course of history. The future was being forged in ways no one could have anticipated. I had just turned ten when Fidel Castro and his followers broke through the Moncada Barracks' gate. I do not recall anybody counting me for the 1953 census. In case they missed me, I was one of the approximately 76.4 percent of Cubans age ten or older who could read and write, one of the approximately 2,985,155 males in the Cuban population, and one of the 71.8 percent of Cubans who were counted as white. Cuba then had 159,200 motor vehicles, 1,000,000 radio receivers, 78,931 TV sets, 193 newspapers, 170,092 phones, and an income per capita second only to those of Argentina and Venezuela in all of Latin America, and comparable to those of the Spain and Portugal of those days. Matanzas province then had 395,780 souls, the city 82,619.[5]

Much can be inferred from statistics such as these about the kind of country Cuba was before Castro. Note, however, only two figures: one million radios and 78,931 TV sets. That boils down to one radio receiver for every six Cubans and one TV receiver for every seventy-five. The latter figure is amazing considering that Cuban television began in 1950, but it tells only part of the story of TV's outreach. In a culture as family- and neighborhood-oriented as Cuba's, the first household on the block to buy a TV set could count on running out of chairs to accommodate the visitors. Of course, these are 1953 figures. Between 1953 and 1958 the ownership of TV receivers trebled, and TV fare grew exponentially. By 1958 TV signals reached every corner of the island. The small screen was ready for larger-than-life Fidel and the world's first media revolution.[6]

Cuban TV pioneered virtually all the formats of Latin American television. Cuban *telenovelas* of the age were memorable, but the commercial jingles were positively adhesive.[7] In the 1970s, a friend of mine sat at the piano in a hotel lobby in Havana to while away half an hour. It occurred to him to play a few TV jingles from the 1950s. As his fingers moved deftly across the keyboard and he started singing, commercial messages of decadent capitalism came back to life. Before he knew it, a crowd had gathered, singing along and volunteering lyrics and anecdotes. Jingle after bubbly jingle sprang forth from the piano to everyone's delight—that is, until two beefy young men from State Security intervened, ordered him to stop, and closed the piano. The crowd dispersed in sullen silence.

Cuba's TV impresarios were aggressively entrepreneurial. The most creative mind in early Cuban television belonged to an adoptive matancero, Gaspar Pumarejo. Born in Santander, Spain, he began his career as an emcee at Radio Matanzas. In the 1940s he moved to Havana in search of a place in the growing and exciting world of Cuban broadcasting. He managed to acquire a languishing station, Unión Radio, which he promptly turned around into a legendary success. One of his runaway hits was essentially a jazzed-up version of Matanzas' "Spirits' Hour" ("La hora espírita") of 1935. The star of the show was "Clavelito," a singer who claimed to effect miraculous cures using a glass of water his listeners were supposed to concentrate on as he performed. André Breton, the surrealist, would have understood. When TV arrived on the scene, Pumarejo was ready with a franchise and a camera. His homespun channel was actually the first to broadcast a black-and-white signal in 1950, and a color signal in 1958. More than a match for Pumarejo, the Mestre brothers of CMQ-TV brought the World Series to Cuba in 1956, relaying the signal via a plane flying in circles over the Florida Straits.

The 1956 attack on the Goicuría Barracks shocked Matanzas, but that summer we went to Varadero as usual. The "Blue Beach," originally a well-kept Cárdenas secret, had become decisively incorporated into the life of matanceros as the twentieth century wore on. Today, Varadero hosts well more than half a million visitors yearly, but in the 1950s it was a world unto itself where bad news from the outside was deep-fried in suntan oil. My grandparents had owned one of the first big timber-framed houses built in Varadero, which they sold shortly before I was born to pay for one of my grandfather's political campaigns. They always lamented the sale of the house, but so be it. Although no longer homeowners on the Blue Beach, my grandparents always rented a big place for the summer, and the whole family would spend the season there for as far back as I can remember (that is, whenever we did not spend the summer at San Miguel de los Baños, the other traditional summer hangout for Matanzas folks).

San Miguel is an idyllic little town next to Jacán Mountain, a 1,200-foot prominence of the Bejucal-Madruga-Limonar range almost in the geographic center of the province. From the summit you can see all the way to Cárdenas and the ocean some thirty kilometers away. Reaching the summit is quite an experience. You do so by a monumental stairway containing all fourteen stations of Christ's Via Crucis, leading at the top to an elegant Calvary and *tempietto* with a marble crucifix.

San Miguel was famous for its hot springs, said to cure a wide range of ailments. The Rev. Abiel Abbot, a visitor to the region in the late 1820s, was the first to report the "sulphurous springs" of the "Hacana" hills.[8] Legend has it that the "discoverer" of the waters was an old slave named Miguel.[9] Afflicted with an apparently terminal stomach ailment and with his legs covered with ulcers, he became useless. In the merciless world of Cuban slavery, he was left to die. Somehow, Miguel found the springs, drank the waters, plastered his legs with the smelly mud, and was cured.

However it was that the curative powers of San Miguel's springs were discovered, by the 1850s their fame was locally secure. Sugar magnates such as Cosme de la Torriente began to frequent the place, although creature comforts were next to nil. In 1868, scientists of the University of Havana conducted a chemical and pharmacological study of the waters and confirmed their therapeutic efficacy for urinary and digestive-tract ailments, arthritis, rheumatism, and certain dermatological conditions. In 1892, the Matanzas provincial government declared the springs to be of public interest and voted to construct an all-weather road. The plan came to nothing because of the War for Independence.

Around 1910, a Havana lawyer, Dr. Manuel Abril, bought the tract of land that contained the two main springs, La Salud and El Tigre, and began to make discreet further land acquisitions in the neighborhood. He had big plans for San Miguel de los Baños, including the development of the springs as a world-class spa inserted into a first-class, thoroughly planned setting.

Nothing but the best was good enough for Dr. Abril. For starters, he toured as many spas as he could possibly visit, from Saratoga Springs to Baden-Baden. By the time the Great War made such travel impossible, he had a pretty good idea of what he wanted. The proposed urbanization had four components: (1) a grand boulevard intended to be flanked by palatial homes; (2) the monumental Via Crucis and tempietto atop the Jacán; (3) the layout and infrastructure of the town, including street paving, water, and sewer; and (4) the boulevard's "bookends": an elegant church dedicated to St. Michael the Archangel at one end and the elegant Hotel Balneario at the other. As a sideline, San Miguel's water was bottled and sold throughout Cuba.

It took fifteen years to achieve the ambitious building plan. The finished Balneario was opulent, a roaring twenties' extravaganza. It was a tropical ver-

sion of the Grand Casino of Monte Carlo, with four cupolas, a palatial stairway, and magnificent leaded-glass windows. To remember it as I do and see it
as it was when I visited in 2003 was a truly depressing experience. It makes one
really wonder. The Balneario was derelict. The leaded windows—what was left
of them—were in shreds, the walls flaking away, the formerly grand bar full
of detritus. In short, a mess. The fountains that once dispensed health were
fouled by algae—or worse. The grand stone mansions along the boulevard
where I learned to ride my bike with great gnashing of teeth and scraping of
knees are in diverse stages of collapse. I could not escape the feel of a ghost
town. To bring this important artifact of pre-Castro Cuba back to its former

Fig. 44. *Above:* Mansions, cottages, and a Via Crucis station at San Miguel de los Baños
(Photos by Miguel A. Bretos, 2003). *Below:* "Villa Teté" in 1921 and today.

splendor would take millions. Meanwhile, a solid social and architectural history of San Miguel awaits the energy of some enterprising scholar.

The good news is that San Miguel's enchanting timber homes are in remarkably good shape after all these years. One built by my great-grandparents Laurentino and Isabel around 1915 was in good condition. They were among the first ten householders at San Miguel. Santa Amalia sugar mill, after all, is eight short kilometers away in Coliseo.   Varadero is another grand artifact of regional history. A thorough study of Varadero's development and significance both before and after the revolution is long overdue. Varadero is located on the narrow Península de Hicacos (or, if you wish, the Peninsula of Coco-plum, as the *hicaco* bush, *Chrysobalanus icaco*, is known in English). The southern shore of the peninsula borders Cárdenas Bay and is largely mangrove swamp, but the northern shore contains some twenty kilometers of one of the world's most spectacular beaches.

Salt had been extracted at the tip of the peninsula since the latter part of the sixteenth century. In the 1870s and '80s people, mainly from Cárdenas, began to take the baths there. In 1885, ten local families applied to the municipality for permission to build modest summer homes. With the advent of independence, Varadero achieved momentum, and a handful of families from Matanzas and even Havana joined the original Cárdenas settlers. Rowing became the thing to do, and two crew clubs were formed, Varadero and Halley (honoring the famous comet due to appear again in 1910). Somebody came up with the idea of a regatta and shells were ordered. The *Halley* had its shell made in Cárdenas, the *Varadero* in Matanzas. The event was held on July 31, 1910. *Varadero* won. The modest match gave origin to two key institutions: the Club Náutico de Varadero and the yearly crew regatta that became one of Cuba's classic sporting events.

In the late 1920s, Varadero caught the eye of Delaware millionaire E. I. DuPont, who initially bought 180 hectares of land and virgin beach for a song. Enchanted with the place, DuPont commissioned a beachside mansion from Govantes and Cabarrocas, one of Cuba's top architectural firms. In 1927 the architects delivered the plans, which artfully interweaved elements of naval design, Spanish baroque, and the Cuban vernacular. The mansion, built on a crag, was finished by 1930 and named Xanadu after the fabled stately pleasure-dome of Coleridge's Kubla Khan.

DuPont enclosed his Cuban Xanadu in a cocoon of privacy: the hicaco groves were relandscaped to suggest a tropical jungle. He had enough land left

Fig. 45. President Federico Laredo Brú arrives in Varadero for Regatta Day 1938 on the Cuban Navy's flagship. Photo by José Luis López.

over, however, to engage in a bit of high-end real estate development. Peñas de Hicacos, S.A., became his corporate instrument to commercialize Varadero's waterfront. DuPont's chief operative in town, a Delaware engineer named L. Paul Edwards, developed a concept of "Cuba's Chautauqua" as a theme for the real estate offer. It made no commercial difference. American buyers may not have cared for a tropical Chautauqua anyway, and Cubans had no idea what Chautauqua was all about. The developed tract sold briskly, mainly to Cubans, for whom the white sand and blue surf were incentive enough. "Chautauqua" became simply "DuPont." Between Peñas de Hicacos and François Larrieu & Co., a Cuban firm with extensive holdings on the peninsula, a lot of Varadero sand changed hands during the 1930s, 1940s, and 1950s. Land values skyrocketed, and Varadero became a veritable laboratory for emerging and exciting new trends in Cuban domestic architecture.

Varadero's second big push forward came during the war years. Both Batista and Grau became frequent visitors. The President of the Republic customarily came on regatta day to give away the cup, usually on a Cuban warship, but

Batista and Grau got into the habit of taking Varadero weekends. Grau built a luxury waterfront home. Exquisite planned suburbs built of *coquina* stone—the Surf, Silva, and Kawama—were developed to accommodate the wave of new visitors and settlers. An airport connected Varadero to the United States by air. More important, Batista proposed in the early 1940s to address the problem of access to Varadero from Havana by means of a new superhighway to be known as the Vía Blanca.

The politics of the Vía Blanca was, to say the least, complex. Before it was completed in the 1950s, access to Varadero from Havana took from four to five hours on the narrow Central Highway via Matanzas, Coliseo, and Cárdenas. From Matanzas it took almost two hours, again via Coliseo and Cárdenas. Only Cárdenas had easy access. *Cardenenses* had felt victimized when the Central Highway bypassed the town in the 1920s. Now, the townspeople feared, they were about to lose preeminent access to a key economic and psychological asset. Varadero, moreover, was within the Cárdenas municipality. How long, they wondered, before an energized Varadero would get its municipal independence? (Answer: it happened in 1976.)[10]

Batista was determined to develop Varadero as part of a vast and ambitious plan to develop the eastern shore of Havana harbor.[11] The centerpiece of the scheme was the Harbor Tunnel, which brought the formerly inaccessible eastern shore to within five minutes of the Presidential Palace in downtown Havana. The tunnel connected with the Vía Blanca leading to the "eastern beaches" and beyond. The route led ultimately to the sandy Cuban Shangri-la, Varadero Beach, some 130 kilometers away.

Two of the largest and costliest highway bridge projects ever undertaken in Cuba, the Bacunayagua and Canímar spans, were built just to get to the Blue Beach. In 1955 a special autonomous agency, ACETVA—Autoridad del Centro Turístico de Varadero—was created to oversee Varadero's transformation. Batista had the good judgment to place one of Cuba's top young architects, Nicolás Quintana, at the head of the design team. Quintana was not a Batistiano by any stretch of the imagination, but Batista understood Quintana was the best, and Quintana saw the opportunity to do some good. He reported to Public Works Minister Nicolás Arroyo, later Cuba's ambassador to Washington and an eminent architect in his own right.[12]

The Batista government completed the Havana-to-Matanzas stretch of the Vía Blanca in 1954; built the Varadero aqueduct and sewer; upgraded the airport; dredged the Paso Malo lagoon to turn the peninsula into an island; built a marina, a bridge, and a new axial avenue through town; and promoted the place. Strict building codes were developed by Quintana's team. The height of buildings, for example, was limited by the mean height of existing pine stands. Streets were landscaped with almond trees. Almonds have been superabundant in Varadero ever since. Girls used them to play kitchen with, boys used them as projectiles. Major efforts were made to control mosquitoes. Sunset in Varadero meant that you had to withdraw behind netting: skeeters had full control of the airspace.

The Vía Blanca put Varadero within an hour and a half of the capital. From Matanzas it was now not quite half an hour to the white sand, but a new issue raised its head: concern about what the expected traffic influx would do to the city center. A civic movement arose seeking to have the Vía Blanca bypass Matanzas altogether. Rather than figuring out how to capture the tourist peso, matanceros would rather not deal with the hassle. The bypass project was actually carried out under the revolution.

Perhaps matanceros feared they would go the way of the hermit crabs. The new roadway cut through all sorts of coastal ecosystems. Crabs by the gazillions had commuted since time immemorial from the shallow waters to the marine terraces lining the shoreline between Matanzas and Varadero. The first couple of years after the Vía Blanca was opened, you could hear the car's tires crunching crabs all the way from the Canímar River to Varadero itself. Unable to sustain the carnage, the crustaceans disappeared. Also victimized by development was the chelonian population, the huge sea turtles known as *caguamas* (*Chelonia mydas*). We would sneak out in the dark of night to watch the lumbering behemoths lay their eggs. Little turtles would be sold as souvenirs, doomed to certain death in some bucket filled with water from the faucet.

Varadero has profound symbolic value matching its economic importance. The Blue Beach has a hold on Cuba's imagination as the island's ultimate Eden. To see one of the spare, impressionistic Varadero scenes by the Matanzas painter Cobo is to understand that immediately. Cobo's sky, sand, surf, and sea grapes are bathed in an intense, almost beatific light. Access to Varadero was the driving force for virtually all development plans for the Havana-Matanzas-Varadero-Cárdenas corridor during the 1940s and 1950s. (One suspects that Varadero's worth as an attractor of U.S. tourist dollars was really an alibi. The Varadero of the '40s and '50s was built by Cuban elites for themselves.)

In the early years of the revolution, access to the chichi resort became a great sign of empowerment for the masses. We spent the 1960 summer season, the last we would spend in Varadero, at a borrowed cabin in the "Yacht Club."[13] The Yacht Club was designed by Quintana's firm, Moenck and Quintana. It was an enclave between the International Hotel and DuPont. The cabana next to ours was sealed. It had belonged to Zoila Mulet de Fernández Concheso, Batista's education minister.

Every night, late enough to be annoying, a caravan of cars would go by the no longer functioning gates, blaring horns and shouting revolutionary slogans. They seemed to be saying: "Get out, your time is up." Many did. A system of *taquillas* (lockers) was set up to accommodate the mass influx to proletarian Varadero. That populist phase ended long ago. The Blue Beach is once again a Xanadu of sorts for powerful elites and an international tourist attraction. The old DuPont mansion is now a restaurant. Varadero today resembles neither Biarritz nor the people's beach. It has become a Cancun clone. As in Cancun, the beach itself is parting ways with the human construct. In my childhood there were only two rocky outcrops on the vast expanse of sand. Today, there are quite a few and the beach is narrower. Nature does not forgive.

Despite all the summer fun, I always looked forward to going home at the end of the season, tanned to blisters and ready for a new school year. My school was one of a handful of private schools in the city—Catholic, Protestant, and secular—that offered what was in hindsight an excellent education, although the premium was not on analytical or critical thinking but on memorization. Teachers taught to the exams but, since the curriculum was very demanding, we still had to cover a lot of ground. So we ended up remembering a lot. The American-style honor system at exams was inconceivable, and monitoring was ferocious.

We were, of course, a privileged group. My mother was a teacher by training and actually taught at a public school in Versalles. Mother was a born educator, and I am sure the greatest satisfactions of her life came to her as "Señorita Teté" the teacher. Every September when the school year began, she bought cartons of notebooks and huge bundles of pencils that she would distribute as the need arose. Mother loved her profession and was totally committed to her calling. She was also chronically frustrated by the hardships her students had to face, which everybody attributed to widespread corruption. A particularly galling issue were the *botelleros* (sinecurists) embedded throughout the public education system. They showed up once a month to collect their pay and would not return until thirty days later.

The Liceo was, well, the Liceo. Before its dissolution in 1960, members would settle down in Cuban rocking chairs in the lounge and enjoy conversation and the life of the street outside the big tall windows, sipping Cuban coffee in the morning and mojitos in the afternoon. A group of senior habitués monopolized the space between five and seven in the evening every weekday. Dressed in impeccable linen guayaberas, they thrived on chitchat and were known as *florones* (wreaths). When the Liceo was confiscated, the florones simply moved across the street to the public benches on the square and carried on.

One entered the Liceo of the 1950s through a foyer opening to an inner courtyard directly ahead. To the right was the elegant Salón Rojo, the "Red Room," where nonmembers had to cool their heels while visiting the building on an errand. The courtyard was cool and verdant with tropical growth and carefully tended areca palms. At the fountain, a marble Pomona struck a pose. The main ballroom opened to the courtyard. It had a Carrara marble floor, heavy plasterwork, and a stage at the end. Huge framed mirrors hung between the tall louvered doors. The scene would have been familiar to Faílde but for the ponderously Baroque German electrical chandeliers, a gift of the Heydrichs of waterworks fame.

The large, elegant Liceo library, heavy with carved Cuban mahogany shelves and reading tables, adjoined the ballroom. Across the hall and opposite the library was the air-conditioned television room. In the 1950s the library was invariably deserted, the TV room invariably crowded. At the end of the courtyard, past the lovely fountain with its saucy Pomona amidst everything that was prim and proper there was a bar, and beyond the bar, a huge room dedicated to billiards, poker, and the ubiquitous dominoes.

The smoked-filled games room was alive with the sound of colliding billiard balls, the rattle of domino chips, the bang of the stiff leather cups used to roll the dice, and loud profanity. Banging the cup hard brought good luck, the louder the better. The noise had driven the chess and checkers crowd to the relative peace of a corner of the ballroom under the big chandeliers.

Not much happened on the stage where the crème of the island's intelligentsia had once pontificated and maestro Faílde had launched the danzón. The occasional children's parties invariably featured Rodeline the Magnificent, a hack local magician in a turban and cape. Once a year Alicia Alonso, Cuba's seemingly everlasting prima ballerina assoluta would come down to give end-of-year awards to the local ballet academy students. The Somavilla Orchestra played onstage at the occasional debutante ball and at the traditional New Year's Ball, an elegant, must-be-attended event for the city's beautiful people.

One particularly memorable moment took place in the late 1950s. Bringing a taste of opera to the Liceo was the dream of a small but dedicated group, and they had somehow arranged for a version of Menotti's *Amahl and the Night Visitors* to be performed at the Liceo by Havana's Auditorium Opera. One of the younger members in the audience, a ruddy fellow we all called "Nero" because he looked a bit like the young Sir Peter Ustinov in *Quo Vadis,* delivered a loud Bronx cheer in the darkened room at a critical point in the performance. He did it for no reason, just for the sheer and very Cuban delight of *choteo*, of being mindlessly irreverent. Nero's resounding *trompetilla* was perfectly timed. It almost became part of the score, seemingly stopping time itself, reverberating to the farthest corners of the august Temple of the Muses to almost everyone's horror. I say almost everyone because there was some laughter, clearly in solidarity with Nero's contribution to the musical experience.[14] The artists were rewarded with what was probably the longest standing ovation they had ever received, but the Liceo was disgraced nevertheless.

In the 1950s, the artistic and literary origins of this clubby setting were hard to find. Yet, it was there that, as a child, I met Ernest Hemingway. The writer was in Matanzas and was due at the Liceo for a brief courtesy visit. My father was asked to greet him and brought me along. I dutifully followed. Hemingway looked courteously unimpressed by the solemn library and the hanging portraits of former Liceo luminaries by Matanzas' eminent portrait artists Esteban Valderrama and Francisco Coro Marrodán. When he was escorted to the bar, however, Hemingway's face lit up. He sat down—it was hot. Before too long he was holding court, banging the dice cup with the best and having a grand old time. Perhaps he sensed something about the Liceo that one cannot describe but that would have been evident to someone of his sensibility: for good or ill, it was Cuban to the core.

18   Return to the City of Rivers

THE FLIGHT FROM Montreal's Dorval Airport to Havana turned
out to be quite pleasant despite my initial trepidation. Raquel and I had booked
with Cubana Airlines, and I was apprehensive about flying in Soviet-made aircraft. I had flown them on a trip to China in the 1970s and it was a truly scary
experience. Later on, traveling through European Russia, I was struck by the
country's material backwardness, the dreariness of daily life, the poor roads,
the nineteenth-century plumbing, and the 1930s telephones. That the Soviets
had managed to convince so many for so long that they were technologically
avant-garde was amazing. Not quite as amazing, however, as the somber real-
ization that my own country had once merrily chosen to jump on that rickety
bandwagon. Poland, Hungary, and Romania had no choice, but Cuba did. It
was the only western country to join voluntarily, not be kidnapped into the
Soviet orbit.

The sight of our aircraft was reassuring. No need to worry: Cubana operated a leased Airbus for the flight. I smiled in the expectation that the ride
would be smooth, the cabin pressure adequate, and the air breathable. I could
even look forward to enjoying the in-flight meal and keeping it down.

I was soon lost in reverie. It was, after all, a solemn transit. I was going back
to my native land, the land of my ancestors, with the longing of an exile, the
anticipation of a child, the curiosity of a visitor, the resentment of a victim
and—I hoped—the objectivity of a scholar. Would I recognize my country
and, just as crucial, would my country recognize me?

Sitting across the aisle from us was Roger, a Canadian man in his thirties. Halfway through the flight Roger tapped me on the shoulder and handed me his copy of the *Toronto Globe and Mail*. "Would you like to read the paper?" he asked. When I looked at the front page I was struck. It was exactly forty-two years to the day since I had left Cuba in 1961. Excited, I told Raquel.

"Congratulations," said Roger. "I am glad for you. That you are going back." Our new Canadian friend was a Cuba enthusiast. He waxed lyrical about the island's charms. "Cubans are the happiest people in the world," he said. "If you get sick Fidel takes care of you, the weather is great, the ladies hot, and Cubans pay no taxes!"

"They might be happier if they had more freedom," I ventured, but Roger was not convinced. He stuck by his assertion that Cuba was a fiscally privileged nation, perhaps unique on the face of the earth, maybe in all of History. "Life is easy in Cuba," he said in parting. He flung his duffle bag over the beefy suntanned shoulder his sleeveless undershirt revealed. "This is all my luggage. I spend most of my time there with little on and remember, Cubans are special. They pay nooo taxes!"

Maybe they should. What strikes visitors to Cuba immediately is the dilapidated, almost derelict condition of many of her cities. Walls bulge and buildings collapse for lack of maintenance. Entire city blocks, especially in Havana, seem grandfathered by the laws of gravity. In that sense, Matanzas is not doing badly. Most of the city as I remembered it stands intact as if frozen in time, although there have been some losses and the general aspect of the town is drab and shabby. Four decades without a fresh coat of paint show. In the aggregate, however, far more of merit has been preserved than lost. The population growth has been dramatic but its impact on the city's historic center has been modest. Of the design and building quality of the postrevolutionary high-rises that ring the city and accommodate this population the less said the better. They are bad architecture compounded by shoddy construction.

Matanzas, a contrived Athens, is a natural Mesopotamia, a place defined by rivers. Heraclitus' ancient words of wisdom about rivers and the certainty of change were therefore very much in my mind as I crossed Concordia Bridge and the Yumurí in reverse on another, this time bright and sunny, August morning. The revolution and its inventor were still in place—was Heraclitus wrong about change? That mattered but little just at that moment. As our car cleared La Cumbre and the wide bay appeared below, I was overcome with emotion. Only the blue sky, the breeze combing the stately palm trees, and the view zooming in as the car sped downhill mattered. Like my last, my first view of Matanzas came to me through a veil of tears.

Mindful of the powerful image of the ever-flowing river, my mind was alertly on the lookout for signs of change. The growth of the port facilities was evident and impressive, as was the city's physical expansion. Matanzas' population today is more than twice what it was in 1958. Other intangible things have changed also. The conversation between the Leader and the people, once vibrant and true whether one liked it or not—I obviously did not—has become a mindless cacophony, a tired litany bounced off every conductive surface. Commander in Chief, give us our orders! Fatherland or death, we shall win! Mr. Imperialist, we have no fear of you! Billboards that formerly bore Camay soap's promise of beauty after the first bar now sold anti-imperialism or the Cubans' resolution "to be like Ché."

Change was apparent in the trivial as well as the fundamental. It was very hot—not unusual for a Cuban August—and I noticed many men in the streets in their undershirts or altogether shirtless, a sin against urbanity in the Matanzas of fifty years ago. Was this a form of exhibitionism by the sexy Cubans, an outcome of cultural change, or simply a sign that clothing was hard to find?

Clearly, the Yumurí had passed a lot of muddy water under the elegant bridge in forty-two long years, but what a pleasant surprise it was to realize upon returning that Matanzas was still populated by matanceros as I remembered them: cordial, polite, a trifle too trusting, generous, and infinitely hospitable. A visit to the house at La Playa where we lived when I was born was a moving experience. The family that now lives there received us with open arms, showed us through it, and seemed almost apologetic that the joinery had to be torn down because of *comején* (termites). While we were talking to the lady of the house her son arrived, a muscular young man about sixteen years old. He was caked with mud. "Where have you been?" asked his mother in mock disgust. "He has been exploring caves," said the little boy that grew up to become me. "How did you know?" asked the young man, surprised.

The wraparound colonnaded porch where somebody had taken a photo of me at age one between my two grandmothers was still there. The avocado trees in the garden were gigantic now, and there were orchids everywhere. I could imagine my grandmother Consuelo with her tools tending to the parterres with good old Calambuco, the gardener, in tow, and my parents as a young couple whispering sweet nothings to each other as the sea breeze played with my mother's hair; so little had changed.

On the way we passed the home of my late granduncle, Laurentino García Jr. The house looked as grand and elegant as in its former life; in fact, it was one of the few buildings in Matanzas showing evidence that paint still existed. Before he left, Junior buried or walled in all kinds of valuables—money, jewels, and whatnot. He and Esther, his wife, died in a home for the elderly in Miami, collecting a welfare check but presentable to the end. Well into their eighties they could still turn out a mean danzón. A serious horticulturist—a passion for gardening ran in the family—my granduncle missed his garden most of all.

It took a day for Junior's bet on the future to collapse. No sooner had they left than a servant passed the word around. A mob descended on the house with pickaxes and shovels, dug up the gardens, and cut holes everywhere. It was a treasure hunt, a free-for-all. Junior's fabled collection of orchids, heliconias, ferns, and tropical flowers—he had some truly exotic specimens—was thoroughly trampled. Restored, the house is now Matanzas' "wedding palace." Two generations of Matanzas couples have tied the knot in Junior's living room. Who knows, maybe there is some stuff still buried there somewhere.

Years later, my father, who was very fond of Junior, gave him a day at Miami's magnificent Fairchild Tropical Gardens as a birthday gift. Junior was as happy as an Easter bunny when they started their exploration of the exotic palms and the strangely shaped, beautiful flowers. He started showing off his vast botanical learning. That is, until they got to a display of heliconias. As my father later recounted, Junior grew somber and had to sit down. Tears streamed down his cheeks. "Are you all right, Uncle?" my father asked. Junior turned his head to his nephew and grabbed his arm. "What we have lost, Pino"—everyone called my father Pino—he said in a voice trembling with sadness. "What we have lost, Pino, what we have lost! Our country, our homes, everything!" The outing was ruined and Junior depressed for days.

An attempt to visit the Casa Cabañas in downtown Matanzas, where I lived as a child, was rather less successful. The family that lives there now was sitting on the sidewalk when I approached them. "This house was built by my grandfather," I said, "and I lived here as a child." "You *did*," answered a trim, beautiful Afro-Cuban lady possibly in her eighties with the bearing of a queen. She had that ineffable, self-assured countenance shared by those who know themselves to be at the core of a culture. The lady's expression left no doubt that any further conversation would be unnecessary, so there was no further conversation beyond a polite farewell. They graciously stood up as I took my leave. Manners are important in Matanzas. I had for many years imagined what such an encounter might be like. Exile and loss not only make you nostalgic, they make you angry. I was surprised that there was no confrontation at all. If anything, I felt a bit embarrassed to have so awkwardly intruded on their privacy.

The visit to the old Liceo was in many ways the culmination of the trip. Rolando Bretos, my father's brother, was the Liceo's last executive director. He had been elected to office only a few months before it was confiscated. Uncle Rolando and board chairman Emiliano Moreno Boskowitz officially handed over the keys to the building and the inventory of its contents on December 18, 1960. Rolando and other Liceo board members showed up that morning in the gala uniform of the Cuban bourgeoisie, the classic *dril cien* white linen suits. They probably fantasized about the day, not too far in the future, when they would take the premises back from the *compañeros* who showed up, predictably, in work clothes or militia uniforms.

It was not to be. The hoped-for liberation went bust on the sands of the Bay of Pigs. An exhibit of relics from the invasion was presented in the Liceo's grand ballroom shortly after the invaders' defeat in April 1961. It included captured weapons, equipment, and even the carbonized remains of a pilot. Revolutions are not for the squeamish. The elegant linen suits must have gone limp in Cuban closets. Too presumptuous for a society wedded to hardship socialism, they were too impractical to take into exile.

Uncle Rolando is buried in Lincoln, Nebraska, next to his wife, Leonor Vidal—my other Aunt Nena—and his sister Consuelo, my darling Aunt Cuca. Aunt Nena's parents are buried there also. The cold sod of the prairie must lie heavy upon their remains. Some day, I hope, they may yet dissolve in the warm, red soil of Matanzas.

Lincoln was their draw in the exile relocation sweepstakes. Like my sister and me, Uncle Rolando and Aunt Nena's two children had come to the United States as unaccompanied Pedro Pan minors in 1961. They were relocated to Nebraska in the care of the Lincoln Diocese's Catholic Charities. When their parents arrived a year later, the family was reunited there. Rolando and Nena landed after a blizzard had dumped one foot of snow on the prairie. Rolando, unfamiliar with ice, fell flat on his behind at the airport. Gifted with a deliciously profane Cuban language, he greeted Nebraska accordingly. Not an auspicious beginning, but in time Rolando grew to love his serendipitous new home. He played the guitar and had a fine singing voice. Whenever the profound sadness of exile got to him, especially on those long, cold, gloomy winter nights, he would strum old boleros.

Their son, Rolando Jr., lives in Lincoln. He is a rugged western outdoorsman who loves to hunt and thinks nothing of getting up at two in the morning to stalk deer in deep subzero temperatures. His sister Leonor—my cousin Nenita—lives in Portland, Oregon, with her Havana-born husband, Luis Navarro. They met and married in Lincoln, where Luis' family had experienced an identical saga. Luis has reached the pinnacle of his profession and was recently inducted into the U.S. Engineering Hall of Fame. They have two children, Luis, like his father a brilliant engineer; and Laura, like her mother a woman of beauty, smarts, and character. Laura has been to Cuba, works to send help to the island through Caritas, and considers herself *muy cubana*.

Many years later, one of the compañeros to whom Rolando and Emiliano Moreno handed over the keys recalled his memories of the Liceo Artístico y Literario de Matanzas' last day. This is what Roberto Santana Milián had to say:

> About 8:30 in the morning I showed up at the Liceo and was received very kindly by a gentleman dressed in a white linen suit. His name was Moreno. I read to him the resolution. Amidst the conversation he mentioned that he believed he recognized me. I answered that it was possible because for many years I had been the bootblack who shined his shoes at the Liceo's entrance.[1]

After one hundred years, the day of the bootblacks had arrived.

The Liceo's Red Room was still red on the day of our visit, a color equally compatible with socialism as with the Victorian decor it once featured. An oversized picture of "Ché" playing chess in his fatigues hung on the wall. The marble floors and plasterwork were still there. The huge German chandeliers donated to the Liceo by the Heydrichs almost one hundred years before were still hanging. Little holes revealed that they had at some point been wired for neon lighting by some hack electrician. The courtyard was as I remembered it minus the potted plants. A trickle of water oozed from the ever-coquettish Pomona's fountain.

The woman in charge of the building was sincere and forthcoming. We were struck by the youth of most of the people we met there that day. Every race known to Cuba was represented. Many seemed to be studying something and had books about them. I immediately sensed a deep affinity towards these wonderful young people, something profound, ineffable, tribal. I wish them the best of all possible Cubas. It is up to them to put it together.

I couldn't imagine—not for a moment—any of them blowing a Bronx cheer at a serious cultural event like Nero had. But—I wondered—would they actually dare to do so at the many crossroads of contemporary Cuban life where that response is eminently warranted though perhaps impolitic and possibly dangerous?

My fellow matanceros were curious about the remote past of their Sala White and excited by my potential as a source. It was as if they were living in a Roman villa and I had suddenly materialized in a toga speaking Latin. Some took notes. We had questions also. The person who left Cuba when he was eighteen and later became me asked to see the library. The Liceo had some twenty thousand volumes in 1960, including a superb Cuban collection and many rare Matanzas imprints. It represented a hundred years of accumulation by the town's elite although, truth be told, not much of consequence had been added to it in the twentieth century.

> "Library? I didn't know there was a library," said a woman.
> "Yes, there was a library," someone else responded.
> "What happened to it?" Nobody knew. Somebody asked where it
> had been.

The person that was eighteen when he left Cuba and later became me walked across the ballroom to the two enormous high-ceilinged rooms where the library had been, the books housed in elegant, glazed dark Cuban mahogany shelves. The shelves had stretched from floor to ceiling with access ladders and an overhang. In a corner, a tall but famously shy French grandfather clock had chimed away the hours melodiously and so discreetly as to be almost inaudible. Two huge matching mahogany reader's tables with exquisitely carved chairs had completed the ménage.

Now the walls were stark white and quite bare. Here and there, rectangular holes revealed where the massive shelves had been anchored. The tables and chairs had long ago vanished. Had the clock gone back to Europe in one of the many antiquarian export sales sponsored by revolutionary authorities, its honorable library service locked up in the inscrutable silence of things?

> "Lo que el viento se llevó," said one of the young men. "Gone with the
> Wind."[2]

Fig. 46. The Liceo Ballroom, ca. 1880. The historic space looked very much like this when the danzón was launched there in 1878. (Courtesy of University of Miami, Cuban Heritage Collection)

A few days later, before our departure, I went to the antiquarian bookstalls in Havana's Plaza de Armas. I saw a book in a familiar dark blue tooled leather binding. On the spine it bore the initials "L de M." I asked the dealer: "Do you have any more from where this came from?"

> "Not right now but I've been selling books with that same binding for years. They come from a former club in one of our provinces."
> "Yes, the Liceo de Matanzas."
> "How do you know? Are you Cuban?"

I smiled. A few months before, my three children, Pilar, Max, and Fernando, had visited Cuba together. Fernando is a marine biologist who has long been involved with conservation research in Cuba and goes there frequently. He looks Cuban, however it is that Cubans are supposed to look, has acquired a Cuban accent, and sports guayaberas. The three went out for dinner, and when they were going back to their hotel rooms, Fernando was intercepted at the door by a no-nonsense agent of State Security.

"Oye. You know that Cubans are not allowed in."

"I am Cuban but I am also a U.S. citizen by birth and a guest at this hotel," answered Fernando.

"Papers."

Fernando was not carrying his U.S. passport, so Pilar and Max had to go to his room and fetch it. Only then was Fernando allowed in. The guard apologized.

I cannot speak for others, let alone my children, but speaking for myself I can answer the bookseller's question categorically: Yes, I am Cuban. It is my fate, which I gladly accept, and also my inheritance, which I joyously embrace, even though being Cuban is not easy. The nature of our dilemma is encapsulated in the motto of the old Cuban republic: *Patria y Libertad*. Fatherland *and* Freedom. We were supposed to achieve both, but for the past fifty years we have had to make do with one or the other.

Whatever their convictions, whether they live on the island or overseas, whether they cheer for the revolution or despise it, Cubans have carried a heavy burden over the past half century, one it is impossible to let go of. I have never come across an ex-Cuban. As to my children and their posterity, only time will tell. I hope the option to be Cuban in a useful way will be available to them some day. When that day comes, I fancy they shall be at least in part matanceros also, and that the Sleeping City, like the Sleeping Beauty of the fairy tale, will be there in their hearts, ready to be awakened by a kiss.

Notes

Chapter 1. One Last *Vuelta*

1. On Forestier's work in Cuba, see Lejeune, "Jean Claude Nicolas Forestier" and R. Ruiz, *Memoria francesa*, 30.

2. An instrumental version of the anthem can be found at <www.archive.org/details/RepublicOfCuba-NationalAnthem> (accessed May 6, 2009).

3. Bergad, *Cuban Rural Society*, 249–50.

4. See Chuffat Latour, *Apunte histórico;* and Perseverancia, *Los chinos*. The charada was used for betting on the numbers' games (*bolita* or *terminales*). Bolita was in effect an illegal lottery (*bolita* refers to the little numbered balls used in the drawings). Winning numbers for terminales were the last two or, in some cases, the last three digits—i.e., "terminals"—of the first, second, and third prizes in the national lottery drawn every Saturday. Bets were placed on numbers to win (*fijo*), to place (*corrido*) or in combination (*parlé*). The charada assigned meanings to numbers, so that 1 stood for "horse," 2 for "butterfly," 3 for "sailor," 4 for "cat," 5 for "nun," and so on. The number 22 stood for "fire," 33 for "vulture," and 95 for "Matanzas." As a mnemonic aid, the 36 numbers of the classic charada are represented on a poster, once ubiquitous in Cuba and now in places like Miami, featuring the numbers and their meanings superimposed on the body of a Chinese man ("el chino de la charada").

This is how it worked: Susana dreamed of a vulture with its wings on fire and bet two pesos on the parlé of 22 and 33. Josefa killed a vulture with her car, saw an omen, and bet five pesos on 33 fijo. Juan, who was turning thirty-three years old that day, bet fifty cents on 33 corrido. The first, second, and third prizes that week were, respectively, 156722, 92333, and 143567. Susana and Juan won; Josefa lost because her number merely placed. See what happened in Matanzas when Bishop Severiano Saínz y Bencomo died in 1937 (chapter 15).

5. For a thorough discussion of the exodus, see Grenier and Pérez, *Legacy of exile*.

Chapter 2. Bay of Slaughters

1. For an excellent synopsis of precontact Matanzas, see Martínez Gabino et al., *Historia aborigen*. In *The Tainos* Rouse opens a window on "the people who greeted

Columbus." For a concise debunking of the myth of native extinction in Cuba, see Yaremko, "*Gente bárbara*."

2. Vento Canosa, *Alma de la ciudad*, 31–34.

3. Marrero, *Cuba: economía y sociedad*, 1:101–2.

4. For early Matanzas Bay see Trelles y Govín, *Matanzas y su puerto*; Ponte Domínguez, *Matanzas: biografía*, 1–20; and R. Ruiz, *Aguas de la ciudad*, 21–26.

5. Díaz del Castillo, *Verdadera historia*, 68–69.

6. Las Casas, *Historia de las Indias*, vol. 2, chap. 31.

7. *Ceiba pentandra* (fam. Bombacaceae) is Cuba's magic tree. Sacred to the Taíno, it is the abode of Iroko, one of the orishas, or deities, of the Afro-Cuban pantheon. Coincidentally, it is venerated also by the Maya of Mexico and Central America.

8. According to Peter Martyr, Vicente Yáñez Pinzón circumnavigated Cuba before Ocampo, and there may have been other, even earlier attempts, but Ocampo's report officially set the record straight (Marrero, *Cuba: economía y sociedad*, 1:101).

9. Ibid., 1:170, 184.

10. Cabrera Infante, *Vista del amanecer*, 18.

11. Trelles y Govín, *Matanzas y su puerto*, 12–13.

12. Lafrery, "Geografía tavole moderna," fol. 64, Library of Congress, Map and Geography Division. See also Cueto, *Cuba in Old Maps*, for a learned, definitive discussion of Cuban historical cartography. Matanzas is covered on pages 197–204.

13. *Islario*, fol. 64321, MSS 98 272n6 Biblioteca Nacional, Madrid.

14. Alexis, son of Alexander II, visited Cuba as part of a tour of the United States in 1871–72.

15. "Cuba. Costa norte."

16. Marrero, *Cuba: economía y sociedad*, 3:93–112.

17. *Afbeeldinghe in wat maniere Den Admirael Pieter Adriaensen Ita twee Rycke Honduras vaerders ver overt* (Anonymous, Dutch, etching, 275 × 366 mm, ca. 1628, British Museum, 1870.0514.2123).

18. See Goslinga, *The Dutch*, app. IV, 496–99.

19. *Verovering vande silver-vloot inde Bay Matanca AD 1628.* (Claes Jansz Visscher, Dutch, etching, 215 × 405 mm, ca. 1628, British Museum 1878.0713.2780). See also Ampzing, *West-Indische Trivmph-basvyne*.

20. Marrero, *Cuba: economía y sociedad*, 3:110.

21. Moreno Fraginals, *Cuba/España*, 92; see also Marrero, *Cuba: economía y sociedad*, 3:109–10.

22. Archivo General de Indias, Seville, Spain (hereafter AGI), Indiferente General, 1870; Marrero, *Cuba: economía y sociedad*, 2:205n.

23. The original version of the song dates to the time of the events. Jan Peter Heike (1809–1876) edited the seventeenth-century lyrics in 1847 The score is by J. J. Viotta (1814–1859). An instrumental version is available at the Memory of the Netherlands site of the Netherlands Royal Library, <www.geheugenvannederland.nl> (accessed May 6, 2009).

1. For seventeenth-century Matanzas, see Macías Domínguez, *Cuba*.

2. Martínez Carmenate, *Historia*, 36–37.

3. Oficiales reales to the Crown, Havana, Feb. 30, 1679. AGI, Santo Domingo, 123.

4. Marrero, *Cuba: economía y sociedad*, 4:148–49.

5. Real cédula, Lisboa, Sept. 16, 1582, AGI, Santo Domingo, 1122, cited in Marrero, *Cuba: economía y sociedad*, 2:124.

6. Between 1700 and 1797 some 142 ships were built at Havana, including the largest ever ship of the line, *La Santísima Trinidad*, lost at Trafalgar in 1805. Harbron, *Trafalgar*, 52–53. On naval construction before 1700 see Marrero, *Cuba: economía y sociedad*, 4:73–96. For an informative overview of Cuba's timber-producing trees, see Fernández Zequeira et al., *Cuba y sus árboles*, 67–84.

7. Martínez Carmenate, *Historia*, 17. See Marrero's numerous references to encomienda in *Cuba: economía y sociedad*, vol. 2.

8. For a thorough discussion of Cuba's early colonial land regime see Pérez de la Riva, *Origen y régimen de la propiedad territorial*. See also Corbitt, "Mercedes y realengos," 262–85, and the material throughout Marrero, *Cuba: economía y sociedad*, especially vols. 2 and 3.

9. Martínez Carmenate, *Historia*, 28–29.

10. Francisco Díaz Pimienta (1594–1652) was one of the most remarkable characters of early Cuban history (see Moreno Fraginals, *Cuba/España*, 87–91).

11. Rodríguez de Ledesma to the Crown, Havana, April 12, 1678, AGI, Santo Domingo, 106. Dutch engravings from 1628 show a small, probably palisaded structure at the lower end of the bay, next to a river.

12. Gage, *English American*, 372.

13. Córdova to the Crown, Dec. 9, 1680, AGI, Santo Domingo, 457. This *legajo,* entitled "Expediente sobre la población y fortificación del puerto de Matanzas, años de 1681 a 1696," is essential to the study of Matanzas' foundation.

14. Córdova to the Crown, May 20, 1684, AGI, Santo Domingo, 457.

15. Real Cédula, April 14, 1682, AGI, Santo Domingo, 457.

16. "Relación de servicios del Maestro de Campo de Infantería Española Don Severino de Manzaneda Salinas de Zumalabe," AGI, Indiferente General, 131. There are several versions of the governor's complete name. His definitive *hoja de servicios,* compiled at the end of his administration in Havana, lists him as I do here, but another, apparently earlier, hoja lists him as Severino de Manzaneda Salinas y Rozas (AGI, Indiferente General, 132). However, the *expedientillo* of his application for a Santiago knightly appointment has him as Severino García de Manzaneda Salazar y Sumalabe. This is understandable. A Santiago application demanded exacting and exhaustive genealogical evidence about *hidalguía* and *limpieza de sangre* (noble lineage and purity of blood). Don Severino may well have enlisted lineages to which succession he was entitled, but which were not normally in use as part of his name, to bolster his case. That would have been the case, for

example, had he been able to document his line within an ancient and prestigious branch of the Garcías, a commonplace surname that nevertheless includes some of the oldest Hispanic lineages. The García motto suggests it: "De García arriba nadie diga" (Higher than García let no one say). Tellingly, the surnames García and Salazar seem to appear *only* in the Santiago application. AHN, Ordenes Militares-Expedientillos, No. 4466.

17. Marrero, *Cuba: economía y sociedad*, 4:168. Manzaneda is to be credited not only with founding Matanzas and Santa Clara, but also with envisioning Cienfuegos.

18. Manzaneda to the Crown, Nov. 8, 1691, AGI, Santo Domingo, 457.

19. Manzaneda to the Crown, Jan. 1, 1693, AGI, Santo Domingo, 457.

20. "Copia de autos hechos de lo que se ha obrado en la nueba población de San Carlos y San Severino de Matanzas, año de 1693." AGI, Santo Domingo, 457.

21. Manzaneda to the Crown, November 3, 1694, AGI, Santo Domingo, 457.

22. AGI, Santo Domingo, 457. The legajo contains a roster of sailings, description and origin of settlers, etc.

23. AGI, Santo Domingo, 457.

24. "Relación de servicios del capitán Diego Méndez de León Illada," AGI, Santo Domingo, 375.

CHAPTER 4. Green Tobacco and a Clever Marquis

1. Testé, *Historia eclesiástica*, 3:167.

2. Martínez Carmenate, *Historia*, 74.

3. On Matanzas tobacco, see Rivero Muñiz, *Tabaco*, 80–85.

4. AGI, Santo Domingo, 499, cited in Marrero, *Cuba: economía y sociedad*, 7:186.

5. Marrero, *Cuba: economía y sociedad*, 7:82–83.

6. Meaning a crucial, definitive moment—"when the chips are down"—the phrase originated from the comparison of the British "redcoat" army tunic with the vivid red and black colors of the pulp and pit of the *mamey* (*Pouteria sapota*), a tropical fruit abundant in Cuba.

7. "Independent Status of the Cities of Santa Maria del Rosario, St. Philip & St. Jago [Bejucal] and Matanzas," National Archives, London, CO/117/2/6. On Matanzas' surrender, see idem CO 117/1/51.

8. Cueto, *Cuba in Old Maps*, 76, 242. There are three known such powder horns bearing images of "Matansia" (Cueto, "Los cuernos de pólvora").

9. AGI, Santo Domingo, 1598"B" contains the metropolitan files on the Florida colonization scheme. Martínez Carmenate's excellent discussion in *Historia*, 100–10, is based on the Matanzas end of this remarkable episode. See also Gold, "Departure of Spanish Catholicism," 377–88.

10. For a thorough, richly documented discussion of Fort Mose and its context, see Landers, *Black Society*.

11. About the Vigía fortress, see Hernández Godoy, "San José de la Vigía"; and Alfonso, *Memorias*, 62–63.

12. *Reglamento para las milicias*, 38, insert 4. For a thorough study of Cuba's military reorganization, see Kuethe, *Cuba, 1753–1815.*

13. Alfonso, *Memorias*, 76–78, note 32 (not paginated).

14. Marrero, *Cuba: economía y sociedad*, 7:193 and Mena and Cobelo, *Historia de la medicina*, 451–52.

15. Tarascas are still used in Corpus Christi processions in Spain and Latin America, famously in Toledo. The dictionary of the Real Academia Española de la Lengua defines a tarasca as "figura de sierpe monstruosa, con una boca muy grande, que en algunas partes se saca durante la procesión del Corpus" (a monstrous serpent figure, with a very large mouth, which in some regions is brought out during the Corpus procession). On the Matanzas tarasca, see Alfonso, *Memorias*, 121. In 1773, two blacks were paid two pesos for carrying the tarasca, and others who dressed up as *diablitos* received five pesos apiece.

16. For the full story of the affair, see Alfonso, *Memorias*, 122–74.

17. Alfonso, *Memorias*, 174. The Spanish text follows: "Dios tenga en su santo reino/al transitorio Giménez./Escarmienten los vivientes/no se fíen de mugeres."

18. Curiously, events were memorialized in much the same way in each episode of *La Guantanamera,* a radio show in Cuba during the 1940s and 1950s. The show, a runaway audience success, combined a radio dramatization of a murder with décimas sung by La Calandria, a well-known vocalist, to the tune of Joseíto Fernández' popular "Guajira Guantanamera." (Long before Pete Seeger mainstreamed Fernández' "Guantanamera" with verses by Martí, in Cuba *cantar la guantanamera* meant to be implicated in a police case, usually involving violent death.)

19. On Valdés see Pérez Cabrera, *Historiografía de Cuba*, 140–47.

20. AGI, Contratación, 5518, N2, R14, March 16, 1773.

21. Santa Cruz y Mallén, *Historia de familias cubanas*, 8:120.

22. *Calendario manual y guía de forasteros*, 84.

23. On the situado and Cuba, see Marichal and Souto Mantecón, "Silver and Situados."

24. "Expediente sobre el robo de un mulo," Sala Primera, Aug. 29, 1796. AGI, Santo Domingo, 1145.

CHAPTER 5. Coffee Cup and Sugar Bowl

1. By 1797 no forests existed within forty-two miles of Havana. In 1828 José Antonio Saco estimated that figure to be one hundred (Bergad, *Cuban Rural Society*, 348 n).

2. Perret Ballester, *Azúcar en Matanzas*, 337.

3. Knight, *Slave Society*, 67.

4. Thomas, *Cuba*, 131–32.

5. For a prolix chronicle of sugar's kingdom, see Ely, *Cuando reinaba su majestad el azúcar.*

6. Marrero, *Cuba: economía y sociedad*, 12:74.

7. Moreno Fraginals, *Cuba/España*, 183.

8. Santa Cruz, *La Habana*, 244–45; Bergad, *Cuban Rural Society*, 348.

9. Cuba's cane-induced ecological disaster has been brilliantly explored by Funes Monzote, *From Rainforest to Cane Field.*

10. For a thorough and enlightening exploration of the economics of slavery in nineteenth-century Cuba see Bergad, Iglesias; and Barcia, *Cuban Slave Market.* They note that a "surge" in slaving occurred precisely between 1853 and 1862, the climax of sugar's expansion in western Cuba (98–99).

11. For a glimpse at the financing of late eighteenth-century mills, see García Rodríguez, *Aventura de fundar ingenios.*

12. See Bergad's discussion in *Cuban Rural Society;* and Perret Ballester, *Azúcar en Matanzas.* The latter's subtitle is, eloquently, *y sus dueños en La Habana.*

13. Bergad, *Cuban Rural Society,* 170–71.

14. Matanzas "city" means the urban core itself and its barrios. Matanzas "district" means the urban core plus its adjacent communities. Matanzas "province" means the modern province of that name.

15. Bergad, *Cuban Rural Society,* 67.

16. Moliner Castañeda, *Cabildos afrocubanos en Matanzas,* 81ff.

17. Perret Ballester, *Azúcar en Matanzas,* 220–22.

18. On the Chinese then and thereafter, see Jiménez Pastrana, *Chinos en Cuba;* Helly, *Idéologie et ethnicité;* and Marrero, *Cuba: economía y sociedad,* 9:123–36.

19. Moreno Fraginals, *Ingenio,* 157–58.

20. Quoted in Bergad, *Cuban Rural Society,* 388–89.

21. Perret Ballester, *Azúcar en Matanzas,* 446.

22. Moreno Fraginals, *Ingenio,* 91.

23. Moreno Fraginals, *Cuba/España,* 98, 186.

24. Perret Ballester, *Azúcar en Matanzas,* 337.

25. Ibid., 38–39.

26. Ibid., 237–40.

27. Abad, "Un siglo de ferrocarriles," 141–42.

28. For a history of Cuban railroads, see Zanetti Lecuona and García Alvarez, *Caminos para el azúcar.* See also Bergad, *Cuban Rural Society,* 107–15; Moyano Bazzani, *Nueva frontera del azúcar,* and Alfonso Ballol, *Ferrocarril de La Habana a Güines.*

29. Zanetti Lecuona and García Alvarez, *Caminos para el azúcar,* 51. A discussion of Matanzas' pioneering lines is found on pages 55–57. See also Perret Ballester, *Azúcar en Matanzas,* 255–71.

30. Abundant biographical and genealogical information on Matanzas' sugar oligarchy can be found in Perret Ballester, *Azúcar en Matanzas,* 300–39. Holders of titles are exhaustively covered in Nieto y Cortadellas, *Dignidades nobiliarias en Cuba.*

31. Perret Ballester, *Azúcar en Matanzas,* 256.

32. Several mill owners who were ennobled, however, took their titles from their mills, as did José Baró y Blanxhart, ennobled as the Marquis of Santa Rita.

33. Cited in Thomas, *Cuba,* 151.

34. Journal of Eulalia Keating, Feb. 28, 1839, cited in Paquette, *Sugar Is Made with Blood,* 61.

35. Abbot, *Letters written in the interior*, 63.

36. Marrero, *Cuba: economía y sociedad*, 13:110.

CHAPTER 6. The Year of the Lash

1. Curiously, the only other historical event commemorated in the charada is the accession and impeachment of President Miguel Mariano Gómez in 1936. The number 36 stands for "Miguel Mariano."

2. Morales y Morales, *Iniciadores*, 1:17, 335.

3. An informative monograph of this region is González Pérez, *Santa Ana–Cidra*.

4. Perret Ballester, *Azúcar en Matanzas*, 190.

5. See Martínez, "Antislavery Courts"; and Bethel, "Mixed Commissions." The Court of Mixed Commission had functioned since 1817 and included from time to time functionaries such as the eminent British-Australian naturalist William Sharp Mcleay (in Cuba 1825–1836), who produced notable entomological illustrations from the Havana and Matanzas regions (Mcleay Family Papers, State Library of New South Wales, Sydney).

6. Thomas, *Cuba*, 194.

7. Rauch, *American Interest*, 40. For a thorough and lucid analysis of Turnbull's role, see Paquette, *Sugar Is Made with Blood*, 150–55, 174–77. Turnbull's own perspectives and observations are cogently articulated in his classic travel account, *Travels in the West*.

8. Corwin, *Spain and the Abolition of Slavery*, 74–78.

9. Barcia, *Seeds of Insurrection*, 25–48.

10. On the Aponte movement see Childs, *Aponte*; on the rebellion's leader's intellectual scope, see the remarkable study by Palmié, *Wizards and scientists*, chap. 1 and appendixes.

11. Thomas, *Slave trade*, 668.

12. There is a fine biography by Urbano Martínez Carmenate, *Domingo Delmonte y su tiempo*.

13. Lobo, *Havana*, 133.

14. On del Monte's prolix epistolary, see Figarola-Caneda, *Centón epistolario,* and the introduction to the 2002 edition by Sophie Andioc. An important collection of del Monte papers is at the Library of Congress (see the Domingo del Monte Collection).

15. Marrero, *Cuba: economía y sociedad*, 13:188–91.

16. An excellent modern study, indispensable for understanding this period and its larger context, is Paquette, *Sugar Is Made with Blood*. In a different vein, see also Rojas, *Harén de Oviedo*.

17. Irish historian Margaret Brehony noted the irony that one of the Irish involved, a Patrick Donegal, arrested under the charge of sabotaging a locomotive, was kin to the captain-general (Brehony, "Irish Railroad Workers in Cuba," 185).

18. See the excellent biography by Castellanos, *Plácido*.

19. Dolores María "Lola María" de Ximeno y Cruz (1866–1934), was a socialite with a

mind of her own and a lively prose. See her extensive autobiographical narrative throughout Ximeno y Cruz, *Aquellos tiempos.*

20. Ibid., 2:48.

21. Ibid., 2:49–53.

22. This aspect of Plácido has elicited considerable criticism. A case in point was Manuel Sanguily's dismissive opinion of the poet, whose authorship of the "Plegaria a Dios" he denies (Paquette, *Sugar Is Made with Blood,* 5, 277).

23. Ximeno y Cruz, *Aquellos tiempos,* 2:55.

24. The Spanish text follows: "Ser de inmensa bondad, Dios poderoso:/a vos acudo en mi dolor vehemente;/extended vuestro brazo omnipotente,/rasgad de la calumnia el velo odioso/arrancad este sello ignominioso/con que el mundo manchar quiere mi frente/. . . . ./Mas si cuadra a tu suma omnipotencia/que yo perezca cual malvado impío,/y que los hombres mi cadáver frío ultrajen con maligna complacencia,/suene tu voz y acabe mi existencia . . . /¡Cúmplase en mí tu voluntad, Dios mío!"

25. Ximeno y Cruz, *Aquellos tiempos,* 2:57.

26. See Paquette, *Sugar Is Made with Blood,* 3–26, 233–65.

27. Bergad, Iglesias, and Barcia, *Cuban Slave Market,* 54–55.

28. See the vivid *Resumen de los desastres ocurridos en el puerto de la Habana.*

CHAPTER 7. Tyre of the Western Seas

1. Ponte Domínguez, *Matanzas: biografía,* 145.

2. For a succinct but thorough discussion of the late-nineteenth-century Cuban economic juncture, see Pérez, *Cuba between Reform and Revolution,* 130–40.

3. See Pichardo, *Itinerario general.*

4. Ponte Domínguez, *Matanzas: biografía,* 102.

5. Ibid., 114–17.

6. In an allusion to *Neptuno* and a salute to steam navigation, Havana's notorious merchant and smuggler extraordinaire, Pancho Marty i Torréns hung a depiction of a steamship in a restaurant he ran at the new Tacón Market. The market itself began to be called Plaza del Vapor, a name that has survived (Torre, *Lo que fuimos y lo que somos,* 83–84).

7. Vivanco, "Entrada del vapor Almendares," in *Paseo pintoresco,* 43–45.

8. *Paseo pintoresco,* 44. The pagination of this edition is erratic because it preserves the pagination of the original, published in installments.

9. Torrademé Balado, *Iniciación a la historia del correo,* 203–6, 297.

10. Hazard, *Cuba with Pen and Pencil,* 270–71.

11. See Cotarelo Crego, *Matanzas en su arquitectura.*

12. For an excellent summary of this period, see R. Ruiz, *Matanzas: surgimiento y esplendor de la plantación.*

13. The old parochial church, upgraded to cathedral status in 1912, suffered major damage when some of the vaulting collapsed in the 1970s due to massive water leakage and

lack of maintenance. Many of the distinctive murals inside have been ruined by mold. Like so much else of Cuba's built heritage, Matanzas' cathedral is severely distressed.

14. *Reseña histórica de Matanzas*, 62.

15. Testé, *Historia eclesiástica*, 3:181.

16. Ibid., 3:182–83. On Navia's scheme, see "Plano de la nueva población llamada de San Alejandro, propiedad de don Eloi Navia," AGI, Santo Domingo, 800, Mapas y planos.

17. Alfonso, *Memorias*, 25–26.

18. On Havana's urban aesthetics and the role of shaded corridors, see Carpentier's *Ciudad de las columnas* enhanced by Graziano Gasparini's revealing photographs.

19. The Beas were originally from Biscay and settled in Matanzas around the mid-nineteenth century. Demetrio Manuel de Bea y Maruri founded the family firm, which in its heyday, owned sugar mills as well. In 1888 Bea was ennobled as the Marquis of Bellamar. My father's first Pontiac dealership, Brecar Motor Company, opened at the building (No. 3 Magdalena Street) in 1949. The space is now the headquarters for Ediciones Vigía, Matanzas' remarkable publishing house.

20. The entrepiso (in Cuba *entresuelo*) initially served as a dormitory for the slaves and, in the 1920s, became the offices of Laurentino García, S.A., my grandmother's family's firm. For a few years in the 1930s the Vallejos (my wife, Raquel's, family) also had offices in the palace, but it was love not neighborliness that brought us together. We met as exiles in Miami many years later. The grand old house is now the Provincial Museum.

21. Dollero, *Cultura cubana*, 167.

22. López Marrero, "Ciudad de los puentes." Julio Sagebién y Tavernier was the top engineer of Matanzas' golden age. In 1857 he was hired by the Aldama-Alonso group to plan the new Havana-Matanzas railway. See "Aprobación del proyecto de ferrocarril de Güines a Matanzas y otros," Archivo Histórico Nacional (Madrid), Ultramar, 45, E (hereafter AHN).

23. Villaverde, "Puentes del Yumurí y del S. Juan en Matanzas," in *Paseo pintoresco*, n.p.

24. Pezuela y Lobo, *Diccionario geográfico*, 4:40.

25. Cabrera Galán, *Ateneo de Matanzas*, 48–53.

26. Villaverde, "Canteras del Yumurí," in *Paseo pintoresco*, n.p.

27. Carley, *Cuba*, 120–22.

28. Abbot, *Letters written in the interior*, 66; García Santana, *Matanzas*, n.p.

29. Murray, *Letters*, 250.

30. *Expediente sobre la construcción del cementerio*, 14.

31. Ibid., 29.

32. Testé, *Historia eclesiástica*, 3:167.

33. Pruna, *Ciencia y científicos en Cuba*, 359–78.

34. Bergad, *Cuban Rural Society*, 358n.

35. "Notes on the Heydrich and García-Amechazurra families," [mss. by Alfredo Heydrich, M.D.], in possession of the author, Québec. On Ferdinand Heydrich's aqueduct operations, see AHN, Aguas, Ultramar, 219, exp 7. I am grateful to the late Alfredo

Heydrich, M.D., of Bellingham, Washington, for numerous conversations about the Matanzas Heydrich clan, and to Carmen García Blanco de Galindo of Matanzas for sharing with me valuable information and moving insights about all manner of kinsfolk, the Heydrichs included.

36. See Tanco Armero, *Viaje . . . a China;* and Yun and Laremont, "Chinese Coolies and African Slaves," 99–122.

37. For a thorough discussion and "mini-biographies" of the Matanzas sugar elite, see Perret Ballester, *Azúcar en Matanzas,* 300–39.

38. Richard Henry Dana Jr., *To Cuba and Back,* 78–79.

39. Ibid., 79.

40. The Spanish text follows: "Si no, de que sirven, San Juan apacible/tus aguas que brillan en manso correr,/tus botes pintados de rojo y de negro,/que atracan airosos a tanto almacén,/y el canto compuesto de duros sonidos/de esclavos lancheros que bogan en pie,/y alzando y bajando las palas enormes/dividen y azotan tus ondas de muer?"

CHAPTER 8. Athens of Cuba

1. Martínez Carmenate, *Atenas de Cuba.*

2. Ibid., 85; Wurdemann, *Notes on Cuba,* 111.

3. Dollero, *Cultura cubana,* 140.

4. R. Ruiz, "Un canario controversial," in idem., *Matanzas: tema con variaciones,* 31–49.

5. Fornet, *Libro en Cuba,* 150.

6. León, *Prensa;* and Moliner Castañeda, *Imprenta.*

7. Cabrera Galán, "Permanencia de la Atenas," 4.

8. Bosch, *Cuba, la isla fascinante,* 65.

9. Cernuda, *Cien años,* 6.

10. Ibid., 7–8, 36–37.

11. Ximeno y Cruz, *Aquellos tiempos,* 2:176–80.

12. Theodore, *Relación de la segunda y tercera ascensión aerostática.* See also Kuhn, "Fiestas and fiascoes," 114n.

13. Marrero, *Cuba: economía y sociedad,* 14:61.

14. Portell-Vilá, "Cham Bom-Biá."

15. Marrero, *Cuba: economía y sociedad,* 14:96–111.

16. Ibid., 14:101.

17. See Leiva Luna, "*La Empresa.*"

18. "Se establece segunda enseñanza en el colegio 'La Empresa' de Matanzas," AHN, Ultramar 30, exp. 30.

19. Between 1870 and 1880, no less than four new private primary schools and two new private secondary schools were authorized for Matanzas city (see AHN, Ultramar 142, exps. 11 and 12; Ultramar 141, exps. 17 and 18). On the suppression of the institutos, see AHN, Ultramar 272, exp. 17.

20. "Establecimiento de una escuela gratuita en Matanzas." AHN, Ultramar 11, exp. 8.

21. Jiménez de la Cal, *Familia Guiteras*.

22. A. Guiteras, *La Eneida*. See also Carbón Sierra, "Antonio Guiteras y su traducción."

23. Pérez Cabrera, *Historiografía de Cuba*, 225–48.

24. Perrier, *Bibliografía dramática*, 63.

25. Vitier, *Lo cubano en la poesía*, 90–98.

26. Holbrook, *American Lyceum*; Bode, *The American Lyceum*.

27. Llaverías, *Catálogo de los fondos del Liceo Artístico y Literario*, v–xxi.

28. Martí, *Obras*, 4:472–76.

29. On the Liceo's agenda and early programming, see Liceo de Matanzas, *Estatutos* and *Anuario de la sección de ciencias físicas y naturales* [1866].

30. Cabrera Galán, *Ateneo de Matanzas*, 12.

31. Ibid., 30–31.

32. On Gundlach's Cuban research, see Dathe, *Johann Christoph Gundlach*.

33. See the exhibition guide by Figarola-Caneda, *Guía oficial*.

34. Cabrera Galán, *Ateneo de Matanzas*, 48–53.

35. O'Connor, *Athens of America*, 108, 119, 148–50.

36. Pérez Arbeláez, *Humboldt en Colombia*, 12.

37. Ximeno y Cruz, *Aquellos tiempos*, 2:39–50.

38. Ballou, *Due south*, 120.

CHAPTER 9. Disguises and Holy Spaces

1. This, of course, is a critical issue with a vast literature. Moreno Fraginals, in a telling anecdote, relates how Captain-General Tacón made the criollos' position in the new pecking order clear to all in terms of palace protocol. Moreno Fraginals , *Cuba/España*, 223–24.

2. Ibid., 216.

3. Tseelon, *Masquerade and Identity*, 1–36.

4. Material cited here and later is from Ximeno y Cruz, *Aquellos tiempos*, 2:155, 168–69.

5. Ortiz, "Cabildos afrocubanos"; and Moliner Castañeda, *Cabildos afrocubanos en Matanzas*.

6. Moliner Castañeda, "Contribución francesa"; R. Ruiz, *Memoria francesa*, 15.

7. Ximeno y Cruz, *Aquellos tiempos*, 2:135 (italics in the original).

8. Marmier, *Lettres sur l'Amérique*, cited in Marrero, *Cuba: economía y sociedad*, 14:274–77.

9. Cuervo Hewitt, *Aché*, 111–78.

10. "Cuba. Costa norte. Bahía de Matanzas," Map 1735.

11. Bolívar Aróstegui, *Orishas en Cuba*, 25–26.

12. The Catalonian text follows: "Rosa d'abril, morena de la serra/de Montserrat Estrel,/Il-lumineu la catalana terra/guieu nos cap al Ciel." Verdaguer, a priest and a key figure of the Catalan nineteenth-century renaissance, was a frequent visitor to Cuba as

a chaplain of the Spanish Transatlantic Company. For an excellent introduction to the history of, and devotion to Our Lady of Montserrat, see *Nigra Sum: iconografía de Santa María de Montserrat*, 15–40.

13. On the condition of Cuban buildings and spaces, see Dalrymple, "Why Havana Had to Die." Although he writes about Havana, his argument has validity for the rest of Cuba, certainly for Matanzas.

14. The subject of Spanish migration to the Americas and to Cuba in particular has an extensive literature. For the former see Sánchez Albornoz, *Españoles hacia América*; for the latter see Maluquer de Motes, *Nación e inmigración*.

15. Moreno Fraginals, *Cuba/España*, 349.

16. See Moreno Fraginals and Moreno Massó, *Guerra, migración y muerte*.

17. Gómez Gómez, "Emigrantes asturianos," in Uría González et al, *Asturias y Cuba*, 21.

18. Gómez Gómez, "Emigrantes asturianos," 27–32.

19. Chávez Alvarez, *Fiesta catalana*, 2. Chávez Alvarez' book is a carefully researched and beautifully written monograph richly evocative of ambiance. See also Catalá and Zaldívar, *De Montserrat a Monserrate*.

20. See Roy, *Catalunya a Cuba*.

21. Cited by Chávez Alvarez, *Fiesta catalana*, 19–20.

22. Ibid., 36.

23. On the image by Joan Roig i Soler, see ibid., 26–32.

24. For an exciting discussion of this theme, see Palmié, *Wizards and Scientists*.

CHAPTER 10. The Tyranny of Nearness

1. Portell-Vilá, *Historia*, 2:121.

2. Despite its age, the best treatment of annexationism is Portell-Vilá's' *Historia*. On the Cárdenas landing, see idem, 1:432–65. See also Rauch, *American Interest;* and Santovenia, *Armonías y conflictos*.

3. Portell-Vilá, *Historia*, 1:375–85.

4. Ponte Domínguez, *Matanzas: biografía*, 189.

5. Portell-Vilá, *Historia*, 1:459. Portell-Vilá remarks that the phrase was "cryptic" and says no more. Portell-Vilá, who was a native of Cárdenas, minimizes López' annexationist aims. Curiously, he reproduces two of López' official documents in facsimile, noting that neither contains any "allusion" to annexation but missing the overwhelming visual fact that Cuba's official coat of arms, as if its contents were not enough, is flanked by both Cuba's flag and the Stars and Stripes, the latter in the position of honor. Ponte Domínguez, a matancero, emphasizes Cárdenas' disappointing lack of support. A Cuban nationalist historian like Portell-Vilá, he also minimizes López' annexationist agenda.

6. For a well-informed discussion of Cuba's national symbology, see Gay-Calbó, *Símbolos de la nación*.

7. On the Teurbe Tolón family's Matanzas roots, see Ponte Domínguez, *José F. Teurbe Tolón y Blandino*.

8. See Montes-Huidobro's critical edition of *El laúd del desterrado*, which features Teurbe Tolón as one of Cuba's key exile poets. Teurbe Tolón's publications include *Los preludios*. He was also the author of a renowned language manual, *The Elementary Spanish Reader and Translator*. See also Carbonell, *Los poetas del laúd del desterrado*.

9. Hazard, *Cuba with Pen and Pencil*, 283.

10. See E. Guiteras, *Guía de la cueva;* Calzadilla Rodríguez, *Cueva de Bellamar;* and especially, Vento Canosa, *Alma de la ciudad*, 115–23.

11. Hazard, *Cuba with Pen and Pencil*, 291–92.

12. Herrera López, *Tren de Guanabacoa*, 37.

13. Hazard, *Cuba with Pen and Pencil*, 272–73.

14. Wurdemann, *Notes on Cuba*.

15. See Jualynne Dodson, "Encounters in the African Atlantic World: The African Methodist Episcopal Church in Cuba" in Castañeda Fuertes, ed., *Between Race and Empire*, 85–89.

16. *Atlanta Constitution*, August 30, 1910, 7.

17. Currier was born in the Virgin Islands. He was considered an expert in Native American missions. The first bishop of Matanzas has a rich bibliography, including *Lands of the Southern Cross* and *History of Religious Orders*.

18. For an authoritative treatment of Matanzas' Protestant history see Ramos, *Panorama del Protestantismo*.

19. For a thorough discussion of that legendary game, see González Echevarría, *Pride of Havana*, 75–77.

20. Dihigo has a fine biography, Bjarkman, *Immortal*. See also González Echevarría, *Pride of Havana*, 180–81.

CHAPTER 11. Las Alturas de Simpson

1. Díaz Ayala, "Historia de la Sonora matancera."

2. Bremer, *Homes of the New World*, 2:364–73.

3. Philip Pasmanick has argued that the décima format makes an appearance at the heart of the rumba itself. See "'Decima' and 'Rumba.'"

4. See Santiago, "Roots Revival."

5. Ortiz, *Instrumentos*, 2:172–233.

6. Ibid., 2:221–22.

7. Ibid., 2:76–114.

8. Vinueza, *Presencia arará*.

9. Cabrera's research in Matanzas was extensive. See *Laguna sagrada de San Joaquín* and *Monte*. On Cabrera's career, see Hiriart, *Lydia Cabrera*.

10. For a succinct biography of Malanga, see Perret Ballester, *Azúcar en Matanzas*, 84.

11. Evora, *Orígenes de la música cubana*, 175.

12. For the remote antecedents of this tradition, see Carpentier, *Música en Cuba*, 50–75.

13. Ortiz, *Instrumentos*, 2:110–35

14. Starr, *Louis Moreau Gottschalk*, 182.

15. Oliver Ruiz, "Música en el proceso de conformación de la identidad."

16. On White, see Faivre d'Arcier, *José White*.

17. Starr, *Louis Moreau Gottschalk*, 183.

18. On Brindis de Salas, known in his day as "the Cuban Paganini," see Toledo, *Presencia y vigencia de Brindis de Salas*.

19. Carpentier, *Música en Cuba*, 100.

20. Perret Ballester, *Azúcar en Matanzas*, 123.

21. Soloni, "Danzón y su inventor." See also Castillo Faílde, *Miguel Faílde*.

22. The Spanish lyrics follow: "Allá en Matanzas se ha creado/un nuevo baile de salón/con un compás muy bien marcado/y una buena armonización./Para las fiestas del gran mundo/con la elegancia y distinción/será el bailable preferido/por su dulce inspiración./Danzonete, prueba y vete./Yo quiero bailar contigo/Al compás del danzonete."

23. Ojeda, "The danzonete."

24. Orovio, *Diccionario de la música cubana*, 349.

25. The literature on La Sonora and its stars is truly massive. Its popularity throughout Latin America is attested by the fact that major works have been published in Costa Rica, Colombia, and elsewhere. See, for example, Zaldívar, *Mito de la Sonora Matancera* and Valverde, *Memoria de la Sonora Matancera*.

26. Orovio, *Diccionario de la música cubana*, 39.

27. Ibid., 455.

CHAPTER 12. Forget the *Maine*!

1. Crowley, *Documentary History of Australia*, 3:533.

2. The literature on Finlay is extensive. See Saladrigas y Zayas, *Tribute to Finlay*, and Pruna, *Ciencia y científicos en Cuba*, 379–412.

3. *The Splendid Little War* was later the title of an influential treatment of the war by U.S. historian Frank B. Freidel.

4. Whether La Demajagua was tiny or merely small is a matter of judgment. In 1860 it was the 1,113th out of 1,365 Cuban mills in terms of productivity. It was nowhere near the Acanas, Tinguaros, and Alavas of Matanzas. Céspedes was not the "rich mill owner" of traditional historiography. His fortune was otherwise based. His thinking, therefore, was not representative, let alone typical, of the western *sacarocracia* (Moreno Fraginals, *Cuba/España*, 274–75).

5. See the discussion of this bizarre incident in Córdova y Quesada's remarkable *Locura en Cuba*.

6. Byrne has a fine biography by Martínez Carmenate, *Bonifacio Byrne*. The original Spanish of the quoted excerpt follows: "Murió de cara al mar aquel valiente/bañado por la luz de la alborada/noble, serena y firme la mirada,/tranquilo el corazón, alta la frente."

7. Halstead, *Story of Cuba*, 254–55.

8. For a précis of their legend, see Santovenia, *Huellas de gloria*, 123–30, 135–38.

9. Stoner, "Women's Rights," 16.

10. For Juan Gualberto Gómez' own account of the events at Ibarra, see Gómez, *Por Cuba Libre*, 313–22.

11. Portuondo, *Historia de Cuba*, 519–21.

12. Placer Cervera, "Acciones navales," 14–18.

13. Kekatos, "Edward H. Amet." See also Musser, *Emergence of Cinema*, 256, 261, 598.

14. For an almost day-by-day account of the hostilities, see Miró Argenter, *Crónicas de la guerra*.

15. Helg, *Our Rightful Share*, 78–82.

16. Pearson. Special Report from Washington, Release May 30, 1966.

17. Weyler wrote an extensive apologia for his term in Cuba. Weyler y Nicolau, *Mi mando en Cuba*.

18. For a thorough and sobering discussion of the war's devastation see Tone, *War and Genocide*. The war's effects on Matanzas are discussed in Bergad, *Cuban Rural Society*, 305–20.

19. See Tone, *War and Genocide*, 193–224, for a discussion of reconcentration and its effects.

20. Schwartz, *Lawless Liberators*, 139–41.

21. Naranjo Orovio, "Creando imágenes," 513.

22. Bretos, "Imaging Cuba," 53–63.

23. Santovenia, *Huellas de gloria*, 212–13.

24. For details of Gómez' death, see Horrego Estuch, *Juan Gualberto Gómez*, 275–82.

CHAPTER 13. The City Sleeps

1. Quesada, *Derechos de Cuba a la Isla de Pinos*.

2. Gómez, *Por Cuba Libre*.

3. See Moreno Fraginals' incisive discussion in *Cuba/España*, 348–53.

4. Wilson (1837–1925) has a very competent biography: Longacre, *Grant's cavalryman*. A retired Civil War veteran, Wilson was recalled to service at the time of the Spanish-Cuban-American War.

5. Pérez, *Essays on Cuban History*, 43; Contreras Llorca et al., *Bibliotecología en Matanzas*, 80; Vento and Ruiz, *Biblioteca pública de Matanzas*, 67–74. On Mrs. Wilson's strange death, see "Mrs. Wilson Burned to Death." *New York Times*, April 29, 1900, 1.

6. González García and Ortega Suárez, *Características generales del espiritismo kardeciano en Matanzas*, note 14.

7. *Reseña histórica de Matanzas*, 28.

8. Ibid., 37.

9. Ibid., 39.

10. For an exhaustive discussion of Cuban tramways, see Allen Morrison, "Tramways of Cuba," remarkable for its thoroughness, depth of information, rigorous scholarship, and accuracy of presentation.

11. The Spanish text follows: "Te quiero porque eres triste,/triste como la tristeza;/te

quiero por tu pobreza/de canario sin alpiste./Te quiero porque trajiste/el verde justo en la sien,/pero te quiero también/por tu Pan que tiene sueño,/por tu porvenir pequeño/de fósforo y henequén."

12. The Spanish text follows: "Matanzas, me cago en tí/y en tu puñetero Pan,/en tu maldito San Juan/y tu sucio Yumurí."

13. Ponte Domínguez, *Matanzas: biografía*, 310–11.

14. Consejo de Administration de la Zona Franca, *Zona Franca*, 5–17.

15. "La Compañía de Jarcia," *La Lucha* (1923), reproduced online at <www.guije.com/pueblo/municipios/matanzas/lucha_negocios/jarcia.htm> (accessed April 24, 2009).

16. For a detailed account of Matanzas' Koreans, see Ruiz and Lim Kim, *Coreanos en Cuba.*

17. Ibid., 39–41.

18. Ibid., 48–49.

19. Interview with Dayton Hedges by the author, West Palm Beach, Florida, October 16, 2007.

20. Levine, *Tropical diaspora*, 76–78.

21. *Matanzas contemporánea*, n.p.

22. *Album de Matanzas*, n.p. Members of the 1925 board were Alberto J. Cohen, president; Roberto Matalón, president ad honorem; Alberto G. Maya, secretary; Isaac Esquenazi, economist; Salomon Ben-Haim, treasurer; Moisés Matalón, comptroller; Julio Haaday, presidente del templo; and Marcos Béhar, Isaac Ben-Haim, Enrique Béhar, Marco Surijón, Elías Ben-Haim, Salomón Matalón, José Surijón, and Salvador Esquenazi, members at large.

23. See Dollero, *Cultura cubana*, 111.

24. The Spanish text follows. "Me desordeno, amor, me desordeno,/cuando voy en tu boca, demorada,/y casi sin por qué, casi por nada,/te toco con la punta de mi seno."

25. Lifelong matancero Federico Uhrbach (1873–1932) was, with his brother and collaborator, Carlos Pío, one of Cuba's exponents of *modernismo*.

26. The Spanish text follows: "Mientras lentamente los bueyes caminan,/las viejas carretas rechinan . . . rechinan . . . ./Lentas van formando largas teorías por las guardarrayas y las serventías./Vadean arroyos, cruzan las montañas/llevando el futuro de Cuba en las cañas/ . . . /Van hacia el coloso de hierro cercano: van hacia el ingenio norteamericano,/y como quejándose cuando a él se avecinan,/cargadas, pesadas, repletas,/¡con cuántas cubanas razones/rechinan las viejas carretas . . . !"

CHAPTER 14. Nightmares and Cold Sweats

1. See Morúa, *Integración cubana*. For two informative biographies of Morúa, see Pérez Landa, *Vida pública*, and Horrego Estuch, *Martín Morúa Delgado*.

2. Bronfman, *Measures of equality*, 67–78.

3. For a general background of the Cuban race situation leading to the 1912 events and the brujo scares, see Helg, *Our rightful share*, especially chapters 6 and 7.

4. For starters on the Cuban Abakuá tradition, see L. Cabrera, *Sociedad secreta Abakuá*.

5. For a statement of the same childhood experience by Matanzas-born folklorist Jorge Luis Rodríguez, see "Muerte de la niña Cecilia," pt. 1, p. 2.

6. There is no agreement about the number of incidents of *brujería* between 1902 and 1920. Chávez Alvarez reports eight; Palmié (*Wizards and scientists*, 212) suggests almost treble that amount.

7. Bronfman, *Measures of equality*.

8. Ortiz, *Los negros brujos*.

9. Chávez Alvarez, *Crimen de la niña Cecilia*, 30–34; Palmié, *Wizards and scientists*, 238.

10. My account of this famous case is based on two well-documented modern studies, Rodríguez' "Muerte de la niña Cecilia," and Chávez Alvarez' *Crimen de la niña Cecilia*. See also Stephan Palmié's illuminating discussion in *Wizards and scientists*, 201–59, and the tendentious but gripping account in Roche y Monteagudo, *Policía y sus misterios*, 225–40.

11. Vento Canosa, "Consideraciones," 85–89. Dr. Vento is also closely associated with Matanzas' other famous "skeleton," the remains of Josefa Margarita Ponce de León y Herdero, found mummified in a niche at the Matanzas' cemetery, kept for years by Dr. Vento in his home, and exhibited in the provincial museum, breaking all attendance records in 1965.

12. Chávez Alvarez refers to this as the "black" version in *Crimen de la niña Cecilia*, 16–18.

13. *El Imparcial*, June 24, 1919, cited in Rodríguez, "Muerte de la niña Cecilia," pt. 3, p. 2.

14. Armando Carnot awaits his biographer. On a trip to Matanzas I visited his former home at Manzano Street. The house has collapsed and is in ruins. Ironically, the only part standing is the front wall bearing a grand commemorative plaque erected to his memory by the people of Matanzas. For a sketch of his life, see Salazar, "Armando Carnot Veulens."

15. Chávez Alvarez, *Crimen de la niña Cecilia*, 174–77.

16. See Thomas, *Cuba*, 556–63.

17. On the events leading to the 1920 crash, see the exhaustive study by Santamaría García, *Sin azúcar no hay país*, especially 55–60.

18. See Laurentino García's obituary in Havana's *Diario de la Marina*, April 24, 1925, p. 6.

19. McAvoy, *Sugar baron*, 75, 153, 159–60. See also Santamaría García, *Sin azúcar no hay país*, 134–35, 154–55, 380.

20. L. Pérez, *Cuba under the Platt Amendment*, 188.

21. In 2003 I visited the mill and was shown around the locomotive yard. Renamed José Smith Comas in 1960, the mill has some of the best-preserved engines in Cuba.

CHAPTER 15. Kilowatts and Revolution

1. Brown, Gauthier, and Meurville. "Georges Claude's Cuban OTEC experiment."

2. García Fernández, "Cuba investiga."

3. "Could sea power solve the energy crisis?" *Daily Telegraph*, 1/8/08.

4. Claude wrote his memoirs, *Ma vie et mes inventions.*

5. See Cousteau and Jacquier, *Français on a vole ta mer*, especially chap. 9.

6. "Sea Power," *Time,* October 20, 1930.

7. For Claude's own report of the proceedings, see Claude, "Power from the Tropic Seas." See also Planas, "Obra de Georges Claude."

8. The Cuban revolution of 1933 has an abundant literature. A good place to begin is Aguilar, *Cuba, 1933.*

9. See Suchlicki, *University Students.*

10. For the revolution of 1933, Guiteras' role, and its aftermath, see Aguilar, *Cuba, 1933;* Ameringer, *The Cuban Democratic Experience*, and Argote-Freyre's in-depth biography of Batista, the first installment of what promises to be a definitive biographical study. On Guiteras, see Jiménez de la Cal's study of the Guiteras family and the works by Tabares del Real and Cabrera.

11. On Saínz see Testé, *Historia eclesiática*, 119–49. When he was appointed Bishop of Matanzas in 1915, Saínz had his hands full with the Mexican Revolution, concretely with the deteriorating position of the Catholic Church in the Yucatan Peninsula. This fascinating history lies at the Archivo Histórico de la Arquidiócesis de Yucatán in Mérida, awaiting a researcher.

CHAPTER 16. Deus ex Machine Gun

1. This chapter, obviously written from a personal but not uninformed perspective, offers a synopsis of an exceedingly important and complex period in the history of Cuba for which there is a truly massive literature. What happened in Cuba in the 1950s has received attention from scholars, mythmakers, ideologues, fiction writers, movie script writers, journalists and all manner of folk. The Cuban government, very much an interested party, has created a relentlessly negative story line of pre-Castro Cuba that is constantly projected in the press, museums, publications, and all means of diffusion and propaganda.

2. For an excellent scholarly treatment of the Auténtico years, see Ameringer, *Cuban Democratic Experience.*

3. Lowinger and Fox, *Tropicana Nights*, 54–55.

4. For a thorough treatment of this period, see García-Pérez, *Insurrection & Revolution.*

5. For a roster of those killed in the action—fourteen in total—see Jiménez de la Cal, *Matanzas*, 68.

6. See Franqui, *Cuba: el libro de los doce.*

7. This raises the issue of death and survival during the insurgency against Batista. In January 1959 *Bohemia* jejunely reported that a total of 22,000 people had perished. This estimate which, in any case, would have been impossible to arrive at with any degree of objectivity that early on, soon became fixed in myth despite its obvious falsehood. Arnaldo Jiménez de la Cal, Matanzas' city historian and a loyal revolutionary, reports that "more than 100 Matanzas-born combatants" were killed. This included the seven Matanzans

killed in the Moncada attack as well as the fourteen dead at the Goicuría (Jiménez de la Cal, *Matanzas*, 68). The variance between myth and body count is impressive.

8. García-Pérez, *Insurrection & Revolution*, 99–109.

9. The complete text follows: "En este lugar sagrado/donde acudió tanta gente/bien esfuerza el mas cobarde,/y se caga el mas valiente."

10. Curiously for figures said to be so crucial to the process as Camilo and Almeida, their actual contributions seem to have engaged very little serious scholarly attention. Contrasted to the massive bibliographies for Castro and Guevara, those for Camilo and Almeida are slender indeed, with the vast majority of the entries being pieces produced by the Cuban government or, in the case of Almeida, written by himself.

11. Ruby Hart Phillips sensed this quality, writing: "As I watched Castro I realized the magic of his personality. . . . He seemed to weave a hypnotic net over his listeners, making them believe in his own concept of the functions of government and the destiny of Cuba" (Phillips, *Island of Paradox*, 406).

CHAPTER 17. Nero's Cheer

1. On May 15, 1943, the Cuban chaser CS-13 under the command of Lieutenant Mario Ramírez Delgado sank Unterseebot-176 in Cuban waters. U-176, commissioned in 1941, had sunk a 45,850 tonnage before she was sent to the bottom (Morison, *History of United States Naval Operations*, 1:190–91).

2. One such volunteer with strong connections to Matanzas was Roberto Esquenazi-Mayo, later on a distinguished Cuban scholar (see *Memorias de un estudiante soldado*).

3. Matanzas city's first distillery was Belcher and Brothers, founded in 1859. Yucayo, the makers of Yucayo rum, began operations in 1900. During the war years no less than ten new distilleries were built in the province in order to meet the emergency. In 1940 Cuba produced 37,269,680 liters of alcohol (45 degrees Gay-Lussac), with Matanzas contributing almost 50 percent of the production. In 1944 the national production reached a whopping 206,225,626 liters (Perret Ballester, *Azúcar en Matanzas*, 233–34).

4. Testé, *Historia eclesiástica*, 5:168–73.

5. For a summary of 1953 census figures, see Cuban Economic Research Project, *Study on Cuba*, 426–41.

6. There is an informative history of ante-revolution Cuban broadcasting: Salwen, *Radio and TV in Cuba*; however, the fascinating history of Cuban radio and TV in the 1930s, '40s, and '50s awaits systematic study.

7. Cuba may well have been the first country outside of the United States where candidates for public office were advertised with TV commercials and jingles. A case in point was Andrés Rivero Agüero's 1958 entry with the theme "Cuba first, and Rivero Agüero president." Of course, ad hoc music had been a component of Cuban politics at least since the classic *Chambelona* of Menocal days.

8. Abbot, *Letters written in the interior*, 33.

9. Information on San Miguel de los Baños is scant. A good place to begin is "Historial de la fundación de San Miguel de los Baños," in *Matanzas contemporánea*, n.p.

10. Portell-Vilá, "Carretera que beneficiará a Varadero," in *Matanzas contemporánea*, n.p.

11. Batista, *Piedras y leyes*, 271–74.

12. For Quintana's relationship with Batista, see "Nicolás Quintana," in *Encuentro de la Cultura Cubana*, 28–30.

13. Excellent photos are reproduced in *Encuentro de la Cultura Cubana*, 35–37.

14. To understand the deeper context of this banal but telling event, see Mañach, *Indagación del choteo*.

CHAPTER 18. Return to the City of Rivers

1. R. Ruiz, *Matanzas: tema con variaciones*, 71.

2. Among other collections lost as a result of confiscation were the archives of Havana's Asturian and Galician Centers and the Asociación de Dependientes, key sources for students of Spanish migration (Moreno Fraginals, *Cuba/España*, 315).

Bibliography

Abad, Luis V. "Un siglo de ferrocarriles," *Diario de la Marina,* Número Centenario (1932): 141–42.

Abbot, Abiel. *Letters written in the interior of Cuba.* Boston: Bowles and Dearborn, 1829.

Academia de la Historia de Cuba. *William Rufus King. Discursos leídos por Thomas W. Palmer y Emeterio Santovenia.* Havana: Siglo XX, 1953.

Aguilar, Luis E. *Cuba, 1933: Prologue to revolution.* Ithaca, N.Y.: Cornell University Press, 1974.

Album de Matanzas. [Matanzas: n.p.], 1925.

Alfonso, Pedro Antonio. *Memorias de un matancero.* Matanzas: Imprenta de Marsal, 1854.

Alfonso Ballol, Bertha. *El ferrocarril de La Habana a Güines. El primer ferrocarril de Iberoamérica.* Madrid: Ferrocarriles de Cuba/Fundación de FFCC Españoles, RENFE, n.d.

Ameringer, Charles. *The Cuban democratic experience: The Auténtico years, 1944–1952.* Gainesville: University Press of Florida, 2000.

Ampzing, Samuel. *West-Indische trivmph-basvyne.* Haarlem: A. Rooman, 1629.

Apuntes históricos de la ciudad de Matanzas e historia del cuerpo de bomberos y del matadero municipal. Matanzas: A. Estrada, 1928.

[Arechabala, José, S.A.]. *José Arechabala en su 75o aniversario, 1878–1953.* [Cárdenas: José Arechabala, S.A., 1954].

Argote-Freyre, Frank. *Fulgencio Batista.* New Brunswick, N.J.: Rutgers University Press, 2006.

Ballou, Maturin. *Due south: Or, Cuba past and present.* New York: Negro Universities Press, 1969.

Barcia, Manuel. *Seeds of insurrection: Domination and resistance on western Cuban plantations, 1808–1848.* Baton Rouge: Louisiana State University Press, 2008.

Basso Ortiz, Alejandra. *Los gangá en Cuba: la comunidad de Matanzas.* Havana: Fundación Fernando Ortiz, 2005.

Batista, Fulgencio. *Piedras y leyes.* Mexico City: Ediciones Botas, 1962.

Beato Núñez, Jorge, and Miguel F. Garrido. *Cuba en 1830. Diario de viaje de un hijo del Mariscal Ney.* Miami: Ediciones Universal, 1973.

Bellin, Jacques Nicolas. *Baye de Matance dans l'isle de Cuba*. [Paris: 1764].

Bergad, Laird W. *Cuban rural society in the nineteenth century: The social and economic history of monoculture in Matanzas*. Princeton: Princeton University Press, 1990.

Bergad, Laird W., Fe Iglesias García, and María del Carmen Barcia. *The Cuban slave market, 1790–1880*. Cambridge: Cambridge University Press, 1995.

Beschreibung von Eroberung der spannischen Silber-Flotta. Amsterdam: Bei Nicolao Jans Fischer, 1628.

Bethel, Leslie. "The mixed commissions for the suppression of the transatlantic slave trade in the nineteenth century." *Journal of African History* 7 (1966): 79–93.

Bjarkman, Peter C. *The Immortal: Martin Dihigo and the baseball legacy of Cuba*. Jefferson, N.C.: McFarland, 2007.

———. *A history of Cuban baseball, 1864–2006*. Jefferson, N.C.: McFarland, 2007.

Blainey, Geoffrey. *The tyranny of distance: how distance has shaped Australia's history*. Melbourne: Sun Books, 1966.

Bode, Carl. *The American Lyceum: Town meeting of the mind*. Carbondale: Southern Illinois University Press, 1968.

Bolívar, Simón. *Carta de Jamaica*. Caracas: Ediciones de la Presidencia de la República, 1972.

Bolívar Aróstegui, Natalia. *Los orishas en Cuba*. Havana: Ediciones Unión-UNEAC, 1990.

Bosch, Juan. *Cuba, la isla fascinante*. Santiago de Chile: Editorial Zig-Zag, 1955.

Brehony, Margaret. "Irish railroad workers in Cuba: Towards a research agenda." *Irish Migration Studies in Latin America* 5, no. 3 (November 2007). <www.irlandeses.org/0711brehony1.htm> (accessed April 29, 2009).

Bremer, Fredrika. *Homes of the New World: Impressions of America*. 2 vols. New York: Harper Brothers, 1853.

Bretos, Miguel A. "Imaging Cuba under the American flag: Charles Edward Doty in Havana." *Journal of Decorative and Propaganda Arts* 22 (1996): 82–103.

Bronfman, Alejandra. *Measures of equality: Social science, citizenship, and race in Cuba, 1902–1940*. Chapel Hill and London: University of North Carolina Press, 2004.

Brown, Martin C., Michel Gauthier, and Jean-Marc Meurville. "Georges Claude's Cuban OTEC experiment: A lesson in tenacity for entrepreneurs." *IOA Newsletter* 13, no. 4 (Winter 2002). <www.clubdesargonautes.org/otec/vol/v0113-4-2.htm> (accessed 1/30/09).

Cabrera, Lydia. *La laguna sagrada de San Joaquín*. Madrid: R, 1973.

———. *El monte*. Havana: Ediciones C. R., [1954].

———. *La sociedad secreta Abakuá narrada por viejos adeptos*. Miami: Ediciones Universal, 2005.

Cabrera, Olga. *Guiteras: la época, el hombre*. Havana: Editorial de Arte y Literatura, Instituto Cubano del Libro, 1974.

Cabrera Galán, Mireya. *El Ateneo de Matanzas: su historia y trascendencia*. Havana: Editorial de Ciencias Sociales, 2000.

———. "Permanencia de la Atenas de Cuba." *Matanzas. Revista Artística y Literaria de la Atenas de Cuba* 4 (2000): 3–7.

Cabrera Infante, Guillermo. *Vista del amanecer en el trópico*. Barcelona: Seix Barral, 1974.

Calcagno, Francisco. *Diccionario biográfico cubano (comprende hasta 1878)*. New York: Imprenta y Librería de N. Ponce de León, 1878.

Calendario manual y guía de forasteros . . . para el año 1795. Havana: Imprenta de la Capitanía General, n.d.

Calzadilla Rodríguez, Iraida. *Cueva de Bellamar: maravilla en una gota de agua*. Havana: Pablo de la Torriente, 1998.

Cantero, Justo Germán. *Los ingenios: colección de vistas de los principales ingenios de azúcar de la isla de Cuba*. Havana: Tipografía de Luis Marquier, 1857.

Carbón Sierra, Amaury B. "Antonio Guiteras y su traducción de La Eneida." *Faventia* 18, no. 1 (1996): 119–28.

Carbonell, José Manuel. *Los poetas del laúd del desterrado*. Havana: Siglo XX, 1924.

Carley, Rachel. *Cuba: 400 years of architectural heritage*. New York: Whitney Library of Design, 1997.

Carpentier, Alejo. *La ciudad de las columnas*. Havana: Editorial Letras Cubanas, 1982.

———. *La música en Cuba*. Mexico City: Fondo de Cultura Económica, 1946.

Carrerá y Heredia, Rafael R. de. *Atlas histórico del progreso de los ferro-carriles de Cárdenas, el Júcaro, Matanzas y el Coliseo en la Isla de Cuba*. Madrid: Imprenta de Tello, 1872.

Castañeda Fuertes, Digna, ed. *Between race and empire: African-Americans and Cubans before the Cuban Revolution*. Philadelphia: Temple University Press, 1998.

Castellanos, Jorge. *Plácido, poeta social y político*. Miami: Ediciones Universal, 1984.

Castillo Faílde, Osvaldo. *Miguel Faílde, creador musical del danzón*. Havana: Ediciones del Consejo Nacional de Cultura, 1964.

Catalá, Francesc, and Alfredo Zaldívar. *De Montserrat a Monserrate: religiosidad, historia, tradición*. Matanzas: Ediciones Vigía, en el muy caluroso agosto de 1996.

Cernuda, Ramón. *Cien años del paisaje cubano/One hundred years of Cuban landscape, 1850–1950. December 2001–February 2002*. Coral Gables: Cernuda Arte, 2001.

Chacón y Calvo, Jose María. *Estudios heredianos*. Havana: Editorial Letras Cubanas, 1980.

Chaunu, Pierre, and Hughette Chaunu. *Seville et l'Atlantique*. 8 vols. Paris: A. Collin, 1955–1959.

Chávez Alvarez, Ernesto. *El crimen de la niña Cecilia: la brujería en Cuba como fenómeno social, 1902–1925*. Havana: Editorial de Ciencias Sociales, 1991.

———. *La fiesta catalana: presencia hispánica en la cultura cubana*. Havana: Editorial de Ciencias Sociales, 1989.

Childs, Matt D. *The 1812 Aponte rebellion in Cuba and the struggle against Atlantic slavery*. Chapel Hill: University of North Carolina Press, 2006.

Chuffat Latour, Antonio. *Apunte histórico de los chinos en Cuba*. Havana: Molina, 1972.

Claude, Georges. *Ma vie et mes inventions*. Paris: Plon, 1957.

———. "Power from the Tropic Seas." *Mechanical Engineering* 52 (December 1930): 1039–44.

"Cobo: un homenaje permanente a Matanzas." *Matanzas. Revista Artística y Literaria de la Atenas de Cuba* 4 (2000): 26–29.

Consejo de Administration de la Zona Franca. *Zona franca del puerto de Matanzas. Free zone of the port of Matanzas.* [Matanzas: 1938].

Contreras Llorca, Caridad, Katherine Siverio Cartaya, and Maridena Cabrera Pérez. *La bibliotecología en Matanzas, 1828–1989.* Matanzas: Ediciones Matanzas, 2005.

Corbitt, Duvon. "Mercedes y realengos: A survey of the public land system in Cuba." *Hispanic American Historical Review* 19, no. 3 (1939): 262–85.

Córdova y Quesada, Armando. *La locura en Cuba.* Havana: Seoane, Fernández y Cía., 1940.

Corwin, Arthur F. *Spain and the abolition of slavery in Cuba, 1817–1886.* Austin: Institute of Latin American Studies, 1967.

Cotarelo Crego, Ramón. "Matanzas, ciudad de puentes." *Matanzas. Revista Artística y Literaria de la Atenas de Cuba* 4 (2000): 8–11.

———. *Matanzas en su arquitectura.* Havana: Editorial Letras Cubanas, 1993.

———. *Teatro Sauto, Matanzas.* [Matanzas: Imprenta de Divulgación de Cultura], 1993.

Cousteau, Jacques-Yves, and Henri Jacquier. *Français, on a vole ta mer.* Paris: R. Laffont, 1981.

Crowley, Frank K. *A Documentary History of Australia.* 5 vols. West Melbourne: Nelson, 1980.

"Cuba. Costa norte. Bahía de Matanzas." Map 1735, scale 1:25000. 2nd ed., Nov. 1, 1983. Havana: Instituto Cubano de Hidrografía, 1984.

Cuban Economic Research Project. *A study on Cuba.* Coral Gables: University of Miami Press, 1965.

Cuervo Hewitt, Julia. *Aché, presencia africana: tradiciones yoruba-lucumí en la narrativa cubana.* New York: Peter Lang, 1988.

Cueto, Emilio. *Cuba in old maps.* Miami: Historical Association of Southern Florida, 1999.

———. "Los cuernos de pólvora de la invasión anglo-americana a La Habana." *Herencia* 13, no. 2 (2007): 69–77.

———. *Mialhe's colonial Cuba: The images that shaped the world's view of Cuba.* Miami: Historical Association of Southern Florida, 1994.

Currier, Charles Warren. *History of religious orders.* New York: Murphy and McCarthy, 1894.

———. *Lands of the Southern Cross: A visit to South America.* Washington, D.C.: Spanish-American Publication Society, 1911.

Dalrymple, Theodore. "Why Havana had to die." *City Journal,* Urbanities section, Summer 2002. <www.city-journal.org/html/12_3_urbanities-why_havana.html> (accessed Jan. 30, 2009).

Dana, Richard Henry Jr. *To Cuba and Back*. Carbondale and Evansville: Southern Illinois University Press, 1966.

Dathe, Wilfried. *Johann Christoph Gundlach (1810–1896). Un naturalista en Cuba. Naturforscher auf Kuba*. Marburg an der Lahn: Basilisken Presse, 2002.

Deschamps Chapeaux, Pedro. *El negro en la economía habanera del siglo XIX*. Havana: Unión de Escritores y Artistas de Cuba, 1971.

Díaz Ayala, Cristóbal. *Cuando salí de La Habana: 1898–1997, cien años de música cubana por el mundo*. San Juan, P.R.: Fundación Musicalia, 1999.

———. *Cuba canta y baila: discografía de la música cubana*. San Juan, P.R.: Fundación Musicalia, 1994.

———. "Historia de la Sonora Matancera y sus estrellas." *Latin Beat Magazine*, February 1997. <www.LatinBeat.com> (accessed Jan. 30, 2009).

———. *Música cubana: del areyto al rap cubano*. San Juan, P.R.: Fundación Musicalia, 2003.

Diaz del Castillo, Bernal. *Verdadera historia de la conquista de la Nueva España*. Mexico: Porrúa, 1968.

Dollero, Adolfo. *Cultura cubana. La provincia de Matanzas y su evolución*. Havana: Imprenta Seoane Fernández, 1919.

Ely, Roland T. *Cuando reinaba su majestad el azúcar: estudio histórico-sociológico de una tragedia latinoamericana*. Buenos Aires: Editorial Sudamericana, 1963.

Encuentro de la Cultura Cubana (special issue on Nicolás Quintana) 18 (Fall 2000).

Expediente sobre la construcción del cementerio general de la ciudad de San Carlos de Matanzas. Matanzas: Imprenta del Gobierno y Marina, 1840.

Esquenazi-Mayo, Roberto. *Memorias de un estudiante soldado*. Havana: Ministerio de Educación, 1951.

Estévez y Romero, Luis. *Desde el Zanjón hasta Baire*. Havana: Tipografía La Revoltosa, 1899.

Estrada y Zenea, Ildefonso. *Mi labor: apuntes para la historia de la isla de Cuba y con particularidad para la de la ciudad de Matanzas*. Mexico City: Tipografía de Amado Loaiza, 1904.

Evora, Tony. *Orígenes de la música cubana: los amores de las cuerdas y el tambor*. Madrid: Alianza Editorial, 1997.

Faivre d'Arcier, Sabine. *José White y su tiempo*. Havana: Editorial Letras Cubanas, 1997.

Fernández Zequeira, Maira, et al. *Cuba y sus árboles*. Havana: Editorial Academia, 1999.

Ferrer, Ada. *Insurgent Cuba: Race, nation and revolution, 1868–1898*. Chapel Hill: University of North Carolina Press, 1999.

Figarola-Caneda, Domingo. *Centón epistolario de Domingo del Monte*. Havana: Siglo XX, 1923.

———. *Centón epistolario/Domingo del Monte*. 2 vols. Havana: Imagen Contemporánea, 2002.

———. *Guía oficial de la Exposición de Matanzas*. Matanzas: Imprenta La Nacional, 1881.

———. *Plácido: contribución histórico-literaria.* Havana: Siglo XX, 1922.

Foner, Philip S. *The Spanish-Cuban-American War and the Birth of U.S. Imperialism, 1895–1902.* 2 vols. New York: Monthly Review Press, 1972.

Fornet, Ambrosio. *El libro en Cuba: siglos XVIII y XIX.* Havana: Editorial Letras Cubanas, 1994.

Franqui, Carlos. *Cuba: el libro de los doce.* Mexico City: Ediciones Era, 1966.

Freidel, Frank B. *The splendid little war.* Boston: Little, Brown, 1958.

"Frustration in Cuba." *Time,* July 7, 1930. <www.time.com> (accessed Jan. 30, 2009).

Funes Monzote, Reinaldo. *From rainforest to cane field in Cuba: An environmental history since 1492.* Chapel Hill: University of North Carolina Press, 2008.

Gage, Thomas. *The English American.* New York: Argonaut Press, 1928.

García Fernández, Hugo. "Cuba investiga sobre el uso de la energía del mar." *Juventud Rebelde,* April 3, 2007. <www.juventudrebelde.cu/cuba/2007-04-03/cuba-investiga-sobre-el-uso-de-la-energia-del-mar> (accessed Jan. 30, 2009).

García Pérez, Gladys Marel. *Insurrection and revolution: Armed struggle in Cuba, 1952–1959.* Boulder, Colo.: Lynne Rienner, 1998.

García Rodríguez, Mercedes. *La aventura de fundar ingenios: la refacción azucarera en La Habana del siglo XVIII.* Havana: Editorial de Ciencias Sociales, 2004.

García Santana, Alicia. "Matanzas: del ideario a la realidad urbana." <http://hispanidadymestizaje.es/ideario.htm> (accessed May 2, 2009).

Gay-Calbó, Enrique. *Los símbolos de la nación Cubana: las banderas, los escudos, los himnos.* Havana: Sociedad Colombista Panamericana, 1958.

Gold, Robert L. "The departure of Spanish Catholicism from Florida, 1763–1765." *The Americas* 22, no. 4 (April 1966): 377–88.

Gómez, Juan Gualberto. *Por Cuba Libre.* Havana: Oficina del Historiador de la Ciudad, 1954.

González Echevarría, Roberto. *The pride of Havana: A history of Cuban baseball.* New York: Oxford University Press, 1999.

González García, Juan Francisco. *Memoria catalana de Matanzas.* Matanzas: Ediciones Vigía [1998].

González García, Rigoberto, and C. Jorge D. Ortega Suárez. *Características generales del espiritismo kardeciano en Cuba y en Matanzas.* <www.socieddespiritistacubana.com> (accessed May 2, 2009).

González Pérez, José Ramón. *Santa Ana–Cidra: historia de una comunidad.* Havana: Departamento de Orientación Revolucionaria del Comité Central del Partido Comunista de Cuba, 1975.

Goslinga, Cornelis C. *The Dutch in the Caribbean and the wild coast, 1580–1680.* Assen: Van Gorcum, 1971.

Grenier, Guillermo, and Lisandro Pérez. *The legacy of exile: Cubans in the United States.* Boston: Allyn and Bacon, 2003.

Guiteras, Antonio. *La Eneida de P. Virgilio Marón.* Barcelona: Imprenta de Jaime Jesús, 1885.

Guiteras, Eusebio. *Guía de la cueva de Bellamar*. Matanzas: Imprenta de la Aurora del Yumurí, 1863.

Guiteras, Pedro J. *Historia de la conquista de la Habana*. Philadelphia: Parry and McMillan, 1856.

———. *Historia de la isla de Cuba*. 2 vols. New York: J. R. Lockwood, 1865–66.

Guiteras de Hoskins, Blanca. "Noticias iconográficas de Pedro José Guiteras." *La Habana Literaria* 2, no. 13 (July 1892): 9–134.

Halstead, Murat. *The story of Cuba*. Chicago: Werner Co., [1896].

Harbron, John D. *Trafalgar and the Spanish navy*. Annapolis: Naval Institute Press, 1988.

Hazard, Samuel. *Cuba with pen and pencil*. London: Sampson Low, Marston, Low and Searle, 1873.

Helg, Aline. *Our rightful share: The Afro-Cuban struggle for equality, 1886–1912*. Chapel Hill: University of North Carolina Press, 1995.

Helly, Denise. *Idéologie et ethnicité: Les Chinois Macao a Cuba, 1847–1947*. Montréal: Les Presses de l'Université de Montreal, 1997.

Hernández Godoy, Silvia Teresita. "San José de la Vigía: historia de una fortaleza." *Triunvirato*, 2nd ser., 2 (2003): 15–24.

Herrera López, Pedro A. *El tren de Guanabacoa a Regla:* monografía. Havana: Ediciones Extramuros, 2003.

———. "El castillo de San Severino y sus proyectos constructivos (siglos XVII y XVIII)." *Triumvirato*, 2nd ser., 2 (2003): 201–10.

Hiriart, Rosario. *Yemayá y Ochún/Lydia Cabrera*. New York: CR, 1980.

Holbrook, Josiah. *American Lyceum, or society for the improvement of schools and diffusion of useful knowledge*. Boston: Perkins and Marvin, 1829.

Horrego Estuch, Leopoldo. *Juan Gualberto Gómez: un gran inconforme*. Havana: Comisión del Centenario, 1954.

———. *Martín Morúa Delgado: vida y mensaje*. Havana: n.p., 1957.

[Jarquín, Manolo]. "Matanceras." *Diario de la Marina*, Apr. 24, 1925, 6.

Jiménez de la Cal, Arnaldo. *La familia Guiteras: síntesis de cubanía*. Matanzas: Ediciones Matanzas, 2004.

———. *Matanzas. Síntesis histórica*. Villanueva i la Geltrú, n.p., 2000.

———. *Principio y fin del bandidismo en Matanzas*. Havana: Ediciones Verde Olivo, 1997.

Jiménez Pastrana, Juan. *Los chinos en la historia de Cuba, 1847–1930*. Havana: Editorial de Ciencias Sociales, 1983.

Kekatos, Kirk J. "Edward H. Amet and the Spanish-American War Film." *Film History* 14, nos. 3–4 (2002): 405–17.

Knight, Franklin W. *Slave society in Cuba during the nineteenth Century*. Madison: University of Wisconsin Press, 1970.

Kuethe, Allan J. *Cuba, 1753–1815: Crown, military, and society*. Knoxville: University of Tennessee Press, 1986.

———. "Guns, subsidies and commercial privilege: Some historical factors in the emergence of the Cuban national character, 1763–1815." *Cuban Studies* 16, no. 2 (1986): 123–38.

Kuhn, Gary. "Fiestas and fiascoes: Balloon flights in nineteenth-century Mexico." *Journal of Sports History* 13, no. 2 (Summer 1986): 111–18.

Landers, Jane. *Black society in Spanish Florida*. Champaign: University of Illinois Press, 1999.

Laplana, Josep de C. "La imatge de la Mare de Déu de Monserrat al llarg des segles." In *Nigra sum: iconografia de Santa María de Montserrat*. Montserrat: Museu de Montserrat, 1995.

Las Casas, Bartolomé de. *Historia de las Indias*. 3 vols. Mexico City: Fondo de Cultura Económica, 1951.

Leiva Luna, Elio. *"La Empresa," el colegio de alma cubana*. Matanzas: Imprenta Estrada, 1944.

Lejeune, Jean François. "Jean Claude Nicolas Forestier: The city as landscape and the great urban works of Havana." *Journal of Decorative and Propaganda Arts* 22 (1996): 150–85.

León, René. *La prensa en Matanzas: cronología y bibliografía*. Charlotte, N.C.: Author, 1990.

Lévi-Strauss, Claude. *The way of masks*. Seattle: University of Washington Press, 1982.

Levine, Robert. *Tropical diaspora: The Jewish experience in Cuba*. Gainesville: University Press of Florida, 1993.

Liceo de Matanzas. *Anuario de la sección de ciencias físicas y naturales*. Matanzas: Imprenta de la Aurora del Yumurí, [1866].

———. *Estatutos del Liceo de Matanzas*. Matanzas: Imprenta de la Aurora del Yumurí, 1860.

Llaverías, Joaquín. *Catálogo de los fondos del Liceo Artístico y Literario de La Habana*. Havana: Publicaciones del Archivo Nacional de Cuba, 1944.

Lobo, María Luisa. *Havana: History and architecture of a romantic city*. New York: Monacelli Press, 2000.

Longacre, Edward G. *Grant's cavalryman: The life and wars of General James H. Wilson*. Mechanicsburg, Pa.: Stackpole Books, 1996.

Lowinger, Rosa, and Ofelia Fox. *Tropicana nights: The life and times of the legendary Cuban nightclub*. Orlando: Harcourt, 2005.

López Marrero, Ignacio. "La ciudad de los puentes: el entorno matancero en sus manos." <www.giron.co.cu> (accessed Jan. 30, 2009).

Macías Domínguez, Isabelo. *Cuba en la primera mitad del siglo XVII*. Seville: Escuela de Estudios Hispanoamericanos, 1978.

[Madden, Richard M.] *Poems by a slave in the island of Cuba*. London: T. Ward and Co., 1840.

Maluquer de Motes, Jordi. *Nación e inmigración. Los españoles en Cuba (siglos XIX y XX)*. Colombres, Asturias: Editorial Júcar, 1992.

Mañach, Jorge. *Indagación del choteo*. Havana: Revista de Avance, 1928.

Marichal, Carlos, and Matilde Souto Mantecón. "Silver and situados: New Spain and the financing of the Spanish Empire in the Caribbean in the eighteenth century." *Hispanic American Historical Review* 74, no. 4 (1994): 587–613.

Marmier, Xavier. *Lettres sur l'Amérique. Canada–Etats-Unies–Havane–Rio de la Plata.* Paris: A. Bertrand, [1851].

Marrero, Leví. *Cuba: economía y sociedad.* 15 vols. Río Piedras: Editorial San Juan, 1972–1992.

Martí, José. *Obras completas.* 25 vols. Havana: Editorial Nacional de Cuba, 1963.

Martínez, Jenny S. "Antislavery courts and the dawn of international human rights law." *Yale Law Journal* 117 (2007).

Martínez Carmenate, Urbano. *Atenas de Cuba, del mito a la verdad.* Matanzas: Ediciones Matanzas, 1993.

——. *Bonifacio Byrne.* Havana: Editora Política, 1999.

——. *Domingo Delmonte y su tiempo.* Maracaibo: Dirección de Cultura de la Universidad del Zulia, 1996.

——. *Historia de Matanzas (siglos XVI–XVIII).* Matanzas: Ediciones Matanzas, 1999.

Martínez Fernández, Luis. *The life and times of a British family in nineteenth-century Havana.* Armonk, N.Y.: M. E. Sharpe, 1998.

Martínez Gabino, Aída G., et al. *Historia aborigen de Matanzas.* Matanzas: Editorial Matanzas, 1993.

Mason, Michael Atwood. *Living Santería: Rituals and experiences in an Afro-Cuban religion.* Washington: Smithsonian Institution Press, 2002.

Matanzas contemporánea. [Havana?: "Editado por el Centro Editorial Panamericano, 1942"].

McAvoy, Muriel. *Sugar baron: Manuel Rionda and the fortunes of pre-Castro Cuba.* Gainesville: University Press of Florida, 2003.

Mena, César A., and Armando Cobelo. *Historia de la medicina en Cuba.* Vol. 1, *Hospitales y centros benéficos en Cuba colonial.* Miami: Ediciones Universal, 1992.

Ministerio de Obras Públicas, Negociado de Caminos y Puentes. *Proyecto para la construcción de la autopista sur de la Península de Hicacos.* Havana: Ministerio de Obras Públicas, 1955.

Miró Argenter, José. *Crónicas de la guerra.* 3 vols. Havana: Instituto del Libro, 1970.

Moliner Castañeda, Israel. *Los cabildos afrocubanos en Matanzas.* Matanzas: Ediciones Matanzas, 2002.

——. "Contribución francesa a la cultura de Matanzas." *Revista del Vigía* 4, no. 1 (1993): 77–82.

——. *La imprenta en Matanzas.* Matanzas: Consejo Nacional de Cultura, 1964.

Montes-Huidobro, Matías. *El laúd del desterrado.* Houston: Arte Público Press, 1995.

Morales y Morales, Vidal. *Iniciadores y primeros mártires de la revolución cubana.* Havana: Cultural, 1931.

Moreno Fraginals, Manuel. *Cuba/España, España/Cuba: historia común.* Barcelona: Crítica, Grijalbo Mondadori, 1995.

——. *El ingenio: el complejo económico social cubano del azúcar.* Vol. 1, *1760–1860.* Havana: Comisión Nacional Cubana de la UNESCO, 1964.

Moreno Fraginals, Manuel, and Manuel Moreno Massó. *Guerra, migración y muerte: el ejército español en Cuba como vía migratoria*. Colombres: Editorial Júcar, 1992.

Morison, Samuel Eliot. *History of United States naval operations in World War II*. 15 vols. Champaign: University of Illinois Press, 2001.

Morrison, Allen. "The tramways of Cuba." <www.tramz.com/cu> (accessed Jan. 30, 2009).

Morúa Delgado, Martín. *Integración cubana*. Havana: Edición de la Comisión Nacional del Centenario de Martín Morúa Delgado, 1957.

Moyano Bazzani, Eduardo L. *La nueva frontera del azúcar: el ferrocarril y la economía cubana del siglo XIX*. Madrid: CSIC, 1991.

Murray, Amelia M. *Letters from the United States, Cuba, and Canada*. New York: Negro Universities Press, 1969.

Musser, Charles. *The emergence of cinema: The American screen to 1907*. New York: Scribner's, 1990.

Naranjo Orovio, Consuelo. "Creando imágenes, fabricando historia: Cuba en los inicios del siglo XX." *Historia Mexicana* 210 (Oct.–Dec. 2003): 511–40.

Nieto y Cortadellas, Rafael. *Dignidades nobiliarias en Cuba*. Madrid: Ediciones Cultura Hispánica, 1954.

Núñez Jiménez, Antonio. *La cueva de Bellamar*. Havana: Editorial Ciudad, 1952.

O'Connor, Thomas H. *The Athens of America: Boston, 1825–1845*. Amherst: University of Massachusetts Press, 2006.

Ojeda, Francisco J. "The danzonete: The creation of a style and the rise of the featured vocalist." *Latin Beat Magazine*, February 2004. <www.LatinBeat.com> (accessed Jan. 30, 2009).

Oliver Ruiz, María Victoria. "La música en el proceso de conformación de la identidad matancera en el siglo XIX." *Revista Atenas*, October 2005. <www.atenas.rimed .cu/Todos_los_n/07-Rev_Atenas_octubre2005/articles/P_Articulo009.htm> (accessed Jan. 30, 2009).

Olivera, Otto. *Viajeros en Cuba, 1800–1850*. Miami: Ediciones Universal, 1998.

Orovio, Helio. *Diccionario de la música cubana. Biográfico y técnico*. Havana: Editorial Letras Cubanas, 1981.

Ortiz, Fernando. "Los cabildos afrocubanos." *Revista Bimestre Cubana* 16, no. 1 (Jan.–Feb. 1921): 5–39.

———. *Contrapunteo cubano del tabaco y el azúcar*. Havana: Jesús Montero, 1940.

———. *Hampa afro-cubana. Los negros brujos*. Madrid: Librería de F. Fe, 1906.

———. *El huracán, su mitología y sus símbolos*. Mexico City: Fondo de Cultura Económica, 1947.

———. *Los instrumentos de la música afrocubana*. 5 vols. Havana: Publicaciones de la Dirección de Cultura del Ministerio de Educación, 1952.

Palmié, Stephan. *Wizards and scientists: Explorations in Afro-Cuban modernity and tradition*. Durham: Duke University Press, 2002.

Paquette, Robert. *Sugar is made with blood*. Middletown, Conn.: Wesleyan University Press, 1973.

Paseo pintoresco por la isla de Cuba. Miami: Herencia Cultural Cubana/Ediciones Universal, 1999.

Pasmanick, Philip. "'Decima' and 'rumba': Iberian formalism in the heart of Afro-Cuban song." *Latin American Music Review/Revista de Música Latinoamericana* 18, no. 2 (1997): 252–77.

Pearson, Drew. Special Report from Washington, Release May 30, 1966. <http://dspace .wrlc.org/doc/bitstream/2041/52754/b19f14-0530xdisplay.pdf> (accessed May 20, 2009).

Pérez, Louis A., Jr. *Cuba between reform and revolution.* New York and Oxford: Oxford University Press, 1995.

———. *Cuba under the Platt Amendment, 1902–1934.* Pittsburgh: University of Pittsburgh Press, 1986.

———. *Essays on Cuban history: Historiography and research.* Gainesville: University Press of Florida, 1995.

———. *Winds of change: Hurricanes and the transformation of nineteenth-century Cuba.* Chapel Hill: University of North Carolina Press, 2001.

Pérez Arbeláez, Enrique. *Humboldt en Colombia.* Bogotá: Empresa Colombiana de Petróleos, 1959.

Pérez Cabrera, J. M. *Historiografía de Cuba.* Mexico City: Instituto Panamericano de Geografía e Historia, 1962.

Pérez de la Riva, Juan. *El café: historia de su cultivo y explotación en Cuba.* Havana: Jesús Montero, 1944.

———. *Origen y régimen de la propiedad territorial en Cuba.* Havana: Siglo XX, 1946.

Pérez Landa, Rufino. *Vida pública de Martín Morúa Delgado.* Havana: n.p., 1957.

Perret Ballester, Alberto. *El azúcar en Matanzas y sus dueños en La Habana: apuntes e iconografía.* Havana: Editorial de Ciencias Sociales, 2007.

Perrier, José Luis. *Bibliografía dramática cubana.* New York: Phos Press, 1926.

Perseverancia, Ramón de. *Los chinos y su charada.* Havana: Imprenta la Primera de Belascoaín, 1894.

Pezuela y Lobo, Jacobo de la. *Diccionario geográfico, estadístico, histórico de la isla de Cuba.* 4 vols. Madrid: Establecimiento Tipográfico de Mellado, 1863.

Phillips, Ruby Hart. *Cuba, island of paradox.* New York: Meyer and Obolensky, [1959].

Pichardo, Esteban. "La ciudad de San Carlos de Matanzas." *Memorias de la Real Sociedad Económica,* 2nd ser., 3 (March 1846): 148–58.

———. *Itinerario general de los caminos principales de la isla de Cuba.* Havana: Imprenta de Palmer, 1828.

Placer Cervera, Gustavo. "Acciones navales en el litoral norte de Matanzas durante la guerra hispano-cubano-americana." *Boletín de Historia Militar* 3, no. 93 (1994).

Planas, Juan Manuel. "La obra de Georges Claude." *Revista de la Sociedad Geográfica de Cuba* 3, no. 4 (Oct.–Dec. 1930): 1–20.

Ponte Domínguez, F. J. *José F. Teurbe Tolón y Blandino.* Miami: San Lázaro Graphics, 1993.

———. *Matanzas: biografía de una provincia.* Havana: Siglo XX, 1959.

Portell-Vilá, Herminio. "Cham Bom-Biá, el médico chino." *Archivos del Folklore Cubano*, 3, no. 2 (1928): 155–59.

———. *Historia de Cuba en sus relaciones con los Estados Unidos y España*. 2 vols. Havana: Jesús Montero, 1938.

Portuondo, José A. *Historia de Cuba*. Havana: Minerva, 1955.

Pruna, Pedro M. *Ciencia y científicos en Cuba colonial. La Real Academia de Ciencias de La Habana, 1861–1898*. Havana: Sociedad Económica de Amigos del País, 2001.

Quesada, Gonzalo de. *Los derechos de Cuba a la Isla de Pinos*. Havana: Imprenta de Rambla Bouza, 1909.

Ramos, Marcos Antonio. *Panorama del protestantismo en Cuba*. San José, Costa Rica: Editorial Caribe, 1986.

Rauch, Basil. *American interest in Cuba, 1848–1855*. New York: Octagon, 1974.

Reglamento para las milicias de infantería y caballería de la Isla de Cuba. Havana: Oficina del Gobierno, 1839.

Reseña histórica de Matanzas, 1508–1941. [Havana: Imp. La Revoltosa, 1941].

Resumen de los desastres ocurridos en el puerto de la Habana y sus jurisdicciones inmediatas, del Departamento Occidental de la isla de Cuba. Havana: Imp. de Vidal y Comp., [1844?]

Rivero Muñiz, José. *El tabaco. Su historia en Cuba*. Havana: Instituto de Historia, 1964.

Roche y Monteagudo, Rafael. *La policía y sus misterios en Cuba*. Havana: La Moderna Poesía, 1925.

Rodríguez, Jorge Luis, "La muerte de la niña Cecilia." <www.afrocuba.org/Anto11/cecilia.htm> (accessed Jan. 30, 2009).

Roig de Leuchsenring, Emilio. *Cuba no debe su independencia a los Estados Unidos*. Havana: Sociedad Cubana de Estudios Históricos e Internacionales, 1950.

Rojas, Marta. *El harén de Oviedo*. Havana: Editorial Letras Cubanas, 2003.

Rouse, Irving. *The Tainos: Rise and decline of the people who greeted Columbus*. New Haven, Conn.: Yale University Press, 1992.

Roy, Joaquín. *Catalunya a Cuba*. Barcelona: Barcino, 1988.

Ruiz, Raúl. *Aguas de la ciudad*. Matanzas: Ediciones Matanzas, 1995.

———. *Los amigos de la cultura cubana*. Matanzas: Ediciones Matanzas, 2006.

———. *Esteban Chartrand: nuestro romántico*. Havana: Editorial Letras Cubanas, 1987.

———. *Matanzas: surgimiento y esplendor de la plantación esclavista, 1793–1867*. Matanzas: Ediciones Matanzas, 2001.

———. *Matanzas: tema con variaciones*. Matanzas: Ediciones Matanzas, 2002.

———. *Memoria francesa*. Matanzas: n.p., n.d.

———. *Retrato de ciudad*. Havana: Ediciones La Unión, 2003.

Ruiz, Raúl, and Martha Lim Kim. *Coreanos en Cuba*. Havana: Fundación Fernando Ortiz, 2000.

Saco, José A. *Colección de papeles científicos, históricos y políticos y de otros ramos sobre la isla de Cuba*. Havana: Dirección General de Cultura, 1960.

Saladrigas y Zayas, Enrique. *A tribute to Finlay*. Havana: Ministry of Health and Social Assistance, 1952.

Salazar, Guillermo Franco. "Armando Carnot Veulens, el médico de los pobres." <www .conexioncubana.net/index.php?st=content&sk=view&id=5496&sitd=317> (accessed April 26, 2009).

Salwen, Michael B. *Radio and TV in Cuba: The pre-Castro era*. Ames: Iowa State University Press, 1994.

Sánchez Albornoz, Nicolás. *Españoles hacia América*. Madrid: Alianza Editorial, 1988.

Santa Cruz, María de las Mercedes de, Countess of Merlin. *La Habana*. Torrejón de Ardoz (Madrid): Cronocolor, 1981.

Santa Cruz y Mallén, Francisco Javier de. *Historia de familias cubanas*. 9 vols. Havana: Editorial Hércules, 1940; Miami: Ediciones Universal, 1986.

Santamaría García, Antonio. *Sin azúcar no hay país: la industria azucarera y la economía cubana, 1919–1939*. Seville: CSIC, University of Seville, 2002.

Santiago, Fabiola. "Roots revival: punto guajiro makes a comeback." *Miami Herald*, February 5, 2004.

Santovenia, Emeterio. *Armonías y conflictos en torno a Cuba*. Mexico City: Fondo de Cultura Económica, 1956.

———. *Huellas de gloria: frases históricas cubanas*. Havana: Siglo XX, 1928.

Schwartz, Rosalie. *Lawless liberators: Political banditry and Cuban independence*. Durham, N.C.: Duke University Press, 1989.

"Sea power." *Time*, Oct. 20, 1930. <www.time.com> (accessed May 2, 2009).

Sociedad Geográfica de Cuba. *Revista de la Sociedad Geográfica de Cuba* 3, no. 4 (Oct.– Dec. 1930).

Soloni, Félix. "El danzón y su inventor, Miguel Faílde." In *Cuba Musical,* by José Calero Martín and Leopoldo Valdés, <www.guije.com> (accessed Jan. 30, 2009).

Starr, S. Frederick. *Louis Moreau Gottschalk*. Urbana: University of Illinois Press, 1982.

Stoner, K. Lynn. *From the house to the streets: Women's movement and social change in Cuba*. Bloomington: Indiana University Press, 1983.

———. "Women's rights and the Cuban republic." *Cuban Heritage* 2, no. 1 (1988): 17–18.

Suchlicki, Jaime. *University students and revolution in Cuba, 1920–1968*. Coral Gables, Fla.: University of Miami Press, 1969.

Tabares del Real, José A. *Guiteras*. Havana: Editorial de Ciencias Sociales, 1990.

Tanco Armero, Nicolás. *Viaje de la Nueva Granada a China y de China a Francia*. n.p.: Simón Racon, 1861.

Testé, Ismael. *Historia eclesiástica de Cuba*. 5 vols. Burgos: Tip. de la Editorial El Monte Carmelo, 1969.

Theodore, Adolphe. *Relación de la segunda y tercera ascensión aerostática de D. Adolfo Theodore*. Puerto Príncipe: Imprenta de Gobierno y Real Hacienda, 1831.

Thomas, Hugh. *Cuba: The pursuit of freedom*. New York: Harper and Row, 1971.

———. *The slave trade: The history of the Atlantic slave trade, 1440–1870*. London: Phoenix, 2006.

Toledo, Armando. *Presencia y vigencia de Brindis de Salas.* Havana: Editorial Letras Cubanas, 1981.

Tone, John L. *War and genocide in Cuba, 1895–1898.* Chapel Hill: University of North Carolina Press, 2006.

Torrademé Balado, Ángel. *Iniciación a la historia del correo en Cuba.* Havana: Imprenta La Habanera, [1945?].

Torre, José María de la. *Lo que fuimos y lo que somos ó La Habana antigua y moderna.* Havana: Spencer, 1857.

Trelles y Govín, Carlos M. *La ciudad de Matanzas y su puerto desde 1508 hasta 1693.* Matanzas: Imprenta Estrada, 1932.

———. *Matanzas en la independencia de Cuba.* Havana: Imprenta Avisador Comercial, 1928.

Treserras, José A. *Historia de Matanzas.* Vol. 1, *Matanzas y Yucayo.* Matanzas: Junta de Cultura y Turismo, 1943.

Tseelon, Efrat, ed. *Masquerade and identity: Essays on gender, sexuality and marginality.* London: Routledge, 2001.

Turnbull, David. *Travels in the west. Cuba; with notices of Porto Rico, and the slave trade.* London: Printed for Longman, Orne, Brown, Green, and Longmans, 1840.

United States Army. *Annual Report of Brigadier General James H. Wilson, U.S.V., Commanding the Department of Matanzas and Santa Clara.* Matanzas: n.p., 1900.

Uría González, Jorge, et al. *Asturias y Cuba en torno al 98.* Barcelona: Editorial Labor, 1994.

Valdés, Antonio José. *Historia de la isla de Cuba y en especial de La Habana.* Havana: Imprenta de La Cena, 1813.

Valverde, Umberto. *Memoria de la Sonora Matancera.* Cali: Editorial Caimán Récordes, 1997.

Vázquez, Ricardo. *Triumvirato. Historia de un rincón azucarero de Cuba.* Havana: Departamento de Orientación Revolucionaria, 1972.

Vento, Saúl and Raúl Ruiz. *La Biblioteca Pública de Matanzas.* Havana: Editorial de Ciencias Sociales, 1980.

Vento Canosa, Ercilio. *El alma de la ciudad.* Matanzas: Ediciones Matanzas, 1991.

———. "Consideraciones sobre el caso de la niña Cecilia." <http://hispanidadymestizaje.es/cecilia2.htm> (accessed April 26, 2009).

Verovering vande Silver-vloot inde Bay Matanca K. 1628. Amsterdam: Nicholas Visscher, 1628.

Vinueza, María H. *Presencia arará en la música folclórica de Matanzas.* Havana: Casa de las Américas, [1989].

Vitier, Cintio. *Lo cubano en la poesía.* Havana: Instituto del Libro, 1970.

Weyler y Nicolau, Valeriano. *Mi mando en Cuba (10 febrero 1896 a 31 octubre 1897); historia militar y política de la última guerra separatista durante dicho mando.* 4 vols. Madrid: F. González Rojas, 1910–11.

[Wurdemann, J. G. F.]. *Notes on Cuba, by a Physician.* Boston: James Munroe and Co., 1844.

Ximeno y Cruz, Dolores María de. *Aquellos tiempos. Memorias de Lola María.* 2 vols. Havana: Colección de Libros Cubanos Raros y Curiosos, 1928.

Yaremko, Jason. "'*Gente bárbara*': Indigenous rebellion, resistance and persistence in colonial Cuba, c. 1500–1800." *Kacike: Journal of Caribbean Amerindian History and Anthropology.* <www.kacike.org/Yaremko.html> (accessed Jan. 30, 2009).

Yun, Lisa, and Ricardo Rene Laremont. "Chinese coolies and African slaves in Cuba, 1847–74." *Journal of Asian American Studies* 4, no. 2 (June 2001): 99–122.

Zaldívar, Mario. *El mito de la Sonora Matancera.* San José, Costa Rica: Litografía IPECA, 1999.

Zanetti Lecuona, Oscar, and Alejandro García Alvarez. *Caminos para el azúcar.* Havana: Editorial de Ciencias Sociales, 1987.

Index

War of independence. *See* independence war

Watchtower Square. *See* Vigía Square

Weyler y Nicolau, Valeriano, 184. *See also* reconcentration

White y Laffite José: career, 158–60; on postage stamp, 160; reception in his honor, 124

Wilson, James H., Gen., as U.S. military governor, 190–91

Winters, Rev. McHenry, 146

Women, education of, 109

World War II, impact on Matanzas, 246

Ximeno, Lola María de: describes 1855 festival, 121; describes Día de Reyes, 126–27; and Plácido, 84; on values and esthetics of the "Señorío," 122–24;

Ximeno y Uzaola, José Matías de, 125–26

Yambú. *See* rumba

Yemayá, offerings to, 18. *See also* Afro-Cuban religion

Yucatec Mayas, as virtual slaves, 100

Yucayo Rum (distillery), 287n3

Yumurí (Babonao)River: ciénaga (swamp) marks limit of *traza*, 42; Concordia bridge inaugurated, 173; crossed in reverse, 261

Yumurí Valley, 18, 52

Zafra, 60–63

Zayas y Alfonso, Alfredo (fourth president), 224

"Zilvervloot": capture of, 24; lyrics, 270n23

Miguel A. Bretos is retired from the National Portrait Gallery, Smithsonian Institution, where he was a senior scholar. He is the author of four books, including *Iglesias de Yucatán* (1992) and *Cuba and Florida: An Exploration of a Historical Connection, 1593–1991* (1991).